Houston

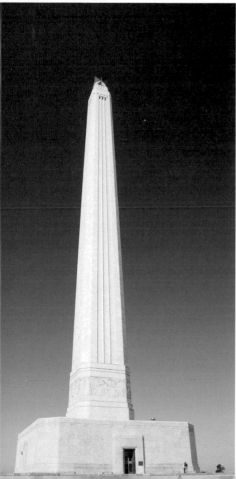

Page 1: Stately Houston City Hall.

Page 2: (top) Downtown Houston cityscape on a summer day; (bottom left) Statue of Sam Houston in Hermann Park; (bottom right) Ferris wheel at the Houston Rodeo.

Page 3: (top) Rice University campus in Houston; (bottom left); San Jacinto Monument at the San Jacinto Battleground State Historic Site in La Porte, TX; (bottom right, upper) Great Egret with fish at Armand Bayou Nature Center in Pasadena, TX; (bottom right, lower) Dawn at Brazos Bend State Park in Needville, TX.

Page 4: (top) Houston skyline at sunset; (bottom) Wells Fargo Plaza skyscraper.

INSIDERS' GUIDE® TO
HOUSTON

INSIDERS' GUIDE® TO

HOUSTON

SECOND EDITION

LAURA NATHAN-GARNER

INSIDERS' GUIDE

GUILFORD, CONNECTICUT
AN IMPRINT OF GLOBE PEQUOT PRESS

All the information in this guidebook is subject to change. We recommend that you call ahead to obtain current information before traveling.

INSIDERS' GUIDE ®

Editor: Kevin Sirois
Project Editor: Heather Santiago
Layout: Joanna Beyer
Text Design: Sheryl Kober
Maps by XNR Productions, Inc. © Morris Book Publishing, LLC

ISBN 978-0-7627-8130-0

Printed in the United States of America
10 9 8 7 6 5 4 3 2 1

CONTENTS

Directory of Maps

ABOUT THE AUTHOR

Native Houstonian **Laura Nathan-Garner** lives with her husband, daughter, and a slightly neurotic beagle in Houston. By day, she edits *Focused on Health* (mdanderson.org/focused), the online healthy living newsletter of The University of Texas MD Anderson Cancer Center. She is also the author of *Day Trips from Houston* (13th edition) and has written for *Redbook, Cooking Light,* and other national publications.

ACKNOWLEDGMENTS

Writing a book about a city as big as Houston can be intimidating. Equally intimidating: Realizing how much the city has changed in the 3-plus years since I wrote the first edition of *Insiders' Guide to Houston*. Luckily, I've had some pretty Houston-savvy people to turn to while writing and updating this book. Though they are too numerous to name, I'm grateful to the many friends, friends of friends, coworkers, and family members who, over the last 3 years, have shared favorite new restaurants, shops, museums, and events. Many of you have also set me straight, knowingly or unknowingly reminding me about stores having moved, restaurants getting new chefs, admission fees going up, and even road closures and name changes. Your recommendations, pointers, and reminders, no doubt, have made this book more well-rounded and representative of Houston.

Special thanks to the staff at Globe Pequot Press, especially my editor Kevin Sirois, who helped see this book through from start to finish, and Amy Lyons, who provided large doses of insight and guidance when I wrote the first edition and trusted me enough to get the job done again. I'm grateful to my family, especially my parents and brothers, who've been my cheerleaders from the beginning. I'm also incredibly thankful for Ricky, whose curiosity about the world makes projects like this more fun and whose patience, wisdom, and support makes completing them possible. And perhaps more than anyone, I'm indebted to this book's quiet heroine—our daughter, Lilah, who allowed me to deliver this book to my editor before I delivered her.

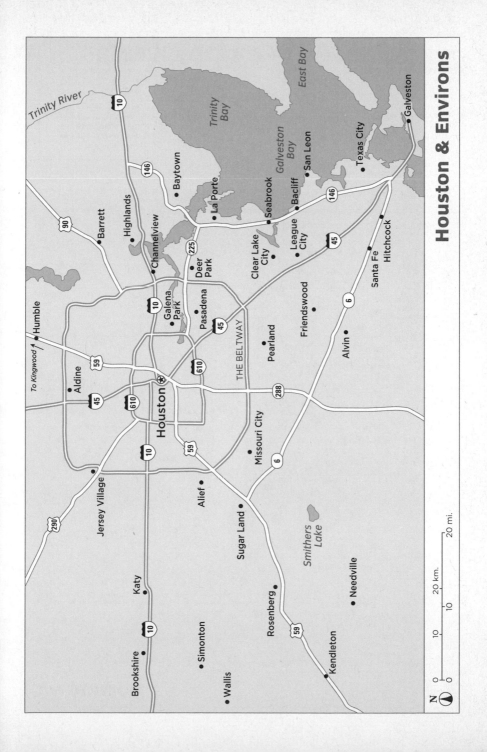

Houston & Environs

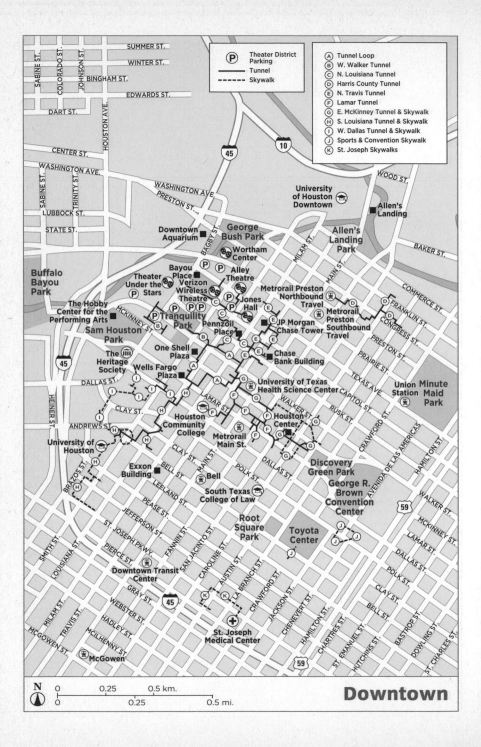

Downtown

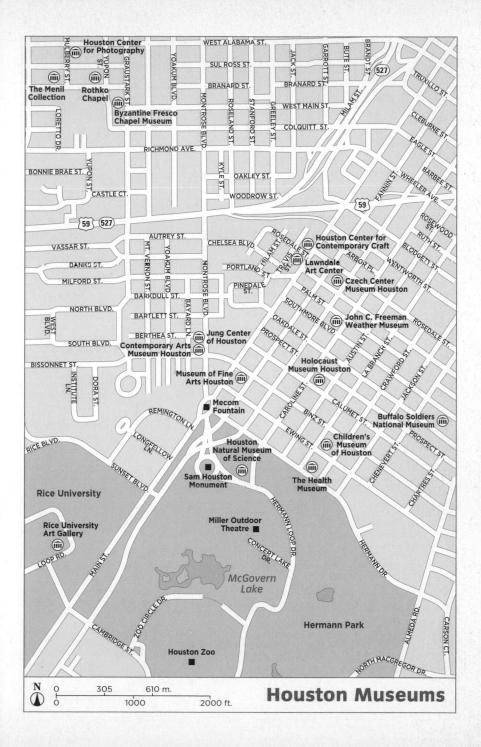

Houston Museums

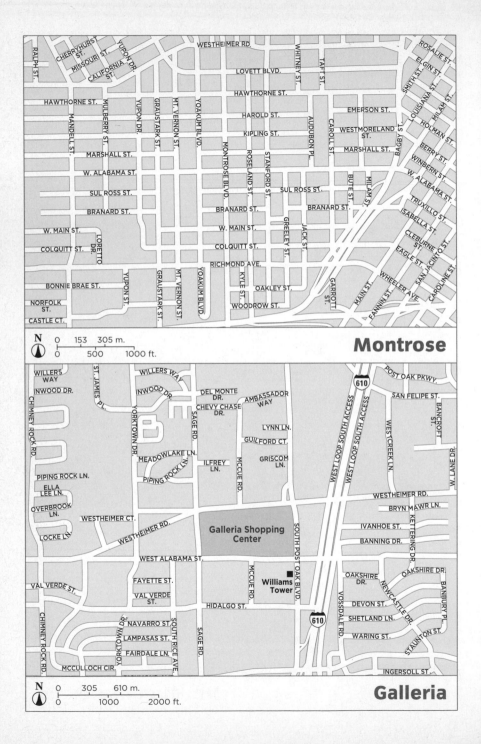

Montrose

Galleria

INTRODUCTION

A few years ago, the man seated next to me on a plane asked where I was from. "But you don't sound like you're from Houston," he said when I told him. I laughed a little—one of those genuine, but somewhat forced laughs of someone who's heard this before. Then I told him what seems so obvious to me: Houston's a big city and people here don't have the thick, drawn-out accents that you might find in smaller towns around Texas. "Well, everyone I know from Houston has an accent," he said. I wondered how many people from Houston he'd actually met.

Looking back, there's some truth to what each of us said. Houston is a big city filled with people who buck every stereotype that outsiders might have about Texans and Houstonians. In fact, for someone visiting from a more homogenous area, we Houstonians might bear a slight resemblance to a United Nations assembly with our many different accents, beliefs, rituals, and skin tones. Of course, Houston also has its share of people like my companion in row 12 had met—those with deep Southern twangs, as well as ranchers who ride horses and breed livestock.

It's this kind of diversity that makes this city so rich with culture. You'll see this at annual events like the International Festival, the Art Car Parade, the Livestock Show and Rodeo, and the Shakespeare Festival, as well as at our first-class museums and in our performing arts companies' unparalleled performances. You'll taste this diversity in our cuisine, which spans from the requisite barbecue and Tex-Mex to chic new American options that have landed our chefs James Beard Award nominations and praise in foodie bibles like *Gourmet, Bon Appetit*, and *Wine Spectator*. You'll see it at our pro football, basketball, and baseball games, where fans paint their faces and wear their pride on their chests and heads. You'll see it in the faces of the families who flock to our parks on sunny days. And if you're a shopper, prepare yourself: You'll see it in our stores that sell everything from Prada and Tiffany to rare antiques and vinyl records to one-of-a-kind handbags. You'll even see it in our hospitality, which many discovered when Houston opened its arms to thousands of people displaced by Hurricane Katrina in 2005. These are just a few of the thousands of reasons so many of us call Houston home, even when our current addresses lie elsewhere.

Having been born and raised in Houston, I thought I knew most of what there is to know about this city. But in the course of writing the first edition of this book and speaking to other Houstonians, I discovered there's so much more to love: A bat colony. An art car parade. A funeral museum. A velodrome. A house made of beer cans. A taco joint that makes s'mores tacos. A bookstore that only sells murder mysteries.

Then, I wrote the second edition of this book. And guess what? A lot had changed in just 3 years, and during that time I'd discovered even more new restaurants, shops, bars, farmers' markets, and events—some new, some just new to me.

That's the beauty of Houston. With so many new places and activities popping up and older ones just waiting to be found, it's tough to get bored here.

Of course, if you've spent a lot of time in Houston (or anyplace for that matter), it's easy to forget about or overlook some true gems. That's what happens when we fall into the routine of everyday life.

But as I tell friends who've moved away and wonder why I returned to Houston, this city is filled with treasures and quirks just waiting to be discovered. So whether you're a longtime Houstonian, a new resident, or just passing through, cast aside what you think you know about Houston and prepare to be pleasantly surprised.

HOW TO USE THIS BOOK

You've heard the saying: "Everything is bigger in Texas." Houston is no exception. With the city itself spanning nearly 600 square miles and the surrounding suburbs and exurbs adding another 8,000-plus square miles, there's a lot of ground to cover here. All of the possibilities—where to eat, which theater company to watch, where to shop, where to stay, which festivals to attend—can seem overwhelming, even if you've lived here for years.

That's where this book comes in. Whether you're in town for a weekend, a week, a month, or a lifetime, consider this your personal tour guide for Houston. In the self-contained chapters that follow, you'll find information on almost everything you might want or need to know about Houston—where to stay or live, where to eat and go out at night, where to see a great theater performance, and countless other details. How you read these chapters is up to you: Every trip— or decision to live in a new city—is a little different, so this book is designed to allow you to easily jump around and use the chapters that you need most. Each chapter includes options for every taste and budget, making this something of a *Choose Your Own Adventure* guide. Of course, feel free to read this book from cover to cover if you find it helpful.

The book begins with a look at Houston's history. Even if you already know a thing or two about the city, you're likely to find a few things you don't know. Perhaps you know that Augustus Allen and his brother John founded the city, but do you know how they lured prospective residents to live here? Or did you know that Houston was once the railroad capital of Texas? Check out the "History" chapter to learn even more about this city's intriguing past and present.

After you've gotten a feel for Houston's history, you might want to figure out how you're going to get to and around the city. That's where the "Getting Here, Getting Around" chapter comes in. If you need a place to stay, be sure to check out the "Accommodations" chapter, too.

Afterward, follow your stomach to the "Restaurants" chapter for a sampling of some of Houston's best culinary offerings. Trying to decide where to go after dinner? Be sure to check out the "Nightlife" chapter, which includes something for every mood and taste—pubs, bars, wine bars, live music venues, dance clubs, country-and-western dance clubs, gay bars, movie theaters, and readings.

If it's the arts you love, look at the "Performing Arts" chapter for some of Houston's best theater, ballet, opera, and music offerings, many of which can be found downtown in Houston's 17-block Theater District. And be sure to check out the "Museums" chapter, which showcases everything from the requisite (but outstanding) fine arts and natural history museums to the one-of-a-kind Rothko Chapel, the Holocaust Museum, and even a funeral museum.

Whether you're here a day, a week, or a lifetime, you're probably wondering what you should put on your list of must-sees. Flip to the "Attractions" chapter to find some of this city's gems, including NASA's Space Center Houston, the San Jacinto Battleground State

Historic Site, and the downtown tunnel system. Also check out the "Annual Events" chapter, which highlights some of the city's best annual festivals, parades, and events ranging from the Houston Livestock Show and Rodeo to the International Festival to the Bayou City Arts Festival. Annual events are organized by month so you can flip to the month you're in town and see what's happening during your stay. Kids in tow? Be sure to check out the "Kidstuff" chapter, which will point you toward Houston's many kid-friendly attractions, theaters, events, and activities like ice-skating and bowling.

Looking for a good place to run or have a picnic? Check out the "Parks" chapter. You'll learn about some of the city's best parks, including several off-leash parks where you can take your favorite dog. For ideas on where to relax or enjoy your favorite recreational activity, flip to the "Recreation" chapter, which highlights some of the best places to partake in everything from skateboarding to camping. You'll also find a list of gyms and yoga studios. Prefer to watch other people play sports? Check out the "Spectator Sports" chapter to find out how and where to see Houston's many professional sports teams in action. You'll even learn about Houston's annual bowl game and greyhound and car racing venues.

Need to buy something, or just like to shop? Either way, be sure to peruse the "Shopping" chapter, where you'll find some local gems.

If you're moving to the Houston area or already live here, be sure to check out the blue-tabbed pages at the back of the book. There you will find the **Living Here** appendix that offers sections on relocation, child care, education, and health care.

In each chapter, you'll find **Insiders' Tips** (represented by an ■), which offer up useful information and tips you might not find elsewhere. Sprinkled throughout the book are **Close-ups,** which offer insight into some of the most intriguing—and often idiosyncratic yet endearing—aspects of Houston.

You'll also find listings accompanied by the ✳ symbol—these are our top picks for attractions, restaurants, accommodations, and everything in between that you shouldn't miss while you're in the area. You want the best this region has to offer? Go with our **Insiders' Choice.**

As you consult these pages, keep in mind that this book is meant to be a starting point for your trip or move. Houston is a huge city, and no chapter is exhaustive in recommendations or information. Often, favorite spots are those discovered by accident, so don't be afraid to stray from this book when deciding what to do here. There are so many great restaurants, shops, clubs, bars, and attractions in this city that you just might stumble upon something really special. Also bear in mind that some recommendations and information may be out of date by the time you read this book. New businesses are constantly popping up, while others move or close their doors. Even long-standing shops, restaurants, clubs, theaters, and attractions often change their hours or days of operation, so call ahead before heading out to see the city.

With that in mind, start exploring Houston—whether in your chair (or airplane seat) as you read this book or as you try to navigate your way around the city. Odds are, once you get to know Houston, you'll start to love it.

AREA OVERVIEW

Sure, you've visited—or even lived in—big cities. But it can be tough to grasp exactly just how big a city can be until you've spent some time in Houston, the county seat of Harris County. Sitting just 50 miles from the Gulf of Mexico, this low-lying city spans some 634 square miles. That's enough space to hold New York, Boston, Seattle, San Francisco, Seattle, Miami, *and* Washington, D.C. And that's just what lies inside Houston's city limits. Add in neighboring cities such as Baytown and Sugar Land and the eight counties that make up the Houston-Galveston-Brazoria Consolidated Metropolitan Area, and the Greater Houston area spans more than 8,778 square miles—an area slightly smaller than Massachusetts but larger than New Jersey. Most of this land is—or was—forests, swamps, prairies, or marshes. Buffalo Bayou, the birthplace of Houston, passes through the city, running from the western suburb of Katy into downtown and then east into the Houston Ship Channel. Three Buffalo Bayou tributaries can be found around Houston: Braes Bayou runs along the Texas Medical Center; Sims Bayou runs through downtown, as well as south of Houston; and White Oak Bayou flows through the Heights neighborhood. The combination of these bayous, the city's flat land, and frequent rain makes flooding a common occurrence.

WHO LIVES HERE?

This isn't keeping many people away, though. Houston's population has swelled over the last couple of decades, with a growing number of people coming here for the mild winters, a relatively low cost of living, and unrivaled opportunities in the aerospace, medicine, and energy sectors. In fact, Houston is one of the country's fastest-growing metropolitan areas. Now home to nearly 6 million people, the Houston metropolitan area's population grew by a whopping 26 percent between 2000 and 2010.

And this population is incredibly diverse. In fact, Houston is home to a substantially larger percentage of blacks, Hispanics, Latinos, and foreign-born residents than the rest of Texas. According to the 2010 US Census, just over a quarter of Houston residents identify themselves as white persons not of Hispanic origins. Maybe that's not surprising given the city's proximity to Mexico and Latin America. But here's something you might not expect from Houston: More than 90 different languages are spoken here, and nearly 28 percent of Houston residents were born abroad. And thanks in part to the large number of colleges and universities here, Houston has one of the country's youngest populations: The median age is just under 33 years old.

AREAS COVERED IN THIS BOOK

The vast majority of this book focuses on activities and spots inside the City of Houston since these tend to be more centrally located and attract more people. The majority of destinations in the city limits can be found inside Loop 610, a major local freeway that circles around the heart of the city, including downtown. Houstonians often refer to locations in terms of whether they are inside or outside the Loop. For this reason, the neighborhoods in this chapter are categorized as either "Inside the Loop" or "Outside the Loop."

Admittedly, talking in terms of "Inside the Loop" and "Outside the Loop" isn't always the most ideal way to discuss the Greater Houston area. Houston has dozens of neighborhoods, and the Greater Houston area is filled with dozens of suburbs and exurbs. While it's impossible to discuss every Houston neighborhood and suburb in the space of a chapter, it is equally impossible to talk about Houston without mentioning some locations and destinations outside the city limits. This chapter highlights a few of the larger suburbs and neighborhoods, particularly those that are home to attractions listed elsewhere in this book.

In this chapter, more distant suburbs and neighborhoods are classified under broader ordinal categories, such as "Northwest" or "East." Because Houston is so large and is home to so many neighborhoods and suburbs, these ordinal directions serve to keep you from becoming overwhelmed: You can look at a map and find a location relative to where you are. These overarching, ordinal categories include both neighborhoods in Houston (but outside the Loop) and suburbs located outside the city limits. Don't worry, though: Suburbs here have been identified as such. This chapter includes the distance from downtown to these suburbs, so you have a better sense of how far you'll be traveling if you decide to visit the more distant reaches of the Houston area.

CLIMATE

Thanks to its Gulf Coast location and the forests, swamps, and prairies in the area, Houston's climate qualifies as humid subtropical. On average, the city gets about 48 inches of rain a year, which makes for more than a few bad hair days.

Winters here are mild, so you probably won't need more than a light jacket. If you're just visiting, you're unlikely to see snow, and on the off chance that you do, it probably won't stick. Since 1939, the city has had just 14 measureable snowfalls. January temperatures reach a high of about 62°F on average; lows average about 41°F.

i Find out the day's weather forecast by calling the local weather line at (713) 630-0222.

Visiting during the summer? Be sure to pack sandals, shorts, sleeveless or short-sleeved shirts, and plenty of sunscreen. Temperatures tend to get up to a sweltering 94°F in July. If that doesn't seem too hot, keep in mind that the relative humidity on summer mornings is about 90 percent, with the humidity falling to about 60 percent in the afternoons. Now for the good news: You'll be hard-pressed to find a place in Houston that isn't air-conditioned—rental cars included.

Uh-O-Zone

On days when high ozone levels are particularly likely, the Texas Commission on Environmental Quality issues ozone watches, advising children, the elderly, and adults with breathing problems or lung disease to stay indoors. Wondering if there's an ozone day on the horizon? Find out by watching or listening to the local weather.

INSIDE THE LOOP

Bellaire/Meyerland/Braeswood/Southside Place

Bellaire, Meyerland, Braeswood, and Southside Place all sit in the southwestern part of the Loop and spill over west of Loop 610. These neighborhoods are predominately residential and are filled with large trees and a mix of older homes and newer mansions. There are also some retail developments and restaurants in the area. If you're looking for the city's Jewish community, you'll find it here. The Bellaire/Meyerland/Braeswood/Southside Place area is home to 2 major synagogues, the Jewish Community Center, and good kosher bakeries.

Downtown

Houston's bustling downtown district is located in the center of the Loop. It is bounded by I-10 on the north, Bagby Street on the west, Chartres Street on the east, and US 59 on the south. Since Houston's founding in 1836, downtown has been the city's primary area for commerce and municipal activities. Downtown is home to City Hall and Allen's Landing, the spot where the Allen brothers arrived in and first settled Houston. The skyscrapers here are the headquarters of some of the world's largest corporations, including Continental Airlines, El Paso Corporation, Shell Oil Company, and Halliburton. Downtown is also the location of the George R. Brown Convention Center, which hosts dozens of conventions each year in its 1.2 million square feet of exhibit and meeting space.

For many years the only real entertainment downtown had to offer were the world-class ballet, opera, and theater performances in the Theater District. There were some nice restaurants in Market Square, an area dating back to the 1800s, but these weren't great evening destinations unless you were attending the theater afterward.

i Need directions or advice on where to go and what to see in Houston? Visit the City of Houston Visitors Center on the first floor of City Hall Mon through Sat from 9 a.m. to 4 p.m., or call the center at (800) 4-HOUSTON.

So people typically left downtown after work and stayed away on the weekends. Over the last decade or so, though, the city has revitalized downtown to make it a more enticing place to play and even live. Many new restaurants and clubs, an aquarium, a movie theater, and a number of residential lofts and luxury apartments have opened in the area.

In 2004, the city introduced a new light-rail system that runs through downtown along Main Street. More lines—and a Fannin Street station—are planned for the coming years, which will make it even easier to get around downtown. Dubbed METRORail, the light rail makes it particularly easy to get to two of Houston's newest sports stadiums—Minute Maid Park (baseball) and the Toyota Center (basketball and hockey)—as well as to the many festivals that are held downtown each year. Most of these festivals take place at one of the parks downtown and a growing number of festivals and other events are held at Discovery Green, a Central Park–like green space that opened in 2008 and has quickly become the hub of downtown recreation. All of these attractions are discussed elsewhere in this book. Information about the Downtown Aquarium can be found in the "Attractions" chapter; the parks, including Discovery Green, are listed in the "Parks" chapter. The stadiums are discussed in the "Spectator Sports" chapter, the Theater District is discussed in the "Performing Arts" chapter, and the METRORail is discussed in the "Getting Here, Getting Around" chapter.

i Using a GPS to navigate your way around town? Enter the appropriate suburb name rather than "Houston" for destinations located outside of Houston city limits.

The Heights

Located northwest of downtown, the Heights is bounded by Loop 610 on the north, I-10 on the south, Yale and Oxford Streets on the east, and Blair and Dian Streets on the west. Whether you're looking for charm, community, or independent spirit, you'll find it in the Heights. This relatively small neighborhood dates back to 1896, when it was established outside what were then the city limits. Built above White Oaks Bayou, the neighborhood is named for the fact that, with an elevation 23 feet higher than that of downtown, it was the highest point in the city.

Today this spirited community is home to a number of thrift shops, art galleries, plant nurseries, and special events.

i On the first Saturday of the month, head to the First Saturday Arts Market in the Heights to check out local artists' work, listen to music, eat street food, and mingle with area residents. The free-to-attend market is held at 548 W. 19th St. from 11 a.m. to 6 p.m., rain or shine. Learn more at firstsaturdayartsmarket.com.

Midtown

Bounded by I-45 on the north, US 59 on the south, SH 288 on the east, and Bagby Street on the west, Midtown sits on the southwest edge of downtown. After being run-down for many years, this neighborhood has received a big makeover and become one of the hippest areas in town. A younger crowd flocks to Midtown partly for the prime location, partly to be near some of the hottest bars, lounges, restaurants, and events in the city. Remnants of Midtown before the makeover are still evident, though. The area remains home to a large Vietnamese population, whose presence is evident in the neighborhood's numerous Vietnamese restaurants, businesses, and even street names.

Montrose

Montrose is bounded by Allen Parkway on the north, US 59 on the south, Bagby Street on the east, and Shepherd on the west. It is Houston's most eclectic neighborhood, thanks in part to the neighborhood's proximity to the Museum District and Midtown, as well as the Rice and St. Thomas Universities. Montrose is perhaps best known for its large gay and lesbian population, but the area is also home to and frequented by plenty of students, artsy types, families, and young professionals. This pedestrian-friendly neighborhood is filled with independent shops and thrift stores and trendy restaurants and bars, making it a popular place to shop and socialize. Montrose is also the site of one of the city's biggest parades—the Gay Pride Festival and Parade in June. Learn more about the parade in the "Annual Events" chapter.

Museum District

Nestled between West University and Montrose, the Museum District is home to 17 of Houston's best museums. The district covers a 1.5-mile radius from the Mecom Fountain, a three-pool-high fountain that stands in the traffic circle at the entrance to Houston's prized Hermann Park. Inside the park, you'll find the Houston Zoo, a beautiful Japanese garden, the Houston Museum of Natural Science, and the Miller Outdoor Theatre. Rice University is located right across the street from the park.

The Museum District has a sophisticated feel, with trees and well-manicured landscaping lining many of the streets. This makes for enjoyable scenery if you opt to go museum hopping—a walkable option, if the weather's nice. The Contemporary Arts Museum, Museum of Fine Arts, Museum of Natural Science, Health Museum, Children's Museum, and Holocaust Museum are all within a few blocks of one another. Ten of the museums in the district are free, and all except one offer free admission days or hours. Each September, the area hosts Museum District Day (page 187), when the museums offer free admission and shuttle service, as well as special family-friendly programming. The Museum District is easily accessible by METRO bus and lightrail, as well as via US 59, TX 288, Main Street, and Fannin Street. Learn more about the Museum District in the "Museums" chapter.

River Oaks

River Oaks is one of Houston's ritziest neighborhoods, centrally located just east of the Galleria and west of Shepherd between US 59 on the south and Buffalo Bayou on the north. The area was developed by Michael and William Hogg, the sons of former Texas governor Jim Hogg. Along with their sister Ima, the Hoggs oversaw the building of Bayou Bend, a beautiful manse and gardens on Buffalo Bayou. Today the Museum of Fine Arts Houston owns the Hoggs' River Oaks home and gardens. The Hogg manse isn't the only magnificent house in the area, though. During the spring, River Oaks homes are surrounded by azaleas, which people from across the city pay to see as part of the River Oaks Garden Club Azalea Trail. This affluent area is also home to a number of independent restaurants, bakeries, and boutiques. Many of these can be found in the River Oaks Shopping Center, as well as in Highland Village, an upscale shopping area located along Westheimer.

Texas Medical Center

Sitting adjacent to Hermann Park and across the street from Rice University, the Texas Medical Center—aka the Medical Center or TMC—is the world's largest medical center with 49 medicine-related institutions. Although there are some restaurants and housing around the Medical Center, this area revolves around the hospitals, which you can learn about in the "Health Care" chapter.

Close-up

The Wards

In and around downtown and east Houston sit six wards, each named for its ward number (First Ward, Second Ward, and so on).

These wards represent former political subdivisions that date back to the late 1830s, shortly after the city's founding. At that time, the Allen brothers and other civic leaders divided the city into four geographic political districts, calling them wards. Over the next four decades, two additional wards were added. None were defined based on population. Rather, it was natural and major thoroughfares—Buffalo Bayou, Congress Street, and Main Street—that demarcated each of the six areas.

Today, the wards don't hold any true political significance, but the neighborhoods are still known by their ward numbers. And, because most of the wards' residents are minorities, some of these areas have a reputation for being poor and crime ridden. Yet, many of the wards have been undergoing a revitalization, allowing some of the old homes in the area to be restored. Still, this rebirth has been slow for some, with Hurricane Ike wreaking significant damage on some of the wards in 2008. Below is a breakdown of the six wards:

Located northwest of downtown just north of Congress Avenue and west of Main Street, the **First Ward** is situated alongside the Theater District. Historically a working-class neighborhood, the First Ward is now home to a mix of Latino, black, and white residents. The Old Jeff Davis Hospital—Houston's first hospital—is located in the First Ward. Today, this neoclassical-style building has shed its status as a hospital and been turned into artists' lofts.

The **Second Ward** lies between Buffalo Bayou on the north and railroad tracks on the south and between Lockwood Avenue on the east and Congress Street on the

Most of the hospitals here are located off Fannin Street, Main Street, or Holcombe Boulevard and are easily accessible on the METRORail.

Upper Kirby & Greenway Plaza

Just north of West University and south of River Oaks lies the area known as Upper Kirby. It is bounded by Westheimer on the north, Westpark on the south, Shepherd on the east, and Buffalo Speedway on the west. Even if you don't have a map, you can usually tell when you're in the neighborhood: Red British-style telephone booths and red street signs dot Upper Kirby.

Much like the neighborhoods that surround it, Upper Kirby is fairly trendy and upscale, with a mix of commercial developments, private homes, and apartments. With its numerous bars, pubs, and restaurants, Upper Kirby is a popular spot to hang out or meet up with friends. The downside? Parking spaces can be tough to come by, especially on evenings and weekends.

The part of Upper Kirby located along US 59/Southwest Freeway is known as Greenway Plaza. The area is named after a series of office buildings just off the freeway. Today these buildings are joined by a number of luxury apartments, condos, and west. Once a white, upper-class area, the Second Ward lost many of its residents to other suburbs after World War II. It is now home to a large Latino population, as well as industrial buildings and some lofts.

Settled by freed slaves following the Civil War, the **Third Ward** is a historically black neighborhood. It's home to both Texas Southern University and the University of Houston. After many years of being run-down, the Third Ward has gotten a significant physical and emotional makeover with the help ofan innovative community art program called Project Row Houses. You can learn more about Project Row Houses on page 127 of the "Museums" chapter.

Nicknamed Freedman's Town, the **Fourth Ward** was founded by freed slaves. Located along the edge of downtown in what is now Midtown, this ward was once the hub of black culture in the city. Over the years, though, it became run-down. Today, lofts, apartments, restaurants, and bars are beginning to replace the old shotgun-style houses and housing projects.

Freed slaves created the **Fifth Ward** out of parts of the First and Second Wards. Located just northeast of downtown, the Fifth Ward sits north of Buffalo Bayou and east of its Little Oak Bayou Tributary. It's the city's oldest black neighborhood, but it has attracted large Latino, Asian, and immigrant populations over the years. In fact, about a third of today's Fifth Ward residents are of Latin or Hispanic origin. Although the Fifth Ward has one of the city's highest populations of ex-felons, it also has areas filled with organic gardens and blooming flowers.

Created out of the northern portion of the Fourth Ward, the **Sixth Ward** sits along downtown's western edge. It is home to the area's largest concentration of Victorian-era homes, making it the first Houston neighborhood to be added to the National Register of Historic Places in 1978. Many run-down homes here have been restored, but some are at risk of being bulldozed.

townhomes, as well as a strip center with a growing number of restaurants and shops.

Washington Corridor

The Washington Corridor—aka Washington Avenue—is arguably Houston's hottest neighborhood. It sits just south of The Heights and just north of the Fourth Ward and River Oaks. This rapidly developing area is bounded roughly by the West Loop 610 South on the west, I-45 on the east, I-10 along most of the northern part of the neighborhood, and Allen Parkway and Memorial Park along the south.

While a large number of apartment and condo renters, as well as homeowners, call the area home, even more people call the area home to their favorite hangouts. The neighborhood's main street—Washington Avenue—is lined with some of the city's trendiest restaurants and bars.

West University & Rice Village

Technically, West University—also known as West U and West University Place—spans from Bissonnet Street to Bellaire Boulevard/Holcombe Boulevard between Community Drive on the west and Kirby Drive on the east, but "West U" is sometimes used to describe the area as far east as Main Street, where Rice University lies. The area is home to some beautiful, pricey houses, as well as endless restaurants and shops. Many of these are located on or just east of Kirby in Rice Village, a retail area located just a few blocks west of Rice University. Also known as the Village, it has expanded in recent years to include about 4 main blocks between Rice and University Boulevards on the north and south and Kirby and Greenbriar on the east and west. Many chain stores like Ann Taylor and Banana Republic have moved in. Still, a number of local restaurants, bars, pubs, and stores—particularly women's boutiques—can be found around the Village.

i Parking spaces are tough to come by in Rice Village. Visit during off-peak weekday hours if you want to avoid searching for an elusive spot.

OUTSIDE THE LOOP

West

Galleria & Uptown

Located just off West Loop 610 South, the Galleria area is anchored by the Galleria, Houston's most distinguished mall, which sits at the intersection of Westheimer Road and Post Oak Boulevard. Just a couple of blocks away stands the third-tallest building in the city—Williams Tower—and a unique water wall, which is listed in the "Attractions" chapter.

The Galleria is home to an ice-skating rink, restaurants, and elite stores such as Louis Vuitton, Tiffany, Nordstrom, Neiman Marcus, and Dylan's Candy Bar, as well as mall staples such as Banana Republic, Gap, Abercrombie & Fitch, and Macy's. More great shopping can be found across the street

and in the blocks surrounding the Galleria, particularly on Westheimer on either side of Loop 610 and on Post Oak Boulevard.

A few blocks north of the Galleria at Post Oak Boulevard and Loop 610, you'll find the Uptown Park development, which is home to several higher-end boutiques and restaurants. Several hotels and a growing number of residential developments also dot the area. Because the Galleria area offers easy access to US 59, Loop 610, and I-10, as well as to River Oaks and other neighborhoods inside the Loop, many out-of-town visitors choose hotels in this area.

On Thanksgiving evening, many Houstonians and their Thanksgiving guests flock to the Galleria area to watch the lighting of the Christmas trees along Post Oak. This popular event, which you can learn more about in the "Annual Events" chapter, also includes special holiday entertainment, snacks, and even a fireworks display.

Depending on the route you take, the Galleria is about 8 miles west of downtown.

Memorial

Located south of the Katy Freeway between West Loop 610 North and West Beltway 8, Memorial is one of Houston's wealthiest and most beautiful neighborhoods. Large homes and tall pine trees line the residential portions of Memorial. Many great restaurants and shops make their homes in the area, as do some low-rise business offices. Popular shopping areas here include the recently renovated Memorial City Mall, which has a skating rink and a giant carousel; Town & Country Village, a well-manicured open-air shopping area; and City Centre, a chic new mixed-use urban development. Don't be surprised if you see a familiar-looking face when you're out and about in the Memorial area: Among the area's residents are Roger Clemens, former president George H. W. Bush, and former First Lady Barbara Bush. Memorial is about 12 miles from downtown.

Katy

One of Houston's most popular suburbs, Katy has a long history as an agricultural town and continues to produce rice today. Katy is composed of several master-planned communities and golf courses. More restaurants and retail developments have been cropping up here in recent years. The most notable of these is Katy Mills Mall, a mixed retail and outlet mall. Located off the Katy Freeway, Katy is about 25 miles from downtown.

East

Houston Ship Channel

Located east of Beltway 8, the Houston Ship Channel is the hub of the city's industrial and shipping activity. It comprises a large part of the Port of Houston and feeds into the Gulf of Mexico. As one of the country's busiest ports, the Ship Channel is used to transport general cargo, petrochemical, grain, and other products to destinations around the country and the world. Many oil refineries are located along the channel, which has been widened several times to accommodate larger ships. The sheer amount of industrial activity and ships passing through here makes for some unpleasant odors and high ozone levels. Located along the length of the Ship Channel are the USS Texas, which was used during both World Wars, and the San Jacinto Monument, the site where Texas revolutionaries defeated Mexican troops to secure Texas's independence in 1836. Both the USS Texas and the San Jacinto Monument are located in the San Jacinto

Battleground State Historic Site in the town of La Porte; learn more about these sites in the "Attractions" chapter. The Ship Channel is about 25 miles east of downtown.

Baytown

Baytown sits on the east side of the Ship Channel, about 27 miles from downtown. While there are plenty of homes in this independent city, the area is perhaps best known for its many oil refineries and rubber and chemical plants. Baytown is also home to Royal Purple Raceway, a motor-racing complex that you can learn more about in the "Spectator Sports" chapter. Baytown residents and visitors—as well as their cars and bicycles—can travel across the Houston Ship Channel on the Lynchburg Ferry, which was used to transport Texas revolutionaries to the Battle of San Jacinto in 1836.

North

The north side of Houston is home to George Bush Intercontinental Airport, the city's largest airport, which sits just north of Beltway 8. Much of this area is devoted to airport operations, as well as to hotels and rental car companies. There are also several neighborhoods and suburbs north of Houston.

Spring

Spring lies about 22 miles north of downtown on I-45 and falls into Houston's extraterritorial jurisdiction. Once home to the Orcoquiza Native Americans, this predominately residential area has seen tremendous growth in the last few decades, with several new residential developments popping up. The area is home to many retail developments. Perhaps the most notable of these is Old Town Spring, which houses shops in Spring's oldest buildings. Spring is also home to the popular water park SplashTown, which you can learn about in the "Kidstuff" chapter.

Conroe

Located about 40 miles north of downtown on I-45, Conroe is the county seat of Montgomery County. It's also home to Lake Conroe, one of the most popular places in the area to go boating, fishing, and waterskiing. While many people come here only on weekends and during vacations, the permanent population has grown dramatically in recent years as the Greater Houston area has expanded.

The Woodlands

Located about 30 miles north of downtown off I-45, The Woodlands offers a serene reprieve from city life. The master-planned community is heavily wooded and elegantly landscaped, making it a popular place for the fairly well-off to call home. In recent years The Woodlands has become home to a growing number of restaurants and retail establishments, including The Woodlands Mall. Cynthia Woods Mitchell Pavilion, an outdoor amphitheater that hosts some of the city's biggest concerts, is located in The Woodlands; find out more about it in the "Nightlife" chapter.

Northeast

Kingwood

Located off US 59, Kingwood is a master-planned community that dates back to the 1970s. However, it wasn't officially annexed by Houston until 1996. While Kingwood is a master-planned community, the villages within it boast a variety of architectural styles. However, the neighborhoods here are all filled with pine trees and oaks. Although

Kingwood is predominately a residential neighborhood, there are also many retail developments and restaurants, including a growing number along US 59. Kingwood is about 23 miles from downtown.

South

Pearland

Located about 20 miles south of downtown on TX 288, Pearland is one of the country's fastest-growing suburbs. The population is more than 80 percent white and predominately white-collar. Many residents work in the Medical Center or downtown. This master-planned community occupies three different counties—Harris, Fort Bend, and Brazoria. Pearland has no major industries of its own, though the area boasts several retail developments, restaurants, and parks.

Southeast

Head southeast of downtown along I-45, and you'll find William P. Hobby Airport. Drive a little farther, and you'll find some of the area's most popular recreational areas, as well as some industrial areas.

Pasadena

Pasadena is located east of the Houston Ship Channel, about 20 miles southeast of downtown, and is filled with odor-emitting refineries and shipping-related businesses. Although there are some million-dollar homes in the area, most Pasadena residents are blue-collar workers who play a central role in Houston's industries. About half of Pasadena's residents are Hispanic or Latino. The city, which is largely shaped by its industries, is home to an annual strawberry festival and to Armand Bayou Nature Center, a beautiful nature reserve listed in the "Parks" chapter.

Bay Area

Situated between Houston and Galveston, the Bay Area is the name used to refer to a collection of communities along Galveston Bay. The crown jewel of these communities is Clear Lake. This wealthy master-planned community is home to a large population of engineers, thanks to its proximity to Houston's petrochemical plants, Lockheed-Martin, Boeing, and NASA's Johnson Space Center. Clear Lake is also home to a lake of the same name, which empties into Galveston Bay. The area is one of the best and most popular places in the Houston region to go boating, sailing, fishing, and waterskiing. Most of Clear Lake is located in Houston, but a small part lies in Pasadena's jurisdiction.

Drive just a few minutes south of Clear Lake, and you'll find yourself in Kemah. This small fishing town is home to some colorful little cottages and shops—and the Kemah Boardwalk Entertainment District, which boasts restaurants, carnival rides, boardwalk games, shops, an aquarium, and other family-friendly entertainment. You can learn more about the boardwalk in the "Attractions" chapter. Like other parts of the Bay Area, Kemah endured significant damage from Hurricane Ike, but most of the boardwalk attractions have been repaired and reopened. Clear Lake is located about 20 miles from downtown; Kemah is about 30 miles from downtown.

Galveston

Galveston sits on the Gulf of Mexico, making it a popular place to go to the beach, surf, sail, water-ski, fish, and enjoy other water-based activities. The island is also home to many hotels, seafood restaurants, and touristy shops, making this a hotspot for Houstonians and other tourists looking to escape for a week or a weekend. Many of the residences here are beach houses, occupied only on weekends and during the summer. Once Texas's most bustling port, much of Galveston was destroyed by the Hurricane of 1900. While the city rebuilt after that storm, some parts are still rebuilding from Hurricane Ike, which destroyed hundreds of homes and businesses and killed many who didn't heed evacuation orders. Galveston is about 45 miles from downtown.

Southwest

Alief

Located west of West Beltway 8, Alief is one of Houston's most diverse areas, with a large population of Latin American and Asian immigrants, blacks, and people of Caribbean, African, and Middle Eastern origins. Many Louisiana residents who fled Hurricane Katrina moved to this area. There are some good hole-in-the-wall restaurants and ethnic shops in Alief, which is home to part of the city's Chinatown, as well as Little Saigon. In recent years, Alief's seen quite a bit of crime and gang violence, with a murder rate that is 480 percent above the national average. Alief is about 15 miles from downtown.

Sharpstown

Located between Beltway 8 and Loop 610, Sharpstown was considered a trailblazer among master-planned communities when it was founded in the 1950s. Today, though, many of the buildings—including apartments, homes, retail stores, and restaurants—look pretty outdated. The area, which is home to large Asian and Latin

Houston Vital Statistics

Founded: 1836 (incorporated in 1837)

Area codes: 713, 281, 832

Population (in 2010): 2.1 million inside the city limits; 5.95 million in the Houston Metropolitan Statistical Area, which includes the suburbs and exurbs

County: Harris

Counties in the Houston-Galveston-Brazoria Metropolitan Statistical Area: Harris, Fort Bend, Montgomery, Brazoria, Galveston, Liberty, Waller, Chambers

Nicknames: Space City, Bayou City, Clutch City

Average temperatures:

  January: 62°F (high), 41°F (low)

  July: 94°F (high), 74°F (low)

Average annual rainfall: 48 inches

Major commercial airports: George Bush Intercontinental Airport, William P. Hobby Airport

Major colleges and universities: Rice University, University of Houston, Texas Southern University, University of St. Thomas, Baylor College of Medicine, South Texas College of Law, University of Texas Health Science Center at Houston, Houston Baptist University, Prairie View A&M College of Nursing

Major area businesses: NASA, Texas Medical Center, El Paso Corporation, Shell Oil US Division, Landry's Restaurants, Halliburton, Marathon Oil, Pennzoil, Sysco, Gulf South Pipeline Company, Schlumberger Technology Corporation, Shipley Do-Nuts, BP America, Pappas Restaurants, ConocoPhillips, CITGO Petroleum, CenterPoint Energy, Al's Formal Wear, Apache Corporation

Daily newspaper: *Houston Chronicle*

Alternative newsweekly: *Houston Press*

Sales tax: 8.25 percent

Hotel tax: 17 percent

Famous sons and daughters: Musicians Beyoncé and Solange Knowles, Kenny Rogers, and Lyle Lovett; Dell Computer founder Michael Dell; WordPress creator Matt Mullenweg; race car driver A.J. Foyt; journalists Dan Rather and Walter Cronkite; Broadway star Tommy Tune; actors Dennis and Randy Quaid, Patrick Swayze, Isaiah Washington, Hilary and Haylie Duff, Renee Zellweger, Salma Hayek, Chandra Wilson, Jennifer Garner, and Alexis Bledel; filmmaker Wes Anderson; basketball stars Clyde Drexler and Rashard Lewis; NFL football star Vince Young; baseball star Nolan Ryan

Famous residents: Former US president George H. W. Bush and former First Lady Barbara Bush; former US Secretary of State James Baker; filmmaker, aviator, and billionaire Howard Hughes; baseball stars Roger Clemens and Andy Pettitte; gymnast Mary Lou Retton; NBA basketball coaches Avery Johnson and Jeff Van Gundy; televangelist and pastor Joel Osteen; *Project Runway* winner Chloe Dao

Visitor Information

Greater Houston Convention and Visitors Bureau
City Hall
901 Bagby, Ste. 100
(713) 437-5200
visithoustontexas.com
The Greater Houston Convention and Visitors Bureau is responsible for attracting conventions and tourists to the Houston area. Call or visit the website for more advice on where to go, what to do, where to stay, and where to eat in Houston. The visitors bureau is located downtown in City Hall.

Explore Houston! Visitors Center
George R. Brown Convention Center, Level 2
1001 Avenida de las Americas
(713) 853-8000
(800) 427-4697
houstonconventionctr.com
Attending a convention at the George R. Brown Convention Center? Be sure to stop in at the Explore Houston! Visitors Center. They'll help you with with dinner reservations, touristy questions, and airline, concert, and theater tickets. Added bonus: The Visitors Center sells Houston souvenirs for just about everyone on your list.

Many of the Houston suburbs also have their own visitor bureaus or chambers of commerce that assist

newcomers. The contact information for the largest suburbs' visitors bureaus are:

Bay Area Houston Convention and Visitors Bureau
913 N. Meyer Rd., Seabrook
(281) 474-9700
(866) 611-4688
visitbayareahouston.com

Galveston Island Visitors Center
2328 Broadway, Galveston
(888) 425-4753
galveston.com/cvb

Katy Visitor and Tourism Bureau
23501 Cinco Ranch Blvd., Ste. B206, Katy
(281) 391-5289
katychamber.com

Lake Conroe Area Convention and Visitors Bureau
505 W. Davis St., Conroe
(936) 522-3500
conroecvb.net

Old Town Spring Visitors Bureau
606 Spring Cypress, Spring
(281) 288-2355
shopspringtexas.com

Fort Bend Chamber of Commerce
445 Commerce Green Blvd., Sugar Land
(281) 491-0800
fortbendchamber.com

The Woodlands Convention and Visitors Bureau
2801 Technology Forest Blvd.,The Woodlands
(281) 363-2447
thewoodlandscvb.com

American immigrant populations, makes up part of Houston's Chinatown. Here you'll find a number of ethnic restaurants and grocery stores, as well as many apartments, residential developments, and some single-family homes.

Stafford

Located predominately in Fort Bend County, Stafford is known for being a business-friendly community. Among the businesses located here: Tyco, UPS, and Texas Instruments. Retail businesses, hotels, and restaurants can also be found by the dozen in Stafford, where the sales tax is 0.5 percent lower than that of surrounding cities. There are many single-family homes in the area, but the people working here outnumber Stafford residents.

Sugar Land

Once a sugar plantation and the home of Imperial Sugar's headquarters, Sugar Land is now one of Houston's most highly regarded suburbs. An independent municipality, Sugar Land is a master-planned community filled with larger homes, golf courses, and country clubs. Nearly 60 percent of residents are white, about a quarter are of Asian descent, and more than a couple are famous athletes. As with other master-planned communities in the area, the bulk of businesses here are retail and restaurants. Sugar Land is about 20 miles from downtown, just off US 59.

GETTING HERE, GETTING AROUND

Between the hundreds of domestic and international flights departing from and arriving at Houston's two airports each day and the many interstate and state highways that run through the city, Houston is accessible from just about anywhere. Once you get to town, you'll need a car—that is, unless you're staying (and don't plan to leave) downtown, where you can walk, take cabs, and ride METRORail. Downtown options aside, Houston is a sprawling metropolis without a sprawling public transportation system. Sure, the city has a bus system, but the frequent stops and traffic mean you could spend an hour or more traveling from point A to point B, even if points A and B are just a few miles apart. The city has a light-rail system, too, but it doesn't venture into the suburbs, much less to areas inside the Loop like the Galleria, River Oaks, the Heights, or Montrose. You can take cabs around the city, but the cost adds up quickly. And, in most cases, you'll have to call ahead to schedule a pickup.

When trying to get your bearings in Houston, keep in mind that downtown is at the center of the city and that the city's major freeways—I-10, US 59, and I-45—intersect there. Heading south of downtown will take you to Freeport on the Gulf of Mexico; heading southeast will take you to William P. Hobby Airport and to Galveston, which is about a 45-minute drive from Houston. Heading north of downtown will take you to Dallas, which is about a 4-hour drive from Houston. Go east of downtown and you'll wind up in the Houston Ship Channel area. Heading west from downtown? You'll soon be on your way to Memorial Park, Memorial, Katy, and eventually San Antonio—about a 3-hour drive from Houston.

BY CAR

When you're driving around Houston during rush hour, there's one thing you can always expect: traffic on major freeways. And we're talking serious traffic here. During weekday mornings and in the early evening, it can take twice—or sometimes even three times—as long as usual to reach your destination.

No matter where you're headed, it's nearly impossible to avoid the freeways if you spend more than a few days—or even hours—in Houston. But here's some good news: You probably won't use most of these freeways or tollroads, at least not if you're spending your time in the city's central areas. So, instead of overwhelming you with highways you'll probably never use, the next few paragraphs highlight just the major freeways and tollroads. Keep in mind that this is just a starting point. Before hitting the road, spend some time looking at a map to get a better feel for the city's layout.

Toll Road Driving Made EZ

While you *can* get around without ever driving on a toll road here, it's sometimes quicker to include a toll road—or two—in your route. Houston's toll roads may be set up a little differently from those you've encountered before, though. That's because Houston has tollbooths at the toll road entrances as well as pass-through tollbooths, which require you to pay a toll even after you've paid the initial entry toll. This means you may have to stop and pay tolls two or three times in the course of a drive. Tolls vary, but they typically run somewhere between 30 cents to $1.50 for cars; vehicles with three or more axles pay higher tolls.

i Use your EZ Tag to park in the on-site garages at George Bush Intercontinental and William P. Hobby Airports. This way, you can skip the hassle of waiting in line to pay the cashier.

Want to avoid the hassle of rummaging through your wallet for money at tollbooths? If you're here to stay, your best bet is to purchase an EZ Tag. (EZ tags can't be used on rental cars since they can't be transferred from vehicle to vehicle.) Just stick the tag on your windshield and drive through the EZ Tag lane. A camera will scan your EZ Tag and automatically deduct the toll from your account. An EZ Tag will cost you a one-time activation fee of $15, plus a minimum credit or debit card payment of $40, from which your toll charges will be deducted. You can purchase an EZ Tag online or by visiting one of the four EZ Tag stores. Call (281) 875-3279

to find these locations, or visit the EZ Tag registration website (hctra.org). The website also includes a downloadable map with the toll roads' entry and exit points and toll plazas.

TxTag and EZ Tag can be used interchangeably in Houston. The only difference is that TxTag stickers can be used statewide. So, you might want to buy one if you're in Texas long-term and plan to travel around the state a lot. Want to buy a prepaid TxTag sticker? Visit txtag.org or call (888) 468-9824.

i Find out about road closures and traffic pile-ups around town by visiting Houston Transtar's website: traffic.houstontranstar.org.

Freeway & Toll Road Cheatsheet

Here's the lowdown on the freeways and toll roads you'll almost inevitably encounter—or at least hear about:

Loop 610—aka the Loop—runs around central Houston, which includes downtown, the Medical Center, Montrose, the Museum District, Midtown, West University, Braeswood, the wards, and the Heights, among other areas. The northern part of the Loop is known as the North Loop, the southern part is called the South Loop, the eastern side is known as the East Loop, and the western side—which runs along the Galleria and Bellaire—is known as the West Loop.

Sometimes, an additional ordinal direction is added to the name of the Loop to describe a more specific location. Here are some examples:

- North Loop West refers to the section of the north loop between US 290 and I-45.
- North Loop East runs between I-45 and US 90.
- East Loop North is the section of the East Loop between US 90 and I-10.

- East Loop South runs between I-10 and TX 225.
- South Loop East is the section of the South Loop between TX 225 and TX 288.
- South Loop West runs between TX 288 and the South Post Oak Road spur.
- West Loop South is the section of the West Loop between the South Post Oak spur and Buffalo Bayou.
- West Loop North runs from the Buffalo Bayou and US 290.

US 59, which cuts through the Loop, runs from northeast to southwest Houston and along the eastern side of downtown. The section in the northeastern part of the city is called the Eastex Freeway; the section running from downtown to the southwestern suburbs is called the Southwest Freeway.

I-45 cuts through the northern part of the city before running along the western side of downtown and then veering southeast. I-45 North will take you to the northern suburb of The Woodlands and eventually to Dallas, about 4 hours north of Houston. I-45 South will take you to William P. Hobby Airport, the Bay Area, Space Center Houston, and ultimately, Galveston.

i Tune in to AM 740 or AM 1610 on your radio for the latest traffic and weather updates.

I-10, which runs from California to Florida, cuts east-west through the upper half of the Loop and intersects with both I-45 and US 59 downtown. The section of I-10 running east from downtown to the Ship Channel is called the East Freeway, or the Baytown East Freeway. The recently widened stretch of I-10 that runs west from downtown to Katy is called the Katy Freeway. The Harris County Toll Road Authority recently

added managed lanes to the Katy Freeway between 610 West and TX 6, a state highway that runs from the Texas-Oklahoma border to just northwest of Galveston and intersects with I-10, Westheimer Road, FM 1960 (an old farm-to-market road), and US 290.

The **Katy Freeway managed lanes** run both eastbound and westbound from 5 to 11 a.m. and 2 to 8 p.m., Mon through Fri. The managed lanes are part toll road, part HOV lane (which we'll get to shortly). This means vehicles with two or more people can drive in the managed lanes for free.

i Have two or more people in your car? Drive in the left managed lane of the Katy Managed Lanes. Driving solo with your EZ Tag or TxTag? Stay in the right managed lane.

Don't have passengers to keep you company? You can drive in the managed lanes by paying a toll. There aren't any tollbooths for these lanes, though. You must have a toll tag—either an EZ Tag (local) or a TxTag (statewide), and the cost of the toll will be deducted each time you drive in a managed lane. Tolls range from 30 cents to $1.60, depending on the time and direction you're driving in. Visit hctra.org to download a map of the managed lanes' entry and exit points.

Houston has a second loop made up of the **Sam Houston Tollway,** the **Sam Houston Parkway,** and **Beltway 8.** This intermediate loop circles the more distant reaches of the city, including the area near George Bush Intercontinental Airport on the north, the Houston Ship Channel on the east, and southern exurbs like Sugar Land on the south. It also intersects with I-10 just west of Memorial and east of Katy, making this a popular place to enter the toll road and head to Intercontinental Airport from the west side of town. Each side of the Beltway, as this Texas state highway is often called, is referred to by its compass direction (East Belt, for example). The northern, southern, western, and southeastern sides of the loop are called the Sam Houston Tollway or Beltway 8; the northeastern side is referred to as Sam Houston Parkway. The beltway primarily runs on frontage roads; the tollway section obviously requires a toll. Tolls along the Sam Houston Tollway range from 75 cents to $2, though they're typically 75 cents or $1.

HOV Lanes: Your Rush Hour Ally

Toll roads aren't your only allies when battling traffic. The city also strives to encourage carpooling and curb traffic with several so-called HOV lanes that run along the interior of most major freeways and highways. To drive in an HOV lane, you must have at least two people riding in the car, including the driver. In most cases, concrete separators will tip you off as to where these lanes lie; along US 59 South, HOV lanes are distinguished only by painted diamonds in the lane. Many HOV lanes accommodate inbound traffic during the morning rush hour from 5 to 11 a.m., then switch to accommodate outbound traffic from 2 to 8 p.m. A map of HOV lanes and schedules can be downloaded from ridemetro.org/schedulesmaps/hov.aspx.

i Want a carpool buddy? METRO maintains a database of local commuters who want to carpool. Visit METRO's website (ridepro.ridemetro .org/ridepro/service.asp) to find other commuters who live and work near you.

At the time this book went to press, METRO was working on making the HOV lanes along I-45 (Gulf Freeway) into HOT (High-Occupancy Toll) lanes. This will allow drivers without passengers to use the HOV lanes for a toll. The tolls will vary by the time of day and traffic volume. METRO will sell HOT lane toll tags at ridemetro.org, or you can use your EZ Tag to pay. You can learn more about the coming HOT lanes at ihate houstontraffic.org.

i Want to drive in the HOV lane on US 290/Northwest Freeway during rush hour? Unless you're willing to pay, you must have three passengers. Cars with just two occupants are required to pay $2. Prefer to just pay the $2? You'll need to register by calling (713) 224-7433 to register and learn more.

BY PLANE

Houston is home to two commercial airports—George Bush Intercontinental Airport (IAH) and William P. Hobby Airport (HOU). Together they served more than 49.5 million passengers in 2010. Between the two airports, you can find service to nearly 200 international and domestic destinations on just about every national and international airline.

Recent renovations at both airports make for a relatively pleasant airport experience. They're clean, easy to navigate, and are full of new restaurants and shops.

The larger of the two airports, George Bush Intercontinental, is located in north Houston, about 23 miles north of downtown and 27 miles northeast of the Galleria. Hobby Airport is located in the southeast part of the city, about 7 miles south of downtown and 16 miles from the Galleria. If that seems like a quick ride to your destination, keep in mind

Houston Roadways

Here are a few other Houston roadways worth knowing:

The east-west highway **US 290** runs northwest, intersecting with both Loop 610 and the Sam Houston Tollway. You can take US 290 straight to the Texas capital of Austin, which is about 2.5 hours northwest of Houston by car.

FM 1960 is an old farm-to-market road that intersects with US 290 and TX 6 in northern Harris County. It primarily travels east.

Westheimer Road, sometimes referred to as **FM 1093** on signs, is a major road that runs east-west from the Westpark Tollway to downtown, where it turns into Bagby Street. Westheimer runs parallel to I-10, which lies to its north. The Galleria mall sits on Westheimer, which goes under West Loop 610 South and through River Oaks, Montrose, and Midtown.

Just south of Westheimer is the **Westpark Tollway,** which runs relatively parallel. The Westpark Tollway runs from Westpark Drive on the west to **TX 99,** which will eventually make a third loop around the Houston metropolitan area. Tolls here range from 35 cents to $1.25, but there are no tollbooths. You must have an EZ Tag to drive on the Westpark Tollway. If you drive on the tollway without an EZ Tag, you'll get a ticket in the mail.

The **Hardy Toll Road** runs from I-45, just north of the city, to Loop 610, near central Houston. For the most part, the 22-mile Hardy Toll Road runs parallel to I-45. Toll charges range from 75 cents to $1.50 for cars; EZ Tag users get a 25-cent discount on each Hardy Toll Road toll.

TX 288 runs south from downtown to Freeport, Texas, along the Gulf of Mexico. 288, as it's known, will also take you to the southern Houston suburb of Pearland.

US 90 overlaps with I-10 from Katy to roughly the East Loop Freeway, where US 90 then heads northeast and becomes known as the Crosby Freeway.

that 60 mph doesn't always translate to 1 mile a minute here. Houston freeways can get pretty congested, especially during rush hour. So, if you're staying 30 miles from the airport, give yourself an hour to get there. And be sure to account for the extra time you will need to park and return your rental car (if you're driving), check your luggage, go through security, and get to your gate in time. The airlines usually recommend arriving an hour and a half before takeoff, but it's a good idea to arrive at least 2 hours early if you're traveling during peak travel holidays.

Even though both Houston airports have plenty of security lines and ticket counters, there's almost always a line during the winter holidays and big travel weekends.

Where to Park

Parking at the airport? Both Intercontinental and Hobby offer plenty of on-site and off-site parking options, whether you're parking for a few hours or a few days. One of the cheapest—and greenest—options is the city-owned ecopark, whose shuttles run on clean natural gas instead of diesel fuel. Parking in

Airlines Serving Intercontinental Airport

Airline	Phone Number	Website	Terminal(s)
AeroMexico	(800) 237-6639	aeromexico.com	D
Air Canada	(888) 422-7533	aircanada.com	A
Air France	(800) 237-2747	airfrance.com	D
Alaska Airlines	(800) 252-7522	alaskaair.com	A
American Airlines	(800) 433-7300	aa.com	A
British Airways	(800) 247-9297	britishairways.com	D
Delta Air Lines	(800) 221-1212	delta.com	A
Emirates	(800) 777-3999	emirates.com	D
KLM Royal Dutch Airlines	(800) 447-4747	klm.com	D
Lufthansa	(800) 399-5838	lufthansa.com	D
Northwest Airlines	(800) 225-2525	nwa.com	A
Qatar Airways	(877) 777-2827	qatarairways.com	D
Singapore Airlines	(800) 742-3333	singaporeair.com	D
TACA	(800) 400-8222	taca.com	D
United Airlines	(800) 864-8331	united.com	A, B, C, E
US Airways	(800) 428-4322	usairways.com	A
VivaAerobus	(888) 935-9848	vivaaerobus.com	D

Intercontinental's ecopark lot will cost you $2.77 plus tax for up to 3 hours and $4.62 plus tax (uncovered parking) or $6.47 plus tax (covered parking) for 3 to 24 hours. Hobby has two ecopark lots. Depending which lot you park in, you'll pay either $1.85 plus tax or $2.77 plus tax for up to 3 hours, and $5.44 plus tax or $7.39 plus tax for up to 24 hours. Intercontinental's ecopark lot is located at JFK Boulevard and Greens Road as you approach the terminals. Hobby's ecopark lot is on-site and within walking distance of the terminals. Look for the blue and green signs.

George Bush Intercontinental Airport

Previously called Intercontinental Airport, Houston's largest and busiest airport was renamed to honor the 41st US president and Houston resident George H. W. Bush in 1997. Houstonians tend to refer to the airport—abbreviated IAH—as "Intercontinental" or "Bush Intercontinental." Currently, Intercontinental, which is located off the Hardy Toll Road, is served by 17 commercial airlines, as well as several passenger charter airlines. Because this bustling airport is one of United/Continental Airlines' biggest hubs and Houston is the largest major city near Mexico and Latin America, more than 700 flights depart from Intercontinental each day. These flights offer nonstop service to more than 176 domestic and international destinations.

i Need help navigating the airport—or making plans once you leave the airport? Get help at one of the Visitor Information Centers on the baggage claim levels of Terminals A, B, and C at Intercontinental.

To accommodate its many airlines and passengers, Intercontinental has five terminals, lettered A through E. Passengers leaving Houston on international airlines depart from Terminal D. International inbound flights provided by Continental Airlines arrive in Terminal E. Customs and Border Protection are also located in Terminal E on the second floor.

Traveling between terminals? Hop on the Inter-Terminal Train for a quick connection between terminals B, C, and E. Signs for the train are located in the ticketing areas and terminals.

i Arriving on an international flight? Grab a free-to-use luggage cart in the customs area. The carts aren't allowed on Intercontinental's Inter-Terminal Train.

Intercontinental's many amenities make the airport seem like a city unto itself. You'll find more than 50 restaurants and bars here, ranging from McDonald's and Chili's Too to healthier options like Upper Crust and The Real Food Company to homegrown favorites like Pappas Bar-B-Q, Pappadeaux Seafood Kitchen, and Pappasito's Cantina. You'll also find gift shops selling everything from Houston and Texas paraphernalia to luxury handbags and perfumes. Other amenities include an interfaith chapel, a currency exchange booth, and multilingual service representatives. Since Intercontinental is one of United/Continental Airlines' hubs, you can often find last-minute weekend getaway flights between Houston and locations around the country, as well as South America, for as little as $139 round-trip. Visit continental.com and go to "Deals & Offers" to find current deals.

William P. Hobby Airport

After stints as Houston Municipal Airport and Howard R. Hughes Airport—yes, that Howard Hughes—Houston's oldest commercial airport was renamed in 1967 to honor former Texas governor William P. Hobby. Abbreviated HOU, Hobby is just 7 miles south of downtown Houston off I-45/Gulf Freeway, making this a more convenient airport for many visitors and Houstonians. With just six passenger airlines, one charter service, and no international flights currently serving Hobby, it's not nearly as congested as Intercontinental. All six airlines—Southwest, AirTran, JetBlue, Delta, Frontier, and American—fly out of the Central Concourse. Together, they provide nonstop or direct service to more than 34 destinations around the United States.

Hungry? At Hobby, you've got your pick of more than a dozen dining and drinking establishments, most located in the concourse. Your options range from popular local joints like Barry's Pizza, Pappasito's Cantina, and Pappas Burgers to national chains like Wendy's and Subway. Got time to kill? Stop by the 1940s Air Terminal Museum, which commemorates the old terminal's classic art-deco architecture as well as its role in early aviation.

i Picking someone up at the airport? At both airports, you can avoid circling the terminal while you wait by parking in the free passenger pickup waiting lot. Just remind your passenger to call and let you know when he or she has arrived.

Other amenities include the usual suspects: newsstands, gift shops, an interfaith

Rental Car Agencies
Serving Intercontinental & Hobby Airports

Agency	Phone Number	Website
Advantage Rent A Car		
(IAH only)	(800) 777-5524	advantage.com
Alamo	(888) 826-6893	alamo.com
Avis	(800) 331-1212	avis.com
Budget	(800) 527-0700	budget.com
Dollar Rent a Car	(866) 434-2226	dollar.com
Enterprise	(800) 736-7222	enterprise.com
Hertz	(800) 654-3131	hertz.com
National	(888) 826-6890	nationalcar.com
Thrifty	(877) 283-0898	thrifty.com

chapel, a currency exchange booth, and multilingual special service representatives.

From the Airports to the City

Need transportation from the airport? At both airports, visit the information desk on the baggage claim level for help. Or head out the door and a ground transportation agent can help you find taxis and limos.

Car Rental

Eight national rental car agencies serve Houston's two airports; one additional agency—Advantage Rent A Car—serves only Intercontinental. Most rental car agencies have more drop-off and pickup locations around the city, though these locations usually have fewer cars available—and often close earlier—than the airport locations.

To rent a car at Hobby, head down to the baggage claim level and find the booth for your preferred agency. Once you pay, an agent will send you outside to catch a shuttle to the appropriate pickup lot.

At Intercontinental, the nine rental companies share a consolidated rental car facility.

To get there, just follow the rental car signs and head outside after picking up your bags in baggage claim. Then hop on one of the white and maroon buses marked Rental Car Shuttle and take a free 5-minute ride to the facility, where you'll find your agency's office and car lot. Returning a rental car at the airport? Give yourself at least an extra 15 minutes to drop off the car.

i Don't have GPS on your phone? Save yourself a headache and rent a GPS at the car rental agency. Otherwise, you may give yourself a headache trying to navigate your way through Houston's unfamiliar jam-packed freeways.

Taxis & Limousines

City ordinances require Houston cabbies to charge $2.50 for the first $\frac{2}{11}$ mile and 17 cents for each additional $\frac{1}{11}$ mile. (That translates to $4 for the first mile and $1.87 for each additional mile.) The meters calculate waiting at a rate of 33 cents per minute, or up to $20 per hour. There's an additional $1

Taxi Zone Rates

To/From Intercontinental Airport

Daytime Zone	Rate
North Houston, 610 North	$38
Downtown	$44.50
Galleria, Greenway Plaza, MedicalCenter, Memorial, River Oaks	$51
Reliant Center area	$55
Hobby Airport	$62
West Memorial, Bear Creek	$69
Ellington Airport, Westside	$74.50
NASA, Space Center Houston	$88.50
Kingwood	$28.50
Willowbrook	$35

To/From Hobby Airport

Daytime Zone	Rate
Medical Center, Ellington Field, Southeast Houston	$27
Downtown	$22
The Heights, Greenway Plaza	$33
Galleria, North Loop	$46
Spring Branch, Town & Country	$52
Dairy Ashford	$59.50
Area of I-10 West, TX 6	$68.50
Intercontinental Airport, Greenspoint	$60.50
NASA, Space Center Houston	$31.50
Kingwood	$73
Willowbrook	$67.50

*Remember to add $1 to the zone rate if you're taking a cab between 8 p.m. and 6 a.m.

surcharge for all trips that start between 8 p.m. and 6 a.m.

Now for some good news: You'll only be charged one fare if you're riding with one or more other passengers. Even better: you'll be charged either a metered or a flat zone rate—whichever is less. For cabs to and from Intercontinental, daytime rates range from $28.50 to $88.50, depending on the zone. For cabs to and from Hobby, daytime rates range from $22 to $73. Gratuity isn't included in the zone rates.

If you take a cab to or from the aiport and choose the metered option instead of a flat rate, beware: cab drivers can add an additional $2.75 fee for departures from Intercontinental and $1.25 for departures from Hobby.

Heading back to the airport or need a cab or limo to get around town? Always call ahead to reserve your ride. There are more than 2,200 cabs in Houston, but taxi stands are rare unless you're downtown. Here you'll find the phone numbers and websites for several taxi, town car, and limo companies. In many cases, you can make a reservation online or over the phone.

A1 TRANSPORTATION TAXI, LIMO & TOWN CAR SERVICE
(866) 416-1975
a1transportationtaxi.com

AFC CORPORATE TRANSPORTATION
(713) 988-5466
afchouston.com

EXECUCAR
(800) 410-4444
execucar.com

LIBERTY CAB
(713) 695-6700
libertycab.net

RIVER OAKS LIMO & TRANSPORTATION
(832) 203-7622
riveroakslimo.com

i Age 60 or older? Don't be coy about your age. Cab drivers here give seniors a 10 percent discount.

TAXIS FIESTA
(713) 225-2666
taxisfiesta.com

TOWNE CAR HOUSTON
(713) 236-8877
townecarhouston.com

UNITED CAB
(713) 699-0000
unitedcab.com

YELLOW CAB TAXI
(713) 236-1111
yellowcabhouston.com

i Taking a cab around downtown? Take advantage of "Six in the City." Every cab ride that starts and ends downtown costs a flat rate of $6.

Airport Shuttles

Don't want to shell out money for a cab, limo, or rental car? Here are a few options for getting to and from the airport and around Houston:

SuperShuttle's blue and yellow vans provide ground transportation to and from both airports. Because it's a shared-ride service, though, you won't reach your destination as quickly as you would by taking a cab. That is, unless you opt for SuperShuttle's more expensive ExecuCar service. SuperShuttle prices vary, but shared rides usually cost between $20 and $30 with an advance reservation; gratuity isn't excluded. Discounts are available for groups and round-trip purchases. Catch a ride on SuperShuttle by going to the company's desk in the baggage claim area or save a few dollars by making reservations in advance at (800) 258-3826 or supershuttle.com.

Houston's bus service, **METRO,** offers daily service from downtown to Intercontinental and vice versa via the local Route 102 bus. One-way fare costs $1.25. For route and schedule information, call (713) 635-4000 or visit ridemetro.org.

Some hotels—especially those near the airport—offer complimentary shuttle service for their guests. Call ahead to find out if yours does. Hotels farther away from the airport rarely offer service to and from the airport, but they may provide transportation to attractions and restaurants within a 3-mile radius of the hotel.

BY TRAIN & BUS

Amtrak

The local Amtrak station—abbreviated HOS—sits on downtown's northwestern edge at 902 Washington Ave., just off I-45. The station provides service on the Sunset Limited route, which runs from Los Angeles to New Orleans, with stops in San Antonio, Tucson, El Paso, and other locations on the southern edges of California, Arizona, New Mexico, Texas, and Louisiana.

i Before stepping onto the METRO-Rail platform, make sure you have a paid ticket. These are paid-fare zones, so you can receive a class C misdemeanor and a fine of up to $500 for waiting on the platform without a ticket.

Heavy luggage? Breathe easy: You can get free baggage assistance and check bags here. Free short-term and long-term parking is available; there's also a taxi stand. The full-service station is very clean, has an indoor waiting area, and is fully wheelchair accessible.

For a schedule or to purchase tickets, call (800) 872-7245 or visit amtrak.com.

Greyhound

There are five Greyhound stations in Houston, plus a few more in the exurbs, including Conroe, Humble, and Katy. The main Houston Greyhound station is located just north of downtown at 2121 S. Main St.; the ticket counter and station here are open 24 hours. Other locations are located in Northwest, Southeast, and Southwest Houston, though most aren't open all night. Greyhound buses also stop at the Amtrak station, listed above, but there are no bus ticketing or baggage facilities at that location. Greyhound Bus Line information, including addresses of additional Houston stations, is available by calling (800) 231-2222 or (713) 759-6565 or visiting greyhound.com.

BY FERRY

Spending time in the Baytown area? You may need to take the Lynchburg Ferry. It carries passengers and their cars across the Houston Ship Channel so they can get to and from Houston. One of the fleet's two ferries departs every 5 to 10 minutes from 4:30 a.m. to 8 p.m. Mon through Fri and from 11 a.m. to 6:30 p.m. on weekends. The ferry is closed on major holidays.

To set sail for a free 7- to 10-minute trip to the other side, just drive onto the ferry at 1001 S. Lynchburg Rd. in Baytown. The ferries hold 12 cars at a time. Call (281) 424-3521 for more information.

BY PUBLIC TRANSPORTATION

Houston's public transportation options are improving, but they still aren't nearly as abundant or efficient as those of other large cities like New York, Chicago, and San Francisco. The Metropolitan Transit Authority, better known as METRO, runs the city's public transportation, which includes bus service and a new light-rail system.

By Bus

METRO buses run all over Harris County and most routes travel on local streets, with stops every other block or so. Coupled with Houston traffic, this can make for some very slow travel if you have far to go, especially if you need to switch bus lines. To speed up their commute, some people ride their bikes for part of the way and then board a bus with the bike to travel longer distances.

Park & Ride

METRO's Park & Ride service is another option for those who want to spend a little less time on the bus. Commuters park their cars for free at a designated Park & Ride location and take the bus to work. (The exception to this "free" rule is the Fannin South Park & Ride lot, which charges a daily parking rate of $2.50.)

There are 26 Park & Ride lots in Harris County. Prices to ride the Park & Ride buses vary depending on where you are traveling, but you will pay somewhere between $2 and $4.50 to ride. Discounts are available for seniors.

By Vanpool

Don't want to put miles on the car but also don't want to take the bus? METRO Star—the agency's vanpool service—may be your best bet. Participants drive to the Park & Ride station, where they meet up with other people who work in their area and ride together in a METRO-owned van. Call (888) 606-7433 to learn more or to sign up for METRO Star's free matching service.

i Forget putting change in parking meters. Many Houston meters now allow you to pay using your cell phone. Visit parkmobile.com to set up your account, then use the mobile app or call the number on the meter signs to pay for parking whenever you see a meter that says "Parkmobile."

By Light-rail

Houston's METRORail system, which opened in 2004, provides service between downtown, the Museum District, Hermann Park, Rice University, the Houston Zoo, and Reliant Park. The METRORail begins running at 4:30 a.m. on weekdays and at 5:30 a.m. on weekends. The train runs until midnight Mon through Thurs, until 2:20 a.m. Fri and Sat, and until 11:40 p.m. Sun. Riding from one end of the current red line to the other takes about 30 minutes. Five additional rail lines will open in 2014, making it even easier to get around the downtown area.

For METRORail and METRO bus routes, Park & Ride locations, or schedule information, call (713) 635-4000 or visit ridemetro .org. METRORail and local METRORail and METRO bus fare costs $1.25 per trip.

Fare Pricing & Payment

A discounted fare of 60 cents is available for for seniors, disabled persons, Medicare cardholders, and full-time students with a Metro Q Fare Card photo ID. The fare includes free transfers for up to 2 hours after you board your first bus or train. You may pay for a ride on a METRO bus in cash or with a Q Card ride pass, which can be purchased at retailers including Valero gas stations and Fiesta, Randalls, and Kroger grocery stores. METRORail riders must have a Q Card or a METRORail ticket, which can be purchased from the ticket vending machines located on all the rail platforms. Although you won't be asked for your ticket when you board the train, an officer may get onboard to make sure you have one. A complete list of retailers that sell Q Cards can be found on the METRO website.

HISTORY

Houston's history begins a lot like that of other US cities founded in the first half of the 1800s: Some entrepreneurs headed west, hoping to strike it rich. Their names? Augustus Chapman Allen and John Kirby Allen.

Their story—Houston's story—began in August 1836, when the two entrepreneurial brothers arrived in Texas, looking to establish a port city.

THE BEGINNING

The Allen brothers, who hailed from New York City, wanted to build a city where a stream called the Buffalo Bayou met the San Jacinto River. This location wasn't far from where Texas revolutionaries had defeated the Mexican army to win the decisive Battle of San Jacinto—and Texas's independence—just 4 months earlier. When they couldn't strike a deal to buy this fertile land, the Allen brothers headed a little farther west, following the Buffalo Bayou to where it merges with White Oak Bayou. Wanting to build a port city, the duo sought a place where other countries and parties could meet to trade, and the narrow bayou seemed to provide ample space for ships to enter the city and turn around. The Allens decided to build their city in this spot and purchased about 6,600 acres of land here for $9,000. Today, the area is known as Allen's Landing.

Simply discovering an ideal place for a city wasn't enough, of course. The Allens needed residents, people who'd pay to live on their land. On August 30, 1836, the brothers placed an ad in the Texas newspaper *Telegraph and Texas Register*, inviting people to purchase lots in their new town for relatively low prices. The ad promised abundant timber and grassland in the coastal plains town. It also declared that the new town would become the "great interior commercial emporium of Texas." In case this wasn't enough to lure people to the new city, the Allens also suggested that ships from New York and New Orleans could sail up Buffalo Bayou to the city, which boasted cool breezes. This last part, as any Houstonian can tell you, bordered on false advertising: Houston is hot and humid most of the year.

The brothers' ad referred to the new city as the "Town of Houston." The name Houston was already familiar to many Texans. The city's namesake—General Sam Houston—had led the Texas revolutionaries to victory and helped Texas become an independent nation in April 1836. General Houston's army—Texians, they were called—had been defeated at the Alamo in San Antonio on March 6, and that defeat and the "Remember the Alamo!" battle cry it inspired had led many colonialists to join the Texas revolutionaries. Six weeks later, on April 21, 1836, Houston and his army snuck up on the Mexican army as it took a siesta at San Jacinto, an area just southeast of what is now Houston. In less than 20 minutes, General Houston and his army captured the Mexican president and general Antonio López de Santa Anna and captured or killed hundreds of other Mexicans. Within 3 weeks, Santa Anna signed peace treaties agreeing to Mexico's pullout of what is now Texas. Sam Houston, meanwhile, became a national hero and got a city named after him. While the Allen brothers' sales skills convinced 12 people to move to their new city as of January 1, 1837, having the general's name attached couldn't have hurt either.

THE CAPITAL YEARS

With big visions for their little town, the Allen brothers convinced the still-new Texas Congress and then-Texas president Sam Houston to move the Republic of Texas capital from nearby Columbia to Houston. On May 1, 1837, the Texas Congress met in Houston for the first time. One month later, on June 5, 1837, the congress granted the incorporation of the City of Houston. James S. Holman, an agent who worked for the Allen Brothers' Houston Town Company, was named the city's first mayor. Shortly after becoming an incorporated city, Houston was named the county seat of Harrisburg County. The county was renamed Harris County in 1839.

Houston's tenure as the capital of Texas was short-lived. When Mirabeau B. Lamar became Texas's second president in 1839, he had the capital moved 2 hours northwest to Austin, which is the capital today. Still, the Allen brothers kept pushing forward to make their city a world-renowned port. In 1840, Houston established a chamber of commerce to promote shipping and trade along

the Buffalo Bayou. Shortly thereafter, Mayor John Andrews and the city aldermen established the Port of Houston Authority, which oversaw the regulation of slips, wharves, and roads of neighboring Buffalo Bayou and White Oak Bayou.

Houston became the capital again in 1842, but only briefly. Three years later, in 1845, the Republic of Texas was annexed by the United States, becoming the 28th state to join the Union. At the same time, Houston's future was beginning to look dreary. Some residents weren't thrilled about becoming US citizens; some worried about the new state's financial situation. To make matters worse, a deadly yellow fever and cholera outbreak hit the Midwest, and the port city wasn't producing the kind of trade the Allen brothers had envisioned. This may have been partly because Houston's credibility faded when it lost its status as capital. It didn't help that the Buffalo Bayou wasn't nearly as easy to navigate as the city's founders had thought or hoped. Frequent rainstorms created so much mud that it was nearly impossible to reach the city by land. To make matters worse, Francis R. Lubbock, who rode the first steamship to Houston in 1837, lamented that the branches that filled Buffalo Bayou made it nearly impossible to see the town.

i The site of the Texas army's victory at San Jacinto is now marked with a towering monument and museum. Both are open to the public. Find out about visiting the San Jacinto Battleground State Historic Site on page 138.

Despite these problems, most Houstonians stuck around. Like so many Americans in those days, they held out hope—in this case, hope that the city would eventually become the trading hot spot that the Allen brothers had envisioned.

BIRTH OF THE RAILROADS

Houston's early settlers soon got their wish. Thanks in part to the new chamber of commerce and the port authority, business began picking up, with frame buildings popping up around what's now the downtown area. In 1842 the Texas legislature authorized the city to clean up the Buffalo Bayou so it would be easier to navigate. The chamber of commerce, meanwhile, began a channel improvement project that led to repeated attempts to widen Buffalo Bayou so that ships could get in and out more easily.

The waterways are just one part of Houston's story during those early years. The chamber of commerce recognized that people had to be able to get around and move agriculture and other goods if Houston was to become a major city. So, the chamber helped develop the state's first railroad—Buffalo Bayou, Brazos & Colorado Railroad. The chamber also established Texas's first telegraph line. The railroad, which began providing service in 1853, was only the second railroad west of the Mississippi River and the first part of what is now the Southern Pacific Railroad. Other railroads followed and, within a few years, Houston's railroads were connected with Galveston's. Houston railroads also connected with other rails in the state, earning Houston the nickname "city where 17 railroads meet the sea." The new railroads shipped out agricultural products and lumber from East Texas's piney woods and brought in cotton from nearby plantations.

All of this shipping activity inspired optimism and confidence in Houstonians and Texans. Streets were paved with shells, Buffalo Bayou was dredged deeper, and the population and the local economy were growing. But in 1859, the city suffered a big blow: a fire raged through town, destroying many homes and businesses. Still, Houston continued trading, thanks to the railroads.

THE CIVIL WAR YEARS

Two years after that devastating fire, the people of Texas voted to secede from the Union, and Governor Sam Houston was forced out of office for refusing to join the Confederacy. The Union blockaded the Texas coastline at the beginning of the war and siezed nearby Galveston in October 1862. Three months later, on January 1, 1863, Confederate general John Magruder surprised Union troops with a quick offensive that allowed the Confederacy to reclaim Galveston. Magruder used Houston to get his troops organized for the Battle of Galveston, which was waged both on land and at sea. No fighting ever took place on Houston soil, though.

That's not the only reason January 1, 1863, was a day for the Texas history books. That New Year's Day also happened to be the day that President Abraham Lincoln's Emancipation Proclamation was supposed to take effect. But Houston's railroads and telegraphs weren't sufficient to get the word out that the slaves were freed—certainly not when Texas was under Confederate control. Not until June 19, 1865, did the news spread that slaves in Texas were emancipated. That's when Union general Gordon Granger and some 2,000 federal troops arrived in Galveston to reclaim Texas and announce the slaves' liberation. Slaves throughout Galveston—and soon Houston—celebrated in the streets. The date of Granger's arrival and proclamation became known as Juneteenth and continues to be celebrated in Texas, 28 other states, and Washington, D.C.- today.

Texas's economy took a big hit when the Civil War ended in 1865, and Houston suffered another yellow fever outbreak 2 years later. But somehow the fledgling city defied the odds. New brick buildings were cropping up, more streets were paved with shells, and in 1876 public schools opened for children ages 8 to 14. There were so many railroads traveling through the city that, by 1890, Houston was regarded as Texas's biggest railroad hub.

Buffalo Bayou was also getting a makeover. In 1869 civic leaders established the Houston Ship Channel Company, which was tasked with digging a channel and dredging Buffalo Bayou deeper to make it easier for ships to navigate and turn around. During the last decade of the 19th century, the rest of the world finally got access to the Port of Houston. Yet the older and more easily accessible Port of Galveston remained the state's most bustling port.

PORT DOMINANCE

The Port of Houston's struggle to match the traffic of Port of Galveston came to an abrupt end in September 1900. That's when a hurricane—known as the Hurricane of 1900—struck Galveston. The devastating storm killed an estimated 8,000 people and destroyed millions of dollars' worth of property and infrastructure. Galveston worked to rebuild its port, but no amount of rebuilding could fix the damage done by such a fierce storm: inland ports, as the hurricane

demonstrated, are far better protected than those along the Gulf Coast. With that, Houston soon became Texas's leader in trade and industry.

This major economic development wasn't lost on the rest of the country. Between 1900 and 1910, Houston's population doubled to 78,000, and in 1902 President Theodore Roosevelt appropriated $1 million to develop the Port of Houston and turn it into a deep-water port so that bigger ships could visit the area. Congress soon allocated millions more on the condition that Harris County taxpayers pay for the other half of the construction of a 25-foot channel. In November 1914, after 7 years of digging, President Woodrow Wilson pressed a button at the White House, remotely firing a mortar gun and officially opening the Port of Houston to shipping and marine commerce. That port, located on the east side of Houston, is now home to the Houston Ship Channel.

OIL BOOM

At the same time that Houston was making its name as a major national and international port, the city was also staking out another claim to economic prosperity: oil. In 1901, oil was discovered on a salt-dome formation at Spindletop, just east of Houston near Beaumont, Texas. This wasn't just any oil, mind you. The first geyser, produced after salt-dome formation expert Anthony F. Lucas had drilled in the area, blew oil more than 100 feet high. The geyser, which flowed close to 100,000 barrels a day, took 9 days to cap. With that, land prices in the area jumped and major oil companies and entrepreneurs moved in to drill. When they got lucky, they built refining units, pipelines, and storage facilities around the area. Everyone wanted to get a piece of the petroleum pie, and Houston's economy was reaping the benefits.

The discovery of oil at Spindletop couldn't have been more perfectly timed. Because it coincided with the opening of the Houston Ship Channel, the city could easily export its newest asset—an asset that people around the world wanted and needed as automobiles and airplanes were becoming more common. It was also an asset that would become crucial in two world wars.

AIDING THE WAR EFFORT

Trains and ships helped shape much of Houston's early history, so it seems only fitting that airplanes played a role here, too. In 1917, shortly before World War I began, the US government purchased nearly 1,300 acres in southeast Houston to build an air base. Ellington Field, as it was named, served as a flight-training base during World War I. About 5,000 men and 250 aircraft were assigned to the base during the war.

The government closed Ellington Field in 1923, but the Texas National Guard decided to base the 111th Observation Squadron there. The facilities at Ellington Field were becoming quickly outdated, though, and within a few years, the National Guard transferred the squadron to newer facilities at the municipal airport (now William P. Hobby Airport). The military subsequently leased Ellington Field to local farmers, who used the then-overgrown fields as pasture.

Shortly before the US became involved in World War II, it became apparent that the military would need Ellington Field again.

Houston had become a leader in the petrochemical industry, and many petrochemical refineries and manufacturing plants had been constructed along the Ship Channel to build and fuel new ships for the war effort. These refineries and plants, argued US Representative Albert Thomas, needed military protection, and Ellington Field was the most convenient place to base this protection.

Ellington Field was quickly expanded and used to provide advanced training for bomber pilots and house the US Army Air Corps' bombardier school, which was soon replaced with a navigation school. More than five dozen women in the Women's Army Corps were also stationed at Ellington Field, which became a reserve air base when the war ended.

POSTWAR GROWTH & DIVERSIFICATION

During World War II, tonnage levels were reduced and shipping had been halted in the Houston Ship Channel. But Houston's economy managed to stay afloat, thanks to the petrochemical industry, steel manufacturing, shipbuilding, and explosives factories. Once the war was over, though, those wartime factories were no longer needed. So, with tonnage levels back at their normal levels and shipping resumed, Houston's economy again became port-driven. This time, though, the city diversified its offerings to include the natural gas developed here. The Houston-based Texas Eastern Transmission Corporation had laid pipes that could transport gas northward to heat homes during the winter. And just as people up north were getting their winter heat, people down south were introduced to a modern amenity called air-conditioning—an amenity that Houstonians can't imagine living without today. When air-conditioning became available in the 1950s, many companies moved to Houston, which by then was considered home of the energy sector.

Houston's postwar diversification also extended to medicine. In 1945 the M.D. Anderson Foundation founded the Texas Medical Center, positioning the city to become an international leader in medicine and research. As the Texas Medical Center grew in the years that followed, people from around the world visited Houston to get treated for cancer, heart disease, and countless other conditions from some of the world's leading doctors.

SPACE CITY LIFTS OFF

In 1963 the National Aeronautics and Space Administration (NASA) opened its Manned Spacecraft Center 30 miles south of Houston. Renamed the Lyndon B. Johnson Space Center in 1973, the NASA field installation made the aerospace industry an essential component of Houston's economy and earned the city the nickname "Space City." As the Mission Control Center for human space flights and the home base for US astronauts, the Johnson Space Center employed more than 5,000 people in those early days. These weren't the only jobs NASA brought to town. More than 100 companies followed NASA to Houston in the 1960s and 1970s.

The Johnson Space Center was just one of Houston's exciting additions in the 1960s. In 1965 the Astrodome opened. Nicknamed "Eighth Wonder of the World," the Astrodome was the world's first indoor domed sports stadium. From the beginning, the 9.5-acre Astrodome was home to Houston's major league baseball team. Initially named the Colt .45s when they came to town in 1962, the team soon changed its name to the Astros. Like the Astrodome, this name paid homage to Houston's new role in the space industry. The Astros played their first season at the Astrodome on green-painted dirt and dead grass before AstroTurf was installed in 1966. Notably, Mickey Mantle hit the first home run at the Astrodome during an April 9, 1965, preseason game between the Astros and the New York Yankees.

In 1968 the Astrodome became home to a second team—the Houston Oilers, a charter member of the American Football League in 1960. In the years that followed, the Astrodome would host a variety of events, including the 1989 NBA All-Star Game, the 1992 Republican National Convention, the annual Houston Livestock Show and Rodeo, University of Houston football games, bowl games, the 1971 Final Four, and hundreds of conventions.

BOOMTOWN

For years after World War II, Houston's population grew considerably—and not just because people were having babies. Following the war, the city annexed unincorporated areas into the city limits, causing Houston to double in size. While the city would continue to annex other unincorporated areas over the years, the population grew throughout the late 1970s, in part because the economy in the Midwest's rustbelt states had collapsed. Many Midwesterners saw this as a sign that it was time to jump ship, abandon the harsh winters, and follow the jobs. The Arab oil embargo had created plenty of job opportunities in the oil sector, luring many of these Midwesterners to Houston.

"HOUSTON, WE HAVE A PROBLEM"

The 1980s weren't a great time for Houston. In 1983, Hurricane Alicia—a category-3 storm—struck Galveston and Houston, killing 21 people and causing $2.6 billion in damage. It was Texas's first billion-dollar storm. Alicia caused close to two dozen tornadoes and a major oil spill in nearby Texas City. It also blew windows out of many office buildings and stores.

Houston's population boom also came to an abrupt halt during the 1980s. By mid-decade, falling oil prices spelled layoffs and fewer job openings in the oil sector. Some people who worked in the oil business left the industry or even the city.

The explosion of the space shuttle Challenger in 1986 didn't help. For several years after that, the entire aerospace industry was in disarray, as government officials and the public questioned the safety and future of human space flight. Financial cuts and negative perceptions of the aerospace industry hurt Houston at a time when a recession was already squeezing the economy.

BASKETBALL, BUSHES & THE EARLY 1990S

At the end of the 1980s and during the early 1990s, Houston gained some positive PR and a little economic boost, thanks to its hospitality. In 1989 the NBA hosted its annual All-Star Game at the Astrodome, with 44,735 people in attendance. The following year, then-president and Houston resident George H. W. Bush hosted international financial leaders at the 16th annual G-7

Summit, which was held at Rice University. Two years later, the GOP held its Republican National Convention at the Astrodome, where the convention renominated Bush and his vice president, Dan Quayle. After the duo lost the general election to Bill Clinton and Al Gore, Bush and First Lady Barbara Bush moved to Houston, where they've often been spotted cheering on the city's football, basketball, and baseball teams over the years.

CLUTCH CITY

Houston sports fans had a chip on their shoulders for many years: None of our major sports teams had ever won a national title. Sure, we'd come close a few times: The Astros had put up a good fight in the National League Championship Series in 1986, and the Rockets had made it to the NBA Finals in 1981 and 1986. But Houston didn't get a world championship until June 22, 1994, when the Houston Rockets basketball team defeated the New York Knicks in game seven of the NBA Finals. And they'd defied some pretty steep odds to do it. In the second round of the playoffs against the Phoenix Suns, the Rockets had blown leads and lost their first two games. A giant headline on the front page of the *Houston Chronicle* had dubbed Houston "Choke City," a reminder of the many times that Houston's basketball, football, and baseball teams had come close to a big win, only to fall short. Yet the 1994 Rockets team, led by now-Hall of Famer Hakeem Olajuwon, showed tenacity and came back to beat Phoenix in seven games, rallying the city around them. After they won the next two series—and the city's first championship—the Chronicle ran a front-page headline that read "Clutch City." With that, the city had a new nickname, and the team had a new rallying cry. National commentators didn't pick—or even seem to want—the Rockets to win the championship that year. But this team had done it in the most unfathomable way and 1 million Houstonians gladly celebrated the Rockets in their victory parade that summer. The following year the Rockets made a trade to bring native son Clyde Drexler home to play for the team and did it all over again: They blew the first two games against Phoenix in the second round before going on to win the city's second major championship—and raise a new rallying cry: "Double Clutch."

STADIUM MANIA & THE DOWNTOWN REVITALIZATION

The Rockets' championships gave Houstonians a taste of victory and the city's other sports teams something to aspire to, but the sweet taste of victory was short-lived for Houston sports fans. In 1997 the owner of the city's professional football team—the Houston Oilers—moved the organization to Tennessee, leaving Houstonians without a football team. (For Houstonians, cheering for the nearby Dallas Cowboys is unthinkable.) In their bid to convince the NFL to award Houston an expansion team, the city and Houston Livestock Show and Rodeo officials proposed building a new stadium. In October 1999 the NFL awarded Houston an expansion team and the 2004 Super Bowl, to be held in the new stadium.

The new arena, known as Reliant Stadium, sits beside the Astrodome and boasts the NFL's first retractable roof. The new team—the Houston Texans—played their first game at Reliant Stadium on September 8, 2002, upsetting the cross-state rival Dallas Cowboys in a game that remains a treasured piece of Houston sports history. To say Houstonians love their new football team is an understatement. Even though the team didn't go to the playoffs until the 2011 season—nearly a decade after the franchise played its first game in the city—they've always sold out home games.

The Texans weren't the only team in town to get a new stadium. In 2000 the Astros moved downtown to the city's first retractable-roofed stadium. Initially, the new stadium was called Enron Field, named for Houston-based energy company Enron. But after Enron collapsed the following year, mired in scandal and inflated profits in the second-largest bankruptcy ever, the city's baseball stadium needed a new name. In 2002 the Houston-based fruit juice company Minute Maid stepped up to the plate, acquiring the naming rights and renaming the stadium Minute Maid Park.

The following year the Houston Rockets and the Houston Aeros hockey team moved downtown to the Toyota Center. The new downtown stadiums commanded the attention of their home teams' respective leagues, with Minute Maid Park named the site of the 2004 MLB All-Star Game and the Toyota Center named the site of the 2006 (and later the 2013) NBA All-Star Game. The Astros also earned local and national attention in 2005, when they went to the World Series for the first time in the franchise's 45-year history. The team ultimately got swept by the Chicago White Sox, but Houstonians almost didn't seem to care. They were just happy to finally get a taste of life near the top of Major League baseball.

Bringing the excitement of professional baseball and basketball downtown played a big role in the city's effort to make over the downtown area. Along with a huge influx of new restaurants, lofts and luxury apartments, and, significantly, the city's first light rail lines, the new baseball and basketball stadiums helped transform downtown into a place where Houstonians wanted to live and play, not just work. Even better: the addition of the light rail made it easier for Houstonians to travel between downtown and some of the city's biggest attractions, including Reliant Stadium and Hermann Park. Of course, with downtown's makeover, Houstonians no longer had to leave downtown to enjoy green space. In 2008 several blocks worth of concrete were turned into an enchanting park called Discovery Green, giving families and business people a serene escape from the urban hustle.

STORMY WEATHER

Tropical Storm Allison

During the first decade of the 21st century, Houston weathered some exceptionally torrential storms. In 2001 Tropical Storm Allison dumped more than 37 inches of rain on some parts of the city, causing severe flooding and teaching many Houstonians the value of flood insurance. Twenty people were killed, and the city suffered billions of dollars' worth of damage.

Hurricane Katrina

Four years later, in 2005, Houston provided shelter for 150,000 people who fled Hurricane Katrina. About 25,000 Louisianans who had been staying at the Superdome in New Orleans were put up at the Astrodome; many others stayed elsewhere in the Reliant Center complex. Events at the Astrodome were canceled for the rest of the year, even though the evacuees moved out of the Astrodome and into local apartments or the neighboring Reliant Arena by mid-September. Many young Katrina evacuees enrolled in schools around the city, as many families decided to call Houston home. Others returned to Louisiana or elsewhere in the region.

Hurricane Rita

With Katrina still fresh on Houstonians' minds, the city's residents fretted when meteorologists predicted that the category-5 Hurricane Rita would strike the Houston area. In what became the largest urban evacuation in US history, about 2.5 million Houstonians evacuated in anticipation of the storm's landfall in late September 2005. The freeways were so congested that it took Houston evacuees up to 20 hours to make the 2.5-hour drive to San Antonio. In the end Rita did little damage to Houston. But schools were closed for days after the storm so evacuees could return home without another extreme traffic buildup.

Hurricane Ike

On September 13, 2008, Hurricane Ike hit Galveston before rolling into Houston. Ike was only a category-2 storm by the time it struck the Texas coast, but it was the third most destructive hurricane to ever hit the US. The reason? Its high winds, subsequent rain and flooding in parts of the city, and the passage of the storm's eye right over the city. Galveston officials ordered mandatory evacuations, warning residents that they would "face certain death" if they stayed behind. Thousands defied these orders, though, and many

Close-up

Important Dates in Houston History

1836: Texas wins its independence from Mexico; Houston is founded by the Allen brothers.

1837: Houston is incorporated and named the capital of Texas and the county seat of Harrisburg County.

1839: Harrisburg County is renamed Harris County; Texas capital is moved to Austin.

1840: Houston Chamber of Commerce is established.

1845: Texas is annexed by the US.

1853: Buffalo Bayou, Brazos & Colorado Railroad begins providing service, becoming Texas's first railroad.

1859: A major fire destroys many Houston homes and businesses.

1861: Texas secedes from the Union.

1862: The Union takes control of Galveston.

1863: Confederate general John Magruder and his troops reclaim Galveston in the Battle of Galveston.

1865: Union general Gordon Granger arrives in Galveston and announces slaves' liberation.

1869: The Houston Ship Channel Company is established.

1876: Houston public schools are established.

1900: Hurricane of 1900 hits Galveston, killing 8,000.

1901: Oil is discovered at Spindletop.

1902: President Theodore Roosevelt appropriates $1 million to make the Port of Houston a deep-water port.

1914: The Port of Houston opens.

1917: Ellington Field opens as a flight-training base for the military.

1930: Houston is the most populous city in Texas.

1945: The Texas Medical Center is founded.

1963: NASA opens the Manned Spacecraft Center, 30 miles southeast of Houston.

1965: The Astrodome opens.

1973: The Manned Spacecraft Center is renamed Lyndon B. Johnson Space Center.

1983: Hurricane Alicia strikes Galveston and the Greater Houston area.

1986: Space shuttle *Challenger* explodes, hindering Houston's aerospace industry; the Astrodome hosts the MLB All-Star Game.

1989: The NBA All-Star Game is played at the Astrodome.

1990: Houston hosts the 16th G-7 Summit.

1992: Houston hosts the Republican National Convention.

1994 and 1995: Houston Rockets basketball team wins its first two NBA championships—the city's first professional sports championships.

1997: Houston elects its first black mayor, Lee Brown; Houston's football team, the Oilers, moves to Tennessee, leaving the city without a pro football team.

2000: The Houston Astros baseball team leaves the Astrodome and moves downtown to Enron Field, the city's first retractable-roofed stadium.

2001: Tropical Storm Allison kills 20 people and floods Houston after more than 37 inches of rain fall on parts of the city; Houston-based Enron collapses.

2002: Enron Field is renamed Astros Park, then renamed Minute Maid Park; Houston's new pro football franchise, the Houston Texans, play their inaugural season and christen the new Reliant Stadium.

2003: The Houston Rockets basketball team and Houston Aeros hockey team move downtown to the Toyota Center.

2004: Super Bowl XXXVIII is played at Reliant Stadium; the MLB All-Star Game is played at Minute Maid Park.

2005: 150,000 Hurricane Katrina evacuees flee to Houston in August; in September 2.5 million Houstonians evacuate to avoid the impending landfall of Hurricane Rita; the Houston Astros play in their first World Series.

2006: The NBA All-Star Game is played at the Toyota Center.

2008: Hurricane Ike hits Galveston and Houston.

2009: Houston elects its first openly gay mayor, Annise Parker.

2011: Houston, along with the rest of Texas, experiences the worst drought in Texas history; NASA ends its manned space program, resulting in thousands of layoffs at Johnson Space Center; Continental officially merges with United Airlines and moves the company's headquarters to Chicago.

2012: The Houston Texans play and win their first playoff game, the city's first NFL playoff game in 18 years; the Houston Dynamos get their own Major League Soccer stadium—the city's first.

paid the price with their lives. Thousands more Galvestonians and others in low-lying areas around Houston lost their homes. Although fewer people died in the City of Houston, the damage was still devastating. Many parts of the city didn't have power for 2 or even 3 weeks, preventing most schools from reopening for nearly 2 weeks after the storm. The high winds, flooding, fallen stoplights, and falling trees damaged or destroyed thousands of homes and businesses, many of which went under or couldn't reopen for months—or in some cases, a year or two—until they rebuilt. The wind broke windows throughout downtown office buildings, including the JPMorgan Chase building—the city's tallest building—and tore huge holes in the roof at Reliant Stadium, forcing the Houston Texans to delay one game and play the rest of the season with an open roof.

At the time, the damage seemed overwhelming, with no end in sight in some parts of the city. But today, Houston has almost entirely recovered, with most of the damage repaired within weeks, or in some cases, a few months. In some ways the storm provided an opportunity for Houstonians to demonstrate their hospitality and bond with their neighbors. Many Houstonians who had air-conditioning or didn't sustain damage opened their homes to those who did and gave their time and resources to help their community. In Galveston and outlying areas closer to the coast, however, the rebuilding process didn't happen quite as quickly, in part because the city's oceanfront was hit with the highest of tides, which swept away or flooded homes, possessions, and businesses.

DIVERSIFICATION & TODAY'S ECONOMY

After the 1980s recession, Houston learned its lesson and diversified its economy, relying less on the petroleum industry and focusing more on the aerospace, health-care and biotechnology, technology, and education industries. At the same time the city has remained a big player on the international scene, serving as a major trading port between North and South America (particularly in the NAFTA era) and as a major hub for flights to Latin and South America, as well as Asia and Europe. Conventions also benefit the local economy: In 2010 the city hosted some 237 conventions, events, and shows, bringing in $467.8 million.

The fact that Houston hasn't allowed a single industry to define it has served the city well, especially after Hurricane Ike and during the recession that began in 2008. While Houston hasn't been immune to layoffs or declining housing prices, it has fared better than most of the country. The reasons? A large, relatively recession-proof health-care/biotechnology sector, as well as the city's role in education, technology, and international trade.

It's no wonder, then, why Houston was recently identified as one of the best places to find a job and—thanks to a combination of job openings, pay, and affordability—rated the best city for new college graduates by *Businessweek*.

DESERT DAYS

Big changes came to the local landscape in 2011. Hometown airline and major Houston employer Continental officially merged with United Airlines, resulting in the layoffs of more than 500 employees and sending the company's CEO and corporate headquarters to Chicago. And the end of the manned space program during the summer of 2011 meant the layoffs or forced retirement of an estimated 4,000 employees and contractors at another major Houston employer—NASA's Johnson Space Center.

But perhaps the biggest long-term hit to the city's landscape came in the form of the worst drought in Texas history. With more than 30 days of temperatures over 100 degrees and barely 11 inches of rain by August, the Houston area was forced to turn to Lake Conroe and even Dallas' wastewater to supply drinking water. This water shortage meant mandatory water restrictions in many parts of the city, but those were a mere inconvenience compared to wildfires outside the city, billions of dollars in lost livestock and crops, and millions of dead trees—including one-fourth of the trees at the heavily wooded Houston Arboretum & Nature Center in Memorial Park.

ACCOMMODATIONS

Need a place to stay? You've got lots of choices here. The Greater Houston area boasts more than 60,000 hotel rooms, not to mention RV parks, hostels, and even a few chic bed-and-breakfasts. The vast majority of Houston accommodations are hotels and most are chains, many with multiple locations around the area.

You can find accommodations here in a range of prices and with a variety of bells and whistles. Most hotels offer free cable, local phone calls, and some sort of shuttle service. About half throw in free high-speed Internet, while others charge a daily or per-stay fee to get online. A few have kitchenettes and some include breakfast in the price of your stay. Just about all hotels here are wheelchair accessible.

In many cases, you can bring your four-legged friends along for the trip; one hotel even has special doggie beds. Some pet-friendly hotels charge an extra fee for your furry friends to spend the night, but many don't.

Every hotel here offers parking, though many charge anywhere from $6 to $25 to park your car each night. Parking costs tend to be on the higher end if you're staying in the Galleria, Medical Center, and downtown areas. Many Houston hotels are smoke-free; these have been identified as such in the listings that follow.

OVERVIEW

Plan to see a bit of the city? Your best bet is to stay in the Galleria area or downtown. These centrally located areas offer easy access to restaurants, shopping, and almost any place you want to go inside the Loop. The Galleria hotels are just a 15-minute drive from Reliant Park, downtown, the Texas Medical Center, the Museum District, and Hermann Park. Downtown hotels are even closer to these locations and within walking distance of the George R. Brown Convention Center, Discovery Green, Fortune 500 companies, Minute Maid Park, the Toyota Center, and the Theater District.

In town for the Houston Livestock Show and Rodeo, a Houston Texans football game, the Texas Bowl, or some other event at Reliant Center? You might find it more convenient to stay at one of the hotels in the Medical Center or the West Loop.

Prefer something off the beaten path? Consider some of the eclectic accommodations in the Montrose and Museum District area. Or, if you prefer to camp in your RV, try one of the RV parks along South Loop 610, just minutes from Reliant Center and the Texas Medical Center.

This chapter offers a sampling of some of the most centrally located accommodations in the Houston area, organized by neighborhood. This is hardly a comprehensive list, but it should give you plenty of options so you don't have to spend hours online searching for a place to rest your head. For additional accommodations, visit visithoustontexas .com or the website of your preferred hotel chain.

Price Code

Prices are based on a one-night stay in one standard room. Please note: In a few cases, this chapter includes price ranges, such as $$–$$$. This means that the hotel has some rooms available in the lower price bracket but many options—particularly suites—cost more. Keep in mind that hotel rates often change and may be higher during the holidays or other peak times, including during the Houston Livestock Show and Rodeo in late February and March. The rates listed here don't include the Houston hotel tax, which is 17 percent.

$ .... Less than $100
$$ .... $100 to $200
$$$ .... $200 to $300
$$$$ .... More than $300

Quick Index by Cost

$$$$
St. Regis Houston,
  Galleria, 50

$$$–$$$$
Hotel ZaZa, Museum
  District, 53
The Westin Galleria
  Houston, Galleria, 50
The Westin Oaks Houston,
  Galleria, 50

$$$
Doubletree Guest Suites,
  Galleria, 48
Hilton Americas—Houston,
  Downtown, 45
Holiday Inn Express,
  Downtown, 46

$$–$$$$
Alden Hotel, Downtown, 44
Four Seasons Downtown,
  Downtown, 45
Hotel Icon, Downtown, 46

The Houstonian Hotel, Club
  & Spa, Memorial, 52
Intercontinental Houston,
  Galleria, 49

$$–$$$
Hilton Houston Plaza/
  Medical Center, Medical
  Center, 51
Hilton Houston Post Oak,
  Galleria, 48
Hotel Derek, Galleria, 48
Hotel Sorella CityCentre,
  Memorial, 52
Hyatt Regency,
  Downtown, 46
Inn at the Ballpark,
  Downtown, 47
The Lancaster,
  Downtown, 47
Marriott Houston West
  Loop by the Galleria,
  Galleria, 49
Modern B&B, Montrose, 52

Renaissance Houston
  Hotel Greenway Plaza,
  Greenway Plaza, 51
Sheraton Suites Houston,
  Galleria, 50

$$
Best Western Downtown
  Inn & Suites,
  Downtown, 44
Best Western Plaza Hotel &
  Suites at Medical Center,
  Medical Center, 51
Doubletree Hotel
  Houston Downtown,
  Downtown, 45
Holiday Inn Hotel & Suites
  Houston Medical Center,
  Medical Center, 51
Lake View RV Resort,
  Medical Center, 52
Magnolia Hotel Houston,
  Downtown, 47
Omni Houston Hotel,
  Galleria, 49

$–$$
Athens Hotel Suites,
Downtown, 44
Hampton Inn & Suites,
Houston Medical Center/
Reliant Park, South
Loop, 53

$
Comfort Inn Downtown,
Downtown, 45
Candlewood Extended Stay,
Galleria, 47
Homestead Houston/
Galleria Area, Galleria, 48

Houston International
Hostel, Museum
District, 53
South Main RV Park, South
Loop, 54

DOWNTOWN

ALDEN HOTEL $$–$$$$
1117 Prairie St.
(832) 200-8800
aldenhotels.com
Business travelers seeking luxurious downtown accommodations naturally flock to the Alden Hotel. Each of the 97 suites here boasts a chic contemporary decor, a well-lit work area, granite-walled bathrooms, pillow-top mattresses, 400-thread-count Egyptian-cotton sheets, and plush down pillows and comforters. Other highlights include complimentary high-speed Internet, plasma TVs, plush terry cloth robes, a 24-hour gym, and 24-hour room service. Free shuttle service is offered within a 3-mile radius of the hotel. During your stay, be sure to dine at Alden's restaurant, *17, where local ingredients play a starring role in the creative, award-winning American cuisine. Prefer something more laid-back? Grab drinks and more casual fare at Alden's The Sam Bar.

ATHENS HOTEL SUITES $–$$
1308 Clay St. at Caroline St.
(713) 739-1960 (Information)
(888) 759-4466 (Reservations)
athenshotelsuites.com
With just 23 suites, this family-owned place offers the look and feel of a European hotel.

Each suite has a washer and dryer, as well as a kitchenette with a full-size refrigerator, microwave, oven, and coffeepot. Cable, Internet, breakfast, and maid service are also included. Depending on your needs and price range, you can choose from executive, deluxe, and standard suites. Athens Hotel Suites is located in the heart of downtown, just a short walk from the George R. Brown Convention Center, the Theater District, the Toyota Center, City Hall, Minute Maid Park, and the METRORail.

BEST WESTERN DOWNTOWN INN &
SUITES $$
915 W. Dallas
(713) 571-7733
bwdowntown.com
Located on the west side of downtown, Best Western Downtown is a good option if you don't want to shell out a lot of money and don't expect a lot of frills. No matter which of the 75 suites you stay in, you'll get free parking, high-speed Internet, cable, and a hot breakfast, as well as use of the exercise room and Jacuzzi. The hotel doesn't have any smoking rooms and doesn't allow pets. Best Western Downtown offers free shuttle service to and from downtown.

COMFORT INN DOWNTOWN $
5820 Katy Fwy.
(713) 869-9211
choicehotels.com

Comfort Inn Downtown shouldn't ever be mentioned in the same sentence as "luxury hotel," but it's an option if your top priorities are a central location and saving money. Located just a few minutes from the Downtown Aquarium and other downtown attractions, the Comfort Inn Downtown offers a good location for a fraction of the price of most downtown hotels. The 90 rooms here include free continental breakfast, free local calls, free high-speed Internet, and daily newspaper delivery. There's also an outdoor pool. Some rooms have microwaves and refrigerators; laundry facilities are available onsite.

DOUBLETREE HOTEL HOUSTON
DOWNTOWN $$
400 Dallas St.
(713) 759-0202
doubletree1.hilton.com

When location matters, the Doubletree Houston Downtown delivers. This newly renovated hotel is located on the edge of downtown, putting you within walking distance of many big downtown firms and attractions, including the Theater District, Sam Houston Park, Minute Maid Park, the Toyota Center, the Downtown Aquarium, and the METRORail. The hotel is also connected to the downtown tunnel system, making it easy to get around. (Learn more about the tunnel system on page 135.) The Doubletree Houston Downtown has 350 guest rooms, including large rooms and full suites. Every room and suite includes the Doubletree's signature Sweet Dreams beds and floor-to-ceiling windows, many

of which offer great views of Sam Houston Park or the downtown skyline. The hotel has a fitness center, and high-speed Internet is available in all rooms for $10.95 per day. All rooms are nonsmoking, though there are smoking areas outside. Pets up to 75 pounds are allowed here, though you'll be charged a nonrefundable $100 fee to bring along your furry friend.

✳FOUR SEASONS
DOWNTOWN $$–$$$$
1300 Lamar St.
(713) 650-1300
fourseasons.com/houston

Want to bask in luxury in the heart of the city? This is the place to do it. The Four Seasons's 20 floors boast 404 swanky guest rooms, including 12 suites. Every room comes with the usual Four Seasons amenities—cushy beds, flat-screen TVs, CD/DVD players, wireless Internet, terry cloth robes, and twice-daily housekeeping service. When you leave your room, you've got options galore: a visit to the spa, fitness center, pool and hot tub, or the award-winning Italian restaurant Quattro. Bringing the kids? They'll get their own taste of luxury in the form of nightly milk and cookies, pint-size robes, and goodie bags. Babysitting is also available.

✳HILTON AMERICAS—HOUSTON $$$
1600 Lamar St.
(713) 739-8000
hilton.com

With 1,200 guest rooms, Hilton Americas—Houston is the area's largest convention hotel. It's actually connected to the George R. Brown Convention Center, making it the perfect place to stay if you're here for a convention or trade show. Guests enjoy the amenities and great beds for which the

ACCOMMODATIONS

Hilton is known, plus a heated pool; the Skyline Spa & Health Club; three bars and lounges; the hotel restaurant, Spencer's for Steaks and Chops; and high-speed Internet throughout the hotel. Many rooms offer striking views of downtown and Discovery Green, an enchanting park and activity hub located just across the street. Added bonus: the green-minded hotel was the first in Texas to achieve a Green Seal certification for its commitment to the environment. If you seek space or extra luxury, consider staying in one of the hotel's two presidential suites, two chairman suites, or 36 one-bedroom and two-bedroom suites. The hotel is located within walking distance of Minute Maid Park, the Toyota Center, the METRORail, and great restaurants. Pets are permitted.

HOLIDAY INN EXPRESS $$$
1810 Bell St.
(713) 652-9400
hiexpress.com
Seeking a prime downtown location without a ton of frills? You'll find it at this Holiday Inn Express, just a few blocks from the George R. Brown Convention Center, Discovery Green, Minute Maid Park, Toyota Center, and tons of restaurants. Since the hotel's only been open since 2001, the 114 rooms here are in great shape. Like other Holiday Inn Expresses, this one offers a free breakfast buffet, high-speed Internet and cable, and daily housekeeping. There's also a business center, a whirlpool, and a small workout room.

✳HOTEL ICON $$-$$$$
220 Main St.
(713) 224-4266
hotelicon.com
Hotel ICON may be part of the Marriott family, but this celebrity magnet is probably

unlike any hotel you've stayed at before. Located in the 1911 Union National Bank building, this "it" hotel features neoclassical architecture blended with intrepid contemporary designs. The 12-floor hotel has 135 guest rooms, including 9 suites. Guests can take advantage of the luxury spa, oversize personal safes, a 24-hour fitness center, free Wi-Fi, limo service, and valet dry cleaning. Hotel ICON is located on the METRORail line and within walking distance of major corporations' headquarters, Minute Maid Park, the Toyota Center, George R. Brown Convention Center, and the Theater District. The hotel is smoke-free; pets are allowed.

HYATT REGENCY $$-$$$
1200 Louisiana St.
(713) 654-1234
hyattregencyhouston.com
Beauty and location are the big selling points for this 30-floor atrium hotel. The 977 contemporary rooms here boast great views of downtown, as well as Portico bath products, high-speed Internet, Hyatt Grand Beds, and access to the 24-hour fitness center and outdoor pool. Imperial, presidential, and VIP grande suites are available. Take in the perfect sunset by riding the elevator up 33 stories to Spindletop, an upscale glass-walled seafood restaurant that sits atop the Hyatt Regency and rotates every 45 minutes. Or fill your belly at Shula's Steakhouse or Einstein Bros Bagels and More. The Hyatt Regency is located within walking distance of Sam Houston Park, City Hall, the Theater District, dozens of restaurants and Fortune 500 companies, and Houston's baseball and basketball stadiums. Babysitting is available.

INN AT THE BALLPARK $$-$$$
1520 Texas Ave. at Crawford St.
(713) 228-1520
innattheballpark.com

Looking for big-city amenities and plenty of personal space for relaxing or working? You'll find both at this hotel just across the street from Minute Maid Park. No matter which of the 200 luxury rooms or suites you stay in at Inn at the Ballpark, you'll enjoy evening turndown, 24-hour room service, free coffee, AVEDA bath products, free Wi-Fi and transportation, safe deposit boxes, and in-room spa services. Inn at the Ballpark is owned by the Landry restaurant family, which also owns the nearby Downtown Aquarium. Suites start at $300 for those who want even more space. When you're ready to leave your room, relax in the 4-story bar and lounge or enjoy a fancy dinner at Vic & Anthony's Steakhouse, which you can learn more about on page 89.

THE LANCASTER $$-$$$
701 Texas Ave.
(713) 228-9500
thelancaster.com

There's a reason *Condé Nast Traveler* called The Lancaster "one of the best places to stay in the world." Houston's oldest boutique hotel prides itself on paying attention to all the little details of your stay, even going so far as to host a complimentary wine hour Monday through Thursday from 5:30 to 6:30 p.m. Each of the 84 rooms and 9 suites offers an historic European feel with brass door knockers, marble vanities, and four-post wooden beds covered with high-end bedding. You'll also enjoy free Wi-Fi, free car service, in-room massage service, and 24-hour room service. Prefer to get out of the room to eat? Dine in The Bistro, where

you'll find signature dishes like crab cakes and grilled lamb meatballs.

✳MAGNOLIA HOTEL HOUSTON $$
1100 Texas Ave.
(888) 915-1110
magnoliahotelhouston.com

Long gone are this building's days as the home of the Houston Post-Dispatch and headquarters for Shell Oil. Today, one of Houston's most chic contemporary hotels occupies 1100 Texas Ave., and its poshness shines in everything from the velvet curtains to the rooftop pool and Jacuzzi. No matter which of the 314 guest rooms or suites you stay in, you'll enjoy free breakfast each morning and free domestic beer, house wine, and soft drinks every evening. Other perks include a 24-hour fitness center, free Wi-Fi, car service, a bedtime cookie buffet, and a billiards room. Magnolia Hotel Houston is just a few blocks from Fortune 500 companies' headquarters, Minute Maid Park, Discovery Green, the George R. Brown Convention Center, and the Toyota Center.

GALLERIA

CANDLEWOOD EXTENDED STAY $
4900 Loop Central Dr.
(877) 834-3613
candlewoodsuites.com

In town for a few weeks? Or on a tight budget? This Candlewood Extended Stay is a popular choice that will put you just about 0.5 mile south of the Galleria for lower-than-Galleria prices. Each of the 122 rooms and 24 suites here include a full kitchen, and housekeepers tidy up the rooms once a week. During your stay, you'll also have access to the small workout room, free laundry facilities, and the movie lending library. You can bring up to two pets under 80 pounds, though you'll be charged a small nightly fee. Parking is free.

✳DOUBLETREE GUEST SUITES $$$
5353 Westheimer Rd.
(713) 961-9000
doubletree1.hilton.com

Located just a block from the Galleria and its 350-plus fine shopping and dining options, Doubletree Guest Suites is a great place to stay if you're planning to do some serious shopping or just want to stay in a central location. The 380 rooms here include newly renovated suites, which are perfect for stays with the family. The hotel features the usual Doubletree amenities—cushy beds, great chocolate chip cookies, Wi-Fi, and sophisticated decor. Every room also includes a microwave and a mini refrigerator and many rooms include a 32-inch TV. Sunbathers and swimmers can take advantage of the outdoor pool and whirlpool spa, or work out at the state-of-the-art gym. Pets are permitted. This is a nonsmoking hotel.

✳HILTON HOUSTON POST OAK $$-$$$
2001 Post Oak Blvd.
(713) 961-9300
hilton.com

Sitting just 1 block from the Galleria and just a few blocks from Uptown Park, Hilton Houston Post Oak offers the convenience and amenities you've come to expect from this popular hotel chain. It also boasts luxury, which helps explain why this is such a popular spot for weddings and receptions. The 448 guest rooms include minibars, safes, high-speed Internet, and plush bedding. During your stay, take advantage of 24-hour room service, the business center, a fitness center, as well as The Brittany

Bar (a British-style pub), The Promenade (a casual American restaurant), and, of course, room service. Complimentary shuttle service is available within a 3-mile radius of the hotel. Pets up to 75 pounds are permitted for a nonrefundable $75 fee. Smoking is prohibited.

HOMESTEAD HOUSTON/GALLERIA AREA $
2300 W. Loop South
(713) 960-9660
homesteadhotels.com

The newly renovated rooms at Homestead Houston cater to those who are in town for a few weeks, as well as those looking for an inexpensive place to stay for a night or two. The studio suites here include full kitchens, complete with utensils and cookware. There are also on-site laundry facilities. Housekeeping is provided once every 7 days, but you can get your room cleaned more often for $10 per service. Need to get online? Wi-Fi costs $4.99 per stay. Guests can bring one pet for $25 per day, up to a maximum of $150. Van transportation is available within a 3-mile radius. Advance payment is required.

HOTEL DEREK $$-$$$
2525 W. Loop South
(713) 961-3000
hotelderek.com

True to Texas, the Hotel Derek prides itself on being elegant yet comfortable, and at that the hotel succeeds. You'll quickly feel at home in any of the 314 contemporary guest rooms. Your stay includes plush beds, high-speed Internet, in-room safes, complimentary overnight shoe shine, a 24-hour fitness center, daily newspaper delivery, free shuttle service within a 3-mile radius, and the sight of the rosy-faced couples who get married here each week. The elegant Valentino Restaurant offers artful Italian fare. Prefer something a bit more fun and casual? Head to Vin Bar, whose tapas-style menu features cured meats, international cheeses, raw fish, a growing selection of vegetarian options, and wines galore. Hotel Derek is located across the street from the Galleria, offering easy access to some of the city's best shopping and restaurants.

INTERCONTINENTAL
HOUSTON $$–$$$$
2222 W. Loop South
(713) 627-7760
ichotelsgroup.com

You'll enjoy countless amenities at this Galleria-area hotel. Among them: access to the business center, a full-service gym, same-day dry cleaning and laundry service, live entertainment, and a whirlpool and outdoor pool. Each of the 485 guest rooms and 13 suites includes cable and satellite TV, morning newspaper delivery, a coffee and tea maker, and plush bathrobes. High-speed Internet costs an additional $10.95 per day. Don't want to venture down to the Galleria for your next meal? Feast on global cuisine at The Restaurant, or enjoy a martini and tapas at The Bar.

MARRIOTT HOUSTON WEST
LOOP BY THE GALLERIA $$–$$$
1750 W. Loop South
(713) 960-0111
marriott.com

This newly renovated 13-floor hotel has 299 guest rooms, plus 2 suites. No matter which room you rest your head in, you'll enjoy lavish down bedding, large safes, flat-screen TVs and cable, coffee, and tea. In-room wireless Internet costs $12.95 per day, but you can get free Wi-Fi in the lobby. On-site dining options include Alexander Restaurant, which cooks up Southwestern fare, and the Fairway Lounge, which serves American dishes. Exercise options include an indoor atrium pool and a fitness center. The hotel is near the Galleria shopping area, as well as Memorial Park's running and biking trails. Free shuttle service is available to the Galleria mall. The hotel is smoke-free.

✳OMNI HOUSTON HOTEL $$
4 Riverway
(713) 871-8181
omnihotels.com

Though it's just a 3-minute drive from the Galleria, the Omni Houston is serenely tucked away from the hustle-and-bustle of Houston's biggest shopping area, making it a great place to sneak away for a weekend—or even get married. (I speak from experience here!) And it's so beautifully decorated inside that you'll probably wonder how the rates could be so low compared to Houston's other luxury hotels. The hotel has 378 newly renovated guest rooms, including 33 suites, and most offer great views of Houston or the hotel's 2 outdoor swimming pools. Every room includes an ample sitting area, as well as marble baths, plush robes, nightly turndown service, free Wi-Fi, and daily newspaper delivery. If that's not enough pampering for you, get a massage at Mokara Spa or get your nails and hair done at Cerón Salon. Hungry? Enjoy a meal at NOÈ, an award-winning restaurant that serves eclectic American dishes; or take in a view of the meadow while you eat breakfast at Cafe on the Green. Afterward, dance the night away downstairs at the Black Swan nightclub. Special kid-friendly amenities are available.

SHERATON SUITES HOUSTON $$-$$$
2400 W. Loop South
(713) 586-2444
sheratonsuiteshouston.com

The Sheraton Suites is just a 2-block walk from the Galleria mall and restaurants. All 281 suites here come with free high-speed Internet, plush bathrobes and slippers, and two flat-screen televisions. Professionals have easy access to fax machines and copiers here, too. There's an Omaha Steakhouse on-site, but there are plenty of better restaurants nearby. See the "Restaurants" chapter for suggestions.

*ST. REGIS HOUSTON $$$$
1919 Briar Oaks Ln.
(713) 840-7600
starwoodhotels.com

This hotel used to be the Ritz-Carlton. Despite the name change, you can still expect the same luxurious accommodations and great service, not to mention a convenient location right between the Galleria and the exclusive River Oaks neighborhood. The Starwood-owned St. Regis has 232 spacious rooms and suites with floor-to-ceiling windows, high-speed Internet, safes, and top-of-the-line linens. The hotel, which is known for its butler service, offers 24-hour room service, a fitness center, twice-daily turndown service, and a spa. Dining is available in the Zagat-rated Remington Restaurant; The Remington Bar features live music on Friday and Saturday nights. There's also an intimate wine room and an afternoon tearoom. Dogs are welcome.

THE WESTIN GALLERIA HOUSTON $$$-$$$$
5060 W. Alabama
(713) 960-8100
starwoodhotels.com

A popular spot for meetings, weddings, and bar and bat mitzvah parties, The Westin Galleria is adjacent to the Galleria mall. All 487 rooms and 23 suites include Starwood Hotels' signature Heavenly bedding, coffeemakers with Starbucks coffee, and bathrobes. You can even request a special Heavenly Bed for your dog. High-speed Internet is available for $9.95–$14.95 per day, depending on the speed you choose. Need to work out? You can exercise in the hotel gym or jog along nearby running paths. The hotel offers a running map with a 3-mile and a 5-mile route. Children's programming and babysitting are also available.

THE WESTIN OAKS HOUSTON $$$-$$$$
5011 Westheimer at Post Oak Blvd.
(713) 960-8100
starwoodhotels.com

Yes, there are two Westins at the Galleria, and yes, both are connected to the mall and share the same phone number. But they're not the same hotel: If you reserve a room at The Westin Galleria, they won't be able to find your name over at The Westin Oaks. Both hotels charge almost the same rates, and the 406 rooms and 9 suites here offer basically the same perks and accommodations as those at The Westin Galleria—the Heavenly bedding, a gym, dog beds, babysitting service, and children's programming. Many rooms at this location also include Jacuzzis.

GREENWAY PLAZA

**RENAISSANCE HOUSTON HOTEL
GREENWAY PLAZA** $$-$$$
6 Greenway Plaza East
(713) 629-1200
marriott.com

Centrally located off US 59, this Marriott-owned hotel is just minutes from River Oaks, Montrose, West University, Rice University, the Museum District, and the Texas Medical Center. The airy rooms here are decorated with contemporary furniture and bold colors. And, thanks to the floor-to-ceiling windows, you can get some great views of the downtown skyline from many of the 382 guest rooms and 6 spacious suites. Every room includes cable and bathrobes. High-speed Internet access is available for $12.95 a day. Pets are allowed for a refundable $100 deposit. This is a smoke-free hotel.

MEDICAL CENTER

**BEST WESTERN PLAZA HOTEL &
SUITES AT MEDICAL CENTER** $$
6700 S. Main St.
(713) 522-2811
bestwesterntexas.com

Need to be near a relative or friend in the hospital? This Best Western is a good option. The hotel is located within walking distance of Baylor Clinic, Methodist Hospital, and Texas Children's Hospital, and just a short drive from MD Anderson Cancer Center, VA Hospital, Memorial Hermann, Ben Taub, and St. Luke's. It's also just a block from the METRORail station, giving you easy access to the nearby Museum District. The rooms are typical Best Western; the few frills include free high-speed Internet access and hot breakfast, as well as a microwave and satellite TV in every room. There's also

an indoor pool and exercise room. The hotel's 125 rooms and suites include 25 wheelchair-accessible suites. Free shuttle service is available to and from all of the Texas Medical Center hospitals. This is a nonsmoking hotel.

**HILTON HOUSTON PLAZA/MEDICAL
CENTER** $$-$$$
6633 Travis St.
(713) 313-4000
hilton.com

This stylish hotel boasts a prime Medical Center location that offers easy access to Rice University, Hermann Park, Reliant Center, the Museum District, and all of the Texas Medical Center hospitals. Each of the 141 luxurious suites and 42 deluxe guest rooms features a wet bar, comfy bedding, cable, and panoramic views of the city. High-speed Internet access is available for a fee. Fitness buffs can take advantage of the outdoor pool and private jogging track. Free shuttle service can take you to the area hospitals and medical facilities. Babysitting is available. This is a nonsmoking hotel.

**HOLIDAY INN HOTEL & SUITES
HOUSTON MEDICAL CENTER** $$
6800 S. Main St.
(877) 859-5095
holidayinn.com

Modern decor and a convenient location make this a good option if you're in town for medical treatment or visiting a patient at a hospital in the Texas Medical Center. Added bonus: guests are just a short drive from Rice University, Hermann Park, the Museum District, and Reliant Park. There are 287 guest rooms, and 215 of them are suites, so there's plenty of space to spread out. Every room includes free high-speed

Internet access and cable; the suites include full kitchens with cookware and utensils. The recently renovated fitness center includes top-notch cardio equipment and weights. Free shuttle service is available with 24-hour notice.

LAKE VIEW RV RESORT $$
11991 S. Main St.
(713) 723-0973
lakeviewrvresort.com
Park your RV at this highly rated resort and stay in one of the fully furnished cabins or park models. Among the perks here: free barbecue and picnic areas, propane, a walking track, a pool and Jacuzzi, fitness and recreation rooms, free high-speed Internet, a fishing lake, and free shuttle service to the Texas Medical Center. There's also daily maid service. Rentals are available by the day, week, or month. Pets aren't allowed.

MEMORIAL

HOTEL SORELLA CITYCENTRE $$–$$$
800 Sorella Ct.
(713) 973-1600
hotelsorella-citycentre.com
This trendy new hotel sits right in the middle of the CityCentre complex, putting you just steps from hip bars, restaurants, and shops. But between Hotel Sorella's plush beds, chic decor, state-of-the-art spa and fitness center, and the musical performances at the Monnalisa Bar, there's a good chance you may never want to leave the hotel. All 244 rooms and suites feature custom-designed beds, walk-in showers, floor-to-ceiling windows, spacious work desks, and free Wi-Fi. Plus, your stay includes continental breakfast. And if you want to stick around the hotel for lunch, dinner, or Sunday brunch, the acclaimed menu at Bistro Alex should satisfy your hunger.

**✷THE HOUSTONIAN HOTEL,
CLUB & SPA** $$–$$$$
111 N. Post Oak Ln.
(713) 680-2626
houstonian.com
Houston is full of luxury hotels, but none is quite like The Houstonian. Located just 5 minutes from the Galleria and practically across the street from Memorial Park, this lavish hotel sits on 18 wooded acres, some of which are used for running and walking trails. This makes for a tranquil setting, no matter which of the 289 elegantly decorated rooms you stay in. Every room boasts floor-to-ceiling views of the woods and vibrant landscaping, high-speed Internet, an electronic safe, oversize work desks, and terry cloth robes. Unwind while you swim in the pool and gaze at the waterfalls, or get your hair and nails done or get a massage at Trellis, The Spa. You'll also get access to Redstone Golf Club and the Houstonian Fitness Club—widely considered one of the country's best private gyms. Guests enjoy several dining options, including the Gazebo by the pool and American cuisine with a Mediterranean twist at Olivette. Transportation to the nearby Galleria is also available.

MONTROSE

MODERN B&B $$–$$$
4003 Hazard
(832) 279-6367
modernbb.com
Modern B&B lives up to its name, blending Houston's cosmopolitan style with the cozy feel of a bed-and-breakfast. Each of the 8 guest rooms in this contemporary 4-story

building features lively contemporary decor and art. Guests have access to free Wi-Fi, cable, a guest kitchen, exercise equipment, a guest office, and a hip, high-ceilinged gathering area filled with modern furniture, books, and a fireplace. A hot organic breakfast is also included in your stay. And, thanks to Modern B&B's location in the heart of Montrose, you'll have easy access to the Museum District, Hermann Park, Rice University, Rice Village, Upper Kirby, the Texas Medical Center, and some of the city's best restaurants.

MUSEUM DISTRICT

*HOTEL ZAZA $$$–$$$$
5701 Main St.
(713) 526-1991
hotelzaza.com/houston

Forbes has described Hotel ZaZa as one of the 10 best business hotels in the world. And that's fairly accurate: ZaZa is a good place to stay for business, but it's an even better place to stay for pleasure. Located in what was previously the Warwick Hotel, ZaZa caters to the young, hip, and wealthy with a style all its own. The hotel indulges guests with fluffy bedding, plasma TVs, leopard-print carpets, plush robes, and exquisite views. ZaZa's more than 300 guest rooms include several Concept Suites, which are decorated with themes ranging from Casa Blanca (Moroccan-inspired decor) to "Houston, We Have a Problem"(contemporary icy blue and gray decor that is reminiscent of the moon). Hungry? The Monarch Restaurant & Lounge here is a popular draw, thanks to its breakfast and brunch options; cocktails, like the Moulin Rouge and the Blue Mojito; salads; sushi; and stylishly presented entrees. The menu includes plenty of fish and steak fare, but

you can also get burgers, sandwiches, and fries. The Monarch also offers bottle service, giving you access to a long list of fine wines. ZaZa is located in the heart of the Museum District, just a block from Hermann Park and the Museum of Natural Science.

HOUSTON INTERNATIONAL HOSTEL $
5302 Crawford St.
(713) 523-1009
houstonhostel.com

Houston International Hostel sits right in the heart of the Museum District, just a short walk from Hermann Park and Rice University. If you've stayed in a hostel before, you know what to expect: several bunk beds packed into a room, a communal kitchen, and a common room. There are also lockers to store your stuff in, 3 bathrooms with hot showers, a laundry room, and a few computers. It's not anything fancy, but it's tidy and the beds are comfortable. Plus, with rates starting at less than $20 a night, a stay here is dirt cheap. The hostel has mandatory lockout hours from 10 a.m. to 5 p.m. and midnight to 8 a.m., so you'll have to hang out elsewhere during the day and return before midnight. The office is only open from 8 to 10 a.m. and 5 to 11 p.m. each day, so call to make your reservations accordingly.

SOUTH LOOP

HAMPTON INN & SUITES, HOUSTON MEDICAL CENTER/ RELIANT PARK $–$$
1715 Old Spanish Trail at Fannin
(713) 797-0040
hamptoninn.com

Attending an event at Reliant Center or spending some time at the Texas Medical Center? Here's a conveniently located option that's not too hard on the wallet. This Hampton Inn's 120 guest rooms include Cloud Nine luxury bedding and free high-speed Internet. Other perks include a business center, swimming pool, fitness center, free hot breakfast, and free self-parking. This is a nonsmoking hotel.

i Many Houston hotels have staff members who speak several different languages, including Spanish. If you need someone to translate for you or a companion, inquire at the front desk.

SOUTH MAIN RV PARK $
10100 S. Main
(713) 667-0120
smrvpark.com
Located at the intersection of South Main and I-610, the South Main RV Park is just a mile from Reliant Center (home of the Houston Texans and the Houston Livestock Show and Rodeo), 2.5 miles from the Texas Medical Center, and 7 miles from downtown. This securely gated, well-maintained RV camp includes several shaded areas, concrete patios, paved streets, free local phone calls and wireless Internet, cable TV, laundry facilities, and, of course, 20/30/50 amps. The park is managed on-site. Skip the Houston traffic by taking the park's free shuttle service to the Medical Center and nearby shopping areas.

RESTAURANTS

Foodies, you've come to the right place. Houston's cuisine (and appetite) rivals the likes of New York, Chicago, and Los Angeles. And we've got close to 9,000 restaurants—including some James Beard Foundation Award nominees—to prove it. Even better: the average meal here costs an average of $32.53 for 2 people—well below the national average of $35.10.

No matter when you dine out here, you probably won't ever really eat alone. Houstonians, after all, eat out more than residents of any other city in the country (4 times a week, compared to the national average of 3.2 times).

So, what's there to eat in this city?

The thousands of restaurants here cover every kind of cuisine you could want: American, Greek, Spanish tapas, Middle Eastern, Italian, steak, pizza, Southern and Cajun, vegetarian, hot dogs and burgers, every kind of Asian food imaginable, sandwiches and bagels, breakfast and brunch fare, Texas barbecue, seafood from the Gulf of Mexico, and, of course, Tex-Mex—that is, Mexican food with a Texas twist. If you're looking for a fun place to socialize, cap off a great meal, or satisfy your sweet tooth, you've also got your pick of exceptional dessert and coffee shops.

OVERVIEW

With nearly 9,000 restaurants in Houston, it's impossible to list all of the great ones in the space of a chapter. In the pages that follow, you'll find some of Houston's hottest and, in my opinion, best restaurants. Restaurants, as well as dessert options and coffee shops, are organized by cuisine type, with only the most central, original, or most popular location listed here. Additional locations are mentioned in the listings and can be found by visiting the restaurant website.

The restaurants listed here range from highly expensive to dirt cheap, but most fall somewhere in between. The majority of Houston restaurants offer at least a few vegetarian options. You'll also find plenty of

places to dine with children; the barbecue, burger, and hot dog restaurants are particularly good candidates for family meals. Houston restaurants are usually open 7 days a week for lunch and dinner, and many serve brunch on weekends. I've flagged restaurants that are closed on certain days or for certain meals. But you should still call ahead to double-check a restaurant's hours since these often change.

Also keep in mind that the Houston restaurant landscape changes constantly. By the time you read this book, some restaurants listed here may have moved or closed. So it's a good idea to call ahead before your visit.

RESTAURANTS

Houston restaurants tend to fill up on Friday and Saturday nights. Many fill up on weekdays, too. Pricier restaurants usually take reservations, so call ahead if possible.

Price Code

The following prices are based on a meal for two, without drinks, appetizers, desserts, tax,

or tip. Prices are also based on averages only and assume guests eat at least one meat entree.

$	Less than $15
$$	$15 to $30
$$$	$30 to $50
$$$$	More than $50

El Tiempo, Washington Corridor, Mexican & Tex-Mex, $$$, 96

Empire Cafe, Montrose, Coffee Shops, $–$$, 74

Empire Turkish Grill, Memorial, Middle Eastern, $$, 86

Escalante's, River Oaks, Mexican & Tex-Mex, $$$, 94

Fadi's Mediterranean Grill, Memorial, Middle Eastern, $, 86

Field of Greens, Upper Kirby, Vegan & Vegetarian, $$, 96

Fountain View Cafe, Galleria/ Uptown, Breakfast & Brunch, $, 70

Frenchy's Chicken, South Central, Cajun & Southern, $, 72

Fu Fu Cafe, Sharpstown/ Chinatown, Asian, $, 66

Gelato Blu, Washington Corridor, Dessert, $, 79

Goode Company Taqueria & Hamburgers, West University, Burgers & Hot Dogs, $$–$$$, 72

Goode Company Texas Barbeque, West University, Barbecue, $$, 69

Goode Company Texas Seafood, West University, Seafood, $$$, 89

Grotto, Galleria, Italian & Pizza, $$$, 81

The Grove, Dowtown, American, New American & Eclectic, $$$–$$$$, 59

Haven, Upper Kirby, American, New American & Eclectic, $$$, 62

Hobbit Cafe, Upper Kirby, American, New American & Eclectic, $$, 62

The Hot Bagel, Montrose, Delis, Bagels & Sandwiches, $, 75

House of Pies, Upper Kirby, Dessert, $, 79

Hugo's, Montrose, Mexican & Tex-Mex, $$$, 93

India's, Galleria/Uptown, Asian, $$, 64

Indika, Montrose, Asian, $$$, 65

Irma's Southwest Grill Downtown by the Ballpark, Downtown, Mexican & Tex-Mex, $$–$$$, 91

James Coney Island, Upper Kirby, Burgers & Hot Dogs, $, 71

Jonathan's The Rub, Memorial, American, New American & Eclectic, $$$, 59

Kahn's Deli, Rice Village, Delis, Bagels & Sandwiches, $$, 76

Kata Robata Sushi & Grill, Upper Kirby/Greenway, Asian, $$$, 68

Katz's Deli, Montrose, Delis, Bagels & Sandwiches, $$, 75

Kenny & Ziggy's, Galleria/ Uptown, Delis, Bagels & Sandwiches, $$–$$$, 74

Kim Son, Downtown, Asian, $$, 64

Kiran's, River Oaks/Highland Village, Asian, $$$$, 65

Lankford Grocery & Market, Midtown/Montrose, Burgers & Hot Dogs, $, 71

La Vista, Galleria, Italian & Pizza, $$$, 81

Le Mistral, West Houston/ Energy Corridor, French, $$$–$$$$, 80

Little Pappasito's, Upper Kirby, Mexican & Tex-Mex, $$$, 95

Lupe Tortilla Mexican Restaurant, Upper Kirby, Mexican & Tex-Mex, $$$, 95

Madras Pavilion, Upper Kirby/Greenway, Asian, $$, 68

Mark's American Cuisine, Montrose, American, New American & Eclectic, $$$$, 61

Max's Wine Dive, Washington Corridor, American, New American & Eclectic, $$$, 63

Mi Luna, Rice Village/West University, Tapas, $$, 90

Moeller's Bakery, Braeswood, Dessert, $–$$, 77

Morningside Thai, West University, Asian, $$, 68

New York Bagel & Coffee Shop, Fondren Southwest, Delis, Bagels & Sandwiches, $, 74

Nidda Thai Cuisine, Montrose, Asian, $$, 65

Niko Niko's, Montrose, Greek & Mediterranean, $$, 81

Nino's, Midtown, Italian & Pizza, $$$, 83

Nit Noi Thai, Memorial, Asian, $$, 64

Oishii, Upper Kirby/ Greenway, Asian, $–$$, 68

Onion Creek Coffee House Bar & Lounge, The Heights, Coffee Shops, $–$$, 73

The Original Ninfa's On Navigation, Second Ward, Mexican & Tex-Mex, $$$, 95

Pappadeaux Seafood Kitchen, Upper Kirby, Seafood, $$$, 88

Pappas Bar-B-Q, Medical Center, Barbecue, $$, 69

Pappas Bros. Steakhouse, Galleria, Steak Houses, $$$$, 89

Pappas Burger, Galleria, Burgers & Hot Dogs, $$, 71

Pappas Seafood House, Montrose, Seafood, $$$, 88

Paulie's, Montrose, Delis, Bagels & Sandwiches, $$, 76

Pepper Tree Veggie Cuisine, River Oaks/Highland Village, Vegan & Vegetarian, $$, 96

Pho One, Westchase, Asian, $–$$, 69

Picnic, Rice Village, Delis, Bagels & Sandwiches, $, 76

Pico's Mex-Mex, Bellaire/ Meyerland, Mexican & Tex-Mex, $$–$$$, 91

Pink's Pizza, The Heights, Italian & Pizza, $$, 81

Prego, West University, Italian & Pizza, $$$, 85

Pronto Cucino, Montrose, Italian & Pizza, $$, 84

Rajin Cajun, Upper Kirby/ Greenway, Cajun & Southern, $$–$$$, 72

Reef, Midtown, Seafood, $$$–$$$$, 87

Restaurant RDG + Bar Annie, Galleria, American, New American & Eclectic, $$–$$$$, 59

Ruggles Cafe Bakery, West University/Rice Village, American, New American & Eclectic, $$–$$$, 63

Ruggles Green, River Oaks, American, New American & Eclectic, $$, 61

Rustika Cafe & Bakery, West University, Dessert, $–$$, 80

Salento, Montrose, Coffee Shops, $–$$, 74

Saltgrass, Memorial, Steak Houses, $$$, 89

Southwell's Hamburger Grill, Galleria, Burgers & Hot Dogs, $, 71

Sprinkles Cupcakes, River Oaks, Dessert, $, 79

Star Pizza, Upper Kirby, Italian & Pizza, $$, 84

Stone Mill Bakers, River Oaks, Delis, Bagels & Sandwiches, $$, 77

Sweet Lola Yogurt Bar, Midtown, Dessert, $, 78

Swirll Italian Yogurt, Galleria/Uptown Park, Dessert, $, 78

T'afia, Midtown, American, New American & Eclectic, $$$–$$$$, 60

Taco Milagro Restaurant & Beach Bar, River Oaks, Mexican & Tex-Mex, $$, 94

Tacos A Go-Go, Midtown, Mexican & Tex-Mex, $, 91

Taste of Texas, Memorial, Steak Houses, $$$, 90

Three Brothers Bakery, Braeswood, Dessert, $–$$, 77

Tiny Boxwood's, River Oaks, American, New American & Eclectic, $$–$$$, 62

Tony's, Upper Kirby, Italian & Pizza, $$$$, 84

Tony Mandola's, River Oaks, Seafood, $$$, 88

Torchy's Tacos, Montrose, Mexican & Tex-Mex, $, 94

Treebeards, Downtown, Cajun & Southern, $–$$, 72

Trevisio, Medical Center, Italian & Pizza, $$$, 82

Uptown Sushi, Galleria/ Uptown, Asian, $$$, 64

Vic & Anthony's Steakhouse, Downtown, Steak Houses, $$$$, 89

Yia Yia Mary's, Galleria, Greek & Mediterranean, $$$, 80

AMERICAN, NEW AMERICAN & ECLECTIC

Downtown

THE GROVE $$$–$$$$
1611 Lamar
(713) 337-7321
thegrovehouston.com

Tucked on the south end of Discovery Green, this urbane restaurant makes eco-friendly dining chic. The Grove maintains its own herb and tomato garden and recycles and composts just about everything used—or not used—in the restaurant. The Grove describes its food as "American Rustic." For lunch that means the likes of wood-grilled vegetable skewers, skirt steak, ceviche, a fried-oyster BLT, and a lamb burger topped with goat cheese. The more extensive dinner menu includes big and small plate options, as well as a tasting menu. Save room for dessert—say, the Texas pecan and brown butter cake topped with vanilla ice cream, a strawberry rhubarb turnover with homemade crème fraîche, or the chocolate espresso torte with candied kumquats and cinnamon anglaise. The Grove offers an extensive selection of beer, wine, liquor, and specialty drinks, including Champagne Mangos Cosmos, mojitos, ginger margaritas, and Summers in Bombay, which was featured in GQ. Call or go online to make reservations.

i Heading to the theater after dinner? Order off The Grove's pre-theater dinner menu, which includes a starter, an entree, and dessert for $35 per person.

Galleria

RESTAURANT RDG + BAR ANNIE $$–$$$$
1800 Post Oak Blvd. at Ambassador Way
(713) 840-1111
rdgbarannie.com

Chef Robert Del Grande is something of a celebrity among foodies, and it's easy to see why when you visit this recently renamed, rebranded, and relocated restaurant and bar. The place is divided into two über-swanky dining areas, and both are places to be seen—and eat an inspired meal. Downstairs in the BLVD Lounge you can drink cocktails and eat hors d'oeuvres while sitting on a cushy sofa. Upstairs you can dine in either the RDG Grill Room, which serves steaks, seafood, and some of the city's finest Southwestern dishes, or Bar Annie, which serves less-fancy fare like burgers and onion rings. The restaurant serves dinner 7 days a week; lunch is served Mon through Fri; brunch is available on Sun. The ever-popular happy hour is offered Mon through Fri from 4 to 7 p.m.

Memorial

✳**JONATHAN'S THE RUB** $$$
Memorial
9061 Gaylord
(713) 465-8200
jonathanstherub.com

Lobster sliders. Blackened shrimp & grits. Mac & cheese with 5 cheeses and Applewood bacon. Stuffed quail. These are just a few of the reasons so many people are willing to stand in line to get a seat at Jonathan's The Rub. Good service helps, too. Closed Sunday.

Midtown

T'AFIA $$$–$$$$
3701 Travis
(713) 524-6922
tafia.com

T'afia chef Monica Pope, a 2007 James Beard Award nominee, has won praise from *O, The Oprah Magazine, Travel + Leisure, Bon Appetit, Fortune*—and countless Houstonians. Among the reasons: Pope's creativity, her chic lounge and restaurant, and her commitment to local food and farmers. Whether you eat in the bar or the restaurant, you'll order from a constantly changing menu featuring in-season food that largely comes from the Houston area. On any given night, that might mean tasty chickpea fries; redneck pimento mac 'n cheese; cremini sliders with cambazola; dal with okra, longbeans, and fresh peas; or South Texas anteolope loin with milled Yukon Gold potatoes, steamed greens, and salsa verde. T'afia only serves dinner, except on Friday when Pope offers a special 3-course lunch for $22 per person (tax, tip, and drinks not included). T'afia is fairly small and can fill up, especially during Friday lunch and on Friday and Saturday evenings, so call or go online to make a reservation. Closed Sunday and Monday.

Montrose

BABA YEGA $$
2607 Grant St., at Missouri
(713) 522-0042
babayega.com

It may be named after a witch, but Baba Yega is quite charming, thanks to the cozy house it calls home and the Montrose locals who keep returning for more. The menu is filled with healthy options like smoked turkey sandwiches topped with brie, grilled trout, a veggie club, and other vegetarian dishes. Visit during lunch from 11 a.m. to 2 p.m. and get unlimited trips to the hot buffet and salad bar for just $11. Or head over for Sunday brunch and get your fill of eggs, meat, veggies, brown rice, and lox and bagels for $19.95.

✳BARNABY'S CAFE $$
604 Fairview St.
(713) 522-0106
barnabyscafe.com

Charmed by dogs? You'll almost certainly be charmed by Barnaby's, too. Here furry friends are considered special (outdoor) guests and large Milk-Bones are free for the taking after your meal. Named after the owner's childhood sheepdog, this funky, bold-hued restaurant serves up good sandwiches and burgers (including a couple of meatless variations), as well as an eclectic mix of baby back ribs, meat loaf, General Tso's chicken, lasagna, and burritos. Whatever you order, the waffle fries with blue cheese aren't to be missed. Head next door to Baby Barnaby's (602 Fairview; 713-522-4229) for breakfast or brunch 7 days a week. The Midtown location (414 W. Gray; 713-522-8898) also serves breakfast on Saturday and Sunday mornings from 8 to 11 a.m. The breakfast dishes at both locations cover the basics—eggs, pancakes, waffles, bacon. Barnaby's has additional locations in Memorial and River Oaks.

i Forget *Restaurant Week*. In Houston, we have *Restaurant Weeks*—or rather, the entire month of August. That's when many of the city's best restaurants offer special menus and donate a portion of the proceeds to the Houston Food Bank. Learn more at houstonrestaurantweeks.com.

✳MARK'S AMERICAN CUISINE $$$$
1658 Westheimer Rd.
(713) 523-3800
marks1658.com

Looking for a romantic dinner spot? Or just want to eat the best food in town? Head straight to Mark's. You'll savor each bite beneath gold ceilings and among hand-painted deco walls in this renovated 1920s church. Mark's uses only the freshest ingredients so the menus are seasonal, and there's a good chance that the list of specials will be even longer than the printed menu. In fact, the specials change throughout the day, depending on what has just arrived from suppliers or just been prepared in the kitchen. Most of the artfully presented dishes here revolve around beef, seafood, or chicken, but you can ask for vegetarian options, too. Whatever you order, save room for dessert like the Coffee Toffee or Homemade Snicker's Bar. And ask for wine suggestions; the waiters here excel at finding the perfect bottle for the flavors in your meal. Mark's serves lunch and dinner, although lunch is only served on weekdays. Call for reservations.

River Oaks

✳BACKSTREET CAFE $$$
1103 S. Shepherd Dr.
(713) 521-2239
backstreetcafe.net

Backstreet Cafe gets its charm partly from its location inside a 1930s house, partly from its lovely patio and garden, and partly from its first-rate seasonal American food. Year-round, the menu here is filled with sophisticated comfort foods—dishes like red corn chicken enchiladas, jalapeño fettucine, grilled rib eye with mashed potatoes, and chicken milanesa served with green bean salad and bacon mac and cheese. If you're dining here early in the summer, don't miss the special heirloom tomato menu. On the weekends from 11 a.m. to 3 p.m., the Backstreet Cafe serves brunch dishes like migas, breakfast pizza, and crawfish grits cakes and eggs. Vegetarian or vegan? Ask about the Backstreet Cafe's delicious options. Call or visit the website for reservations.

i **Dining at Backstreet Cafe on Sunday night? Order off the Farmer's Market Sunday Supper Menu. This special menu changes from week to week and feaures foods that chef Hugo and his team handpick at the weekend farmers' markets.**

DAILY REVIEW CAFE $$
3412 W. Lamar
(713) 520-9217
dailyreviewcafe.com

Bold colors and airy space make this a good place to enjoy a drawn-out meal with a friend you haven't seen lately. The extensive menu is filled with a mix of salads, soups, pastas, seafood, poultry, pizzas, and, on Saturday and Sunday, brunch dishes. Sit on the patio when the weather's nice. Closed Monday.

✳RUGGLES GREEN $$
2311 W. Alabama
(713) 533-0777
rugglesgreen.com

Ruggles Green is Houston's first certified "green" restaurant, which means everything is made with organic, all-natural, hormone-free, preservative-free products. Even if you don't consider yourself "green," you'll probably find something you like on the menu since good flavor is a top priority here.

Among the menu options: burgers of the meat, veggie, and turkey varieties; grilled panini; soups; salads; tasty wood-fired pizzas; and pastas such as the popular quinoa mac & cheese and quinoa spaghetti and turkey meatballs. This casual, family-friendly spot also serves kids' favorites like burgers, chicken tenders, mac and cheese, and grilled cheese. Ruggles Green offers a selection of organic wines and gluten-free beers. There's a second location at CityCentre in Memorial.

✳TINY BOXWOOD'S $$–$$$
3600 W. Alabama at Saint St.
(713) 622-4244
tinyboxwoods.com

Breakfast, brunch, dinner, lunch: Tiny Boxwood's does it all—and does it all so well. Located at the Thompson & Hanson Nursery, this chic restaurant has a rustic French feel made even better by the large windows that make you feel a little like you're eating amid the flowers and plants just outside. The short dinner menu consists of French-inspired salads, fish and meat dishes (think red fish with grits), and outstanding eclectic pizzas made in a wood-burning oven. Breakfast options include a variety of homemade pastries and egg dishes. The weekend brunch includes must-try migas, a morning meat and cheese board, quiche, and egg-topped pizzas. Lunch includes a variety of salads and sandwiches, including a delicious grilled gouda and pesto sandwich. Tiny Boxwood's serves some of the city's best desserts—including heavenly chocolate chip cookies—so save room. Or, just stop in for dessert and drinks at the bar. This popular spot doesn't take reservations, and there's usually a line out the door for brunch and lunch on the weekends after 10 or 10:30 a.m. Closed for dinner on Sunday and all day Monday. A second

location, Tiny's No. 5, recently opened in West University.

Upper Kirby

HAVEN $$$
Upper Kirby
2502 Algerian Way
(713) 581-6101
havenhouston.com

This relative newcomer on the Houston culinary scene bills itself as a seasonal kitchen, with a mix of New American, Southern, and Cajun influences. The menu features lots of local produce, as well as animals raised in the area. Visit during lunch for the $10 blue plate specials, which vary by day and season. Dinner options also change seasonally; recent winter options have included pan-roasted oysters, crispy pig trotter fritters, free-range chicken with bacon spaetzle and Brussels sprouts, and quail with jalapeño sausage dressing and green tomatoes. Visit for brunch on the weekends, when options include shrimp corn dogs with lemonade and Tabasco mash remoulade, the fried farm egg sandwich with bacon and Swiss on grilled sourdough, and migas with chateau loin of beef. Haven doesn't offer many vegetarian options, but that's slowly changing. Call or go online for reservations. Closed for dinner on Sunday.

HOBBIT CAFE $$
2243 Richmond Ave.
(713) 526-5460
myhobbitcafe.com

True to its name, Hobbit Cafe draws decorative and culinary inspiration from *Lord of the Rings*. Among the names of sandwiches served here: Frodo, Gandalf, and Fatty Lumpkin. But there's more to eat at Hobbit Cafe than just sandwiches. The restaurant also serves up tasty soy and black bean burgers, as well as nonvegetarian options like chicken salad, quesadillas, and burgers made with beef. Visit for brunch on Saturday and Sunday from 10:30 a.m. to 2 p.m. and feast on apple/gingerbread pancakes, beef fajitas and eggs, a variety of omelettes, homemade juices, and the requisite mimosas.

Washington Corridor

✳BEAVER'S $$
2310 Decatur St.
(713) 864-2328
beavershouston.com
This fun, unpretentious restaurant is another product of famed Houston chef Monica Pope. Unlike Pope's more upscale restaurant, T'afia, (page 60), Beaver's serves much more downhome food, though it's equally creative. The menu is filled with the likes of tots n' shots (green chile-pimiento cheese risotto tots, red pepper coulis, and virgin Bloody Mary), Beaver Cakes (basmati rice, goat cheese, sweet and spicy peppers and homemade kimchi), po'boys, meat loaf sandwiches, barbecue chicken and dumplings, and barbeque smoked daily with oak and maple. Wherever possible, Beaver's uses food from local farmers and producers. Not hungry? Beaver's patio and bar are also popular spots to kick back and have a drink, whether you prefer beer, wine, or one of the restaurant's "Dam 'Big' Cocktails." Beaver's opens at 11 a.m. and closes at 9 p.m. Sun and Tues through Wed and at 11 p.m. Thurs through Sat. Closed Mon.

MAX'S WINE DIVE $$$
4720 Washington Ave.
(713) 880-8737
maxswinedive.com
Never eaten fried chicken or venison tamales with wine? Max's Wine Dive beckons you to change your ways. Named one of the "Hot 10" wine bars in the country by *Bon Appetit*, this popular spot serves fried chicken, Kobe burgers, fried Gulf Coast oysters, salads, mac n'cheese tossed in truffle cream, and boatloads of wine. Max's is open until 11 p.m. on Sun and Mon, midnight Tues and Wed, and 2 a.m. Thurs through Sat. Max's serves brunch starting at 10 a.m. on Sat and 9 a.m. on Sun. The place can get noisy and crowded, so call for reservations.

i Max's Wine Dive can be pretty pricey. Save money by going during happy hour (4 to 7 p.m. Mon through Sat) or "reverse" happy hour (10 p.m. to midnight Tues and Wed and midnight to 2 a.m. Thurs through Sat).

West University & Rice Village

BENJY'S $$$
2424 Dunstan, at Kelvin
(713) 522-7655
benjys.com
This posh restaurant/lounge serves well-presented, eclectic dishes like nut-crusted salmon salad, pistachio-crusted goat cheesecakes, margarita surf and turf, and sweet potato risotto with brussel sprouts, as well as a good espresso tres leches. The Sunday brunch here is especially popular. No matter when you plan to eat at Benjy's, make reservations. This small place fills up quickly. For a reprieve from the noise, order a drink from the lounge and sit on the patio upstairs. Benjy's has a second location in the Washington Corridor.

RUGGLES CAFE BAKERY $$–$$$
2365 Rice Blvd.
(713) 520-6662
rugglescafebakery.com

Part bakery, part restaurant, Ruggles serves fresh, made-to-order food. Entrees here range from shrimp tacos to a turkey Reuben to a spicy black bean burger to the warm-baked, Texas–goat cheese salad. Top your meal off with tres leches, the Strawberry Bomb (angel food cake topped with mascarpone, whipped cream, and fresh strawberries), or the fresh fruit tart. When the weather's nice, dine or sip a cup of tea on the patio.

ASIAN

Downtown

KIM SON $$
2001 Jefferson St.
(713) 222-2461
kimson.com
With three restaurants, banquet halls, and kiosks scattered throughout Houston, this family-owned Vietnamese and Chinese food restaurant is practically a Houston empire. While part of Kim Son's success can be attributed to the Vietnamese community, the food also deserves a lot of credit. The menu is an overwhelming 13 pages long, with highlights including Vietnamese crepes, black-peppered soft-shell crabs, noodle salad, and spring rolls. Can't decide what to eat—or want lots of options? Try Kim Son's expansive buffet. The restaurant has two additional locations in Alief and Stafford; both serve what many consider the best dim sum in town and boast extensive buffets. Call ahead for reservations at the downtown location.

Galleria & Uptown

INDIA'S $$
5704 Richmond Ave.
(713) 266-0131
indiasrestauranthouston.com

Among the best Indian restaurants in town, India's serves up authentic curries, tikkas, kebabs, masalas, and a large selection of naans. One of the biggest draws here is the all-you-can-eat lunch buffet, which will cost you around $15. You can certainly find larger Indian buffets, but this one offers plenty of solid options for carnivores and vegetarians alike.

UPTOWN SUSHI $$$
1131 Uptown Park Blvd.
(713) 871-1200
uptown-sushi.com
This trendy Asian fusion and sushi restaurant is one of those places you might expect to see *Sex and the City's* Carrie Bradshaw. It's a place to see and be seen—and eat fresh sushi. The menu consists of Asian fusion dishes like wasabi caviar tuna, lobster tempura, and eggroll prawns, as well as unusual sushi rolls like the Bahama Breeze, which includes onion ring and peppercorn tuna topped with lobster salad mix, cilantro, wonton skin, and spicy miso dressing. Prefer sushi staples? Don't worry: The menu includes plenty of standard rolls and sashimi options. The bar offers the requisite sake and wine, plus several specialty martinis, like the Belgium White Chocolate Martini and the Key Lime Pie Martini.

Memorial

NIT NOI THAI $$
6395 Woodway Dr., at Voss
(713) 789-1711
nitnoithai.com
Since opening in Rice Village in 1987, Nit Noi Thai has expanded to several locations around the city. Each restaurant serves Nit Noi's special sauce, which is made fresh each morning at this location. The extensive

menu offers plenty of choices, including delicious pad thai, spring rolls, and curry dishes. Portions are large, so sharing is a good idea. Service can be slow at this location. Nit Noi has several other locations, including Nit Noi Cafes downtown and in Midtown; the cafes have smaller menus and focus primarily on lunch.

Midtown

✳CALI SANDWICH & FAST FOOD $
3030 Travis
(713) 520-0710
As my husband Ricky described this place: "It's not much on the eyes, but the food's great and It's cheap." That last part might actually be an understatement. Three dollars will buy you one of the best tofu banh mi sandwiches around, and just a few dollars more will buy you an array of noodle dishes. The sesame balls are also worth a try—if they have any left when you order. The place fills up at lunchtime, so arrive before noon to avoid the crowds. Service is pretty quick at lunch, but it can be pretty slow in the evenings and on weekends when the place is fairly empty.

Montrose

✳INDIKA $$$
516 Westheimer Rd.
(713) 524-2170
indikausa.com
There's a good reason why this Indian fusion restaurant has won praise from foodie bibles like the *Zagat Survey* and *Gourmet:* Chef Anita Jaisinghani blends fresh, local, and organic ingredients with traditional Indian ingredients to give Indian food a creative spin. And if the artfulness and flavor of her dishes are any indication, she more than

succeeds. The menu changes seasonally; recent dishes have included tandoori quail, crabmeat samosas, Indian black garbanzo and pumpkin soup, and a roasted portobello layered with spinach puree, butternut squash, garbanzo masala, and goat cheese. Visit for brunch on Sunday, when $25 will get you an unlimited sampling of dishes like pooris with sautéed mixed vegetables and paneer, a variety of pooris, chicken liver and onion masala on brioche, and dark chocolate ginger tart. Indika often fills up, so call ahead or make reservations online. Closed Mon.

i Want to learn to make your own Indian food? Indika chef-owner Anita Jaisinghani offers cooking classes on the fourth Sunday of each month. Learn about upcoming classes on Indika's website: indikausa.com.

NIDDA THAI CUISINE $$
1226 Westheimer Rd.
(713) 522-8895
niddathai.com
You'll be hard-pressed to find someone who doesn't like Nidda Thai Cuisine. This popular Montrose restaurant is known for its curries and coconut Tom Kha Gai soup. The Chu Chee Eggplant—battered and topped with red curry sauce—is also a big hit. Visit during lunch and get a full meal with your choice of tofu or chicken for $6.95.

River Oaks/Highland Village

KIRAN'S $$$$
4100 Westheimer Rd.
(713) 960-8472
kiranshouston.com
Lavish decor and quality food make Kiran's a popular Indian restaurant among those willing to part with a decent chunk of money.

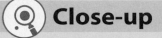

Close-up

Follow That Food Truck!

You don't have to visit a restaurant to eat gourmet food here. More and more food trucks are driving around Houston to serve up everything from cupcakes to banh mi sandwiches to burgers and tacos. And yes, thanks to Houston's strict food codes, it's perfectly safe to eat the food.

Most food trucks stop in different locations throughout the day and night. So, you've got to be in the right place at the right time to catch them.

Your best bet? Follow the food trucks on Twitter. Or find out where they are—and where they're headed next—at foodtrucksmap.com/houston. Here are some of Houston's most popular food trucks. Visit their websites, where applicable, for menus and prices.

Bernie's Burgers. berniesburgerbus.com, @BerniesBurgers. This yellow school bus serves made-from-scratch fries and burgers with names like "Detention," "Homeroom," and "The Pre-Schoolers." Everything's topped with freshly made condiments.

Good Dog Food Truck. gooddogfoodtruck.com, @gooddoghotdogs. Good Dog gives an American favorite a gourmet makeover with made-from-scratch condiments, local artisan buns, and Texas-made hot dogs.

H-town StrEATS. facebook.com/Htownstreats, @htownstreats. Polenta fries, Frito pie dogs, and grilled tofu tacos with green papaya slaw are just a few of the globally inspired H-town StrEATS.

Melange Creperie. melangecreperie.wordpress.com, @MelangeCreperie. This truck usually serves its Paris-style crepes at the corner of Westheimer and Taft in Montrose. Choose two or three sweet or savory fillings, including many local ingredients.

The menu includes traditional tikis, vindaloos, saags, and samosas, as well as unique dishes like Onion Bhaji (vidalia with chickpea flour and spinach) and paneer wraps made with naan and vindaloo aioli. Don't be surprised if chef-owner and namesake Kiran stops by your table to chat. Kiran's is closed for lunch on Saturday and for lunch and dinner on Sunday. The restaurant serves high tea the second Saturday of the month from 3 to 5 p.m.

Sharpstown/Chinatown

FU FU CAFE $
9889 Bellaire Blvd., at Corporate Dr.
(713) 981-8818
Some of Houston's best Chinese noodles and soups can be found at Fu Fu Cafe, where you can have your soup served in a bowl or in a dumpling. You can also choose from several nonsoup dishes like green beans with pork, as well as a long list of pan-fried dumpling options. The restaurant tends to be packed, so arrive early for lunch or dinner,

MMM . . . Cupcake. mmmcupcake.net, @MMMCupcakeTruck. MMM . . . Cupcake serves up happiness with cupcake flavors like strawberry, vanilla chai, red velvet, cookies-n-cream, chocolate, peanut butter, and orange zest.

Oh My Gogi. ohmygogi.com, @OhMyGogi. Oh My Gogi serves up Korean barbecue/Mexican fusion food. Think Korean barbecue tacos, kimchi quesadillas, and lots of Sriracha sauce.

Oh My! Pocket Pies. ohmypocketpies.com, @OhMyPocketPies. Breakfast, savory, and dessert pies are Oh My! Pocket Pies' bread and butter. Choose from a variety of fillings and original, whole wheat, or vegan dough.

Phamily Bites. phamilybites.com, @phamilybites. Satisfy your next Vietnamese food craving with a banh mi sandwich, chargrilled pork skewers, or a cup of pho.

Pi Pizza Truck. facebook.com/Pi.PizzaTruck, @pipizzatruck. Order pizza by the slice or the pie in varieties like Who's The Mac (bacon, mac & cheese, and mozzarella) and Porky's Revenge (slow roasted pulled pork, mozzarella, and jerk coleslaw).

The Waffle Bus. thewafflebus.com, @TheWaffleBus. The Waffle Bus whips up all things waffle, including Nutella and banana waffle sandwiches, waffle burgers, and smoked salmon waffles with dill cream cheese.

Zilla Street Eats. zillastreeteats.com, @ZillaStreetEats. Zilla's ever-changing menu includes the likes of chicken n' waffles, fried Nutter Butters, Dr Pepper braised short ribs, and mac n' cheese.

or plan to wait. Fu Fu Cafe is open until 2 a.m. Sun through Thurs and 4 a.m. on Fri and Sat.

Upper Kirby & Greenway

✳**AKA SUSHI HOUSE**　　　　$$
2390 W. Alabama St.
(713) 807-7895
akasushi.net
Aka Sushi House may sit in a strip center, but the classy red and black decor will quickly make you forget that. The menu here boasts

tasty miso soup with clams, as well as some great rolls, including the signature Nautilus Roll, the Tsunami Roll (shrimp tempura, grilled eel, crab, and mango), and the Crater Roll (baked roll with crab meat and baked scallops). Perhaps the biggest draw here is AKA Hour (Mon through Fri from 3 to 7 p.m. and 9 p.m. to close and all day Sat and Sun). That's when the restaurant discounts many of its rolls and drinks, making this place a bargain.

BLUE FISH HOUSE $$
2241 Richmond Ave.
(713) 529-3100
bluefishhouse.com

This recently renovated sushi bar serves Pan-Asian fare and very fresh sushi in a casual atmosphere. Vegetarian? You'll find plenty of options here, including the U Pick It Tofu, where the chef mixes tofu and vegetables with your choice of sauces, like Japanese curry, spicy lime, and hot balsamic. U Pick It options are also available for chicken, beef, pork, and a variety of fishes. Visit during lunch for some really cheap—and filling—options such as the Blue House Beef Bowl, tofu steak, and Udon It This Time (stir-fried udon noodles with mixed vegetables and garlic sauce). Call for reservations on Friday and Saturday evenings. Blue Fish House has additional locations in Sugar Land and The Woodlands.

KATA ROBATA SUSHI & GRILL $$$
3600 Kirby
(713) 526-8858
katarobata.com

Though the food here tends to be overpriced and the portions fairly small, Kata Robata has lots of loyal fans. Many keep returning for the Cucumber High (vodka, cucumber, and lime) and the lychee martini, as well as the chic decor and the ramen. Others are impressed with the sushi rolls, the sashimi, and the fairly arful presentation of the food. And die-hard fans flock here once a month for Umami, the restaurant's special tasting dinner. Previous dinners have included dishes like tiger blowfish prepared sashimi-style, Japanese deer, and blank squid ink pasta with octopus. Usually, Umami are held on the second Sunday of the month. Kata Robata often fills up on Friday and Saturday nights, so call or go online to make a reservation.

✳MADRAS PAVILION $$
3910 Kirby
(713) 521-2617
madraspavilion.us

Madras Pavilion is nothing fancy, but the food is solid and inexpensive, especially for vegetarians and those craving hard-to-find South Indian food. The restaurant has locations across Texas and the surrounding states, but the chain began here in Houston. The popular lunch buffet includes a constantly changing array of North and South Indian dishes, including many vegetarian options. All of the food served at this location is kosher. Madras Pavilion has a second location in Sugar Land location; not all the food at that location is kosher.

OISHII $–$$
3764 Richmond Ave.
(713) 621-8628
oishiihouston.com

This hole-in-the-wall may not have the best decor in town, but the food and rolls are good for the price. The menu includes standard sushi fare, as well as unique rolls like the David Roll and the Go Deep Roll. The menu also includes nonfish options. Visit during happy hour, and get buy-one-get-one-free specials and really cheap beer and wine. The place tends to fill up around 6:30 on Friday and Saturday evenings, so show up early to avoid a wait.

West University

✳MORNINGSIDE THAI $$
6710 Morningside Dr.
(713) 661-4400
morningsidethai.com

Don't be put off by the often-empty parking lot at Morningside Thai. Those who have discovered this little restaurant love the flavorful dishes, especially curries like the pineapple shrimp curry. Lunch specials range from $7.45 to $9.45. Tofu can be substituted in most dishes. Closed Sunday.

Westchase

PHO ONE $–$$
11148 Westheimer Rd., at Wilcrest
(713) 917-0351
pho-one.com
In the mood for some Vietnamese noodles? Check out Pho One. They serve some of the best pho noodle soup and bahn mi in town, as well as vermicelli patties, beef stew, and vermicelli salad bowls. The menu includes plenty of vegetarian options. The service here is great, too.

BARBECUE

Medical Center

PAPPAS BAR-B-Q $$
8777 S. Main
(713) 432-1107
pappasbbq.com
Pappas Bar-B-Q is owned by the Pappas restaurant family, which also owns steak, seafood, and Tex-Mex restaurants around Houston and elsewhere in Texas. This local chain may not serve the best barbecue in town, but it's definitely one of the most popular restaurants of its ilk. The Texas-style barbecue here is lean and slowly smoked, and it's a big hit when served on top of baked potatoes. Don't want beef or pork? Rest assured: You've got lots of chicken and turkey options here. Portions are Texas-size, so you may want to share. This location is

a good option if you're near the Medical Center or Reliant Center. There are more than a dozen other locations in the Greater Houston area, including two downtown; most of the other locations are in outlying areas.

> **i** Stuck downtown with no time to grab lunch? Call Pappas Bar-B-Q's downtown delivery line (713-759-0039) and get barbecue brought right to you.

Montrose

DEMERIS $$
2911 S. Shepherd
(713) 529-7326
demeris.com
Since 1964, the Demeris family has been synonymous with barbecue. This Houston staple serves beef, ribs, sausage, ham, turkey, and chicken, as well as burgers, fajitas, and salad. Dining in a group? Or have a big appetite and can't decide on just one meat? Order the barbecue dinner, which includes two sides and your choice of one to four meats. Demeris has additional locations in Sharpstown and Northwest Houston.

West University

✳GOODE COMPANY TEXAS
BARBEQUE $$
5109 Kirby Dr.
(713) 522-2530
goodecompany.com
This is the place to go for some of the best barbecue in town. All of the duck and pork ribs, sausage, pepper chicken, and brisket are slowly smoked over mesquite. Among the most popular dishes: the huge brisket sandwich. Food here is served cafeteria-style.

Whatever you order, be sure to try Goode Company's homemade jalapeño cheese bread and the pecan pie. The restaurant has additional locations in Memorial and Northwest Houston.

BREAKFAST & BRUNCH

Many Houston restaurants serve brunch, but most of these also serve lunch and/or dinner. So if none of the breakfast or brunch options listed here appeal to you, be sure to check out some other restaurants, including Tiny Boxwood's (page 62), Backstreet Cafe (page 61), The Hot Bagel (page 75), New York Bagel (page 74), Kenny & Ziggy's (page 74), Tacos A Go-Go (page 91), Torchy's Tacos (page 94), and Indika (page 65).

Galleria & Uptown

FOUNTAIN VIEW CAFE $
Galleria/Uptown
1842 Fountain View Dr.
(713) 785-9060
The Fountain View Cafe is a cafe in name, but it feels like more of an old-school diner, serving greasy breakfast food and sandwiches from morning until afternoon. Visit on the weekend and you're likely to have to wait in a long line to order and find a seat.

Memorial

THE BUFFALO GRILLE $
1301 S. Voss Rd., at Woodway
(713) 784-3663
thebuffalogrille.com
The Buffalo Grille serves breakfast, lunch, and dinner, but breakfast is the best reason to eat here. The long menu includes a long list of egg options—huevos rancheros,

migas, and omelets among them—as well as french toast and pancakes. You'll also get your choice of hash browns or grits. There's some outdoor seating, but it can be tough to come by on weekends, when there's typically a line out the door. Buffalo Grille has a second location in West University.

i Want to sit outside at Buffalo Grille's Memorial location? Avoid the area directly under the trees. The resident birds often mistake these tables for a bathroom.

Midtown

THE BREAKFAST KLUB $$
3711 Travis St., at Alabama
(713) 528-8561
thebreakfastklub.com
"If breakfast is the most important meal of the day, why not have it twice?" That's the motto at the Breakfast Klub, which serves some of the best breakfast in town until 2 p.m., 6 days a week. Frankly, it'd be tough to actually eat breakfast here twice a day: On Saturday, there's always always a line out the door, and most of the food is covered in gravy and/or fried. Signature dishes include the catfish and grits as well as the wings and waffle platter. The Breakfast Klub even offers breakfast sandwiches as well as its own version of Green Eggs and Ham, complete with spinach, chives, and bell peppers. Don't want breakfast food? The Breakfast Klub dishes up several lunch sandwiches and salads—except on Saturday, when breakfast is your only option. Avoid a long wait by visiting during the week. Closed Sunday.

BURGERS & HOT DOGS

Galleria

✳BECKS PRIME $$
2615 Augusta
(713) 266-9901
becksprime.com

Whether you're a vegetarian or a carnivore, this casual local chain is a don't-miss spot. Becks Prime uses only the freshest meat, which makes for some of the best burgers in town. Other hits include one of the best homemade black bean burgers around, the grilled ahi tuna sandwich with feta cheese and cucumbers, the grilled veggies, the fries (especially the sweet potato fries), and the thick milk shakes. Sit outside at one of the picnic tables and enjoy the shade. Becks Prime has 12 locations around the city, including one in Memorial Park.

PAPPAS BURGER $$
5815 Westheimer Rd., at Bering
(713) 975-6082
pappasburger.com

With several big-screen TVs, Pappas Burger is a great place to cheer on your favorite team while eating a big half-pound burger or indulging in a little chicken-fried steak or fried catfish. Prefer something less greasy? Try the grilled tuna niçoise salad or a grilled portobello sandwich. This family-friendly joint also has a kids' menu.

SOUTHWELL'S HAMBURGER GRILL $
5860 San Felipe St.
(713) 789-4972
southwells.com

Southwell's isn't anything fancy, but people keep returning because the burgers are solid—and cheap. You can even swap the meat patty on any burger for a veggie patty.

Other options include chicken and salads, as well as tasty milk shakes. Be sure to try the waffle fries. Southwell's has additional locations in Memorial, the Medical Center area, and the Heights.

Midtown/Montrose

LANKFORD GROCERY & MARKET $
88 Dennis St.
(713) 522-9555
lankfordgrocery.com

Once featured on Food Network's *Diners, Drive-ins and Dives*, many consider the burgers at this hole-in-the-wall to be the best in town. The short menu boasts just a few burgers, including the Grim Burger topped with mac & cheese, bacon, fried egg, and jalapeño. You can get sandwiches and salads here, too, but it's the burgers that woo the crowds. Lankford is open for lunch from 10 a.m. to 3 p.m. daily; it also serves breakfast Mon through Fri from 7 to 10:30 a.m. and Sat from 7 a.m. to noon. Bring cash because they don't take plastic here.

Upper Kirby

JAMES CONEY ISLAND $
3607 S. Shepherd Dr.
(713) 524-7400
jamesconeyisland.com

Ask almost any Houstonian where to find the best hot dog in town and you'll probably get the same answer: James Coney Island. When it opened in 1923, James Coney Island was a two-brother-run hot dog stand; today, there are more than 20 locations around the Greater Houston area. In addition to several different hot dogs, the menu includes burgers, corn dogs, chicken strips, and chili.

There's almost always a line at lunchtime, but it tends to move quickly.

> **i** Kids 10 and younger eat free at James Coney Island on Wednesday from 4 p.m. to close.

West University

GOODE COMPANY TAQUERIA & HAMBURGERS $$–$$$
4902 Kirby Dr.
(713) 520-9153
goodecompany.com

This laid-back joint is a good place to go with the kids or when everyone can't agree on what to eat. The menu includes mesquite-grilled burger and mesquite-grilled chicken options, hot dogs, kid's dishes, salads, enchiladas, and tacos that can be topped with salsa at the condiment bar. Other hits include the chocolate cinnamon shakes and the homemade desserts. The restaurant also serves breakfast favorites like pecan waffles, huevos con chorizo, and eggs with everything from catfish to quail.

CAJUN & SOUTHERN

Downtown

TREEBEARDS $–$$
315 Travis, on Market Square
(713) 228-2622
treebeards.com

Long before the downtown revitalization ushered in new restaurants and entertainment, there was Treebeards. Since 1978, this downtown staple has been a popular spot to lunch on Southern and Cajun dishes, like duck and seafood gumbo, jerk chicken, chicken-fried steak, pot roast, vegetarian red beans and rice, cheese grits, corn bread

dressing, and mustard greens. Treebeards has additional locations downtown at the Cloister at Christ Church Cathedral (1117 Texas Ave.; 713-229-8248) and in the downtown tunnels at 1100 Louisiana (713-752-2601). There's also a take-out location in the tunnels at 801 Louisiana (713-224-6677). All locations are open for lunch Monday through Friday; hours vary by location.

South Central

FRENCHY'S CHICKEN $
3919 Scott, at Wheeler
(713) 748-2233
frenchyschicken.com

Cajun and Creole influences rule at this local fast-food chain, which serves what many consider the best fried chicken in town. Sides include dirty rice, collard greens, corn muffins, and bread pudding. There's often a wait. Bring cash; they're not big on credit card transactions at Frenchy's. This flagship location is near the University of Houston; Frenchy's has several other locations.

> **i** Craving Cajun and Creole food for breakfast or lunch? Try the Breakfast Klub, located in Midtown and listed in the "Breakfast & Brunch" section of this chapter.

Upper Kirby & Greenway

✳RAJIN CAJUN $$–$$$
4302 Richmond Ave.
(713) 623-6321
ragin-cajun.com

The flavorful boiled crawfish might be the biggest draw at this casual joint, but the oysters, po'boys, and fried shrimp are also good. The family-style seating, HDTVs airing sports events, and good food make this the kind of place that you come for dinner and stick around for a couple of hours. Rajin Cajun has additional locations in the Memorial area, downtown, and Sugar Land.

COFFEE SHOPS

The Heights

✳ONION CREEK COFFEE HOUSE BAR & LOUNGE $-$$
3106 White Oak Blvd., between Studewood and Heights Blvd.
(713) 880-0706
onioncreekcafe.com
The comfy couches and tables, as well as an outdoor patio, make Onion Creek a fun place to grab a cup of coffee during the day or hang out with friends in the evening. Some come for the coffee or the alcohol; others come for the occasional live music or to munch on a sandwich, burger, salad, pizza, or panini. Onion Creek also serves breakfast every morning. Be prepared to wait if you order food, though. The kitchen is small and this popular coffee shop usually has several orders in the queue. Onion Creek opens daily at 7 a.m. and stays open until mightnight Sun through Tues and until 2 a.m. Wed through Sat.

Montrose

✳AGORA $
1712 Westheimer Rd.
(713) 526-7212
agorahouston.com
Agora has frequently been named the city's best coffee shop by Houston Press, and it's easy to see why. From the replicas of ancient art hanging on the walls to the live belly dancing, this quirky Greek-inspired coffee shop is charming and unpretentious. There

are plenty of tables for those who want to drink a cup of gourmet coffee, read Agora's free periodicals, and use the free Wi-Fi. Those hanging out in groups can make use of the couches or sit on the patio. Agora serves beer, wine, port, coffee, and then some. It's open daily from 9 a.m. to 2 a.m.

✳BLACK HOLE COFFEE HOUSE $
4505 Graustark St. at Castle Ct.
(713) 528-0653
Once a convenience store, Black Hole has been reincarnated as a hip hangout and workspace for students and young professionals, who visit for the coffee but often stay for food and pastries. Black Hole tries to use locally sourced coffee and food whenever possible. Between the local art lining the walls and books by local authors available for purchase, and the Poison Pen Reading Series that's frequently held here, Black Hole has a very artsy vibe—and a local one at that. The coffee shop is open daily from 6:30 a.m. to midnight.

ⓘ Need to do your laundry? Drop it off at Graustark Laundry (4506 Graustark St., 713-529-9028) while you visit Black Hole. This dog-friendly Laundromat provides self-service and quick wash-and-fold service at reasonable prices.

✳BRASIL $-$$
2604 Dunlavy St.
(713) 528-1993
brasilcafe.net
This funky coffee shop is a great place to caffeinate in the morning, unwind after a long day, or catch up with friends. In addition to the requisite coffee, tea, and Italian sodas, Brasil serves wine and beer, pizza, pasta,

salad, burgers, and sandwiches. The menu includes several good vegetarian options. Local musicians often play here, and it can get loud. On cool evenings, take advantage of the patio seating. Brasil opens daily at 7:30 a.m. and closes at midnight Mon through Sat and at 11 p.m. on Sun.

DIRK'S COFFEE $
4005 Montrose Blvd.
(713) 526-1319
dirkscoffee.com
Dirk's makes some strong coffee, espresso, and specialty drinks. The shady patio makes this a great place to people watch, study, or, if you prefer, play board games.

✳EMPIRE CAFE $–$$
1732 Westheimer Rd.
(713) 528-5282
empirecafe.net
More hip than your neighborhood Starbucks, this friendly neighborhood cafe is a great place to grab a cup of coffee—or wine, beer, or a mixed drink—with a friend. You can also order breakfast dishes, as well as pasta, panini, soup, salad, and an array of tempting cakes and other desserts. There's tons of outdoor seating. Empire opens daily at 7:30 a.m. and closes at 11 p.m. on Fri and Sat and 10 p.m. Sun through Thurs.

SALENTO $–$$
Rice Village
2407 Rice Blvd.
(713) 528-7478
salentowinecafe.com
By night, Salento is a wine bar, but by day, it's a great coffee shop. In fact, it's the kind of coffee shop where people linger, thanks to the good music, free Wi-Fi, a solid food menu, and good wine, beer, and coffee

drinks made with only single origin and medium dark roast coffee.

DELIS, BAGELS & SANDWICHES
Downtown

ANTONE'S $
801 Capitol, at Travis St.
(713) 224-4679
Need to grab a sandwich to go? You'll find tons of already packaged sandwiches at Antone's, along with made-to-order po'boys and Mediterranean treats like stuffed grape leaves and baklava. The sandwiches here may not be the very best in town, but with options like a slice of Gouda on your sandwich, they're definitely among the most original. Antone's has several locations.

Fondren Southwest

✳NEW YORK BAGEL & COFFEE SHOP $
9720–4 Hillcroft St.
(713) 723-8650
Tasty breakfast options abound at New York Bagel & Coffee Shop. This kosher deli and bakery serves everything from corned beef hash sandwiches to eggs with crispy homefries to whitefish, gefilte fish, and challah. The bagels are the best reason to come here, though. They're big, fluffy, and—if you arrive at the right time—hot.

Galleria & Uptown

✳KENNY & ZIGGY'S $$–$$$
2327 Post Oak Blvd.
(713) 871-8883
kennyandziggys.com
Looking for a nice Jewish deli? Head directly to Kenny & Ziggy's. This popular New York–style delicatessen has a menu with more than 200 items, many with witty names

like "Fiddler on the Roof of Your Mouth" (a triple-decker sandwich with corned beef and pastrami) and "Luck Be a Latke" (brisket sandwiched between two potato pancakes). The menu includes standard Jewish and New York–deli fare: lox and bagels, blintzes, matzo brei, potato pancakes, whitefish, and pickled herring among them. Other options include eggs, burgers, sandwiches, salads, schnitzels, Philly cheesesteaks, and meatballs. Save room for dessert, especially a slice of chocolate babka, or, if you prefer, chocolate-dipped macaroons, Boston cream cake, an array of pies, or a Belgian waffle topped with three—yes, three—scoops of ice cream, hot fudge, caramel sauce, whipped cream, and cherries. The restaurant cures and pickles all of the meat and bakes all of its own bread. Want some whitefish, rye bread, or a cheesecake for the house (or hotel)? Kenny & Ziggy's will gladly pack it up for you. Catering is also available. Kenny & Ziggy's is open daily for breakfast, lunch, and dinner until 9 p.m.; the restaurant opens at 7 a.m. Mon through Fri and 8 a.m. on weekends. The place is particularly crowded on Saturday and Sunday mornings so arrive early or plan to wait in line.

Montrose

✳BROWN BAG DELI $
2038 Westheimer Rd.
(713) 807-9191
thebrownbagdeli.net
If you've eaten at a Which Wich?, you're familiar with the Brown Bag Deli concept: You grab a brown bag, check off the kind of bread, meat, cheese, and toppings you want, and hand the bag to the resident sandwich maker, who then makes you a huge sandwich. Meat options include

turkey, ham, roast beef, and salami; nonmeat options include egg salad, tuna with pecans, pimento cheese, and PB&J. Everything here is fresh and the bread—jalapeño cheese bread included—is homemade. Want something to go with your sandwich? Choose from potato chips, chocolate chip cookies, rice crispy treats, and sides, like red potato salad and fresh fruit. Brown Bag Deli has additional locations in Rice Village, downtown, and Northwest Houston.

✳THE HOT BAGEL $
2009 S. Shepherd Dr.
(713) 520-0340
hotbagelshop.bravehost.com
The Hot Bagel is a bit of a dive, but the bagels more than make up for the surroundings. The shop bakes more than two dozen flavors of bagels, which range from sesame, poppy, and everything bagels to less mainstream flavors, like sea salt, sun-dried tomato, and cinnamon apple. All of these can be topped with about 10 different flavors of cream cheese, including fat-free, lox, and honey walnut varieties. Deli sandwiches are also available. This long-standing Houston establishment often has a line out the door on weekend mornings, so show up early or be prepared for a short wait. There's very little seating, so you may want to order your bagels to go.

KATZ'S DELI $$
616 Westheimer Rd.
(713) 521-3838
ilovekatzs.com
Katz's isn't the best deli in town, but it's certainly good—and open 24 hours, 7 days a week. The extensive menu includes half-pound deli sandwiches and loads of specialty sandwiches, including Meat Loaf

Mania, Grilled Salmon Hero, and Yankee Pot Roast. Any sandwich can be made on Katz's homemade rye, challah (braided egg bread), French, or whole wheat bread. The restaurant also serves a hodgepodge of American entrees like fried chicken, pasta, and salad, as well as traditional Jewish dishes like matzo ball soup, potato pancakes, bagels and lox, and kugel. Among the biggest draws are the fried pickles and the breakfast dishes, which are served all day. There's a full bar. Katz's has a second location with a less-extensive menu—and no late-night hours—in Conroe.

✳PAULIE'S   **$$**
1834 Westheimer Rd.
(713) 807-7271
pauliesrestaurant.com
This neighborhood restaurant is worth a crosstown trip. The exposed brick walls and the art on them create a cozy atmosphere in which to eat and drink lemonade, beer, or wine. Paulie's has a great selection of salads, soups, and sandwiches, ranging from Italian hoagies to grilled-shrimp BLTs, meatball sandwiches, and grilled portobello sandwiches topped with red bell peppers and goat cheese. Save room for dessert, whether you prefer cannoli or some of the prettiest sugar cookies in town. Paulie's is open from 11 a.m. to 9 p.m. Mon through Sat. Closed Sun.

i Need to feed a crowd at lunchtime? Call Paulie's 24 hours ahead of time to order box lunches that are sure to please. For $9 to $11.75, you'll get a sandwich, pasta and fruit salad, a cookie, and bottled water.

Rice Village

KAHN'S DELI   **$$**
2419 Rice Blvd.
(713) 529-2891
kahnsdeli.com
Kahn's Deli has been recognized by just about all of the big restaurant raters—Zagat, AOL City Guide, and Citysearch—and their sandwiches deserve a lot of the credit. Among them: pastrami, roast beef, corned beef, tuna melts, chicken salad, and three different kinds of Reubens. Kahn's also makes one-of-a-kinders like the Soho (smoked turkey breast with melted cheese, cranberry sauce, lettuce, and tomato on wheat bread) and the Village Special (chargrilled chicken and vegetables, olive tapenade, and sundried tomato pesto on ciabatta bread). You'll find lox and bagels here, too, along with breakfast options ranging from challah french toast to eggs to wraps. Beer lovers, take note: Kahn's recently added more than 60 craft beers to its menu; they'll also fill your growler to go. Kahn's is open daily for breakfast and lunch.

✳PICNIC   **$**
1928 Bissonnet
(713) 524-0201
picnicboxlunches.com
Looking for a quick, tasty lunch option near the Museum District? This cheerful neighborhood deli, bakery, and coffee shop is a good choice. Everything at Picnic is made fresh, including the delicious salads, sandwiches, breads, and cookies. Seating is true to the restaurant's name: there are just a few long wooden picnic tables, and you'll get your food in a plastic basket. Picnic is open from 10 a.m. to 5 p.m. Mon through Fri and 10 a.m. to 4 p.m. on Sat. Closed Sun.

Picnic's sister restaurant, The Raven, is just a few doors down in the same shopping center; it boasts a more extensive menu and slightly more upscale indoor and patio seating options.

River Oaks

✳STONE MILL BAKERS　　　　$$
2518 Kirby at Westheimer
(713) 524-6600
stonemillbakers.com

It's no secret why there's a long line at Stone Mill Bakers during lunchtime: This sandwich shop and bakery serves up great sandwiches on homemade bread. The bread selection changes daily, but there are always several options, ranging from rye and multigrain to cranberry, corn bread, and challah. Try the whole wheat Dakota bread, which includes sunflower seeds, pumpkin seeds, sesame seeds, and millet. The sandwiches here are big, so consider saving half or sharing. There's a second location in Memorial.

DESSERT

Braeswood

MOELLER'S BAKERY　　　　$–$$
4201 Bellaire Blvd.
(713) 667-0983
moellersbakery.com

Since 1930, this Houston bakery mainstay has made some of the city's best cookies, petit fours, orange rolls, almond logs, danishes, and cakes galore. They don't all look like something you'd see on the Food Network's *Ace of Cakes*, but most of Moeller's desserts more than make up for it in taste.

✳THREE BROTHERS BAKERY　　　$–$$
4036 S. Braeswood Blvd.
(713) 666-2253
3brothersbakery.com

This family-owned kosher bakery has provided the sweets for local Jewish events for five generations, but non-Jews also know they can count on Three Brothers for stellar desserts. Three Brothers makes delicious petit fours, cookies, cupcakes, pastries, wedding cakes, and some creative sheet cakes, including some featuring the face of the person of honor. Three Brothers' pecan pie was named "the best America has to offer" by *Country Living*. The bakery also makes bagels and Jewish baked goods like challah and, for Purim, *hamantaschen*. Diabetic? Good news: Three Brothers also makes sugar-free treats. Three Brothers recently opened a second location in Memorial across the street from Memorial City Mall.

Galleria & Uptown Park

CRAVE CUPCAKES　　　　$
1151–06 Uptown Park Blvd.
(713) 622-7283
cravecupcakes.com

Cupcake lovers, take note: Crave Cupcakes bakes some of Houston's best—and most elegant-looking—cupcakes. Among the flavors: candy bar, banana, cranberry orange, Nutella, and white chocolate macadamia nut; Crave even sells breakfast cupcakes. Gluten-free? Crave has a cupcake just for you—a rich dark chocolate cupcake with chocolate butter cream frosting and chocolate sprinkles. There's a tiny bit of seating both inside and outside the bakery. Single cupcakes cost $3.25; one dozen costs $36. Breakfast cupcakes cost $2.50 each. Local delivery is available; place orders at least 24 hours ahead of time. Crave has a second location near Rice Village.

*DESSERT GALLERY BAKERY AND CAFE $-$$
1616 Post Oak Blvd.
(713) 622-0007
dessertgallery.com

There are desserts and then there are Dessert Gallery desserts—delicacies so decadent that you should break your diet for a bite or two. Chocoholics will find plenty of options here, from the ultrarich Turtle Candy Cake to the flourless Everyone's Favorite Mousse Cake to the Chocolate Concorde Cake. Also worthy of a taste are nonchocolate offerings like the heavenly Lemon Vacherin, which pairs meringue with lemon mousse; the Toffee-licious Cake; and the French Vanilla Cake. Cakes are available by the slice or whole. Other dessert options include chocolate-covered Oreo truffles, French macaroons, gourmet cupcakes, and seasonal treats. Dessert Gallery also makes sandwiches and salads. Sit in one of the Dessert Gallery's plush chairs and play a board game while you savor your dessert and a cup of coffee or Italian soda. Or sit outside and watch the cars drive by. The Dessert Gallery has a second location in Upper Kirby.

SWIRLL ITALIAN YOGURT $
5000 Westheimer Rd.
(713) 552-0863
swirlls.com

At Swirll, you can serve yourself a dozen different flavors of frozen yogurt—pomegranate, green apple, cookies and cream, and country vanilla included. Top yours with fresh fruit, Fruity Pebbles, or mochi, then savor the taste and ambience while sitting in a big comfy orange chair. You can even bring your laptop and use the free Wi-Fi. Swirll has five additional locations around town.

Midtown

*ACADIAN BAKERY $
604 W. Alabama St.
(713) 520-1484
acadianbakers.com

If you love chocolate—and love desserts with a little texture—a stop at Acadian Bakery is an absolute must. (Just ask Margaret Thatcher, Arnold Schwarzenneger, Bill and Hillary Clinton, and George Bush, who are all among the bakery's clients.) The Brownie Chocolate Mousse Cake is to die for, especially if you get it with the chocolate ganache. Like the other tasty cakes here, it's available by the slice. Or, if you call ahead, you can order a cake that serves anywhere from a few people to a few hundred. The bakery itself isn't much to look at, but there's plenty of seating, so you can eat your cake and, if you prefer, a sandwich with one of the bakery's popular homemade buns. Acadian Bakery is open from 9 a.m. to 4:30 p.m. Mon through Fri and 9 a.m. to 2 p.m. on Sat. Closed Sun.

SWEET LOLA YOGURT BAR $
304 W. Gray
(713) 521-1333
sweetlolayogurtbar.com

Plenty of places in Houston dish out frozen yogurt, but no one does it quite like Sweet Lola. You'll find only four flavors of yogurt here, and they vary from season to season. Among the recent flavors: Sugar Plum Berry, Cinnamon Crème, and Dark & Dreamy Chocolate. The real reason Sweet Lola has so many loyal fans, though, isn't the yogurt itself but the toppings. Sure, you can choose fresh fruit or sprinkles, but why would you when faced with alternatives like home-made brownie crumbles, sea salted peanut butter croutons, and lollipops?

River Oaks

THE CHOCOLATE BAR $–$$
1835 W. Alabama
(713) 520-8599
theoriginalchocolatebar.com
Chocolate in the shapes of tools. Chocolate and orange ice cream. Brownie lollipops. Chocolate-topped tres leches. These are just a few of the chocolate treats available at The Chocolate Bar, where, as the slogan suggests, "Every hour is happy hour." In addition to a variety of chocolate cakes and cookies, this chocoholic's heaven sells more than a dozen flavors of ice cream—all of them incorporating chocolate in some way. There's plenty of seating if you want to dine in. The Chocolate Bar has a second location in Rice Village.

✴SPRINKLES CUPCAKES $
4014 Westheimer
(713) 871-9929
sprinkles.com
You'll often find a line out the door at this tiny Highland Village cupcake shop. Flavors range from the expected red velvet to more unusual flavors like cinnamon sugar to dog cupcakes. Some flavors are available daily; others like the delicious peanut butter chocolate, as well as the mocha cupcake, are only available on certain days. Occasionally, Sprinkles whips up themed cupcakes (think s'more-flavored), which are available for a limited time. Cupcakes cost $3.50 each or $39 per dozen. Go online to order some for pickup or delivery.

Indian Twist

In the Upper Kirby or River Oaks area? Stop by **Pondicheri** for dessert. Though the food at this Indian restaurant is lacking in flavor, the desserts are spectacular. Whether you order a chocolate hazelnut basil cookie or a chocolate oatmeal chili one, you're sure to be wowed (2800 Kirby Dr., 713-522-2022, pondichericafe.com).

Upper Kirby

HOUSE OF PIES $
3112 Kirby Dr.
(713) 528-3816
houseofpies.com
This diner is definitely a dive, but it serves great pies (and other diner food) 24/7. That's probably why it's a perennial favorite, especially among students and other nocturnal types. Diabetics, take note: House of Pies makes sugar-free pies. There's a second location a couple miles west of the Galleria.

Washington Corridor

GELATO BLU $
5710 Memorial Dr.
(713) 880-5900
gelatoblu.com
Love gelato? You'll find some of Houston's best at this very blue little shop. Flavors range from standard gelato fare, like pistachio, to Orange Push Up. Gelato Blu even serves gelato shakes. Not into gelato? Try the smoothies, coffee, or sandwiches.

West University/Rice Village

BERRIPOP $
2339 University Blvd., Ste. A
(713) 592-9600
berripop.com

Cheery colors decorate this popular yogurt shop—and, if you like, your yogurt. More tart than sweet, the frozen yogurt here comes in unusual flavors like black cherry, green tea, and raspberry pomegranate. Toppings range from fresh fruit, like mango, pomegranate, and blackberries, to Cap'n Crunch. Berripop has several other locations around the city.

RUSTIKA CAFE & BAKERY $-$$
3237 Southwest Fwy.
(713) 665-6226
rustikacafe.com

Rustika serves an array of soups, salads, breakfast dishes, crepes, and tacos, but the baked goods are the real reason to come here. Stop in for a huge slice of cheesecake, dulce leche, and chocolate raspberry mousse cake are just a few of your choices. Or pick up an almost-too-pretty-to-eat cookie, lemon square, or—on Friday—a challah.

FRENCH

Rice Village

✳CAFE RABELAIS $$-$$$
2442 Times Blvd.
(713) 520-8841
caferabelais.com

Step into this charming little restaurant, and you'll feel like you've escaped to a Parisian cafe. The menu, written on a chalkboard, includes a variety of French-inspired sandwiches (all with fries), salads, quiches, and cheeses, but perhaps the biggest winner here are the mussels. Closed for lunch on

Mon and all day Sun. Cafe Rabelais' owners have a second pricier restaurant, Brasserie Max & Julie, in Montrose.

West Houston/Energy Corridor

LE MISTRAL $$$-$$$$
1400 Eldridge Pkwy.
(832) 379-8322
lemistralhouston.com

It's far from many parts of Houston, but most people agree that Le Mistral is worth the drive, especially if you're looking for someplace romantic. This elegant restaurant infuses its foods with flavors from a variety of French regions. That includes Burgundy snails, *foie gras*, Mediterranean mussels, and steaks and fish made in a variety of ways. Save room for the Grand Marnier soufflé with spicy orange sauce, the individual chocolate soufflé, or Crepe Suzette. Want to sample all of chef David Denis's best creations? Try the tasting menu. Mistral serves lunch and dinner on weekdays, dinner only on Saturday, and brunch and dinner on Sunday. Call for reservations.

GREEK & MEDITERRANEAN

Galleria

YIA YIA MARY'S $$$
4747 San Felipe
(713) 840-8665
yiayiamarys.com

All of the options can feel a little overwhelming at this Pappas-owned restaurant. But just about everything—from the moussaka to the Greek salad to the pita to the souvlaki—is worth a try. Can't decide on something or don't want to spend a lot of money? Order a few mesas (appetizers) like the baked feta, roasted eggplant dip, and spanakopita.

There's a line to order at lunch, but it tends to move quickly.

> **i** Get your fill of authentic Greek food at the Original Greek Festival in October. Find details in the "Annual Events" chapter.

Montrose

*NIKO NIKO'S $$
2520 Montrose
(713) 528-0966
nikonikos.com

Niko Niko's is nothing fancy, and you'll eat off paper plates. But, boy, is it good. Whether you want stuffed grape leaves, Greek meatball gyros, pita bread with falafel and hummus, or some sweet Greek pastries, you'll find some of the best in town here. You'll even find gyro breakfast pitas—or Greekfast, as Niko Niko's calls its breakfast selection. Service is pretty quick, although you may have to wait in line to order and look around for a table if you visit during a peak time. The extensive menu and laid-back family atmosphere make this a good place to bring kids. Breakfast is served daily and until 1 p.m. on weekends. Niko Niko's has a second location with a smaller menu downtown in Market Square.

ITALIAN & PIZZA

Galleria

GROTTO $$$
4715 Westheimer, at West Loop 610 South
(713) 622-3663
grottorestaurants.com

This member of the Landry's Restaurants family continues to be one of the most popular upscale Italian spots in town. Bold-colored murals and plates line Grotto's walls, giving this noisy restaurant a festive atmosphere. Choose from one of the many savory pizza, pasta, meat, chicken, or seafood dishes, or pick a few items from the antipasto bar. Save room for one of the sinfully rich Italian pastries or cakes and consider sampling one of Grotto's many Italian wines. Call or go online to make reservations, especially if you're dining on the weekend. Grotto has a second location in The Woodlands.

LA VISTA $$$
1936 Fountain View Dr.
(713) 787-9899
fatbutter.com

La Vista's slogan is "Where it's all good," which speaks to the quality of the food as much as to the laid-back atmosphere. You won't find many traditional Italian dishes here, but you will find options from all the usual Italian food groups—pasta, pizza, meat, chicken, and seafood. La Vista prides itself on serving up unique flavors. There's a pork tenderloin dish, for instance, that's crusted with cinnamon, coffee, and cumin. There's also a pizza topped with mushrooms, Asiago cheese, sweet sugar, caramelized onions, and sage. La Vista has quite a bit of patio seating, complete with a view of the parking lot. The restaurant doesn't take reservations, so there's often a wait. La Vista is BYOB, with a $5 corkage fee. Lunch is served Mon through Fri and dinner is served here daily.

The Heights

*PINK'S PIZZA $$
1403 Heights Blvd.
(713) 864-7465
pinkspizza.com

Thin-crust pizza plus fresh premium ingredients make for some mighty good pizza here. While you can get your standards like cheese pizza or pepperoni pizza here, Pink's specializes in more unusual pizzas. The Freshetta, for instance, has garlic, feta, spinach, sun-dried tomatoes, bacon, marinated chicken, and fresh tomatoes; the Luigi combines Canadian bacon, Gorgonzola, mozzarella, portobello mushroom, apple, roasted garlic, pesto sauce, and sun-dried tomato. Can't find a pizza that appeals to you? Just name your own toppings. Specialty 12-inch pizzas cost $16.99; specialty 16-inch costs $20.99. Standard cheese pizzas cost less. Grinders, Philly cheesesteaks, and other sandwiches and pasta dishes are also available. Pink's has three additional locations, including one in West University and one in Midtown. Free delivery is available in certain areas.

Located at the top of the John P. McGovern Texas Medical Center Commons Building, Trevisio offers world-class dining in the Texas Medical Center. A water wall stands at the restaurant's entrance, hinting at the simple yet sophisticated decor and food that is yet to come. Dishes here include the likes of granseola (polenta-crusted crab cake with spinach, corn, shiitake mushrooms, jumbo lump crab, and bianco sauce), rapini e salsiccia pizza (rapini mushrooms, Italian sausage, marinara, and mozzarella), and tortellini stuffed with smoked duck and ricotta, dried cherries, and toasted pistachio bianco sauce. Trevisio has a vegetarian menu; just ask for it. On a cool evening, sit outside on the patio and take in some great views of the area. Trevisio is open for lunch Mon through Fri and dinner only on Sat; the restaurant is closed on Sun. Call for reservations.

Houston Culinary Tours

Want an inside look at some of Houston's best food from some of the city's most renowned chefs? Sign up for one of the Houston Culinary Tours. Recent tours have highlighted oysters, Southern food, and local farms and farmers' markets. Learn about upcoming tours at houstonculinarytours.com.

Medical Center

TREVISIO $$$
6550 Bertner
(713) 749-0400
trevisiorestaurant.com

Memorial

✳CIRO'S ITALIAN GRILL $$
9755 Katy Fwy., at Bunker Hill
(713) 467-9336
ciros.com

Ciro's serves Italian food done right: The dishes here tend to be simple and include pizzas made in a wood-burning oven, pasta, soup, and entrees like eggplant parmigiana and veal scallopini. The dishes here are pretty large, but you can order the pastas and salads in smaller sizes. Watching your weight? Look for the "Great Taste: No Waist" dishes on the menu. Whether you're dieting or not, be sure to try the tasty flat bread. Brunch—including $2 mimosas, sangria, and bellinis—is served from 11 a.m. to 3 p.m. on weekends.

Midtown

DAMIAN'S CUCINA ITALIANA $$$
3011 Smith, between Elgin and Tuam
(713) 522-0439
damians.com

Couples wanting a romantic evening often seek refuge in the quiet yet elegant atmosphere of Damian's. From the wall murals to a menu filled with dishes like spaghetti Bolognese, Damian's is one of Houston's most authentic Italian restaurants. The menu includes flavorful pasta dishes aplenty, as well as veal, fish, chicken, and the requisite minestrone soup and antipasti. Damian's is owned by Bubba Butera and Frankie Mandola, whose family members run several great restaurants in Houston and Austin. Dress appropriately: Damian's requires business casual attire and will turn you away if you show up in shorts and/or a t-shirt. Call for reservations. Lunch is served Mon through Fri; Damian's serves dinner Mon through Sat. Closed Sun.

*NINO'S, VINCENT'S, GRAPPINO DI NINO $$$
2817 W. Dallas (Nino's)
(713) 522-5120
2701 W. Dallas (Vincent's)
(713) 528-4313
West Dallas at Eberhardt (Grappino Di Nino)
(713) 522-5120
ninos-vincents.com

The Mandola family has three restaurants located next door to each other on West Dallas: Vincent's, Nino's, and Grappino di Nino. All three serve basically the same menu, which includes a range of pastas, wooden-oven baked pizzas, salads, meat, and fish. Vincent's is known for its rotisserie-cooked chicken. There's also an extensive wine selection. It's a good idea to call ahead for reservations, although you can always head to one of the other two if you can't get a table at the restaurant of your choosing. Nino's is slightly dressier than the other two restaurants, which are casual. That said, you won't usually find people wearing tank tops, shorts, and tennis shoes at any of the restaurants.

Montrose

DA MARCO $$$$
1520 Westheimer
(713) 807-8857
damarcohouston.com

Celebrating a special occasion? Or just want to taste some of the best food in town? Make a reservation at Da Marco. Widely regarded as one of Houston's best restaurants—if not the best—Da Marco serves up eclectic Italian dishes that are sure to wow. Among them: ravioli with ricotta, egg, and truffles; gnocchi, wild boar sausage, and fava beans; pizza with prosciutto, burrata, and eggs; grilled octopus, arugula, orange, and fennel; and whole roasted fish. Save room for dessert—whether you prefer something sweet like the sour cream chocolate torte or some of Da Marco's flavorful cheeses. This beloved restaurant fills up even on weekdays, so call ahead to nab a table as early as possible. Closed Sun and Mon.

*DOLCE VITA $$-$$$
500 Westheimer
(713) 520-8222
dolcevitahouston.com

Chef Marco Wiles says pizza is one of his favorite things to cook and eat, and it shows in the the food he serves up at this Montrose staple. From the crust to the toppings, the pizzas here are first-rate, with eclectic options including the taleggio (taleggio cheese, arugula, pears, and truffle oil), the vongole (clams, garlic, cherry tomatoes, and mozzarella), and zucca (butternut squash, pancetta, smoked buffalo mozzarella, and red onion). The home-made pastas are also outstanding and, like the pizzas, can easily be shared by two people. Start your meal with one of the tasty Italian cheeses or appetizers like the shaved Brussels sprouts with pecorino. The vibrantly painted walls and laid-back atmosphere make this a great place to dine with friends, kids, or the whole extended family.

i Dolce Vita only offers valet park-ing, but you can almost always find free parking on one of the side streets nearby.

PRONTO CUCINO $$
1401 Montrose
(713) 528-8646
pronto-2-go.com

Like other members of the acclaimed Man-dola restaurant family, Pronto serves classic Italian dishes that Houstonians have come to expect from the owners. The menu con-sists largely of pasta, chicken, salad, and fish dishes; Pronto also serves panini and pizza squares. Unlike most of the other Mandola restaurants, this one caters to the take-out crowd as well as people who have no problem walking up to the counter to order their meal. Pronto has two additional loca-tions—one on the border of West University and Braeswood, the other in Memorial's CityCentre complex.

Upper Kirby

CARRABBA'S ITALIAN GRILL $$$
3115 Kirby Dr.
(713) 522-3131
carrabbas.com

There's a good chance that you've eaten at Carrabba's before since the restaurant has more than 200 locations in 27 states. But you probably haven't been to the original restau-rant, which is located right here in Houston and is still operated by the Carrabba family. The food here may not be the best Italian in town, but it's still pretty good. The menu is filled with pasta, steaks and chops, pizza, and soups and salads. You've also got your pick of several specialty dishes, like the Stuffed Shrimp Mandola (shrimp stuffed and baked with Italian-style crab dressing) and Chicken Bryan Texas (grilled chicken topped with goat cheese, sun-dried tomatoes, and basil butter).

STAR PIZZA $$
2111 Norfolk St.
(713) 523-0800
starpizza.net

Love deep dish, Chicago-style pizza? Star Pizza is worth a try. All the pizzas here are made with fresh ingredients, and you'll find options ranging from the standard cheese pizza to specialties like the Joe (spinach and onions) and Starburst Deluxe (pepper-oni, ground beef, mushroom, green pep-per, onion, cheese, and sausage). No matter which pizza you choose, you can opt for a whole-wheat crust. Don't want pizza? There are also plenty of salads, pastas, and sand-wiches to choose from here. Service can take awhile since each pizza is made fresh. Free delivery is available to nearby locations. Star Pizza has a second location, Star Pizza II, in the Washington Corridor.

TONY'S $$$$
3755 Richmond Ave.
(713) 622-6778
tonyshouston.com

After making its home in the same Post Oak Boulevard location for more than 30 years, Tony's moved to its current home in 2005. With that move came $5 million in renovations—and the same great service, first-class dishes, and incredible wine selection that Houstonians have come to expect from owner Tony Vallone. The new location is something of a museum, with works of art by the likes of Robert Rauschenberg and Texas sculptor Jesús Moroles. The menu, too, is worthy of a museum—one of the culinary variety, that is. The chef uses the freshest ingredients to make meticulously presented dishes, like the crab-meat tower, lobster bisque, slow-roasted sea bass, crisp roast duckling, truffled macaroni and cheese, and 30-day aged Snake River Kobe beef. If you've got any dietary restrictions, the chef can usually accommodate them. For rehearsal dinners, birthdays, business meetings, and other special events, Tony's private rooms seat anywhere from 8 to 100 people. Dress is formal attire. Call for reservations.

West University

✻PREGO $$$
2520 Amherst St.
(713) 529-2420
prego-houston.com
This sister restaurant to the Backstreet Cafe and Hugo's is modeled after the neighborhood trattorias found in Italy. Elegant yet contemporary, Prego has received countless awards and write-ups in magazines ranging from *Bon Appetit* to *Money Magazine*. The reason? Chef John Watt uses the freshest ingredients to produce unique flavors and dishes, such as polenta-crusted oysters, roasted red pepper and poblano cream soup with crème fraîche, pumpkin seed–crusted red snapper, and stone-oven pizzas made

with whole milk mozzarella. You'll also find a tempting selection of risottos, chicken, meat, vegetarian, and eclectic pasta dishes, as well as mouthwatering desserts. Prego has an extensive wine selection. Diners here tend to dress up a little, so leave the jeans, shorts, and flip-flops at home. Call ahead for reservations.

LATIN & SOUTH AMERICAN

Rice Village & West University

AMAZÓN GRILL $$
5114 Kirby Dr.
(713) 522-5888
cordua.com
This sister restaurant to the fancier Churrasco's and Américas serves up great Latin fusion fare in a casual, family-friendly setting. The restaurant operates self-serve style: Walk up to order your meal, then grab your own drinks and, if you want, a salad. The menu includes chicken and beef options, burgers, wraps, sandwiches, salads, and seafood, as well as the Cordúa restaurant family's signature plantain chips. Sides include great sweet potato and yucca fries. There's a separate kids menu, which includes cotton candy with every meal. Kids also love the s'mores, which you make right at your table. Sit outside on the patio when the weather's nice. Delivery is available to nearby locations.

River Oaks

✻AMÉRICAS $$$$
2040 W. Gray
(832) 200-1492
cordua.com
From the moment you enter Américas, you'll understand why this restaurant is so special. Chicago architect Jordan Mozer designed it

to resemble South America, with an exqui-site mosaic tree, walls resembling Machu Pic-chu, and handblown glass chandeliers that look like flowers. The food itself is also great, with many options borrowed from sister res-taurant Churrasco's. The steaks and seafood are big draws, as are the appetizers, which include the likes of corn-smoked crab fingers with herbed yuca polenta and jalapeño lime sauce, ceviche served in a pineapple, and empanadas. There's also a prix-fixe option for those willing to spend a little more. Every meal comes with some of Américas' bot-tomless plantain chips and sauces. Américas serves lunch Mon through Sat, dinner daily, and brunch on Sun from 10:30 a.m. to 3 p.m. The $29 brunch buffet includes a carv-ing station; omelets; a ceviche, shrimp, and salad bar; a crepe bar and desserts aplenty; endless mimosas and Bloody Marys are $12. Call or go online to make reservations. The attire is dressy. There's a second location in The Woodlands.

Montrose

✳CHURRASCO'S $$$$
2055 Westheimer
(713) 527-8300
churrascos.com
For 20 years Churrasco's has set the bench-mark for Latin American food in Houston. Owned by the Cordúa restaurant family, this is a sister restaurant to Américas, Amazón Grill, and Artista in the Hobby Center for the Performing Arts. The elegantly decorated Churrasco's tends to feel intimate even when it is crowded. Every meal starts with some of the restaurant's signature plantain chips and chimichurri sauces. The restaurant is perhaps best known for its eponymous Churrasco—a charcoal-grilled center-cut beef tenderloin

steak. Other popular dishes include plantain-crusted chicken and shrimp, the empanadas, and the yucca fries. Looking for a nonmeat option? Try the Cubana—a rich, black-bean soup served in a sourdough bread bowl lined with a unique cheese sauce. Although it's listed on the soup menu, the Cubana is more than enough for an entire meal. What-ever you order, save room for the tres leches. Churrasco's has an extensive wine collection with lots of great Chilean bottles. Call or go online to make reservations. The attire is dressy. There's a second location on the west side of town in Westchase.

MIDDLE EASTERN

Memorial

EMPIRE TURKISH GRILL $$
12448 Memorial Dr., between Gessner
and Benignus
(713) 827-7475
empiretrgrill.com
A peaceful atmosphere and good, inexpen-sive food keep the regulars returning to this neighborhood restaurant. Big winners here include the baba ghanoush (mashed and seasoned eggplant), kebabs, and tomato sauce–topped cabbage rolls stuffed with ground lamb, rice, and herbs. The restaurant also caters to indecisive types with combi-nation appetizer platters that feature five to seven appetizers of your choosing.

✳FADI'S MEDITERRANEAN GRILL $
8383 Westheimer
(713) 532-0666
fadiscuisine.com
To love Mediterranean food is to love Fadi's. This popular Mediterranean restaurant oper-ates cafeteria-style, albeit with more upscale

decor than you'll find at most cafeterias. Entrees—which include sandwich, platter, and sampler options with falafel, kebabs, and/or shawarma—include your choice of fresh sides like balsamic mushrooms, cilantro zucchini, pomegranate eggplant, hummus, or tabouli. Every meal comes with all the warm pita bread and pita chips you can stack on your plate. Portions are huge, but you can order smaller portions of some items at lunchtime. This location is between the Galleria and Memorial areas; there are additional locations in Meyerland, Dairy Ashford, and Sugar Land.

PUB FOOD

Montrose

THE BLACK LABRADOR   **$$**
4100 Montrose Blvd., at Richmond
(713) 529-1199
blacklabradorpub.com
You don't have to leave Houston to feel like you're in London. This popular pub plays the part, from the red British-style phone booth outside to the authentic pub atmosphere inside the ivy-clad brick walls. A fountain and a life-size chess set help provide the ambience for those who dine outside beneath the trees. The Black Lab's extensive menu includes a mix of burgers, soups, salads, quesadillas, zucchini crab cakes, mussels, and—most importantly—traditional pub fare, such as shepherd's pie, bangers and mash, and fish-and-chips. There's also a proper beer selection. The Black Lab serves lunch and dinner daily; brunch is served on Sun starting at 11 a.m.

SEAFOOD

Memorial

✳DENIS' SEAFOOD HOUSE   **$$$**
9777 Katy Fwy., at Bunker Hill
(713) 464-6900
denisseafood.com
This sophisticated Memorial seafood restaurant does seafood your way. That is, your best bet when it comes to ordering is to select one of the fish of the day listed on the chalkboard and tell your server how you want it cooked—blackened, sautéed, or grilled. Other options include gumbo, crab, and boiled crawfish. Although the food is good and the decor striking, Denis' Seafood House is a bit on the pricey side.

Midtown

REEF   **$$$–$$$$**
2600 Travis St.
(713) 526-8282
reefhouston.com
Stepping into Reef feels a lot like stepping into a hot new Manhattan restaurant: This contemporary-chic seafood spot is always packed with people who are just as eager to socialize as they are to try the latest seafood and Southern dishes from Next Iron Chef competitor and Reef owner-chef Bryan Caswell. The constantly changing menu features a variety of in-season fish with creative spins. Recent entrees have included redfish on the half-shell with fried mac & cheese; grilled wahoo with broccolini, orange mustard and jalapeño relish; and Thai-style whole fish. The menu also includes a couple chicken and steak dishes. While the menu is certainly creative, Reef is a little overhyped and overpriced, especially when compared to some of the city's other fine restaurants. Reef is

open for lunch and dinner. Call or go online to make a reservation. Closed Sun.

Montrose

PAPPAS SEAFOOD HOUSE $$$
3001 S. Shepherd Dr., at Alabama
(713) 522-4595
pappasseafood.com
This Pappas restaurant serves all things seafood—étouffée, gumbo, blackened and grilled fish, boiled crawfish, oysters, and lobster—with plenty of fried, blackened, and grilled options. You'll also find Pappas' Famous Greek Salad here, topped with crabmeat or shrimp if you like. All the seafood is flown in daily, and portions are huge. Pappas Seafood House has seven locations around the Houston area.

River Oaks

TONY MANDOLA'S $$$
1212 Waugh Dr.
(713) 528-3474
tonymandolas.com
Tony Mandola's has had multiple restaurants and locations over the last three decades, and this swanky River Oaks spot is the latest incarnation. The fresh seafood here may come from the Gulf Coast, but much of the culinary inspiration comes from the Mandola family's Italian roots and family recipes, as well as New Orleans–style cooking. That makes for a menu filled with the likes of Mama's Gumbo Pizza (dark roux with crabmeat, mozzarella, and parmesan cheese), Sicilian and New Orleans-style po'boys, shrimp and crabmeat spaghetti, and Snapper Martha (grilled snapper topped with shrimp, crawfish tails, and crabmeat sautéed in basil wine butter). Tony Mandola's is open

for dinner seven days a week, for lunch Mon through Sat, and for brunch on Sun from 11 a.m. to 2 p.m. Call or go online to make reservations.

Upper Kirby

*EDDIE V'S PRIME SEAFOOD $$$$
2800 Kirby
(713) 874-1800
eddiev.com
Good service and beautifully presented food make Eddie V's a definite must for seafood lovers who want to go someplace fancy. The menu includes an array of in-season fishes, salads (try the wild mushroom salad or the fuji apple salad), and premium black angus steaks. Sides aren't included with your entree, but order at least one—the truffled mac & cheese. Gluten-free? Just ask for the restaurant's gluten-free menu. Eddie V's is open for dinner daily. Call for reservations. There's a second location in Memorial at CityCentre.

*PAPPADEAUX SEAFOOD KITCHEN $$$
2410 Richmond Ave., at Kirby
(713) 527-9137
pappadeaux.com
One of the city's most popular seafood restaurants, Pappadeaux offers an extensive menu filled with grilled and fried seafood options, some Cajun-flavored fishes, lobster, crab, and even a blackened shrimp, and crawfish fondeaux (fondue). All of the fish are flown in daily. Visit during lunchtime and order off the slightly cheaper lunch menu. There's often a wait to be seated, especially on the weekends, so call for reservations. Pappadeaux has several locations.

West University

GOODE COMPANY TEXAS SEAFOOD $$$
2621 Westpark Dr.
(713) 523-7154
goodecompany.com
Goode Company Texas Seafood serves up seafood with Gulf Coast flair. That makes for a menu fille with gumbo, étouffée, shrimp creole, and mesquite-grilled seafood. You'll also find solid po'boys here, along with handmade shrimp and crabmeat tamales and seafood empanadas. Sides include Southern favorites like fried green tomatoes and hush puppies. The restaurant is a little more upscale than many seafood restaurants, but it's still laid-back. There's a second location in Memorial.

STEAK HOUSES

Downtown

VIC & ANTHONY'S STEAKHOUSE $$$$
1510 Texas Ave.
(713) 228-1111
vicandanthonys.com
Rated one of the city's top steak houses by Zagat, this swanky restaurant sits just across the street from Minute Maid Park, where the Houston Astros play baseball. But don't let its location fool you: Vic & Anthony's exudes high-class ambience, with its huge stained-glass chandeliers and Craftsman-style decor. The steaks are the big draw here, of course, but the iceberg wedge salad, crab cakes and oysters, and seafood dishes also get high marks. Call for reservations, and dress nicely.

Galleria

PAPPAS BROS. STEAKHOUSE $$$$
5839 Westheimer, at Bering
(713) 780-7352
pappasbros.com
The dark paneling and leather booths here are a good indicator that Pappas Bros. Steakhouse is—like other Pappas restaurants—the real deal. Not surprisingly, steak options fill the menu, which options including filet mignon, rib eye, strip steak, peppercorn, veal steak, porterhouse, and lamb chops. Don't want steak? The menu also boasts great seafood options (lobster tail, anyone?) and appetizers ranging from caviar to house-cured salmon and bacon-wrapped scallops. Call or go online for reservations, and be sure to dress nicely.

Memorial

SALTGRASS $$$
8943 Katy Fwy., between Campbell and Voss
(713) 461-6111
saltgrass.com
Saltgrass isn't the city's best steak house, but it's a popular choice for those dining on a budget or with children. The menu includes certified Angus beef steaks and burgers, as well as so-called Ranch Hand Favorites like chicken-fried steak and baby back ribs. Be sure to get your fill of the Shiner Bock Beer Bread. There's often a line to get in on Friday and Saturday evenings so arrive early to avoid a long wait. Saltgrass has more than a dozen locations around the Houston area.

TASTE OF TEXAS $$$
10505 Katy Fwy.
(713) 932-6901
tasteoftexas.com

Dining with children? Or don't want to get dressed up to eat a steak? Check out the Taste of Texas, where the abundant Texas and ranch decor may make you feel like you've left the big city. Choose your own steak cut at the butcher shop, then grab salad, cheese, and bread from the salad bar. Don't want a steak? You've got plenty of alternatives, including burgers, chicken, and steak sandwiches, a tenderloin salad, jumbo grilled shrimp, pecan-crusted chicken, and a veggie platter. Taste of Texas is open for lunch Monday through Friday and dinner daily.

River Oaks

BRENNER'S STEAKHOUSE ON THE BAYOU $$$$
1 Birdsall St., off Memorial near Bayou Bend
(713) 868-4444
brennersonthebayou.com

Rustic yet elegant, Brenner's on the Bayou is widely considered Houston's best steak house—and a popular place to celebrate birthdays, anniversaries, and other milestones. Menu options include the requisite filet mignon, rib eye, and strip steaks, as well as plenty of fish and chicken dishes, all exquisitely presented. Among the biggest nonsteak hits here are the crunchy German potatoes, the apple strudel, and the signature soufflés made with Grand Marnier, Godiva chocolate, and Chambord. With more than 200 bottles of wine, Brenner's offers a wine selection that lays claim to consecutive Awards of Excellence from *Wine Spectator* magazine. Brenner's also serves brunch on Sunday; the rest of the week, the restaurant only serves dinner. Get dressed up, and make reservations online or by phone or online. There's a second location—Brenner's Steakhouse—just west of Memorial.

TAPAS

Rice Village & West University

✴MI LUNA $$
2441 University Blvd.
(713) 520-5025
mi-luna.net

This brightly colored, festive restaurant and bar brings a little bit of Spain to Houston. Mi Luna offers a long list of tapas—appetizers—that include plenty of vegetarian and meat options, both hot and cold. The pizzas and paella are also worth trying. Two or three appetizers per person are usually more than enough, making this a very affordable dining option. Get the full Spanish experience by ordering one of Mi Luna's Spanish wines, or some sangria. On weekdays, happy hour runs from 3 to 6 p.m. and features $5 margaritas and sangritas (a delicious cross between margaritas and sangria) and $3 sangria, Bud Light, and tapas. Visit for Sunday brunch, where you'll enjoy omelets, seafood, homemade desserts, and bottomless sangrias and mimosas. This is an especially fun place to go on Wednesday through Saturday evenings, thanks to the live Latin, flamenco, merengue, or salsa music. In fact, Mi Luna stays open until 2 a.m. on Friday and Saturday nights, so you can dance the night away. There's a second location in Sugar Land.

MEXICAN & TEX-MEX

Bellaire/Meyerland

PICO'S MEX-MEX $$-$$$
5941 Bellaire Blvd.
(713) 662-8383
picos.net

Prefer traditional Mexican fare to the "Tex-anized" version you find at many restaurants here? Try Pico's Mex-Mex. Since 1984, this charming hole-in-the-wall has been serving what it calls Mex-Mex—meats cooked in banana leaves, mole, pickled red onions, queso made with Chihuahua cheese and topped with chorizo. Rest assured: You can also find more traditional Tex-Mex fare here, including enchiladas, fajitas, tacos, and margaritas. From 9 a.m. to 3 p.m. daily, you can even order Mexican breakfast favorites like chilaquiles, huevos rancheros, and migas. Though the menu includes lots of meat, vegetarians can find good options here. The casual atmosphere makes this a good spot for families.

Downtown

IRMA'S SOUTHWEST GRILL DOWNTOWN BY THE BALLPARK $$-$$$
1314 Texas at Austin
(713) 247-9651
irmassouthwest.com

This festive Mexican restaurant is a staple for downtown workers and baseball fans, who know they can count on Irma's for quality Tex-Mex dishes. The waiters don't hand out menus at Irma's, so you have to ask the waitstaff what's cooking—or visit Irma's website to find the relatively short menu. Among the more popular dishes are enchiladas, fajitas, and pork chops with ancho chile sauce. The fresh-squeezed lemonade is also a big hit.

Most entrees, though relatively small, run about $10–$16. Irma's is open for breakfast and lunch Mon through Fri from 8 a.m. to 3 p.m.; it's also open for lunch and dinner starting 3 hours before every Astros home game.

Midtown

✳TACOS A GO-GO $
3704 Main St.
(713) 807-8226
tacosagogo.com

You'll find a lot of breakfast tacos in Texas, but this funky Midtown joint is the place to go for some of the—if not the—very best the Lone Star State has to offer. Name the ingredients for your breakfast tacos. Or choose from huevos rancheros, *migas*, salads, and a full range of tacos on corn, flour, whole wheat, or crispy tortillas. If you're not counting calories—and who can at a Tex-Mex joint?—order a side of chips with your choice of several salsas, delicious queso, or some of the best guacamole in town. Tacos A Go-Go is open Mon through Thurs until 10 p.m. and until 2 a.m. on Fri and Sat; it closes at 3 p.m. on Sun. A second location recently opened in the Heights.

Montrose

EL REAL TEX-MEX $$-$$$
1201 Westheimer at Yoakum
(713) 524-1201
elrealtexmex.com

Located in the restored Tower Theater, El Real is a newcomer on the Houston Tex-Mex scene. But behind the restaurant is a familiar name—celebrity chef Brian Caswell, *The Next Iron Chef* season 3 contestant and chef/owner of the award-winning Midtown restaurant Reef (page 87), among other local

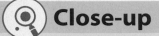 **Close-up**

An Insider's Guide to Tex-Mex

If you're eating Tex-Mex or Mexican food for the first time, you may see some unfamiliar items on the menu. Here's a glossary of some names you're likely to see:

Antojitos: Appetizers or tapas

Botanas: Appetizers

Breakfast taco: Eggs, cheese, and sometimes meat, peppers, or potatoes wrapped in a tortilla; topped with salsa

Cabrito: Young goat, typically very tender

Camarones: Shrimp

Cerveza: Beer

Chalupa: Flat, crispy shell topped with chicken, pork, lettuce, tomatoes, cheese, and/or salsa

Chilaquiles: Fried corn tortillas topped with salsa or mole, cheese, and scrambled or fried eggs

Chili con carne: Chili with meat

Chile rellenos: Stuffed peppers

Chorizo: Spicy pork sausage

Codorniz a las Brazas: Grilled quail

Costillas de Cerdo al Carbon: Pork ribs

Empanadas: Pastry stuffed with ground-up vegetables and meats

Enchilada: Tortilla wrapped around a hot filling, such as cheese, beef, spinach, or chicken and lathered with a sauce

Ensalada: Salad

eateries. El Real serves what Caswell calls vintage Tex-Mex. That translates to dishes cooked in lard, as well as dishes like frito pie, crispy tacos, and puffy tacos. There are also a few vegetarian options, including veggie fajitas and veggie enchiladas. Though the quality of the food often leaves something to be desired, El Real boasts a fun atmosphere, with a big screen set up to watch Houston Texans football games. Added bonus: it's open until 3 a.m. on Fri and Sat nights, so you can stop in and grab a bite after a night out in Montrose.

Fajitas: Grilled strips of steak or chicken eaten in a flour tortilla; usually served with pico de gallo, cheese, and sour cream on the side

Frijoles refritos: Refried beans

Guacamole: Chopped avocado dip peppered with herbs, chopped onions, and chiles

Huevos rancheros: Fried eggs with a tomato-chile sauce

Margarita: Mixed drink made with tequila and lime, served in a salted glass; sometimes includes other flavors such as mango or strawberry

Migas: Eggs scrambled with cheese and corn tortilla strips or chips

Mole: Sauce made of unsweetened chocolate, nuts, and spices; served on top of enchiladas

Mollejas al Ajillo: Sautéed sweetbreads with garlic, Guajillo, and olive oil, typically served with tortillas to make tacos

Pico de gallo: Hot salsa made with tomatoes, onions, chiles, and cilantro

Quesadilla: Two tortillas with cheese between them, served baked

Queso: Cheese dip, often made with Mexican cheese, sometimes includes peppers

Queso con carne: Cheese dip with meat

Salsa verde: Green salsa made with green chiles, garlic, cilantro, and tomatillos; often used on top of enchiladas or for dipping tortilla chips

Sopapilla: Fried pastry topped with honey

Tamale: Corn dough filled with pork, chicken, or vegetables and rolled in a corn husk; served steamed, sometimes with a chile sauce

Tortilla: A flat round bread, usually made of corn, flour, or whole wheat; used to make enchiladas and to accompany dishes such as fajitas and migas

Tostada: Fried tortilla

✳HUGO'S　　　　　　　　　　$$$
1600 Westheimer Rd., at Mandell St.
(713) 524-7744
hugosrestaurant.net
Most food at this acclaimed restaurant—pronounced "ew-goes"—are distinctively not Tex-Mex. Dishes here feature flavors and ingredients found in more central

and southern regions of Mexico, including Oaxaca, Campeche, and Puebla. That makes for dishes like *pan de cazón* (chile-bathed tortillas layered with black beans and grilled shark), *sopesitos* (three masa pancakes topped with duck with mole poblano and served with pork cracklings in salsa verde), *cabrito* (roasted goat meat pulled from the bone), and delicious salmon tacos. Less adventurous types, rest assured: The menu also includes enchiladas, tamales, and chile rellenos, as well as seasonal twists on these Tex-Mex staples. There are plenty of vegetarian options as well. Hugo's award-winning sommelier will help pair your meal with the perfect glass of wine; or try one of the best margaritas in town. Whatever you order, save room for some tres leches, churros, or hot chocolate. The restaurant serves brunch on Sunday. Hugo's is a little nicer than most Mexican restaurants, so leave the flip-flops and shorts at home or your hotel. Hugo's tends to fill up on weeknights, so call for a reservation.

TORCHY'S TACOS $
2411 S. Shepherd Dr.
(713) 595-8226
torchystacos.com
This beloved Austin taco shop recently opened its first Houston location, and it's quickly become one of the hottest tacos stops in town. Credit goes to creatively named tacos like the Trailer Park (fried chicken, green chilies, lettuce, pico de gallo, and cheese with poblano sauce), Brush Fire (Jamaican jerk chicken, grilled jalapeños, mano, sour cream, and cilantro with Diablo sauce), and the Fried Avocado (hand-battered fried avocados with vegetarian refried beans, lettuce, cheese, and poblano sauce). The tacos range from about $3–$4 each. A small parking lot and a big demand for the tacos here can mean a bit of a wait for a space and your tacos, so it's best to visit during non-prime times. Torchy's opens at 7 a.m. Mon through Fri and 8 a.m. on weekends. It's open until 10 p.m. Sun through Thurs and 11 p.m. Fri and Sat.

River Oaks

✳ESCALANTE'S $$$
4053 Westheimer, in Highland Village
(713) 623-4200
escalantes.net
Bright funky decor and an extensive menu make Escalante's a great place to eat Tex-Mex with friends or the kids. Menu highlights include the fajitas, enchiladas, fish tacos, ceviche, and Pat's Mexico City Salad topped with shrimp, pine nuts, walnuts, and a goat cheese medallion. No matter what you order, you'll have an easy time finding something to suit your dietary needs and preferences. Mexican rice, for instance, can be replaced with the vegetarian cilantro rice, and you can choose white, wheat, or corn tortillas for any dish. You can also choose from pinto, charro, or some of Escalante's tasty fat-free refried black beans. Believe it or not, you can even request baked chips instead of the deliciously fattening chips the waitstaff typically serve. Lunch and Sunday brunch specials are available. Service tends to be quick, but you may have to wait up to 45 minutes to get a table on Friday and Saturday nights. Escalante's doesn't take reservations, unfortunately, but you can munch on some chips and sip a margarita at the bar while you wait. Escalante's has additional locations in Memorial, Bellaire/Meyerland, and Sugar Land.

TACO MILAGRO RESTAURANT &
  BEACH BAR $$
2555 Kirby, at Westheimer
(713) 522-1999
taco-milagro.com
Taco Milagro doesn't have the best Tex-Mex in town but the atmosphere, margaritas,

and long list of top-shelf tequilas keep people coming back. There's live music—and often salsa dancing—on Thursday, Friday, and Saturday nights from 9 p.m. to 1 a.m. Those seeking a quieter atmosphere—or the chance to people watch—can find refuge on the patio. The menu includes standard Tex-Mex fare: hard and soft tacos, fajitas, tamales, burritos, and enchiladas, including the less-standard veggie sweet potato and spinach enchiladas.

Second Ward

THE ORIGINAL NINFA'S ON NAVIGATION $$$
2704 Navigation Blvd.
(713) 228-1175
ninfas.com
You're likely to see several Ninfa's restaurants when you drive around Houston, but if you're going to eat at one, make it The Original Ninfa's on Navigation, located just east of downtown. (The other Ninfa's restaurants are no longer related to this one.) Back in 1973 a woman known as Mama Ninfa opened a little hole-in-the-wall here and popularized Tex-Mex. Mama Ninfa and her family no longer own the restaurant, but many people still love the food at this location, whose decor has gotten a makeover. Chef Alex Padilla, a former line cook under Mama Ninfa, serves up enchiladas, handmade tamales, salads, and a variety of tacos—including some with redfish and chipotle mayo. The fajitas are among the most popular dishes, and the margaritas have more than a few fans. Ninfa's on Navigation tends to fill up quickly so plan to wait.

Upper Kirby

✳LITTLE PAPPASITO'S $$$
2526 Richmond Ave.
(713) 520-5066
pappasitos.com
Little Pappasito's isn't a good place to go to for intimate conversation, but that's not why people flock here. No, it's the margaritas, chips, salsa, fajitas, and an endless array of Tex-Mex dishes that keep the crowds returning to Little Pappasito's and the other dozen-plus Pappasito's locations around the city. The menu includes few vegetarian options; even the cheese enchiladas have meat in the sauce. No matter what you order, consider splitting something; portions are huge. Beware: There's usually a wait to get a table.

Although you'll now find Pappasito's as far away as Georgia, the Pappas family-owned chain started here in Houston.

LUPE TORTILLA MEXICAN RESTAURANT $$$
2414 Southwest Fwy., near Kirby
(713) 522-4420
lupetortilla.com
Lupe Tortilla is nothing fancy, but many people consider it one of the best Tex-Mex restaurants in town. The menu includes standard Tex-Mex fare, made with the freshest ingredients and (where appropriate) served with handmade tortillas. The casual, laid-back atmosphere makes this a great place to take young children. Be prepared to wait, though; it often takes up to an hour to get seated here. Lupe Tortilla has ten other locations in the Houston area.

Washington Corridor

✳EL TIEMPO $$$
5602 Washington Ave.
(713) 681-3645
eltiempocantina.com

El Tiempo has a sacred place in Houston Tex-Mex culture: It's owned by the grandson of Mama Ninfa, the woman who brought us the popular Ninfa's restaurants (page 95). The rather pricey menu includes the usual Tex-Mex fare—enchiladas, chalupas, tacos, flautas, quesadillas, salads, fajitas, steak, and seafood. Among the most notable dishes is the Cañonball—an avocado stuffed with shrimp, lathered in melted cheese, then breaded and fried. You'll find some of the city's best margaritas here. There's usually a wait on Friday and Saturday nights. El Tiempo has additional locations in Montrose and Upper Kirby. It's open 7 days a week, but hours vary by location and by day.

VEGAN & VEGETARIAN

River Oaks/Highland Village

PEPPER TREE VEGGIE CUISINE $$
3821 Richmond, at Weslayan
(713) 621-9488
peppertreeveggiecuisine.com

This 100 percent vegan, MSG-free restaurant features a variety of East Asian dishes with Western twists. This translates to the like of their french tofu fries, sesame vegan chicken, General Tso's vegan chicken, sweet and sour vegan fish sticks, and tofu ball spaghetti with

tomato sauce. Can't decide what to order? Opt for the buffet, which features about 18 hot dishes, fresh salad, dumplings, spring rolls, egg rolls, and vegan desserts. The buffet costs just $9.99 on weekdays from 11 a.m. to 2 p.m. and $13.85 all day on Sat and Sun. Closed Mon.

> **i** Find out about the hottest new restaurants and bars by subscribing to Houston Tidbits' e-newsletter at houston.gotidbits.com. You'll also get the skinny on chic new stores and happenings around Houston.

Upper Kirby

FIELD OF GREENS $$
2320 W. Alabama, between Kirby and Greenbriar
(713) 533-0029
fieldofgreenscuisine.com

Health nuts and vegetarians sing the praises of Field of Greens. The restaurant uses largely organic products and has a number of raw food and microbiotic offerings. The menu consists largely of healthy vegetarian fare like a barbecue soy chicken patty, a falafel burger, vegetarian fish tacos, and eggplant parmesan. There are also a few nonvegetarian options, like the grilled salmon burger. Many dishes here are vegan (or can be made vegan), and low-carb, low-fat, and gluten-free options abound. The restaurant is BYOB; there's no corkage fee.

NIGHTLIFE

What's there to see and do in the evenings and wee hours of the morning in Houston? Quite a bit. Scattered around the city are bars, pubs, and lounges that range from chic to dive, from beer to wine to absinthe, and from mellow to deafening. Like to dance? You can get your fix at posh dance clubs that play hip-hop and salsa, authentic country-and-western bars, and several bars that cater to the gay and lesbian community. Or, if you prefer to unwind by listening to music, check out one of the city's many live music venues. You'll find everything from tiny holes-in-the-wall to sophisticated jazz clubs to sports arenas rocking on Bruce Springsteen's latest tour. Many local restaurants also feature a lounge atmosphere and, in some cases, live music. If this appeals to you, take a closer look at the Restaurants chapter and try Taco Milagro Restaurant & Beach Bar (page 94), Uptown Sushi (page 64), Benjy's (page 63), or Mi Luna (page 90). Also take note of coffee shops such as Agora (page 73), Brasil (page 73), Empire Cafe (page 74), and Onion Creek Coffee House Bar & Lounge (page 73)—all of which feature live entertainment (and serve alcohol) in the evening.

COVER CHARGES, AGES & HOURS

Before heading out, take note: Most of the bars and clubs in this chapter require guests to be 21 or older with a valid ID. The legal drinking age in Texas is 21, and most clubs and bars don't let in anyone who is younger. Often Houston clubs and bars charge a cover of anywhere from a couple dollars up to $10 or even $20. This doesn't include drinks or food. Bars often have higher cover charges on weekends and for special events. On the upside, many offer happy hour specials, though hours, days, and discounts vary. For live music venues, purchase your tickets early when possible. Many events—especially those featuring big acts—sell out. Tickets can be purchased at the venue, on the venue's website, or by phone, unless indicated otherwise.

Bars, lounges, and pubs in Houston typically close at 2 a.m. on the weekends and earlier during the week.

BARS, PUBS & LOUNGES

Downtown

EIGHTEEN TWENTY BAR
1820 Franklin Ave.
(713) 224-5535
Popular among the 20-something crowd, Eighteen Twenty Bar has a full bar with reasonably priced drinks, a jukebox, and a popular photo booth. There's plenty of

seating, as well as ample space for standing around. Visit on the first and last Friday of the month and pay $15 to play all the arcade games you want next door at Joystix, a huge video game retail shop, from 9 p.m. to 2 a.m. The bar itself is open daily from 4 p.m. to 2 a.m.

LA CARAFE
813 Congress St.
(713) 229-9399
owlnet.rice.edu/~hans320/projects/lacarafe
Located in a 160-plus-year-old building with some ghost stories of its own, La Carafe is rumored to be the city's oldest bar. It also happens to be a dive. All this seems to make Houstonians love it even more. You'll find a decent selection of wines and beers here, along with creaky seats and an outdoor patio. Bring cash because La Carafe doesn't take credit cards.

Galleria & Uptown Park

THE TASTING ROOM WINE CAFE
1101—18 Uptown Park Blvd.
(713) 993-9800
tastingroomwines.com
With more than 200 different wines on hand at any given time, this casual yet elegant wine bar and wine retail shop is sure to have some kind of vino you'll enjoy. (That is, unless you prefer cheap box wine.) Sit on the patio or relax in the bar, and order food to go along with your drink of choice. Whatever you choose, the waitstaff can help you find the perfect wine to pair with your food. There are additional locations in River Oaks and in Memorial at CityCentre.

Paint and Sip

For a fun night out, grab friends and a bottle of wine, and take a one-night painting class at **Pinot's Palette.** You'll leave with your own rendition of a masterpiece like Van Gogh's *Starry Night.* Pinot's Palette has locations in the Galleria area, Montrose, and Katy. Learn about upcoming classes at pinotspalette.com.

The Heights

BIG STAR BAR
1005 W. 19th St.
(281) 501-9560
bigstarbar.com
Looking for a cheap drink and some billiards in the Heights? Big Star Bar is your place. The bartenders at this dive serve cold beer and specialty drinks named after semifamous people like Fonzi. Other quirky attractions include an outdoor fire pit (seriously), hula-hooping, a jukebox, and an occasional DJ. Big Star Bar is open daily from 4 p.m. to 2 a.m.

THE CORKSCREW
1308 W. 20th
(713) 230-8352
houstoncorkscrew.com
The Corkscrew recently moved to a bigger location, but at heart, it's still a cozy, laid-back wine bar where you can count on the bartenders to chat with you as they pour your drink. You'll find a rotating selection of more than 250 wines here. The menu includes short descriptions of each wine, making the seemingly overwhelming decision of what to order slightly easier. Not a wine person?

The Corkscrew recently began serving liquor for those who need a cocktail. The Corkscrew is open from 4 p.m. to midnight Mon through Thurs, 4 p.m. to 2 a.m. Fri and Sat, and from 2 p.m. to midnight on Sun.

Memorial

HOUSTON TEXANS GRILLE
12848 Queesnbury Ln., in CityCentre
(713) 461-2002
texansgrille.g3restaurants.com
This new sports bar is the hottest place in town—after Reliant Stadium, anyway— to watch Houston Texans football games and other sporting events. Choose from a long list of bottled and draft beers, wines, and mixed drinks, including a few Featherweights (aka low-calorie cocktails). There's also a full kitchen, which serves up gourmet burgers, soups, salads, flatbreads, steaks, and a number of gluten-free options. Houston Texans Grille opens daily at 11 a.m. and closes at midnight Sun through Thurs and 2 a.m. Fri and Sat.

Midtown

13 CELSIUS
3000 Caroline St.
(713) 529-8466
13celsius.com
Named for the optimal temperature at which to store wine, 13 Celsius is one of the city's best wine bars. The sommeliers here know their wines and will help you navigate the impressive list of wines and handcrafted beers, as well as the selection of fine cheeses, meats, and fresh espresso. Almost as impressive as the wine and beer choices is the setting itself: 13 Celsius makes its home in a 1927 Mediterranean-style building intended to pay homage to European wine bars and

bistros. When the weather is nice, sit outside in the courtyard. If you like the wine you order, you can purchase a bottle at retail price to take home. 13 Celsius is open daily from 4 p.m. to 2 a.m.

Montrose

ABSINTHE BRASSERIE
609 Richmond Ave.
(713) 528-7575
absinthelounge.com
Need to satisfy an absinthe fix? Absinthe Brasserie is the place to go. You've got your choice of half a dozen absinthe cocktails here, as well as beer, wine, and mixed drinks like mint juleps, *mojitos,* sangria, and martinis. There's also has a short menu of appetizers, pizzas, and panini. Between the crowds and the DJ, the place can get loud and busy in the evenings. Absinthe Brasserie is open Tues through Fri from 5 p.m. to 2 a.m. and Sat from 7 p.m. to 2 a.m. Closed Sun.

i Absinthe Brasserie isn't marked on the outside, so be on the lookout for the gothic double doors.

*ANVIL BAR & REFUGE
1424 Westheimer Rd.
(713) 523-1622
anvilhouston.com
Sure, you've had cocktails, but odds are you've never had any quite like the ones at Anvil. Local flavors and ingredients are featured in just about every drink here, along with housemade bitters, sodas, liquers, and infusions. The result is strong, precisely mixed drinks like Pliny's Tonic (gin, lime, cucumber, mint, and habenero tincture), Sweet Potato Milk Punch (applejack, sweet potato, whole milk, and cream), and Smoke & Mirrors (rye, fernet, branca, cacao, lemon,

black peppercorn, and egg white). Sure, at $8–$12 a drink, cocktails here can be a bit pricey, but most people who visit this hip, yet handsome bar agree they're worth it. Ditto for the James Beard Award Foundation, which named Anvil owner and self-proclaimed cocktail freak Bobby Heugel a semifinalist in 2011. Anvil is open daily from 4 p.m. to 2 a.m.

BOHEME CAFE & WINE BAR
307 Fairview St.
(713) 529-1099
barboheme.com
Housed in a revamped historic building, this cozy wine bar is a nice place to sip on your favorite drink and unwind with friends. A garden with stone Zimbabwean sculptures surrounds the building while a stucco accent wall and antique light fixtures help liven up the inside. Boheme serves wine; beer; liquor; mixed drinks, like sangria, frozen mojitos, and the popular pinot noir martini; coffee; and a few small food items. Happy hour runs from 7 a.m. to 7 p.m. daily. Boheme is open daily from 6 a.m. to 2 a.m.

✳GRAND PRIZE BAR
1010 Banks
(713) 526-4565
Slightly off the beaten path, Grand Prize boasts two floors (and two patios) of bar goodness. Downstairs, you'll find a pool table, Big Buck Hunter, and a jukebox that plays everything from Guns N' Roses to the latest Beyonce hit. Upstairs, there's loads of retro-looking seating. Whether you order from the upstairs or downstairs bar, you've got your choice of craft and local beers, good mixed drinks, and food ranging from Boudin balls to boarmeat hot dogs. There's often a food truck outside the bar at night,

giving you even more food options. Grand Prize definitely has a hipster vibe, but the crowd is somewhat mixed. Open daily from 4 p.m. to 2 a.m.

POISON GIRL
1641 Westheimer
(713) 527-9929
Quirky vintage decor and pinball machines galore make this Montrose dive an endearing hangout spot. Added bonuses: Poison Girl has good beer, cheap drinks, and a great outdoor patio. On the last Thursday of each month, Poison Girl hosts the Poison Pen Reading Series (poisonpenreadingseries .com), which features readings by local writers. The bar can be hard to spot: Look for the bright pink building with the unassuming "Poison Girl" sign in the window.

WEST ALABAMA ICE HOUSE
1919 W. Alabama, at Hazard
(713) 528-6874
westalabamaicehouse.com
This little ice house isn't air-conditioned. But that's a-okay with many Houstonians who come here for the ice cold beer and conversation. Many even come with their dogs (or, in some cases, cats) in tow. If you get hungry, you can order from the taco truck parked outside the ice house.

River Oaks

DOWNING STREET PUB
2549 Kirby, at Westheimer
(713) 523-2291
downingstreetpub.com
Wondering where to find Houston's most discriminating drinkers and cigar smokers? Look no further than the leather couches at Downing Street Pub. This popular pub boasts nearly 100 single-malt scotches, extensive

wine and beer menus, and a 400-square-foot humidor holding some of the country's finest cigars. There's also a limited food menu for those wanting a snack. Downing Street hosts special tastings throughout the year; call or visit the website to find out about upcoming events. Open Mon through Fri from 10 a.m. to 2 a.m. and Sat and Sun from 5 p.m. to 2 a.m.

MARFRELESS
2006 Pedent, at McDuffie behind River Oaks Theatre
(713) 528-0083
marfrelesshouston.com
This speakeasy isn't easy to find; there's no sign on the outside so you have to know to look for the blue door. The relatively quiet atmosphere and lounge-style seating make Marfreless a good place to go with a small group. The bartenders mix some good drinks, too. Head upstairs and you're likely to find couples getting, uh, cozy. Marfreless is open from 5 p.m. to 2 a.m. Mon through Fri and from 6 p.m. to 2 a.m. Sat and Sun.

Rice Village & West University

✳THE GINGER MAN
5607 Morningside Dr.
(713) 526-2770
houston.gingermanpub.com
The Ginger Man has several locations around Texas and a few on the East Coast, but this Rice Village spot is the original. This pub serves a long list of specialty beers in an unpretentious setting, making it a popular hangout for Rice University and med school students who turn their nose up at the idea of settling for a Budweiser. Sip your beer on the patio when the weather's nice.

Upper Kirby & Greenway

OPORTO CAFE
3833 Richmond Ave.
(713) 621-1114
oporto.us
Inspired by European "gastro bars," Oporto Cafe offers more than 50 wines by the glass, many hailing from Spain, Italy, and Portugal. You'll also find the city's largest selection of Portuguese ports here, along with mixed drinks such as *mojitos,* sangria, and caipirinha. Enjoy hot and cold tapas while you sit at the bar or at one of the tables. Get discounted drinks and tapas during happy hour Mon through Fri from 3 to 7 p.m. Select bottles of wine are half-price on Tuesday evenings.

Washington Corridor

✳BLOCK 7 WINE COMPANY
720 Shepherd Dr.
(713) 572-2565
block7wineco.com
Part-wine retail shop, part-wine bar, Block 7 is a great spot for a date or catching up with friends. While you sip your wine, nibble on one of Block 7's flatbreads, salads, burgers, or appetizers like rabbit sausage with Brussels sprouts leaves. Many of these dishes feature seasonal flavors and locally grown organic foods. There's live music on Sunday. Block 7 is open until 10 p.m. Sun through Tues, 11 p.m. Wed and Thurs, and midnight Fri and Sat. The place can get crowded, so call or go online to reserve a table.

✳BONEYARD DOG PARK & DRINKERY
8150 Washington Ave.
(832) 494-1600
boneyardhouston.com
Want to hit the town with your favorite dog? This bar's for you. Boneyard Dog Park &

Drinkery caters to dogs with its 7,000-square-foot dog park, and to their owners with a bar that serves a large beer and wine selection. There's plenty of outdoor seating—much of it shaded—so you can watch your dog play while drinking your beer. The Boneyard doesn't serve food, but you can often grab a bite to eat from food trucks that pull up outside the bar.

Nightlife Alternatives

Want to skip the bar and lounge scene? You may enjoy attending a reading by a famous author, or taking in a movie at one of the city's eclectic theaters. You might even prefer to cheer on one of the city's sports teams or watch a theater performance. You can learn more about these sorts of options in the **Spectator Sports** and **Performing Arts** chapters, respectively.

COUNTRY-AND-WESTERN DANCING

River Oaks

BLANCO'S BAR & GRILL
3406 W. Alabama, at Buffalo Speedway
(713) 439-0072
houstonredneck.com
If you've got your cowboy or cowgirl boots on and are ready to two-step, head over to Blanco's. Frequently named the city's best country bar by the Houston Press, Blanco's showcases what it calls "live authentic Texas music," as well as jukebox tunes. That means you'll hear plenty of bluegrass, zydeco,

country of all strands, Americana rockabilly, honky-tonk, and oldies. The crowd here is a diverse mix of couples and singles—young and old—in search of a dance partner. Closed on Sat and Sun.

DANCE CLUBS

Galleria

✳BLACK SWAN AT THE OMNI HOTEL HOUSTON
4 Riverway
(713) 871-8181
omnihotels.com/FindAHotel/Houston/Dining/BlackSwan.aspx
One of Houston's best nightclubs can be found in the lower level of the Omni Hotel Houston. Every Friday and Saturday night from 8 p.m. to 2 a.m., DJs play hot dance tunes from the last three decades. The atmosphere is so much fun, in fact, that on any given Saturday night, you're sure to see brides, grooms, and their friends joining the masses on the floor to extend their celebration a little longer.

Midtown

UNION BAR LOUNGE
2708 Bagby St.
(281) 974-1916
unionbarhouston.com
Union Bar Lounge is a cross between a chic lounge and a sports bar. There are several large-screen TVs around the lounge. Sometimes sporting events are on, other times music videos. Union Bar Lounge often features live music. Be prepared if you're here on the weekends: the DJ's been known to get everybody on their feet and dancing.

Literary Readings

Bookworm? You won't want to miss Houston's literary scene. Poetry and prose readings are frequently held here. The most renowned of these are hosted by **Inprint,** a local literary organization that brings several noteworthy writers to town between September and April as part of the **Brown Reading Series.** The authors read from their work, get interviewed on stage, and sign copies of their books. The readings are held at different venues around the city, primarily in the Theater District. Recent authors include Ha Jin, Margaret Atwood, Gary Shteyngart, and Michael Ondaatje. Individual tickets cost $5 and can be purchased through the Inprint website (inprinthouston.org); season tickets are also available. Throughout the year, Inprint hosts book club meetings about the featured authors and their works, readings on the lawn at Discovery Green, and writing workshops. Learn more about Inprint's offerings by calling (713) 521-2026 or visiting inprinthouston.org.

The University of Houston's Graduate Program in Creative Writing also hosts public readings by distinguished faculty, students, and guests. Learn about upcoming readings and other literary events at class.uh.edu/cwp or by calling (713) 743-2255.

Montrose

NUMBERS NIGHT CLUB
300 Westheimer Rd.
(713) 526-6551
numbersnightclub.com
Numbers has been around for years and it's no less of a dive now than it was 15 years ago. Filthy bathrooms and floors don't keep people from coming here to dance, though. Numbers often hosts live shows, and the DJs play a mix of dance tunes that gets big crowds on the floor. The crowd here tends to be fairly young since Numbers is one of the few dance clubs in the city that allows guests under 21.

i When Inprint readings don't sell out, students and seniors ages 65 and older can get in for free by showing up at 6:45 p.m. the evening of the event.

GAY & LESBIAN BARS

Montrose

METEOR
2306 Genesee St.
(713) 521-0123
meteorhouston.com
Comfortable seating, good drinks, and great pop and dance music videos make Meteor what many consider Houston's classiest gay bar. The DJ knows how to fill up the dance floor; in fact, it's not unusual to see people dancing on the tables. Those who need a break from dancing often hang out on the patio. Get $3 well drinks and $3.50 martinis on Friday night. Smoking is off-limits here. There's never a cover charge.

SOUTH BEACH
810 Pacific St.
(713) 529-7623
southbeachthenightclub.com
A huge dance floor, really loud music played by DJs, and black lights make this a popular spot for dancing and flirting. The club attracts a diverse clientele, with people of all races, ages, and sexual orientations hanging out here on any given night. For those who don't want to dance, the front lounge, several bars, and the patio are popular alternatives. Get $3 well drinks all night on Friday. The cover charge here usually runs between $10 and $20, depending on the night; there's no cover charge on Friday before 11 p.m.

LIVE MUSIC

Downtown

RED CAT JAZZ CAFE
711 Franklin St.
(713) 226-7870
redcatjazzcafe.com
This bar and lounge features live jazz—sometimes even during lunchtime—in a hip environment reminiscent of the French Quarter. The Red Cat Jazz Cafe serves mixed drinks, as well as a small selection of wine and beer. If you're hungry, feast on New Orleans–inspired dishes like gumbo, blackened chicken, and okra Creole.

TOYOTA CENTER
1510 Polk St.
(866) 446-8849 (box office)
houstontoyotacenter.com
When it's not being used for Houston Rockets basketball or Houston Aeros hockey games, the Toyota Center hosts some of the city's biggest concerts. Recent acts have included Bruce Springsteen, Eric Clapton, Coldplay, and Nickelback. Parking is available for $15 in the Tundra parking garage next door to the Toyota Center, but you can often find parking on nearby side streets. Purchase tickets by visiting or calling the Toyota Center box office or visiting the Toyota Center website.

VERIZON WIRELESS THEATER
520 Texas Ave.
(713) 230-1666 (box office)
verizonwirelesstheater.com
This midsize concert venue boasts good sound quality and an opportunity to see big-name acts up close. Among those who have recently taken the stage here: James Taylor, the Killers, Deftones, Chris Isaak, and the Indigo Girls. There's reserved seating as well as standing-room-only space. Call or visit the website to purchase tickets. Many shows sell out, so don't wait until the last minute. There's often a line to valet park here, but you can avoid it by parking in the Theater District Parking Garage across the street.

Midtown

THE CONTINENTAL CLUB
3700 Main St.
(713) 529-9899
continentalclub.com/houston.html
Like the Continental Club in Austin, this Midtown joint offers an intimate atmosphere for seeing live music, much of it local. On any given night, you might see a cover band, blues, rockabilly, or ska. There's some space for dancing, as well as a patio for relaxing. On Monday evenings at 7, the Continental Club offers tango lessons.

i Got the munchies? The Continental Club's neighbor, Tacos A Go-Go (713-807-8226), will usually deliver breakfast tacos to bar guests.

SAMBUCA JAZZ CAFE
909 Texas, at Travis
(713) 224-5299
sambucarestaurant.com
Sambuca's actually a dinner club, but many people prefer the music to the food. Live bands and musicians play here every night. Much of the time, as the name suggests, jazz is the featured genre, but on any given night you might hear top 40, classic rock, Latin, or soul. Among the bar's offerings are a long list of specialty cocktails like the Pomtini, Bull's Eye (Belvedere and Red Bull), and the Maker's Manhattan. Visit the website to find out about upcoming performances, then reserve your table online. Most people get dressed up here.

Montrose

CÉZANNE
4100 Montrose Blvd., at Richmond
(832) 592-7464
blacklabradorpub.com/cezanne_about.html
Above the Black Labrador pub (page 87) sits Cézanne, an intimate piano bar featuring some of the best jazz musicians from Houston, New York, and San Francisco. Just how intimate, you ask? There are just 40 seats in this classy wood-paneled bar so expect to get close and personal with your fellow guests as you sip one of Cézanne's renowned martinis. Seating is first-come, first-served, so try to arrive when the doors open at 8:30 p.m. There's a $10 cover and a one-drink minimum. Cézanne is only open on Fri and Sat evenings from 9 p.m. to midnight.

Upper Kirby

GOODE'S ARMADILLO PALACE
5015 Kirby, at Barlett
(713) 526-9700
thearmadillopalace.com
Want some down-home, Texas-style drinking, dining, and evening entertainment? Head over to Goode's Armadillo Palace, where shuffleboard, dominos, billiards, and live Texas music await. Sit on the patio and throw back a few cold beers or sample some whiskey at the whiskey bar. When you get hungry, order Southern delights like wings, fried chicken, or venison chili.

MCGONIGEL'S MUCKY DUCK
2425 Norfolk
(713) 528-5999
mcgonigels.com
Widely considered one of the city's best small live-music venues, the Mucky Duck features live music just about every night of the year. Most musicians who perform at this Irish-themed bar hail from Texas; recent acts have included Randy Weeks, Cory Morrow, Trish Murphy, and Joe Ely. On Monday, the Mucky Duck hosts open-mic night, which attracts everyone from poets to comedians. Signup starts at 6:30. This weekly event is free, but most other shows require tickets, which can be purchased in advance on the website. The only alcohol served here is beer, wine, and champagne. Sit on the patio for a reprieve from the noise.

i Grab a free copy of the *Houston Press* at a local newsstand to find out about upcoming shows in the area. Or visit houstonpress.com.

The Woodlands

CYNTHIA WOODS MITCHELL PAVILION
2005 Lake Robbins Dr., The Woodlands
(281) 364-3024 (box office)
woodlandscenter.org
Take in some of the city's biggest concerts and performing arts events amid lush grass and towering pine trees at the Cynthia Woods Mitchell Pavilion in The Woodlands. Among the big acts recently featured at this outdoor amphitheater: Arcade Fire, Kenny Chesney, and Dave Matthews Band. The Houston Symphony and Houston Ballet also perform here on occasion. General admission seating is available on the lawn for most events; those who want to be closer to the action or to avoid the heat and rain can pay more to sit in the covered amphitheater. Tickets can be purchased through Ticketmaster (ticketmaster.com or 800-745-3000) or in person at the box office. Take note, though: Tickets don't go on sale at the box office until 5 hours after they've gone on sale at Ticketmaster. Free guest parking is available in several lots near The Pavilion; visit woodlandscenter .org/parking.html for a parking map. Be sure to wear comfortable shoes. Most of the parking lots are at least a 5-minute walk from the amphitheater.

i Rain in the forecast? Concerts at the Cynthia Woods Mitchell Pavilion are generally held rain or shine, so bring some rain gear.

MOVIE THEATERS

The Houston area is home to dozens of movie theaters. Many of these are your standard AMC, Cinemark, or Edwards fare, but the city also boasts several unique movie theaters, which are listed here. Showtimes for all local theaters can be found on their respective websites, in the *Houston Chronicle*, or online at movies.yahoo.com or fandango .com. Movie tickets tend to run around $10–$11 for adults; most theaters offer discounts for children and seniors. Some offer student discounts with a valid ID.

Downtown

✳SUNDANCE CINEMAS
510 Texas Ave., at Smith St.
(713) 223-3456
sundancecinemas.com/houston.html
Sundance Cinemas is the best place in town to see independent and foreign-language fims, as well as some of the latest blockbusters. Go online to reserve your seats in the newly renovated theater, and you won't have to worry about arriving early enough to nab the perfect seat. You may, however, want to show up early enough to grab a bottle of wine or champagne at the bar, so you can take it into the theater with you. You can also order freshly made salads, desserts, pizzas, sandwiches, and more traditional concessions like cotton candy and popcorn. Sundance is located in Bayou Place, a downtown dining and entertainment complex with a Hard Rock Cafe, The Blue Fish sushi bar, and Verizon Wireless Theater. Parking is free with ticket validation in the Theater District Garage at Smith and Texas; just make sure you take your parking ticket to the Sundance ticket counter.

Memorial

EDWARDS HOUSTON MARQ*E STADIUM 23 & IMAX

7620 Katy Fwy.

(713) 263-7843

For the most part, the Edwards Marq*e Stadium 23 is a pretty standard theater with oodles of screens. What makes this theater unique is its IMAX screen—the largest such screen in town. The IMAX screen here is typically used for big action flicks like *Spiderman* and *Star Trek*. Tickets to IMAX shows tend to run about $4 more than tickets to the non-IMAX shows. Edwards has a second location in Upper Kirby; it has three 3-D screens.

STUDIO MOVIE GRILL CITYCENTRE

805 Town and Country Ln.

(713) 461-4449

studiomoviegrill.com/townandcountry
.html

Forget about eating popcorn at the movies. At Studio Movie Grill CityCentre, you can watch the latest blockbuster—as well as an occasional classic like *Caddy Shack*—while drinking and dining on burgers, salad, chicken, or quesadillas at a table. A server will bring your order right to your table.

River Oaks

*RIVER OAKS THEATRE

2009 W. Gray

(713) 866-8881

landmarktheatres.com/market/houston/
riveroakstheatre.htm

This old art deco–style theater has been a staple of Houston's independent and foreign-language film scene since 1939. And with just three screens, the theater shows just a handful of movies a day. Some are big flicks like *The Girl with the Dragon Tattoo;* others are more obscure films like Cary Joji Fukunaga's *Sin Nombre.* Visit at midnight on Friday or Saturday night to see old favorites like *Back to the Future, Ghostbusters, Fear and Loathing in Las Vegas,* and *The Rocky Horror Picture Show.*

West Houston

*ALAMO DRAFTHOUSE

West Oaks Mall #429

Westheimer Road at TX 6

(281) 920-9268 (showtimes)

(281) 920-9268 (general contact)

drafthouse.com/westoaks

See one or two movies at the Alamo Drafthouse, and you probably won't want to see a movie anywhere else. Much like the Studio Movie Grill CityCentre, the Alamo Drafthouse serves dinner and drinks in the theater while you watch a movie. But the food, service, and even the movies at the Alamo tend to be better than those at Studio Movie Grill. The Alamo's menu is filled with burgers (including a good veggie burger), nachos, salads, and pizzas, greasy appetizers, beer, wine, and sangria. While many people come here to see blockbuster movies, some of the Alamo's biggest draws are special events, such as quote-alongs for classic movies like *The Big Lebowski* and a *Dazed & Confused* beer dinner, screenings of old favorites like Sixteen Candles, and season-finale watch parties for shows like Glee. The Alamo sometimes even serves thematic food and drinks to complement the featured movie. (Think White Russians for the *Big Lebowski*.) There's a second location in Katy, and additional locations are opening in Midtown and in northwest Houston in early 2013.

Various Locations

AURORA PICTURE SHOW
1524 Sul Ross (organization headquarters)
(713) 868-2101
aurorapictureshow.org
Meet Aurora Picture Show, Houston's nomadic film and video theater. This non-profit micro-cinema screens short films and videos made by noncommercial artists at unique locations and art spaces around the city. Aurora Picture Show also hosts a number of filmmakers, videographers, and curators who come to talk about their work. Ticket prices vary depending on the event and venue, but the organization strives to keep them affordable. There are several free screenings and events throughout the year.

PERFORMING ARTS

When it comes to Houston's cultural scene, the performing arts play a starring role. Only five cities in the country have resident professional companies in ballet, opera, theater, and symphony—and Houston is one of them. Nine acclaimed performing arts organizations—as well as some touring groups—perform downtown in the Theater District, a 17-block area that's only second to Manhattan when it comes to the number of theater seats in a concentrated downtown area. While the Theater District is home to some of Houston's biggest acts, it's hardly the only place to see the performing arts here. Houston is home to many smaller community and professional theaters, as well as Miller Outdoor Theatre in Hermann Park.

OVERVIEW

In this chapter, you'll find a sampling of Houston's abundant performing arts offerings. We've got everything from puppet shows to ballet to theater to Broadway musicals to opera to chamber music to symphony to contemporary music in the classical spirit. Many theaters also offer special performances for children and families; some of the best theaters for kids can be found in the "Kidstuff" chapter.

It's impossible to include all of Houston's performing arts organizations and venues here. So, this chapter features some of the best theaters and companies in their respective genres. These theaters and performing arts companies also tend to attract large audiences. In most cases, this chapter highlights performing arts companies, some of which have their own theaters and others that "borrow" venues. In a couple of cases, specific venues are highlighted since their setting and the breadth of events they host make them attractions in themselves.

Phone numbers listed here are for the box office, which, in most cases, is located at the theater. Exceptions include the addresses of both the theater and box office. All venues listed here are wheelchair accessible, and many offer assisted-listening devices. Call the box office for additional information.

TICKET PRICES

Ticket prices for performances vary. Shows in the Theater District tend to be the priciest, although most theaters offer special prices for students, seniors, children, and larger groups. Tickets for Friday and Saturday evening performances typically cost more than those for weeknights and weekend matinees. In most cases, tickets can be purchased by calling or visiting the theater box office or visiting the theater's website. Tickets at theaters outside the Theater District tend to be fairly inexpensive or even free, but they're often available only by calling or visiting the box office. Price ranges listed here are based on 2011–2012 season ticket costs. Keep in mind that theaters often raise ticket prices from one year to the next. All ticket prices listed are for individual tickets; most local performing arts companies also offer season tickets.

PERFORMANCE DAYS & TIMES

Performance days and times vary. Some venues and groups only offer weekend evening and matinee shows; many have a few weeknight performances. Most theaters—especially those in the Theater District—host shows from September to May or June, then take off a couple months for the summer. Schedules are often released as much as 6 months to a year in advance. Tickets for acclaimed performances, as well as seasonal shows, can be tough to nab at the last minute, so order yours as far in advance as possible.

PARKING IN THE THEATER DISTRICT & ELSEWHERE

Theater District venues are identified as such. Parking for these venues is available in nine Theater District parking garages, which are scattered around this 17-block section of downtown. Parking in these garages costs $7, payable upon entry, on Sat, Sun, city holidays, and after 5 p.m. Mon through Fri. At other times, parking fees are based on an hourly rate. Find the garage closest to the theater you're visiting on the Downtown map (page x). If it's raining or chilly (a rare occurrence, no doubt), get a reprieve by walking through the tunnels that run between the downtown theaters and garages.

Parking at other theaters around the city is typically free and available on-site. Exceptions are included in the listings that follow.

i Find out about the latest off-beat performing and visual arts events in Houston by visiting the Fresh Arts Coalition's website (fresharts .org) or subscribing to their newsletter. This arts collaborative highlights the work and upcoming events of the city's best independent arts groups and organizations.

BALLET

✷HOUSTON BALLET
Wortham Theater (Theater District)
501 Texas Ave., at Smith St.
(713) 227-2787
houstonballet.org
The Houston Ballet is the country's fourth-largest professional ballet group. Led by artistic director Stanton Welch, the ballet's 54 dancers put on more than 70 performances of about 10 different ballets each year. Each season's shows feature ballets ranging from an adaptation of the five-act opera Manon to classics, like *Cinderella* and *Romeo and Juliet*. Among the season's biggest highlights: more than 30 December performances of *The Nutcracker*, many offered at discounted prices. The Houston Ballet occasionally holds shows at Miller Outdoor Theatre (page 115). These performances are free, but they require advance tickets for seats in the covered area. In addition to local performances, the Houston Ballet tours to other cities around the US, Canada, and Europe. The Houston Ballet also has choreographed productions with the Boston Ballet, the National Ballet of Canada, and others.

Houston Ballet Foundation, which runs the ballet, operates a ballet academy, which trains about 300 dancers. More than half of the Houston Ballet's dancers are former academy students.

Tickets to performances are available through the box office. They'll cost you anywhere from about $58 to $152, depending on where you sit and when you attend the ballet. Student and senior? You can get discounted tickets for select performances.

i Want a sneak peek of the upcoming theater season, a backstage tour, or even a chance to meet some of Houston's best ballerinas, musicians, and actors? Attend the free Theater District Open House in August. This daylong, family-friendly event takes place at the main Theater District venues— Alley Theatre, Jones Hall, Wortham Center, and Hobby Center.

MUSIC

DA CAMERA OF HOUSTON
Lillie Cullen Theater at Wortham Center
(Theater District)
501 Texas, at Smith St. (theater)
1427 Branard St. (box office)
(713) 524-5050
dacamera.com

Since 1987, Da Camera has brought Houstonians an assortment of musical styles and sounds, including chamber music and jazz performances by some of the world's best musicians. Many Da Camera concerts connect music with other art forms. Some combine dance and chamber music. Others, like Da Camera's Music and Literary Imagination programs, have paired music

with the stories of literary giants like Franz Kafka and Thomas Mann. This innovative programming has won Da Camera national and international attention, with many of the organization's shows going on tour. Da Camera puts on about 17 performances a year; there's usually just one performance of each show. Da Camera makes its home at the Cullen Theater in the Theater District's Wortham Center, but events are often held at other Houston venues, including the Menil Collection and the Rothko Chapel. Tickets to jazz concerts at the Wortham Center range from $33 to $60; classical concert tickets cost $28 to $55, and tickets to concerts held at the Menil Collection and Rothko Chapel cost $35. Tickets can be purchased online, over the phone, or by visiting the box office. Tickets go on sale at the theater at 6:30 p.m. on the night of the performance. Students and adults over 60 can get in for half price, but only if tickets are purchased by phone or at the box office.

FOUNDATION FOR MODERN MUSIC
1915 Commonwealth (office)
(713) 529-3928
modernmusic.org

Classical music lovers, this one's for you: The Foundation for Modern Music features contemporary music written in the classical tradition by living American composers such as Yoko Ono, Johnson Reagon, and Jerome Kitzke. Sometimes the featured composers even attend the performances, which are held at locations such as the Rothko Chapel and Stages Repertory Theatre. The River Oaks–based foundation also holds an annual competition for teenage composers. Ticket prices vary based on the event and venue.

i Love classical music? Tune into Houston Public Radio's classical station, KUHA on 91.7 FM. This NPR affiliate plays classical music and arts coverage 24/7.

HOUSTON FRIENDS OF CHAMBER MUSIC
Rice University
Stude Concert Hall inside Alice Pratt Brown Hall
6100 Main St.
(713) 348-5363
houstonfriendsofmusic.org
For more than 50 years, Houston Friends of Chamber Music has teamed up with Rice University's Shepherd School of Music to bring outstanding chamber music to Houston. Each year the Houston Friends of Chamber Music board of directors sifts through more than 100 applications from international performing groups to assemble a lineup featuring works by a mix of 18th-, 19th-, and 20th-century composers. There are nine shows a year, all held at Stude Concert Hall on the Rice University campus September through April. Individual tickets cost $60 to $85 for adults, $30 to $60 for seniors 65 and older, and $15 to $25 for students with an ID. All concerts begin at 8 p.m.

✳HOUSTON SYMPHONY
Jones Hall (Theater District)
615 Louisiana St., at Capitol St.
(713) 224-7575
houstonsymphony.org
The internationally acclaimed Houston Symphony is one of the country's oldest performing arts organizations. Each year some 350,000 people come out to listen to the Houston Symphony's 90 full-time musicians perform concerts. Some come for one (or more) of the 18 classical concerts, which have featured the likes of Beethoven's Violin Concerto and Brahms's First. Others come for the nine pops concerts, which have featured rockapella, Broadway tunes, and songs from Billy Joel. The symphony also hosts special events, ranging from talks about different musicians to performances by world-renowned musicians like Yo-Yo Ma. On 4 Saturday mornings each year, the Houston Symphony hosts family concerts for kids ages 4 to 11. Recent family concerts have showcased music from beloved children's movies and stories, like *The Little Mermaid*. Ticket prices vary for different events, but they generally range from $25 to $123. Most concerts are held at Jones Hall; some smaller events are held at other venues, including the Hobby Center's Zilkha Hall, which is located in the downtown Theater District.

OPERA

✳HOUSTON GRAND OPERA
Wortham Center (Theater District)
550 Prairie
(713) 228-6737
houstongrandopera.org
The Houston Grand Opera—also known as HGO—is one of the world's most acclaimed opera companies. Each year HGO puts on six operas—some classics like *La Traviata* and *Tosca*, others debut operas like André Previn's *Brief Encounter*. Since 1973, HGO has commissioned and produced dozens of new operas, 42 of which have made their world debuts in Houston. This innovation—not to mention the accompanying artistic stylings—has won the HGO two Grammy Awards, two Emmy Awards, a Tony Award, and a Grand Prix du Disques. No other opera

company in the world has won all four of these prestigious awards.

HGO always uses supertitles, even for operas performed in English. The company puts on about five performances of each opera. Ticket prices vary, depending on the day and time, but they typically range from $38 to $293.

> **i** Got season tickets but can't make a show? Most theaters allow season ticket holders to exchange their tickets for another performance date or time.

PUPPETRY

BOBBINDOCTRIN PUPPET THEATRE
827 Wendel St. (office)
(713) 259-1304
bobbindoctrin.org

Think puppets are just for kids? Bobbindoctrin Puppet Theatre will change your mind. Since 1995, Bobbindoctrin has been putting on puppet shows that use a combination of rod, shadow, hand, tabletop, and string puppetry and elaborate puppets. Some shows even incorporate masks. The shows here are a combination of newer scripts and original ones written by local playwrights, and few are kid-friendly. All participating artists hail from the Houston area. Previous shows include *Ivan the Fool,* based on Leo Tolstoy's short story; *Oh, Lenin!,* an adaptation of a nonsensical poem by Kornei Chukovski; and sillier titles such as *Got Brains?* and *Sea Monkeys.* During the winter holiday season, Bobbindoctrin produces a puppet festival, featuring a series of short puppet shows. Since Bobbindoctrin doesn't have a theater of its own, shows are often held at nightclubs and museums around the city. Ticket prices vary based on the show and venue.

THEATER

✳ ALLEY THEATRE
615 Texas Ave. (Theater District)
(713) 220-5700
alleytheatre.org

For more than 60 years, the Alley Theatre has been the heart and soul of Houston theater. Each year thousands of Houstonians come to see this Tony Award–winning company perform a gamut of new, rediscovered, classic, and musical plays. Among recent Alley shows: *Cyrano de Bergerac, The Man Who Came to Dinner, The Toxic Avenger,* and Aaron Sorkin's *The Farnsworth Invention.* The Alley even coproduced and premiered *Jekyll & Hyde* in 1990—7 years before the hit show opened on Broadway.

The Alley puts on 11 productions every year, including A Christmas Carol. There are several performances of each show. Ticket prices typically range from $34 to $87, depending on the day and time.

> **i** Want to save money on tickets to the Alley Theatre? Attend a show on Tuesday or Sunday evening, and pay the Cheap Thrills price—$25 or $35, depending on the seat. Cheap Thrills aren't available for holiday shows or other special events.

✳ BROADWAY ACROSS AMERICA
Hobby Center
800 Bagby St. (Theater District)
(713) 622-7469
broadwayacrossamerica.com/houston

Forget Manhattan. You can see the most-talked about Broadway shows right here in Houston. Each year Broadway Across America brings five touring Broadway musicals to the Hobby Center for the Performing Arts. These shows include new hits like *Avenue Q, Spamalot, The Lion King, Jersey Boys,* and *Wicked,* as well as classics like *The Wizard of Oz* and *Mary Poppins.* Some shows are far better than others, but each season includes at least a couple of crowd-pleasers. Tickets can be hard to come by for shows that have received lots of acclaim on Broadway, so buy tickets in advance when possible. Tickets are sold through Ticketmaster and can be purchased by phone, at the Hobby Center box office, or online. Prices range from $30 to $100, depending on the day and time. These prices don't include the $5.50 per ticket surcharge.

i **Seeing a show at the Hobby Center? Dine at Artista on the second floor of the Hobby Center. This sister restaurant of Churrasco's and Américas (listed in the "Restaurants" chapter) dishes up artsy decor and some of the best—and best-looking—Latin food around. Make reservations at cordua .com or by calling (713) 278-4782.**

COUNTRY PLAYHOUSE
12802 Queensbury Ln.
(713) 467-4497
countryplayhouse.org
Since opening in 1956, the Country Playhouse has moved several times, but one thing remains constant about Houston's oldest community theater: It champions quality in everything from well-known plays to first-run plays. All the plays here are performed by locals who audition and work hard to get

their roles just right. Many are performed on the Cerwinske Stage, which seats up to 225 people. Recent shows include *The Best Little Whorehouse of Texas, The Best Christmas Pageant Ever,* and *I Love You, You're Perfect, Now Change.* The Black Box Lab, which previously functioned as a rehearsal space, features rehearsed readings of scripts written by locals. Many of these scripts become full productions. Tickets to Country Playhouse performances range from $12 to $28. The theater is located in Memorial's Town & Country Village shopping center. There's not always someone at the theater to answer the phone, so the easiest way to purchase tickets is to order them online or purchase them at the theater up to 2 hours before the show.

MAIN STREET THEATER
2540 Times Blvd. (Rice Village)
4617 Montrose Blvd. (Museum District)
(713) 524-6706
mainstreettheater.com
When the Main Street Theater entered the local theater scene in the 1970s, its founders sought to entertain Houstonians with more provocative plays and musicals and give more professional thespians training and a stage to show off their skills. More than 30 years later, the Main Street Theater continues to do both for kids and adult audiences alike. Recent shows on the adult-oriented MainStage include *The Light in the Piazza, Urinetown,* the world premiere of *. . . and L.A. Is Burning,* and touring shows like *A Midsummer Night's Dream.* Main Street Theater also offers plays and acting classes for children.

Tickets for MainStage events range from $30 to $40, depending on the day and time. Discounts are available for students, as well as adults 65 and over. Prior to opening night, the theater offers sneak previews for $10.

🔍 Close-up

Society for the Performing Arts

Each year Houston hosts a number of traveling shows. Credit for these traveling shows goes, in part, to the **Society for the Performing Arts** (713-227-4772; spahouston.org).

Credit also goes to the outstanding national and international theater, dance, and music artists and companies that come to town to put on these shows. The selection is always diverse, ranging from orchestras to solo vocalists to gospel choirs to Broadway tunes to contemporary dance groups, operas, jazz, theater performances, and guest speakers. Recent seasons have brought the likes of the Salzburg Chamber Soloists, the bluegrass band Cherryholmes, the Aspen Santa Fe Ballet, and the Virsky Ukrainian National Dance Company. The SPA also offers a Family Fun Series, which features popular kids' acts. Tickets to Family Fun Series events are half-price for kids.

Most events are held at Theater District venues. The full SPA season includes about 17 events. Single ticket prices vary, depending on the event and venue.

Main Street Theater has two locations— one in Rice Village, the other in the Chelsea Market shopping center in the Museum District. The box office is at the Rice Village location. However, at the time this book went to press, the theater was planning to move into a single location at 2540 Times Blvd. So, call before you visit to see if they've moved.

ℹ Attending a Sunday matinee or weeknight show in the Theater District? Arrive about a half hour early and you should be able to find free parking on the street.

✳MILLER OUTDOOR THEATRE
100 Concert Dr., in Hermann Park
(281) 373-3386
milleroutdoortheatre.com
Who said theatergoing had to be an indoor affair? Each year, from March to October, Houstonians flock to Hermann Park's Miller Outdoor Theatre for a cornucopia of free

music, dance, theater, and film events. The shows are put on by local performing arts groups, including the Houston Metropolitan Dance Company, Express Children's Theatre, Theater Under the Stars, the Houston Ballet, the Houston Symphony, Houston Grand Opera, Stages Repertory Theatre, and Miller Theatre Advisory Board. Many of the shows are for young children; recent productions have included The Three Little Pigs and Aladdin.

Two of the biggest highlights here are the Fourth of July celebration, which features the Houston Symphony playing Tchaikovsky's *1812 Overture,* followed by a 16-cannon salute and a fireworks display, and the Shakespeare Festival, which features several performances of two Shakespeare plays each August. You can learn about these two events in the "Annual Events" chapter.

Bring a picnic basket and blankets to watch the show from the amphitheater's

The Performing Arts: Uniquely Houston

Houston is home to dozens of nonprofit performing arts groups, but not all of them have a theater or the resources that their Theater District counterparts do. To help some of these emerging music, theater, and dance groups develop a following, the Hobby Center for the Performing Arts launched **Uniquely Houston** (713-315-2525; thehobbycenter.org). This program provides participating groups with technical, operational, and marketing support. It also gives them a Theater District venue—Zilkha Hall at the Hobby Center—for practicing and performing. The 16 participating groups represent an array of cultures and ethnicities, reflecting the diversity of the city's performing arts offerings. Here are brief descriptions and, where applicable, the websites and phone numbers for the participating programs. Tickets can be purchased by calling the Hobby Center or visiting its box office. Prices vary, but they're typically low.

Ambassadors International Folkloric Ballet
(713) 315-6406
ambassadorsibf.org
This ballet company seeks to preserve traditional folk dances by interpreting traditional dances from Texas, Ecuador, Mexico, and other Spanish-speakingcountries.

Apollo Chamber Players
(832) 496-9943
apollochamberplayers.org
This classical music organization blends unique folk sounds with a variety of ethnic influences.

Ars Lyrica Houston
arslyricahouston.org
Ars Lyrica Houston plays Baroque music—think Handel and Bach—using period instruments. It has put on everything from staged dramas to chamber music programs.

Arts in Motion
thehobbycenter.org
Dancers ages 6 to 19 are the heart and soul of this organization, which performs for children and families at the Ronald McDonald House and other local organizations and events.

Colombian Folkloric Ballet
cfb-usa.org
The Colombian Folkloric Ballet performs ballets, as well as dances from other Latin American countries whose dance forms aren't well represented in Houston. Ballet masters and choreographers from Colombia help stage the annual folkloric performance of "Mi Colombia."

Dominic Walsh Dance Theater
(713) 652-3938
dwdt.org
Dominic Walsh Dance Theater blends classical techniques with more contemporary emphasis on muscular fluidity, intimacy, and sensuality. This makes for some brilliant works by contemporary choreographers, such as Italy's Mauro Bigonzetti (Certe Notti and Come Un Respiro) and Jiří Kylián.

Gente de Teatro
gentedeteatro.org
This theater organization seeks to promote Latin American and Spanish culture by putting on the work of notable Latin American and Spanish playwrights. Among the playwrights whose work has been performed by the organization: Ariel Dorfman, Carmen Pombero, and Mario Vargas Llosa.

Houston Ebony Opera Guild
(713) 335-3800
houstonebonymusic.org
Houston Ebony Opera Guild highlights the work of black choral and opera singers through performances of classic and new operas, as well as concerts composed by black Americans.

Houston Pride Band
(832) 356-7476
houstonprideband.org
This concert band represents Houston's gay, lesbian, bisexual, and transgendered communities and performs at community events and parades throughout the year.

Houston Symphonic Band
houstonsymphonicband.com
Amateurs, semiprofessional, and professional musicians make up this symphonic band, which has toured internationally. The group seeks to make great music accessible to the community for a low cost.

Karen Stokes Dance
karenstokesdance.org
The 10 performers who make up Karen Stokes Dance perform full-length productions and repertory works choreographed by Karen Stokes, whose work is known for quirky movements, strong rhythms, original vocals and, most recently, video projection.

Masquerade Theatre
(713) 861-7045
masqueradetheatre.com
This musical theater company only employs actors and actresses from Houston. They perform both older and newer classics such as *Evita*, *The Producers*, and *The Music Man*.

Music Doing Good
musicdoinggood.org
This group seeks to use its musical talents to raise awareness and money for exceptional health, education, music, and children's charities. The group raises money for these organizations by putting on benefits, luncheons, talks, and performances throughout the year.

Musiqa
(713) 524-5678
musiqahouston.org
This small ensemble of composers and music professors—all hailing from Rice University's Shepherd School of Music and the University of Houston's Moores School of Music—seek to make contemporary classical music fun and engaging for people who might not normally listen to the genre. Musiqa plays four concerts at Zilkha Hall each year, as well as concerts for families, at schools, at the Menil Collection, and the Contemporary Arts Museum Houston.

Samskriti Society for Indian Performing Arts
(281) 265-2787
samskritihouston.org
Samskriti celebrates Indian culture through an array of cultural dance, theater, and music performances.

Virtuosi of Houston
(713) 807-0888
virtuosiofhouston.org
As the country's only youth chamber orchestra, Virtuosi seek to mold Houston's most talented young musicians into professionals and prepare them to attend the best conservatories. Virtuosi perform three concerts each year.

grassy hill. Or take your chances and try to be one of the more than 1,500 attendees—including those in wheelchairs—who get to sit in covered seating at Miller Outdoor Theatre. Since admission is always free, this covered seating is available on a first-come, first-served basis. Even if you want to sit on the grass, be sure to arrive at least a half-hour early. Parking spaces and the best lawn seats tend to fill up quickly. Visit the website for Miller Outdoor Theatre's complete schedule.

STAGES REPERTORY THEATRE
Houston Center for the Arts
3201 Allen Pkwy.
(713) 527-0123
stagestheatre.com
Since opening in the basement of a downtown brewery in 1978, Stages has been committed to producing brave new plays and offering groundbreaking revisions on literary, dramatic, and musical classics. And it's succeeded: the New York Times, the Wall Street Journal, Vogue, and Variety have all praised Stages' innovative theatrical productions.

Each year Stages puts on six shows. Recent shows include Stages artistic director Ted Swindley's international hit musical Always . . . Patsy Cline, Craig Wright's new comedy Mistakes Were Made, and the 2007 Pulitzer Prize–winning drama Rabbit Hole.

Ticket prices vary, although they tend to run between $15 and $35, depending on the day, time, and show. Free parking is available in the Houston Center for the Arts parking lot on the south side of the building on D'Amico Street.

✳THEATER UNDER THE STARS
Hobby Center
800 Bagby St. (Theater District)
(713) 558-8887
tuts.com
Theater Under the Stars—aka TUTS—is considered a gem on the national and international musical scene. Since 1968, TUTS has produced more than 300 musicals, many of them national and international premieres. Musicals that TUTS has debuted include Jekyll & Hyde (in collaboration with the Alley Theatre and the 5th Avenue Theatre of Seattle), Annie Warbucks, Zorro: The Musical, Scrooge, Mame, and the Tony Award–winning redux of Carousel. TUTS also offers its own rendition of new and old musicals ranging from Rent to Annie to Bring It On: The Musical.

TUTS typically puts on about a half dozen shows at the Hobby Center each year; the company or the Humphreys School usually performs a show at Miller Outdoor Theatre during the summer as well. Each show runs for about 2 weeks and includes several matinee and evening performances. Tickets typically range from to $24 to $114, depending on the showtime and day. Purchase tickets online or at the Hobby Center box office.

MUSEUMS

Still struggling to kick that image of Houstonians as boot-wearing folks with a funny twang? A visit to one of our museums should remind you just how cosmopolitan this city really is. In fact, our more than two dozen museums are some of Houston's most prized gems. The Museum of Fine Arts Houston is one of the country's largest art museums, and the Menil Collection holds one of the most noteworthy collections of art assembled during the 20th century. We've also got art museums dedicated to craft, contemporary art, photography, and decorative arts—not to mention the Rothko Chapel, which blends art and religion.

And that's just the art museums. Houston also has several one-of-a-kind history, culture, and science museums. You can learn about the funeral industry at the National Museum of Funeral History, hatred at the Holocaust Museum, and how your body works at the Health Museum. History buff? Be sure to check out the the San Jacinto Battleground State Historic Site (page 138) and Space Center Houston (page 140), each of which boasts artifacts and films that are sure to whet almost any appetite for history.

Houston is also home to a weather museum and a wonderful children's museum, both of which you can learn about in the "Kidstuff" chapter.

OVERVIEW

This chapter highlights Houston's best museums. Seventeen of these are located in the Museum District, an area surrounding Hermann Park and Montrose. All of the Museum District museums are within a 1.5-mile radius of the Mecom Fountain, so several of them are within walking distance of one another. A map of the Museum District can be found on page xi. Parking is available at all Houston museums, but it's limited in some cases. So, if you plan to visit a couple of museums in the Museum District, you may find it easier to take the METRORail to the Museum District stop and walk.

Most museums are closed at least 1 day, if not 2, each week. These closure days are included in the descriptions that follow. Some museums have seasonal hours, so consult the individual museums' websites to double-check this information and find out about special events and exhibits.

i Look for the brown street signs while walking or driving through the Museum District. These will point you toward the major museums in the area, including most of the ones mentioned in this chapter.

Most museums host special fund-raisers and educational programs throughout the year. To learn about upcoming events at

Houston's museums, visit the museums' websites. Or check out the *Houston Press* (houstonpress.com), the *Houston Chronicle* (chron.com), or Houston's daily digital magazine CultureMap (houston.culturemap .com).

All museums are wheelchair accessible unless indicated otherwise.

i Out and about in the Museum District? Use the Museum District's mobile site (m.houstonmuseumdistrict .org) to navigate the area or find out about individual museum events and hours.

Price Code

Many of the museums here are free, so it's possible to get a hefty dose of culture without paying a penny. That said, some museums do charge admission fees, which generally range from about $5 to $15. Most take a dollar or two off the price of admission for seniors, children, and students.

$. . . . . Less than $5
$$ . . . . $5 to $10
$$$ . . . . More than $10

ART MUSEUMS

**CONTEMPORARY ARTS MUSEUM
HOUSTON** FREE
5216 Montrose Blvd., at Bissonnet, just
kitty-corner from the Museum of Fine
Arts Houston (Museum District)
(713) 284-8250
camh.org
The Contemporary Arts Museum Houston makes its home in one of the Museum District's most distinctive buildings. Designed by renowned architect Gunnar Birkerts, the stainless steel building almost appears to be two-dimensional from the street. Inside, though, you'll find plenty of volume and depth. The museum has no permanent collections; its bread and butter are traveling exhibits and thematic exhibits that showcase cutting-edge 20th- and 21st-century art from Texas, the US, and abroad. Recent exhibits have explored the imagery surrounding puppets and showcased the work of local teenagers. During each exhibit, the museum hosts gallery talks that offer a variety of critical (and insightful) views about the work on display. Check the museum website for upcoming lectures and events. While you're here, check out the gift shop. In addition to some fun toys, books, gifts, and home decor, you'll find some unusual jewelry.

Admission is always free, but parking can be tough to come by. During the week, free parking is typically available at the church across the street. There's also limited parking on side streets in the area. Closed Monday and Tuesday.

i Learn about the Museum District's most important sites by taking a 2-mile audio tour as you walk and ride the METRORail through the neighborhood. Download the free audio tour, along with a detailed map, at audisseyguides.com/houston/museum district.html.

FOTOFEST FREE
1113 Vine St., just north of I-10 and
east of N. Main St.
(713) 223-5522
fotofest.org
FotoFest is best known for the huge photography festival and conference it puts on in even-numbered years. (See page 180

Houston CityPass: Your Ticket to Museum and Attraction Discounts

Plan to visit multiple museums and attractions in Houston? Save some money—and avoid ticket lines—by purchasing a Houston CityPass for $39 for adults or $29 for children ages 3 to 11. The pass will get you into the Houston Museum of Natural Science, Space Center Houston, the Downtown Aquarium, either the Museum of Fine Arts Houston or the Children's Museum of Houston, and either The Health Museum or the Houston Zoo. The Houston CityPass can be purchased at citypass.com, or at the ticket desk of any of the aforementioned locations. The pass is only good for 9 days after your first use, though, so use it quickly and often.

chapter for information about the festival.) But between the festivals, FotoFest hosts exhibits and events showcasing some of the most talented contemporary photographers from Texas, the US, and around the globe. Many of these exhibits are curated in collaboration with the Houston Center for Photography.

FotoFest offers free guided tours for all exhibits; most exhibits also feature special talks with the artists and curators. Some of these talks are held at other Houston museums and cultural centers; check the website to learn about upcoming talks. FotoFest interbiennial events and exhibits are free and open to the public. On-site parking is also free.

✳HOUSTON CENTER FOR CONTEMPORARY CRAFT   FREE
4848 Main St., at Rosedale St., 2 blocks south of US 59 (Museum District)
(713) 529-4848
crafthouston.org
From the outside, the Houston Center for Contemporary Craft might not look that impressive. But step inside, and you'll find some of Houston's most intriguing exhibits,

each demonstrating that the making and design of crafts is an intensive process, one with a long and constantly evolving history. Many of the exhibits here showcase objects made from fiber, metal, clay, glass, and wood, and many feature crafters hail from Texas. In fact, you can see many of the featured artists at work in their studios at the center, which provides workspace through its artist-in-residence program. Be sure to visit the center's gift shop—the Asher Retail Gallery. Worthy of an exhibit itself, the Asher Retail Gallery sells meticulously crafted pieces in a variety of media from established and emerging crafters from around the world. Admission is free, and free parking is available on the street and in a wheelchair-accessible lot behind the museum on Travis Street. Closed Monday.

✳HOUSTON CENTER FOR PHOTOGRAPHY   FREE
1441 W. Alabama, at Mulberry St., 1 block south of Westheimer (Museum District)
(713) 529-4755
hcponline.org

Since opening in 1981, the Houston Center for Photography—aka HCP—has displayed the work of some 3,200 established and emerging photographers and educated thousands more. The center doesn't have a permanent collection, but its exhibits are both timely and culturally significant. One recent show highlighted 60 years of photos produced by Magnum Photos, the world's most acclaimed photography cooperative. Another looked at how conflict in the Middle East affects life in the US. And often exhibits here feature work from some of the area's most promising high school–age photographers, as well as participants in the center's outreach programs. One of the biggest draws is the annual Print Auction Exhibition, a free-to-attend auction of prints donated by some of the world's finest photographers.

Admission is free. Parking is available on the street and in the free HCP parking lot. Closed Monday and Tuesday.

i Aspiring photographer? HCP offers more than 200 photography classes on everything from basic digital photography skills to advanced photo editing. Classes fill up quickly, so sign up early at hcponline.org.

LAWNDALE ART CENTER   FREE
4912 Main St., between Portland and Rosedale Streets (Museum District)
(713) 528-5858
lawndaleartcenter.org
Lawndale Art Center is the only museum dedicated to showcasing the work of Houston artists. The center, located in an art deco–style building just a block from the Houston Center for Contemporary Craft, houses four galleries, which offer a combined 20-plus exhibits each year. Informal

talks with the curators and artists accompany many of these exhibits.

The center also hosts several special events, the biggest of which is Dia de los Muertos (Day of the Dead) in early November. To commemorate those who have died, the center offers sugar skull decoration and papier-mâché skeleton workshops, a silent auction, and classical music and dance performances.

Another big draw is the annual 20th Century Modern Market in April. Art dealers from around the country sell ceramics, glass, metal, textiles, furniture, clothes, and other high-quality designs produced during the 20th century.

Admission is always free, but there's a charge for admission to Modern Market events. Parking is available on the street and in the center parking lot. Closed Sun.

✴THE MENIL COLLECTION   FREE
1515 Sul Ross St., between Mulberry and Mandell Streets (Museum District)
(713) 525-9400
menil.org
One of the most significant private art collections assembled during the 20th century is right here in Houston. The Menil Collection houses some 15,000 works of art—paintings, sculptures, photographs, prints, and rare books—that span from antiquity to the Byzantine and medieval eras to African and Oceanic tribes on up to the 20th century. The collection, amassed by John and Dominique de Menil, also includes some of the world's finest examples of surrealism, cubism, and pop art by the likes of Jasper Johns and Andy Warhol. The Menil Collection recently launched the Menil Drawing Institute and Study Center, which collects, exhibits, and studies modernist drawings

by the likes of Paul Cézanne, Paul Klee, and René Magritte.

The Menil Collection holds special events throughout the year; most take place at the main building on Sul Ross Street. On the first Sunday of each month, for instance, The Artist's Eye series features local artists talking about their favorite work from the Menil Collection. Also popular is the Menil/Rice Lecture Series held at nearby Rice University throughout the year. All Menil lectures relate to a theme found in the museum's permanent collection.

Admission is free. So is parking behind the Menil Collection on West Alabama Street between Mulberry and Mandell Streets. Closed Mon and Tues.

i Many Houston museums offer free admission on certain days or at designated times. Find the latest admission-free days and times for museums in the Museum District at houstonmuseumdistrict.org.

✳MUSEUM OF FINE ARTS
HOUSTON $-$$
Caroline Wiess Law Building
1001 Bissonnet St., between Montrose and Main Streets (Museum District)
Audrey Jones Beck Building
5601 Main St., on the corner of Bissonnet and Main Streets (Museum District)
(713) 639-7300
mfah.org
With 57,000 works of art and 300,000 square feet of exhibit space, the Museum of Fine Arts Houston is one of the country's largest art museums. MFAH, as the museum is often called, consists of two main buildings—the Caroline Wiess Law Building and the Audrey Jones Beck Building. Add in the Lillie and

Hugh Roy Cullen Sculpture Garden, some 18 acres of public gardens, the Glassell School of Art, and two houses devoted to decorative arts, and the MFAH practically qualifies as an empire.

The museum's original building—the Caroline Wiess Law Building—dates back to 1924, when William Ward Watkin designed the building in the neoclassical style. Between the late 1950s and mid-1970s, renowned architect Ludwig Mies van der Rohe designed two additions—Cullinan Hall and Brown Pavilion—in the international style. Today the Law Building's galleries house most of MFAH's 20th- and 21st-century pieces; art from Asia, sub-Saharan Africa, and the Pacific Islands; the world's most renowned collection of gold objects; and internationally acclaimed exhibits spanning centuries, continents, and media. Inside the Law Building, you can also watch contemporary and classic flicks in the Brown Auditorium Theatre and research in the nationally renowned Hirsche Library.

In 2000 the MFAH opened the Audrey Jones Beck Building, just steps east of the Law Building. The first major museum designed by Pritzker Prize–winning architect Rafael Moneo, the Beck Building features large lanternlike skylights in the roof, bringing natural light to many of the building's galleries. Inside you'll find exquisite American art, prints, drawings, photographs, a high-ceilinged sculpture court, and special exhibits. The lower levels of the Beck and Law Buildings are connected by a tunnel lined with James Turrell's neon-colored light installation, *The Light Inside*.

There's a lot to see here, so consider taking one of the museum's free tours to learn about the MFAH's permanent collection, special exhibits, art history, and specific

🔍 Close-up

Glassell School of Art

Head a block north of the Museum of Fine Arts Houston's main campus, and you'll find the **Glassell School of Art** (5101 Montrose Blvd., just past Berthea Street; 713-639-7500), MFAH's teaching arm.

Adults take classes through the Studio School for Adults, while young children and teens take classes in the Junior School, the country's only museum school focusing on art education for kids. Both schools offer classes in media ranging from jewelry design to photography to painting to printmaking to art history. Tuition can be pricey, but Glassell does award tuition scholarships to nearly 200 students each year.

This is just one of the ways Glassell strives to make art education accessible to the community. Through the Community Bridge Programs, Glassell offers free workshops at hospitals and community centers to give underserved populations and ill Houstonians the chance to try a variety of artistic media.

Glassell also provides recent art school graduates space and funding to work on their projects for 9 months through the prestigious Core Artist-in-Residence Program. Core artists' work is often displayed at Glassell. Other Glassell exhibits showcase contemporary artists from around the country. Admission is free; so is on-site parking.

Learn about upcoming exhibits and classes at Glassell on the Museum of Fine Arts Houston website: mfah.org.

works or artists. Tours last from 20 minutes to an hour; they're not offered in September.

Before leaving the museum, take a walk through the Lillie and Hugh Roy Cullen Sculpture Garden, located at the corner of Montrose Boulevard and Bissonnet Street. With more than 20 sculptures and other works from 19th- and 20th-century artists like Henri Matisse and Auguste Rodin, this serene garden is the perfect place to contemplate or daydream. The garden is open daily.

A museum ticket gets you into both the Beck and Law Buildings. General admission is $10 for adults and $5 for kids ages 6 to 18 and seniors 65 and older. Kids under 5 get in free. MFAH is included on the Houston CityPass (page 121).

Admission is free on Thursday, though you'll still have to pay for special exhibits. Ticket prices for special exhibits vary, but can surpass $30 per person in some cases.

Free parking is available in lots on Main Street at Bissonnet and Main Street at Oakdale. There's also a four-story parking garage just east of the museum on Binz Street; parking here costs $3.

The Beck Building is closed on Monday, excluding Monday holidays such as Memorial Day and Labor Day.

i Love historic houses? Visit The Heritage Society at Sam Houston Park, where you can tour houses that belonged to Houston's earliest residents and learn about the city's early history.

MUSEUM OF FINE ARTS HOUSTON—
BAYOU BEND $$
6003 Memorial Dr. at Westcott St.
(713) 639-7750
mfah.org/bayoubend

Love American decor? You won't want to miss the Museum of Fine Arts Houston—Bayou Bend. Here you'll find one of the most extensive collections of American decor at the former home of Ima Hogg, the daughter of former Texas governor James S. Hogg.

Built in the late 1920s for Ima and her two brothers, the Hogg manse features 28 rooms, each taking visitors back to another period in American history. Every room is filled with American furniture, ceramics, silver, and wall decor spanning from 1620 to 1870.

After visiting the house, take a walk through the gardens. Credit for this relaxing oasis of color goes largely to Ima Hogg, who planted dozens of flowers, plants, and trees while leaving plenty of green space. Hogg also refused to cut down many of the trees and wild green thickets that comprised an integral part of Bayou Bend.

Admission is $10 for adults and $8.50 for college students and seniors 65 and up. Children 10 to 17 get in for $5; kids 9 and younger get in free but aren't allowed on guided house tours. Admission includes a guided tour or an audio tour. Reservations are required for guided tours.

Admission to the garden—which includes a self-guided audio tour—is $3 for visitors 10 and older and free for kids 9 and younger.

Free parking is available in a public lot on Westcott Street. Closed Monday.

Family Days

Take the kids to Family Days at the Museum of Fine Arts Houston—Bayou Bend on the third Sunday of the month from Sept through May. Highlights include games, music, crafts, and guided tours for the entire family. The best part? It's all free.

RIENZI $$
1406 Kirby Dr., in River Oaks, just east of River Oaks Country Club
(713) 639-7800
mfah.org/rienzi

Obsessed with European decor? Make a trip to Rienzi to see the Museum of Fine Arts Houston's decorative arts holdings, which date back several centuries. The museum makes its home in an exquisite River Oaks house that belonged to philanthropists Carroll Sterling Masterson and Harris Masterson III. Inside is an extensive display of European ceramics dating back to the early 1800s, English portraits, religious paintings from Spain and Italy, Worcester porcelain, and one-of-a-kind pieces of European furniture. The elaborate house sits on 4.4 acres, much of which are filled with gardens—some formal, others filled with native plants such as ferns. Depending on the season, visitors can enjoy dozens of different blooms, thanks to the Garden Club of Houston, which now maintains the gardens.

Guided tours of the house and gardens are available, but reservations are recommended. Admission, which includes the cost of the tour and parking, is $6 for adults and $4 for museum members, seniors 65 and up, college students, and kids 12 to 18 years old.

Kids under 12 get in free. On Sunday, admission is $5 for individuals of all ages, $10 for groups of 2 to 4 people, and $15 for groups of 5 or 6. Admission to the gardens is free. Free on-site parking is available if you take a tour; limited free parking is also available on side streets around Rienzi. Rienzi is closed Mon and Tues; the gardens are open daily.

> **i** Art collector? Houston's got dozens of great art galleries. Many represent artists whose work is showcased at some of the world's most prestigious art festivals and exhibits. Find a list of some of Houston's best galleries in the "Shopping" chapter.

＊THE ROTHKO CHAPEL   **FREE**
1409 Sul Ross St., between Yupon and Mulberry Streets, about 5 blocks west of Montrose Boulevard (Museum District)
(713) 524-9839
rothkochapel.org
This mesmerizing nonsectarian worship space was built after Menil Collection benefactors John and Dominique de Menil visited some of Europe's great churches in the 1950s. Wanting to develop a Houston worship space that would showcase great art, they enlisted architect Philip Johnson to create a chapel to house the paintings of artist Mark Rothko. The resulting octagon-shaped chapel opened in 1969. Inside this nonsectarian worship space hang 14 enormous Rothko paintings. Wooden benches can be used for resting, contemplation, or prayer. The tranquility of the space leads families of all faiths to use the Rothko Chapel for weddings; the chapel also hosts music and spiritual events, as well as guest speakers whose work focuses on social justice and environmentalism.

The Rothko Chapel is open daily. Admission is free, but donations are encouraged. There's free parking on Yupon and Sul Ross Streets. Wheelchair access is located at the north end of the chapel on Sul Ross.

HISTORY, CULTURE & SCIENCE MUSEUMS

＊THE HEALTH MUSEUM   **$$**
1515 Hermann Dr., between LaBranch and Crawford Streets, just east of the Hermann Park Golf Course (Museum District)
(713) 521-1515
thehealthmuseum.org
Fascinated by the body's inner workings? You won't want to miss The Health Museum—one of the country's only museums devoted to health.

Interactive exhibits here make this one of the city's can't-miss attractions—and a place sure to entertain visitors of all ages. Check out your internal organs in real time using a body scanner in "You: The Exhibit." And explore how living in Houston affects the body and how living elsewhere might affect your body differently. Or discover the importance of keeping arteries unclogged, the brain challenged, and bones exercised when you walk through an enormous human body in the Amazing Body Pavilion. You can also watch 4-D films about the body—complete with real scents, rain, lightning, and, of course, surround sound. Or visit the Challenge Gallery and test your reflexes, play Dance Dance Revolution, and try your hands (and brain) at puzzles and games. You'll also find special exhibits, such as "Cells: The Universe Inside Us." The Health Museum often collaborates with the Medical Center to host special events and family-friendly activities.

🔍 Close-up

Project Row Houses

Plenty of museums in Houston will help you appreciate great art, but few show you just how much art changes lives and communities. That's the job of **Project Row Houses**, some 40 houses and other properties spanning 6 blocks in the Third Ward, just southeast of downtown and east of the Texas Medical Center. The organization grew out of a longing among black artists in the Third Ward to use art and creativity to revitalize their poor neighborhood. Seven of these remodeled row houses have been transformed into artist studios and exhibit spaces. Although the exhibits showcase the work of artists from around the world, themes are always relevant to the Third Ward and the lives of its predominately black residents. Outside the exhibit spaces are colorful murals and smiling faces—evidence of Project Row Houses' profound impact on a community that was run-down when the organization launched in 1993.

Each year, Project Row Houses awards free studio space to three local artists, who participate in artist talks and exhibits and lead classes. The organization also sponsors an arts-in-education program, which allows schoolchildren to work with local artists so they can discover their inner artist—or hone already-uncovered talents. Programs are offered after school and in the summer in media such as photography, painting, creative writing, ceramics, music, and dance. There's even a program that helps struggling students with their homework. Project Row Houses also offers residential space to poor single mothers who are trying to finish school and launch a career.

Project Row Houses headquarters is located at 2521 Holman between St. Charles and Live Oak Streets in the Third Ward. Admission to exhibits and artist talks is free, though donations are requested. Parking can be found on the streets surrounding the main office. Closed Mon and Tues. Call (713) 526-7662 or visit projectrowhouses .org to learn about current exhibits and other programming.

Admission costs $8 for adults and $6 for kids ages 3 to 12 and seniors 65 and up. Kids 2 and younger get in free. The museum is also included on the Houston CityPass (page 121). Parking is available in the museum parking lot for $3 with the purchase of an admission ticket. Metered parking is also available along the streets surrounding the museum. Closed Mon, except from June through Aug.

ℹ️ **Need some fresh air during your visit to the sometimes-noisy Health Museum? Head outside to the Sensory Garden for a whiff of the flowers and a few quiet moments on a bench.**

✳HOLOCAUST MUSEUM HOUSTON   **FREE**
5401 Caroline St., about 1 block northeast of Binz St. and 3 blocks southeast of Main St. (Museum District)
(713) 942-8000
hmh.org

Apathy stops at Holocaust Museum Houston. Exhibits here revolve around the Holocaust, but you may leave thinking about hatred and intolerance more broadly.

The Holocaust Museum's permanent exhibit, dubbed "Bearing Witness: A Community Remembers," highlights the stories of Houston residents who survived the

⊙ Close-up

Eyes Wide Open: Orange Show Eyeopener Tours

Among Houstonians, the **Orange Show Center for Visionary Art** is best known for putting on the annual Art Car Parade (page 183). It's also known for celebrating other whimsical forms of art, such as mural art, a renovated Beer Can House (page 132), and the Orange Show Monument, a 3,000-square-foot outdoor monument built with mannequins, wagon wheels, tiles, tractor seats, and other found art.

But that's not all Orange Show offers. Several times a year the Orange Show Center provides an inside look at other unusual art, architecture, homes, and gardens on **Eyeopener Tours.** The goal? To show participants art they might never journey to see—or might never notice. So, some tours focus on Houston neighborhoods such as the Heights, some focus on themes such as glass artists and installations around Houston, and many visit other parts of Texas. Once a year, the Orange Show Center even takes lovers of eccentric art to other parts of the country. Previous trips have visited Wisconsin, Iowa, Minnesota, New Mexico, Ohio, Louisiana, the Carolinas, and Mexico. Whether the tour takes place in town or out, you'll explore public art displays, found art, artists' studios, intriguing architecture and music, and tasty meals. Tours around Houston last a few hours and cost $40 for Orange Show Center members and $60 for nonmembers. Trips outside the city last as long as 5 or 6 days and vary in price.

Want to take an Eyeopener Tour? Call (713) 926-6368 or visit orangeshow.org/tours. Sign up quickly because space is limited. The Orange Show Center is located at 2402 Munger St., 1 block south of the Gulf Freeway.

Holocaust. Using artifacts, photographs, art, written explanations, and a film, this exhibit follows local survivors' lives before the Holocaust, during Hitler's rise to power, and during their time in concentration camps. Also on permanent display are two examples of vehicles used to carry Holocaust victims and survivors. The 1942 World War II railcar is like those used to take millions of Jews and other outcasts to the concentration camps, and a 1942 Danish rescue boat is identical to those used to save more than 7,200 Jews from death.

After seeing these exhibits, you may want some time to reflect, and the museum has several places where you can do just that: the Lack Family Memorial Room, a reflection room with a Wall of Remembrance, a Wall of Tears, a Wall of Hope, and a Memorial Wall for honoring friends and relatives lost in the Holocaust. Meditative types can step outside the Memorial Room and into the Eric Alexander Garden of Hope, a small but beautiful garden that celebrates the memory of the children killed by the Nazis.

Want to learn even more about the Holocaust? Visit the Boniuk Library and Resource Center, which houses more than 4,000 books and 300 videos about World War II, the Holocaust, religion, and anti-Semitism. The library's archives also include thousands of original photographs, journals, letters, and other artifacts available for viewing.

Admission is free, but there's a suggested donation of $5. Guided tours are

available on Saturday and Sunday afternoons. Free parking is available in lots beside
the museum's Caroline Street entrance and
alongside the building on Calumet Street.

i You can take your camera into
just about every museum in town,
but keep the flash off and the fancy
equipment at home to stay on the
guards' good side.

✳HOUSTON MUSEUM OF
NATURAL SCIENCE $$$
**1 Hermann Circle Dr., between Caroline
and San Jacinto Streets in Hermann Park,
just east of Main and Fannin Streets
(Museum District)
(713) 639-4629
hmns.org**
You could tour the Houston Museum of Nat-
ural Science for a day or two and still not see
everything. But you're sure to be intrigued
by what you do see. Here you'll find per-
manent exhibits spanning astronomy and
space, oil and energy, chemistry, paleontol-
ogy, shells, Texas wildlife, dinosaurs, and rare
gems and minerals. Recent special exhibits
have explored the Lucy fossil, the work of Dr.
Seuss, and Jewish soldiers' roles in US wars.

Among the biggest draws here are the
Cockrell Butterfly Center and the Brown
Hall of Entomology, where butterflies flutter
around, sip nectar, and rest inside a simu-
lated tropical rain forest. Brown Hall is filled
with even more live insects and spiders,
including walking sticks, cockroaches, and
tarantulas. If you feel inspired after watch-
ing these creatures, visit the "Insects and
Us" section, where you can learn how to
build your own butterfly garden, ward off
mosquitoes (an essential skill in Houston),
and keep bees.

Other highlights here include the Burke
Baker Planetarium and nature-themed IMAX
films. Most IMAX movies are screened just
once or twice a day, so check the schedule
online or by calling (713) 639-4629. Purchase
tickets in advance and line up early to get
a good seat because IMAX movies often
sell out.

General admission is $15 for adults and
$10 for college students, seniors 62 and up,
and children ages 3 to 11. The museum
is also included on the Houston CityPass
(page 121). Admission to the Cockrell But-
terfly Center, Burke Baker Planetarium, and
Wortham Theater IMAX movies requires
additional tickets, which cost $8 for the
butterfly center for adults, $8 for the plan-
etarium for adults, and $11 for an IMAX
movie for adults. Seniors, students, and chil-
dren under 11 pay $7 to see the butterflies,
$7 to visit the planetarium, and $9 to see an
IMAX movie.

Paid parking is available in the museum
garage on Caroline Street; museum mem-
bers pay $5 and nonmembers who show
their museum ticket stub pay $10. Limited
parking is available on the streets around
the museum. The METRORail stops at the
"Museum District" stop, just 3 blocks from
the museum.

i Want to see a hot new exhibit?
Tickets often sell out days or even
weeks in advance, so buy yours early.
That's especially important for shows
at the Museum of Fine Arts Houston
and the Houston Museum of Natural
Science.

MUSEUMS

i Check out the National Museum of Funeral History's website (nmfh.org) for online-only exhibits and special Web accompaniments to the exhibits hosted at the museum.

NATIONAL MUSEUM OF FUNERAL HISTORY $$
415 Barren Springs Dr., at Ella Blvd., just west of I-45 and George Bush Intercontinental Airport and east of Kuykendahl Rd. in north Houston
(281) 876-3063
nmfh.org

The National Museum of Funeral History, located in north Houston, stays true to its slogan: "Any Day Above Ground is a Good One." This museum has the potential to be depressing, but most guests describe the exhibits as interesting and unexpected. Founded in 1992 by Houston funeral director Robert L. Waltrip, the museum traces the funeral industry's long history with a re-created 1900s casket factory that features artifacts from actual casket factories. Also on display are caskets used around the world and information about the burials of public figures, such as President John F. Kennedy. The museum hosts special exhibits and honors leading funeral and cemetery industry icons in the National Museum of Funeral History Hall of Fame. Perhaps the most amusing—yes, amusing—permanent exhibit here is the collection of over-the-top fantasy coffins created by Ghanaian sculptor Kane Quaye. These coffins resemble animals such as fish, lobsters, and roosters, as well as material objects such as airplanes and cars.

Admission is $10 for adults, $9 for seniors and veterans, $7 for kids 3 to 12, and free for kids under 3. There's free parking in the museum parking lot.

ATTRACTIONS

Houston's museums should be at the top of your list of places to visit, but these are hardly the only must-see sites here. Houston is also home to historic houses, one of the country's best zoos, a house made from beer cans, Space Center Houston, the pivotal battleground of the Texas Revolution, and an unusual tunnel system that's ripe for exploring. And that's not all. In this chapter, you'll learn about more spots that belong on your Houston "to do" list and places that don't fit neatly into other chapters. Several of these locales—City Hall, the Houston Tunnel System, the Heritage Society at Sam Houston Park, and Downtown Aquarium—are located downtown. Others like the Kemah Boardwalk and San Jacinto Battleground State Historic Site aren't technically located in Houston, even though they're among Houston's most definitive attractions. Only one—Williams Tower and Water Wall—is in the Galleria area. Nevertheless, all of these attractions—few as they might seem—are distinctively Houston. You'll find nothing else quite like them, even elsewhere in Texas.

PARKING MATTERS

Attractions that aren't located downtown usually offer free on-site parking. A couple of downtown attractions have their own parking lots; most don't. For these attractions, your best bet is one of the Theater District parking garages, which can be identified from the street by the lavender, aqua, and black Theater District Parking signs. These garages are spread out around the downtown theaters; the most convenient garages for each attraction are identified in the write-ups that follow. The parking fee ranges from free for 10 minutes up to $9 for 3 hours or more. Parking for special events and on weekends and holidays is $7, payable upon entry. A map with the parking garages can be found on page x of this book.

Price Code

Admission to a few Houston attractions is free, but most charge somewhere between $5 and $15, sales tax excluded. Typically, discounts are available for children and guests over 65.

Plan to see several attractions plus a museum or two? Avoid ticket lines and save money by purchasing a Houston CityPass. This $39 pass will get you into Space Center Houston, the Downtown Aquarium, and the Houston Zoo (or The Health Museum)—as well as the Houston Museum of Natural Science and either the Museum of Fine Arts Houston or the Children's Museum of Houston. Learn more about the CityPass on page 121.

Most attractions listed here are open daily, although hours often vary depending on the season. Play it safe by calling ahead.

$. . . . . .Less than $8
$$ . . . .$8 to $12
$$$ . . . . More than $12

THE BEER CAN HOUSE $
**222 Malone St. between Memorial Dr.
and Washington Ave.**
(713) 926-6368
beercanhouse.org

Seen your share of historic houses? You've probably never seen anything quite like Houston's Beer Can House. In 1968 retired Southern Pacific Railroad upholsterer John Milkovisch started inserting marbles, rocks, and metal pieces into redwood and concrete to create landscape art in his yard. Once he'd covered the entire yard, he moved on to the house—only he decided to cover it with some unusual aluminum siding. Over the next 18 years, he covered the entire house with an estimated 50,000 flattened beer cans—all from beers he and his wife, Mary, consumed. After the Milkovischs died, the Orange Show Center for Visionary Art acquired their home and restored it. Today, this one-of-a-kind house is open for public visits. Admission to the Beer House grounds costs $2; guided tours cost $5. The Beer Can House is only open on Sat and Sun from noon to 5 p.m.

i For a close-up look at Houston's architecture, take a guided walking tour on Saturday morning. Several tours are offered, including one through Montrose, one exploring downtown architecture between Hermann Square and Discovery Green, and one along Buffalo Bayou. Tours cost $10. Call the Architecture Center Houston (713-520-0155) or visit aiahouston.org for details.

DOWNTOWN AQUARIUM $–$$$
410 Bagby St., at Memorial Dr.
(713) 223-3474
**aquariumrestaurants.com/downtown
aquariumhouston**

Houston's Downtown Aquarium is home to 8 one-of-a-kind "adventure exhibits," a couple paying homage to the Gulf of Mexico region. The Louisiana Swamp exhibit, for instance, celebrates Texas's eastern neighbor with re-created Gulf Coast marshes and bayous that introduce you to some of the state's slimier residents—alligator snapping turtles, crayfish, spotted gar, and good ol' dwarf alligators.

The Gulf of Mexico exhibit, meanwhile, offers a look at the nurse sharks, snapper, and other aquatic creatures that live around the gulf's offshore rigs. Also not to be missed are the aquarium's international exhibits, which include a sunken temple that showcases a 20-foot tiger reticulated python and other species from a lost Mayan civilization, as well as the white tigers—yes, tigers—that strut around the replicated ruins of an ancient Indian temple.

When all of the marine biology lessons start wearing you or the kids out, head outdoors to play carnival-style games, ride a carousel featuring plastic alligators, or take in some of the best views of the Houston skyline on the Diving Bell Ferris Wheel. Then visit the Aquarium restaurant, where you'll dine surrounded by a 150,000-gallon aquarium. Or visit the Dive Lounge, where you'll find the usual beers and thematically named martinis and specialty drinks like the Redfish Rita, a margarita with cranberry juice.

Aquarium admission is $6.25 for kids ages 2 to 12, $9.25 for adults, $8.25 for seniors 65 and up, and free for kids under

2. Don't be fooled, though. A trip to the aquarium can add up quickly. Rides aren't included in general admission, so you'll pay an extra $2.99 to $4.99 per ride. Want to make a day of it? Buy the All-Day Adventure Pass for $15.99 per person; this allows you to see all of the exhibits and ride as many rides as you want. On-site parking is available for $6; valet parking is available in front of the aquarium for $8.

i While you're downtown, stop by Allen's Landing at 1001 Commerce St. and Main. This is where August C. and John K. Allen landed and laid claim to Houston in 1836. It's often referred to as Houston's "Plymouth Rock."

✳GEORGE RANCH HISTORICAL PARK $$
10215 FM 762, Richmond
(281) 343-0218
georgeranch.org
George Ranch Historical Park is only about 30 minutes southwest of downtown Houston, but it seems like a world away. This 23,000-acre working ranch was the home of Henry and Nancy Jones and three generations of their descendants. Founded in 1824, the ranch actually predates Texas's independence from Mexico.

Tours of each of the four generations' spacious homes put the ranch's 185-year history into perspective: The oldest home, the Henry and Nancy Jones Homestead, features outdoor kitchens, activities like weaving and corn grinding, and crops that you can help harvest. At Polly and William Ryon's post–Civil War home, you'll learn how the ranch expanded after the war and swap stories with a charming actor playing the part of Colonel William Ryon. The Davis Mansion, which dates back to the 1890s, sheds light on the work of sharecroppers and blacksmiths and features an old chuck wagon, a railroad car, and a longhorn pen. Built in the 1930s and inhabited by A. P. and Mamie George, the George Ranch House blends the past with the present as the resident cowboys rope, sort, and tend cattle before sending them off to one of the country's last remaining cattle dipping vats to rid them of fleas and ticks. George Ranch is also home to an authentic general store, actors clad in old-timey garb, and livestock aplenty. You can also grab burgers and sandwiches at the Dinner Belle Cafe. The park is situated around a mile long loop, enabling you to either walk from site to site, or get chauffeured from one stop to the next in a tractor-drawn tram.

Admission is $10 for adults, $9 for seniors 62 and older, and $5 for kids ages 5 to 15. Children 4 and younger get in for free.

Visit on Saturday when you can lunch on barbecue or pork in one of the houses. Menus change to reflect the site. Call to reserve your spot at one of these meals. They cost $12.50 for adults 16 and older, $9 for kids ages 5 to 15, and $4 for kids 4 and younger.

George Ranch Historical Park can be accessed from Houston by taking US 59 South and exiting at Grand Parkway/TX 99. Take a left at Crab River Road/FM 2759; the ranch is about 6 miles down the road. Closed Sun and Mon.

i George Ranch Historical Park aims to keep things authentic, so many buildings aren't air-conditioned. Dress accordingly and be sure to wear comfortable shoes that you don't mind getting muddy.

✴THE HERITAGE SOCIETY AT
SAM HOUSTON PARK   FREE–$$

Sam Houston Park in downtown
Houston
1100 Bagby, between McKinney St. and
Allen Pkwy.
(713) 655-1912
heritagesociety.org

At the northwest edge of downtown sits the beautifully landscaped Sam Houston Park, which is now home to eight carefully restored homes and a church dating back to the 1800s and early 1900s. Thanks to The Heritage Society, it's possible to tour these buildings, each of which has played a distinctive role in Houston's history.

The park dates back to 1900 when Houston mayor Sam Brashier purchased the Kellum-Noble House and land—then considered the edge of town—and turned the area into Sam Houston Park. The Kellum-Noble House—the oldest brick house in Houston—was built in 1847 and became home to one of the city's first private schools. A brick kiln and a sawmill were also operated on the Kellum-Noble property. When the house faced demolition in 1954, locals formed The Heritage Foundation to save it. The Kellum-Noble House is the only restored building in Sam Houston Park that remains at its original site.

The seven other homes and St. John Church, which German farmers built in northwest Harris County in 1891, have been moved here from other locations around the city and Harris County. Among the most notable properties in the park are Yates House, 4th Ward Cottage, Nichols-Rice-Cherry House, Pillot House, and the Old Place.

Yates House was built in Houston's Fourth Ward by former slave, education advocate, and religious leader Rev. Jack Yates in 1870, just 5 years after he was freed. Predating the Yates House is **4th Ward Cottage,** the oldest known "workingman house" in Houston and part of Houston's black "Freedman's Town" neighborhood, where blacks lived, worked, and played in the years after the Emancipation Proclamation was signed. The Greek Revival–style **Nichols-Rice-Cherry House** was owned by William Marsh Rice, whose estate established Rice University. One of the city's first attached kitchens lies in the Victorian-era **Pillot House.** A true log cabin, the **Old Place** dates back to 1823 and is believed to be the oldest building in Harris County. Along with the period artifacts found in each building, you can find hundreds of antique phonographs, textiles, tools, silver, toys, and decorative works in the **Heritage Society Museum** at the corner of Bagby Street and Lamar Street.

Admission to The Heritage Society Museum is free. To go inside the houses and church, you'll need to take a guided tour, which lasts about an hour and 15 minutes. Tours are free for guests 18 and under, $10 for adults, and $8 for seniors 65 and up. Free parking is available off Allen Parkway going into downtown. The parking lot is behind a big white brick building—the Kellum-Noble House. Planning to tour the houses on Sunday? Make reservations since fewer tours are offered that day. Closed Mon.

i Don't have time for a full guided tour? Bring your cell phone and dial a designated phone number in front of each of the restored buildings. For nothing more than a few cell phone minutes, you'll get the Cliffs Notes version of their history.

HOUSTON CITY HALL   FREE
901 Bagby St.
Reflection pool and main entrance
located on Smith Street, between
McKinney Street and Walker Street
(832) 393-0943
houstontx.gov/cao/cityhalltours.html
At just 11 stories tall, Houston's City Hall may look small and insignificant compared to the towering buildings nearby. But don't be fooled: This symbol of Houston government is a spectacular building—one that was criticized for being "ultramodern" when Austin architect Joseph Finger designed it in the late 1930s. The building was also criticized for having private showers for each city council member, as well as a private elevator for the mayor, which some speculate may still be in use.

The art deco–style structure, which was one of the first air-conditioned office buildings, has outlasted that early criticism, making its way into the National Register of Historic Places. City Hall is faceted with Texas Cordova limestone, and the lobby walls are lined with marble. Aluminum medallions of legendary "lawgivers" like Thomas Jefferson, Moses, and Julius Caesar sit above the building's main entryways. Lining the ceiling of the first-floor lobby is a bold-colored, gold-leafed mural featuring the Western Hemisphere, with Houston at its center.

Above City Hall's main front entrance sits a stone sculpture with two men taming a wild horse. It's said to depict people teaming up to govern the world around them. This entrance opens onto a large reflecting pool in Martha Hermann Square, where festivals, concerts, and protests are frequently held.

Free tours of City Hall offer a peek at the city council chambers, the Mayor's Proclamation Room, council offices, the rotunda and reflection pool, and a documentary about Houston. Touring City Hall requires planning ahead, though. Free tours for individuals are only offered on the fourth Thursday afternoon of each month; groups of 10 to 40 people can tour City Hall on the second Monday morning of each month and on the fourth Thursday afternoon. Tour registration ends at noon 2 weeks—yes, 2 weeks—before the scheduled tour. If there aren't enough people signed up for the tour at that point, City Hall may nix the tour altogether. Likewise, if more than 40 people are signed up, you'll have to wait until the next tour date. Tours meet in the City Hall Annex behind City Hall at 900 Bagby St.

Parking is available in several nearby Theater District garages, including two at Rusk Street at Bagby Street, one at Walker at Bagby Street, and one at Capitol Street and Smith. Signs inside the garages will point you toward City Hall and the City Hall Annex.

i Want to relax or just let the kids run around during your visit to City Hall? Pack a picnic lunch and eat on one of the benches around the reflection pool in Martha Hermann Square or across the street at Tranquility Park.

HOUSTON TUNNEL SYSTEM   FREE
Entrances located inside buildings
throughout downtown
houstontx.gov/abouthouston/
exploringtunnels.html
Houston doesn't have a subway system, but Houstonians who work and play downtown still spend time underground. About 20 feet below downtown Houston are 6 miles worth

of tunnels, most of them interconnected. Inspired by New York City's Rockefeller Center, these air-conditioned tunnels link hotels, office buildings, banks, theaters, and City Hall. The tunnel system—or the tunnels, as locals call them—often gets credit for offering a reprieve from the heat, rain, and humidity.

From the beginning, the tunnels have also had a commercial dimension. Entrepreneur Will Horwitz built the first tunnels in the 1930s because he was going to have to excavate the basements of three movie theaters he was building downtown. He figured he might as well build tunnels to connect the theaters, which have since been replaced by The Houston Club and the JPMorgan Chase Tower, both on Capitol Street. Horwitz also opened an arcade and a wine tavern in the tunnels. The tavern and the arcade are now gone, but the tunnels are filled with shops, restaurants, dry cleaners, eyeglass stores, salons, barber shops, printing shops, florists, and just about every other service or shop a busy professional might need. The tunnel system, which connects some 95 city blocks, also links with a number of skywalks and connects most of the major buildings. The Harris County courts, jails, and other legal facilities—all located in northern downtown from Franklin Street on the north to Preston on the south—have their own tunnel system, which doesn't connect to the other downtown tunnels. The Toyota Center, the Downtown Aquarium, Minute Maid Park, and the George R. Brown Convention Center are not part of the tunnel system.

The tunnels can be accessed from street-level stairs, elevators, or escalators inside any building that's part of the tunnel system. Street access is also available at Wells Fargo Plaza, located on Louisiana Street between McKinney and Lamar. Check out the Downtown map on page x to see where the tunnels lie and what buildings they connect.

Most tunnels are only open on weekdays from 6 a.m. to 6 p.m. However, the tunnels connecting Wortham Theater Center, Bayou Place, Jones Plaza, Jones Hall, and the Alley Theatre are also open before, during, and immediately after theater performances.

Take a guided tour of the Downtown Houston Tunnel System through Discover Houston Tours. The 3-hour tours include a 1-hour round-trip ride on METRORail, a walk through the tunnels, and a food stop. Call (713) 222-9255 or visit discoverhoustontours.com for details.

i Visiting the tunnel system? Stop in at the JPMorgan Chase Tower, the tallest building in Texas. Take the elevator to the observation deck on the 60th floor, where you can see Spanish sculptor Joan Miró's colorful "Personage with Birds" and check out Houston from the highest public viewpoint.

*HOUSTON ZOO $-$$
6200 Golf Course Dr., at North
MacGregor Dr. (inside Hermann Park)
(713) 533-6500
houstonzoo.org
The Houston Zoo has an array of exhibits to please the entire family. Home to more than 4,500 animals, zoo's residents represent more than 900 species, including rare breeds like greater kudu, sifaka, and giant eland.

One of the hottest exhibits is the 6.5-acre African Forest, where you can view ostriches, rhinos, chimps, giraffes and other creatures during a 1-hour guided tour (tours must be scheduled 3 weeks in advance and cost $35 for nonmembers and $15 for members). Younger kids won't feel left out, as the John P. McGovern Zoo was designed with little ones in mind. They can interact with sheep and goats, ride the carousel, explore exhibits, or play on the playground to run off some excess energy.

A new and appealing exhibit is the 4-DExperience, which is made up of short 3-D family-friendly films that include effects that stimulate nearly all the senses. For a change of pace, try the water park, where kids can splash and play to cool off and give mom and dad a break.

The zoo is open every day except Christmas. During daylight saving time (from Mar to Nov), the zoo is open from 9 a.m. to 7 p.m., and during Central Standard Time (from Nov to Mar), it is open from 9 a.m. to 6 p.m. Plan ahead, because the last visitors are admitted 1 hour before closing time. Parking is free in the lot on Golf Course Drive. Other parking, for a fee, is available near the Houston Museum of Natural Science, or Memorial Hermann Medical Plaza at 6400 Fannin St. To take the guesswork out of going to the zoo, try taking the METRORail to the Memorial Hermann Hospital/Houston Zoo stop.

i Enjoy free videos and photos of zoo exhibits—complete with real-time GPS coordinates—by downloading the zoo's mobile app on your phone. The free app is available in both the iTunes App Store and Android Marketplace. Just search for "Houston Zoo."

KEMAH BOARDWALK $$$
215 Kipp Ave., Kemah
(877) 285-3624
kemahboardwalk.com
Want to escape the city (or the suburbs) for an afternoon or evening? Join the crowds of Houston families and young couples who head to the Kemah Boardwalk in Kemah, about 30 miles south of downtown. With restaurants, games and rides, souvenir shops, live music, and tranquil views of Galveston Bay, this entertainment district offers something for just about everyone.

Children, for instance, love the Stingray Reef, which allows them to watch—and touch—stingrays as they swim past. Kids—and kids at heart—also love the amusement park. Little ones enjoy riding the two-story carousel, the Kemah Train, and the Balloon Wheel, while older kids and adults get a thrill from scream-inducing rides such as the Broadway Bullet roller coaster and the quick-falling Drop Zone. An all-day ride pass costs $16.99 for guests under 48 inches tall and $19.99 for guests 48 inches and taller. Individual rides cost between $3.50 and $5.99.

You'll find even more thrills onboard the Boardwalk Beast, an open-deck speedboat painted to look like a shark. This 25-minute ride speeds out into Galveston Bay at 40 miles an hour and almost no one gets off the boat dry. But between the music, views, and other entertainment, it's hard to complain. For a slower ride—and alcoholic and non-alcoholic drink options—ride the Boardwalk Beast in the evening. Tickets cost $15 for adults and $12 for kids 12 and under; they can be purchased on-site.

All the restaurants here are owned by Landry's, a popular seafood chain that launched in nearby Katy in the 1980s. Currently, the Boardwalk is home to about 10 restaurants, plus a coffee shop and an ice cream shop. They range from the kid-friendly Pizza Oven, Joe's Crab Shack, and Saltgrass Steak House to the chic Red Sushi. Classic seafood and some of the best views of Galveston Bay can be found at Landry's Seafood House, while good margaritas and decent Tex-Mex can be found at the noisy Cadillac Bar.

To reach Kemah, take the South Loop to TX 225 East, then take TX 146 South to Bayport Boulevard. Take a left at 6th Street and another left at Bradford Street. On-site parking is free on weekdays; on weekends and holidays, you'll have to pay $6 to park in the surface lots or $7 to park in the garage or lot closest to the boardwalk.

i Want to learn about Houston's most architecturally and historically significant areas? Take one of the Greater Houston Preservation Alliance's walking tours on the second Sunday of the month. The docent-led tours cost $10 per person. Learn more by calling (713) 216-5000 or visiting ghpa.org/tours.

*SAINT ARNOLD BREWING COMPANY $

2000 Lyons Ave.
(713) 686-9494
saintarnold.com

Beer aficionados, this one's for you: Saint Arnold Brewing Company is Texas's oldest craft brewery. Named for the patron saint of brewing, Saint Arnold of Metz, Saint Arnold Brewing Company was opened by two Rice University alums in 1994. Today the brewery makes several ales, an IPA, a wheat beer, seasonal pilsners, bocks, ales, and stouts. Saint Arnold also makes its own root beer.

On weekdays from 3 to 4:15 p.m. and on Sat from 11 a.m. to 2 p.m., Houstonians young and old visit to learn about the brewery and its beers—and sample them. Admission costs $7 in cash, and includes a tour of the brewery as well as a tall shooter glass that can be filled with samples during your visit. Weekday tours are offered at 3:30 p.m. On Sat, tours are offered at noon, 1, and 2 p.m. Saturday tours tend to fill up, so arrive at least a half-hour early since the brewery limits the number of people allowed on tours.

Many people bring small kids here so don't worry about getting a babysitter. It's also A-OK to bring a pizza or other food to lunch on before the tour.

The brewery is located in an old three-story brick building just north of downtown.

i Take your own large beer mug to Saint Arnold Brewing Company to get larger samples during your tour.

*SAN JACINTO BATTLEGROUND STATE HISTORIC SITE $–$$

1 Monument Circle, La Porte
Battleship *Texas:* (281) 479-2431
battleshiptexas.org
San Jacinto Museum of History:
(281) 479-2421
sanjacinto-museum.org

The San Jacinto Battleground State Historic Site is a war history buff's dream come true: it's home to the San Jacinto Museum of History, the San Jacinto Monument, *and* the battleship *Texas,* While San Antonio's Alamo may be Texas's most recognizable battle site to non-Texans, the San Jacinto Battleground is just as important. It helped put Houston on the map by landing the city's namesake—General Sam Houston—a spot in history books. This is where General

Houston and his Texas revolutionaries surprised Mexico's General Antonio López de Santa Anna and his army on April 21, 1836, and took control of their camp in a mere 18 minutes. This victory led to Texas's independence from Mexico and the state's eventual annexation by the United States.

That battle—known as the Battle of San Jacinto—is now commemorated by the San Jacinto Monument, which is billed as the world's tallest monument tower. Built in the art-deco style, the 570-foot monument shaft is topped with a 34-foot, 220-ton star made of concrete, stone, and steel. Inside the monument is the San Jacinto Museum of History, which is chock-full of artifacts that span Texas's long history before, during, and after the Battle of San Jacinto. Among the artifacts on display here are Sam Houston's personal dictionary, Mayan art, arrowheads, and manuscripts from New Spain, Texas, the US, and Mexico. The museum is open daily from 9 a.m. to 6 p.m. In the Jesse H. Jones Theatre for Texas Studies, you can also watch *Texas Forever!!*, a film about the Battle of San Jacinto. The 35-minute film is screened every hour on the hour from 10 a.m. to 6 p.m. Tickets cost $3.50 for children 11 and younger, $4 for seniors 65 and older, and $4.50 for adults.

To get the lay of the battleground, take a 500-foot elevator ride to the observation deck near the top of the monument. You'll enjoy a great view of the battleground below and—with the help of the deck's high-powered binoculars—some of the best views of Houston and the Houston Ship Channel. Admission costs $3 for children 11 and younger, $3.50 for seniors 65 and up, and $4 for adults.

If you still haven't gotten your war history fix, visit the battleship *Texas*, which is permanently affixed to the Buffalo Bayou and the Houston Ship Channel. Although the *Texas* is anchored by the battleground, its place in history dates back to World Wars I and II, not the Texas Revolution. The *Texas* was extremely powerful in her day: She was the first US battleship to mount aircraft guns, the first to launch an aircraft, and the first recipient of a commercial radar. Today you can walk around the deck, test out unloaded antiaircraft guns, and see the infirmary, living quarters, mess areas, and other sections of the restored battleship. Admission to the *Texas* costs $10 for ages 13 and up and $5 for seniors 65 and up. Kids 12 and under get in free.

The battleground site is just a few miles south of Houston along the Houston Ship Channel. To get there, drive south on the aptly named Sam Houston Tollway/Beltway 8 and cross the Houston Ship Channel. Then exit TX 225 East/Texas Independence Highway and take the road to La Porte. Exit at Battleground Road and take a left. Stay in the left lane when the road separates, and continue through the park's stone gates.

There's free on-site parking, but the Texas Parks and Wildlife Department charges an additional $1 per person to enter the battleground site. There is no additional charge for admission to the San Jacinto Museum of History or the battleship *Texas*.

i After your visit to San Jacinto Battleground State Historic Site, take a free—if at times industrial-scented—ride on the Lynchburg Ferry, which stops less than a mile from the battleground site. Just drive northeast on Battleground Road/TX 134, and you'll run into the ferry stop.

*SPACE CENTER HOUSTON $$$

1601 NASA Pkwy.
(281) 244-2100
spacecenter.org

Got kids in tow—and little time to see the sites of Houston? Space Center Houston should be at the top of your list. This is the official visitor center of NASA's Lyndon B. Johnson Space Center, home to NASA's Mission Control and the location where all US astronauts train. (And yes, they still train even though the human spaceflight program has ended.)

Space Center Houston offers hands-on and informational exhibits and activities tracing the history of spaceflight. In the Blast Off Theater, you'll feel like you're actually traveling in space. That's because simulated shuttle exhaust blows into the room while large monitors air live updates about the exploration of Mars and astronauts' training activities. Visit the "Feel of Space" exhibit to see how astronauts shower, eat, and live on the space station. Then, head to Kids Space Place to let the kids fly a space shuttle. Other can't-miss exhibits feature old spacesuits, artifacts, and space shuttle hardware.

Get the scoop on each exhibit by taking an Astronaut Audio Tour. These digital tours are narrated by astronaut greats like John Glenn, Gene Cernan, Alan Bean, Shannon Lucid, and Eileen Collins; different versions are available for kids.

General admission costs $22.95 for adults, $21.95 for seniors 65 and older, and $18.95 for kids 4 to 11. Get $5 off by purchasing and printing your tickets online before your visit. Space Center Houston is also included on the Houston CityPass (page 121).

For a little extra dough, you can participate in some of Space Center Houston's exclusive programs:

During **Lunch with an Astronaut,** you'll eat lunch with an astronaut, hear firsthand war stories, and get a personalized lithograph. Tickets for this 1-hour program cost $49.95 per adult and $29.95 per child; your ticket includes general admission to Space Center Houston. Tickets must be purchased in advance; purchase yours online. Spots are limited.

The 4- to 5-hour **Level Nine Tour** will take you inside Mission Control and give you a close-up look at the space vehicle mock-up area, as well as the Space Environment Simulation Lab and the Neutral Buoyancy Lab where the astronauts train. You'll even eat lunch in the cafeteria where astronauts and NASA employees eat. Purchase tickets in advance online. Tours are offered Mon through Fri, but only 12 people are allowed on each one. Tickets cost a hefty $89.95 per person, and kids under 14 are not allowed on the tour.

Space Center Houston is located about 25 miles south of downtown near Clear Lake. To get there, take I-45 south toward Galveston, then take exit 25 for NASA Parkway/TX 1. Drive east and follow the signs for the Johnson Space Center.

> **i** Take note: NASA Parkway was previously named NASA Road 1, so an outdated map or GPS may not account for the name change.

WILLIAMS TOWER AND
WATER WALL FREE

2800 Post Oak Blvd.
(713) 526-6461

It may be only the third tallest building in town, but the Williams Tower is one of the most recognizable buildings in Houston. At 64 stories tall, this Galleria-area tower is visible from points all over the city on clear days. That, along with short buildings surrounding it, gives Williams Tower a leg up on the 75-story JPMorgan Chase building and the 71-floor Wells Fargo Plaza—the city's first- and second-tallest buildings, which blend in among the towering structures that dot the downtown skyline. On clear nights, a light at the top of the Williams Tower beams nearly 40 miles. Unfortunately, security-related concerns have led to the permanent closure of the 51st-floor observation deck, which provided one of the best views of Houston. So, the biggest draw *inside* the Williams Tower is now the building's first-floor art gallery, which features special exhibits of contemporary artists. The gallery is open on weekdays; admission is free.

By far the biggest draw here is the Water Wall, a semicircular fountain that sits amid 188 heritage live oak trees on the tower's south side. The wall is 64 feet tall, with 1 foot for each floor of the Williams Tower. Plenty of picnickers, young families, tourists, and restless teenagers enjoy the Water Wall, but this spot is perhaps most popular among romantics: Plenty of couples have shared their first kiss or gotten engaged or married near the wall, small water droplets splashing on their faces. Water flows down the wall every day from 8 a.m. to 9 p.m., though it does shut off early on occasion.

Located near the intersection of Loop 610 and US 59, Williams Tower and Water Wall is just a block from the Galleria mall. To access the tower and Water Wall from Loop 610, exit at Westheimer Road and head west. Then take a left on South Post Oak. Williams Tower will be on the right, just after you pass West Alabama Street and before you hit Hidalgo Street. Parking is available in the Williams Tower garage on West Alabama Street. During the day, parking costs $2 to $12, depending on how long you stick around. Free parking is available in the garage—as well as on surrounding streets—on weekends and after 6 p.m. on weekdays.

PARKS

With so many miles of freeways and roads, Houston can sometimes look like a concrete jungle. But Houston—or H-town, as we locals sometimes call it—is also home to countless acres of parks and greenery. Today the Houston Parks and Recreation Department maintains some 350 parks, as well as more than 200 esplanades and other green spaces. And that's not even all of the area parks: Just southwest of Houston is a major state park, Brazos Bend State Park, and around the city are more than 50 parks operated by Harris County.

OVERVIEW

With so many parks, you've got a wealth of recreational opportunities here. Want to bike at a velodrome? There's a park for that. Want to practice shooting or go camping? We've got parks where you can do those things, too. Love nature? Get your fill of wildlife watching at Brazos Bend State Park and the Houston Arboretum & Nature Center in Memorial Park. With several parks located along Buffalo Bayou, there are also opportunities to canoe, kayak, or fish right in the middle of the city. Houston's even got skate parks, which you can learn about in the "Recreation" chapter. And of course, many of our parks also have picnic areas, playgrounds, basketball and tennis courts, soccer and baseball fields, off-leash dog areas, and shaded trails for hiking, biking, walking, and running.

The parks here aren't just for solo visits or small gatherings, though: Parks like Hermann Park and Discovery Green bring Houstonians and visitors together for festivals and special events throughout the year. Groups also use the parks for special family or neighborhood events, weddings,

company picnics, and sports tournaments on park fields. Organized events like these require a permit, so contact the Houston Parks and Recreation Department (713-865-4500) if you're planning a sizeable gathering.

The majority of parks here are the smaller neighborhood variety sprinkled throughout the city. Most have publicly accessible playgrounds and some also have pools, tennis and basketball courts, and soccer or baseball fields. Although the playgrounds and other open areas are typically open to the public, pools, athletic courts, and fields are often available only to neighborhood residents or groups that reserve the area in advance.

Because there are so many parks in the Houston area, it's impossible to list and describe them all. The parks in this chapter are among the city's biggest, best, and most visited.

With the exception of Brazos Bend State Park, all of the parks listed in this chapter are located in Houston proper. For a complete list of Houston-area parks, visit the websites of the **Houston Parks and Recreation**

The Price of the Drought: What to Expect

Record drought and heat left many state and local parks in dire straits. Some parks have suffered from wildfires and dead trees. Others have seen their fishing stock depleted or their water dried up. So, if it's still uncharacteristically dry when you read this book, call to make sure the parts of the park you want to visit are currently open.

Department (houstonparks.org), **Harris County** (hctx.net/parks/park.asp), and the **Buffalo Bayou Conservancy** (buffalobayou .org). Maps of the listed parks can be downloaded from their corresponding websites.

Parking is free at most area parks, though you may have to pay for a spot when visiting urban parks like Discovery Green and Hermann Park.

BRAZOS BEND STATE PARK
21901 FM 762, Needville
(979) 553-5102
tpwd.state.tx.us
Located about 30 miles southwest of Houston in Needville, Brazos Bend State Park is a big hit among outdoor enthusiasts. Opened by the state in 1984, this 5,000-acre oasis runs along the Brazos River, which was used to transport cotton and for other commerce in the 1800s. The park's history appears to go back much further, though: Artifacts found here suggest that people have been visiting Brazos Bend State Park for thousands of years.

The park's Brazos River location makes for plenty of camping and fishing opportunities—as well as occasional alligator and freshwater snake sightings. The expansive park is also lined with wooded hiking and biking trails, including the Creekfield Lake Nature Trail, where you can see and learn about different wetlands creatures from interpretive panels. On weekends, the park offers free guided hikes. Visit the Nature Center to participate in an upcoming hike. While you're there, check out the Habits and Niches display, where you can touch and learn more about local wildlife.

General admission to the park is $7; it's $5 per day if you're camping overnight. Kids 12 and under get in free. Camping fees range from $7 to $25 per night for individuals and families, depending on how primitive the campsite is.

i Looking for a fun date night or a family adventure? Head to Brazos Bend State Park on Saturday from 3 to 11 p.m. That's when the Houston Museum of Natural Science–owned George Observatory is open for stargazing. The observatory owns one of the largest publicly accessible domed telescopes, which makes for some unbelievable views of the sky. Tickets cost $5 in addition to the cost of admission to the park. Call (281) 242-3055 for details.

✳BUFFALO BAYOU PARK AND ELEANOR TINSLEY PARK
18–3600 Allen Pkwy. and Memorial Dr., from Shepherd Dr. to Bagby St.
buffalobayou.org/parks.html
Nearly 125 acres of greenbelt and bayou water along Allen Parkway comprise Buffalo Bayou Park. With the park approaching

Canoe & Kayak Rentals

Canoes and kayaks aren't available for rent at Buffalo Bayou Park. But they can be rented by calling one of these companies:

REI
7538 Westheimer Rd.
(713) 353-2582
rei.com

ACK Canoesport
5822 Bissonnet
(713) 660-7000
austinkayak.com

Southwest Paddlesports
26322 I-45, Spring
(281) 292-5600
paddlesports.com

downtown, Buffalo Bayou Park offers magnificent views of Houston's skyline, as well as leisure opportunities aplenty. Many Houstonians run or walk along this greenbelt's trails, which include a number of stretching stations. Public art decorates the park—most notably in the Buffalo Bayou Artpark, which displays public art from the community. Buffalo Bayou flows through the Buffalo Bayou Park, making it possible to canoe or kayak from one of the park's two canoe launches to other locations on the bayou, including downtown's Sesquicentennial Park. (One canoe launch is located on the park's north side; the other is on the south end in Eleanor Tinsley Park, discussed below.)

Other highlights include the Jim Mozola Memorial Disc Golf Course on the park's north side just west of Sabine Street and a section for dogs and their owners to play (2700 block of Allen Parkway at Studewood; see the "Dog Parks" Close-up on page 152). There's also a Mayan-inspired Police Officers'

Memorial, although it's hard to access from most parts of the park. The easiest way to reach the memorial is by parking in the lot at 2400 Memorial Dr.

On the park's south side sits Eleanor Tinsley Park, the site of the city's annual 4th of July Freedom Over Texas fireworks show (page 184). The rest of the year, families visit Eleanor Tinsley Park to play on the playground, admire the Gus Wortham Fountain, let their dogs play, and check out the Mexican free-tailed bat colony living under the Waugh Bridge, located at Waugh Street between Allen Parkway and Memorial Drive. Unless the temperature drops below 50 or the sky is cloudy or foggy, you can see the bats emerge from the bridge at dusk. You'll find the best bat-gazing views on the bridge or the north bayou bank, just east of the bridge in Buffalo Bayou Park.

If you want an up-close look at where the bats live, take one of the Buffalo Bayou Partnership's Bat Colony Pontoon Boat Tours. They're typically offered on the second and fourth Friday evenings of the month. Visit buffalobayou.org or call (713) 752-0314, ext. 4, for details.

i North Lake Conroe Paddling Company offers guided kayaking trips along Buffalo Bayou about once a month. Tours cost $60 per person and include gear rental and mini kayak lessons. Call (936) 203-2697 or visit northlakeconroepaddlingco.com for details.

CULLEN PARK
19008 Saums Rd., just north of I-10
(713) 837-0311
houstontx.gov/parks/ourparks/
cullenpark.html

Located on Houston's west side just east of Katy, Cullen Park sits in Addicks Reservoir, an open flood-zone space used to retain storm water and prevent flooding. The 9,200-acre park rarely floods, though, and is filled with recreational opportunities. Among them: the requisite picnic areas with barbecue grills, baseball and soccer fields, a water playground, and more than 8 miles of hiking and biking trails. The trails take you past beautiful oak trees, a cemetery, and flora, but it's not uncommon for weeds or litter to line the trails. Depending on the season, you might see armadillos, deer, and snakes. Some of these snakes are venomous so watch your step and keep your eyes on young children. Want to practice your archery skills? Take your bow to the archery range on the park's east side at 13751 Clay Rd.

Cullen Park is also home to Alkek Velodrome, a 333-meter outdoor cement track for cyclists. There are only about two dozen velodromes in the country, and people who use them are serious cyclists. So keep the little ones away because cyclists here won't be watching for them.

i **Lock your car and leave valuables at home when visiting Cullen Park. Thieves have been known to spoil parkgoers' fun by breaking into their vehicles.**

✳DISCOVERY GREEN
Downtown between McKinney and Lamar, 1 block east of Austin at La Branch
(713) 400-7336
discoverygreen.com
Discovery Green opened in 2008, but it's already one of Houston's most popular spots. This 12-acre downtown park is the brainchild of former mayor Bill White and the Discovery Green Conservancy, who wanted to convert old parking lots into urban green space that would serve as a recreational hub.

The park is across the street from the George R. Brown Convention Center and just a few blocks from Minute Maid Park, the Toyota Center, and more than a couple towering buildings. But the hustle and bustle of the city feels miles away when you enter Discovery Green, aka Disco Green. Maybe it's the 100-year-old oak trees, the lush grass, and the gardens filled with native plants. Or maybe it's the sight of children and adults navigating their rented remote-controlled sailboats along Kinder Lake.

Discovery Green is loved for more than its trees, grass, gardens, and lake, of course. Kids come here to play on the playground, run through Gateway Fountain, play with remote-controlled sailboats, and ice-skate on the Ice at Discovery Green (page 192) during the winter holiday season. Dogs love to come here to socialize and frolic in the Kinder Large Dog Run and Harriet and Joe Foster Dog Runs. And adults love to run along the 0.5-mile McNair Foundation jogging trail, admire the contemporary art installations, and play chess and bocce, which can be checked out for free from the whimsically decorated Art Carts around the park. Those who stay awhile often bring along a picnic or grab a drink or dinner at The Grove restaurant (page 59) overlooking the park.

Throughout the year, Houstonians flock to Discovery Green for special events and festivals. Among the biggest draws: the Glowarama New Year's Eve celebration (page 193) and the Houston International Jazz Festival (page 186). Also popular is Discovery

Green Flea, a unique market that sells kitsch, vintage, and repurposed collectibles and art; the market is open on the third Saturday of the month.

Yoga and Pilates classes, youth writing workshops, and bike repair workshops are regularly offered here, along with movie screenings, concerts, and theater events. Most, but not all, of these events are free. Visit the website to learn about upcoming events and pricing.

There's metered parking near Discovery Green, but free parking spots can be hard to come by during the summer, for special events, or on the weekend. Paid parking is available in the Convention District Parking garage at 1002 Avenida de las Americas, the Hilton Americas–Houston garage at 1600 Lamar, and the Houston Center garage at 1200 McKinney St. Prices vary.

GEORGE BUSH PARK
16756 Westheimer
(281) 496-2177
pct3.hctx.net/parks/georgebush.aspx
George Bush Park is the largest park run and owned by Harris County. Before being renamed in honor of 41st US president and Houston resident George H. W. Bush in 1997, it was named Cullen-Barker Park. Located in the far western part of the city, the park occupies about half of the 13,500-acre Barker Reservoir, which was built in the 1940s to control flooding. Here you'll find a playground that offers activities for children with physical limitations, two large soccer fields, and six baseball fields, only two of which are available for public use. Gun enthusiasts can also practice their shot at the American Shooting Center, while airplane aficionados can fly model airplanes in the Dick Scobee Memorial Flying Fields, named

after the commander of the space shuttle Challenger, which disintegrated just after launching in 1986.

Miles of biking, running, and even equestrian trails also fill the park, many running along Buffalo Bayou or smaller swamps and bodies of water, where visitors can go fishing. The trails are popular among runners and cyclists who find them easy to navigate. Although the park has trees here and there, shade is scarce.

Also inside the park, on the south end of Westheimer Parkway, is Millie Bush Dog Park, a spacious off-leash area named after George and Barbara Bush's now-deceased springer spaniel. See the "Dog Parks" Close-up on page 152 for details.

✱HERMANN PARK
Fannin Street between North McGregor and Hermann Drive
(713) 524-5876
hermannpark.org
Since opening in 1914, Hermann Park has been one of Houston's most popular recreational destinations. The 445-acre park isn't just a great place to jog, golf, nap, or just enjoy a pretty day; it's also home to three of the city's biggest attractions—the Houston Zoo (page 136), the Houston Museum of Natural Science (page 129), and Miller Outdoor Theatre (page 115).

A giant statue of Sam Houston greets visitors who enter the park from Fannin onto Hermann Drive. To the left is the Houston Museum of Natural Science and, a little farther down, the Houston Garden Center, which is surrounded by more than 2,500 rosebushes. To the right is the bulk of the park, which includes about 2 miles of well-shaded trails for walking and jogging, as well as Miller Outdoor Theatre, the Houston

Zoo, and the Hermann Park Golf Course (page 155).

Another big draw here is McGovern Lake, where children can feed the ducks, birders can watch for migratory birds, and families and couples can ride in four-seat pedal boats, which can be rented from the boathouse across from the zoo for $9 per half-hour. Children 12 and under and adults 65 and over—yes, you read that right—can also partake in some catch-and-release fishing here, but guests ages 65 to 70 must have a Texas fishing license. Visit the website or call for more information on fishing in the park.

Directly north of McGovern Lake is the 740-foot-long Mary Gibbs and Jesse H. Jones Reflection Pool, which is also visible from the Sam Houston statue at the park's entrance. Lined with large oak trees, the reflection pool is a soothing place to walk or picnic. Just west of the reflection pool is the park's simple yet elegant Japanese Garden.

East of McGovern Lake is the Buddy Carruth Playground for All Children, a fun place to have a birthday party or run off some extra energy. Most of the playground equipment can be used by children of all physical abilities, including those confined to wheelchairs. Also popular among children is Bayou Parkland, which offers special educational programs for kids throughout the year.

The Hermann Park Railroad—a red, open-air train—travels around one of the three islands at McGovern Lake. The kid-size train runs from 10 a.m. to 4:30 p.m. on weekdays and 10 a.m. to 5 p.m. on weekends. Rides cost $3 for guests 1 year and older; on weekdays, you can buy an all-day train pass for $6. For an added dose of fun, picnic on the lake's north shore and run through the fountains there.

Visit the Hermann Park website to download a map of the park, which is located across the street from Rice University and within walking distance of the Texas Medical Center and the Museum District. Free parking is available in lots in front of the Houston Zoo, at the Bayou Parkland Pavilion, at the Houston Garden Center, near Miller Outdoor Theatre, and at the golf course clubhouse at the corner of Almeda and MacGregor Streets. Hermann Park is also accessible by taking the METRORail to the Hermann Park/Rice U station.

LAKE HOUSTON WILDERNESS PARK
22031 Baptist Encampment Rd., New Caney
(281) 354-6881
houstontx.gov/parks/ourparks/lakehoustonpark.html
Located northeast of the city in New Caney, Lake Houston Wilderness Park offers outdoor opportunities on and around the human-made Lake Houston. The City of Houston took ownership of the park, which was previously operated by the state, in 2006.

The city continues to develop and expand the park's offerings, which include close to 5,000 acres of forest and 12 miles of trails for hiking and biking. Pine- and cypress-shaded trails offer opportunities to bird-watch, take nature photos, and ride horses, although you'll have to bring your own horse to do the latter. It's common to see snakes slithering along the trail, so watch your feet. Want to learn about plants and animals in the park? Visit the Nature Center for a crash course on different ecosystems, amphibians, invertebrates, reptiles, and butterflies.

The park also offers opportunities to canoe, kayak, and fish for bass, crappie, and catfish in the stocked lake. You're likely to see quite a few boats in the lake, though the lake's boating entry points are not located in the park. See page 164 of the "Recreation" chapter for additional information about water activities on Lake Houston.

Camping is one of the biggest reasons people visit Lake Houston Wilderness Park. That's because Lake Houston Wilderness Park is the only city-owned and operated park that allows camping. Campsites here cater to everyone from primitive campers to city slickers who need their A/C and refrigerator. Want to pitch a tent? You can do that in one of the park's campsites, where you'll also have access to fire rings, picnic tables, and lantern lights. Prefer bunk beds? Stay in one of the park's lodges or cottages, which range from primitive to air-conditioned and heated spaces with kitchens and bathrooms. There are even campsites for people who bring their horses along. Camping fees range from $4 per night per person for a primitive campsite to $160 per night, plus a one-time cleaning fee of $75, for a group of up to 26 people to sleep in the air-conditioned Lazy Creek Cottage. Camping fees don't include the $3 park admission fee that all visitors 13 and older must pay upon entry.

i Celebrate Houston's parks by participating in Hermann Park Conservancy's Run in the Park, held each November. The event includes a 5-mile run and wheelchair race, a 2-mile family walk and a 1K kids' fun run—all in Hermann Park. Learn more in the "Annual Events" chapter.

✳MARKET SQUARE PARK
301 Milam (bounded by Milam, Preston, Travis, and Congress)
(713) 223-2003
marketsquarepark.com
In the 1800s, life in Houston revolved around Market Square Park, which was originally used as an open-air produce market after Augustus Allen donated the land to the city. Over the years, the park became the site of several City Halls, the last of which was demolished in the 1960s. In August 2010, Market Square Park reopened, again making its mark as a gathering place for Houstonians and their four-legged friends. This downtown park charms Houstonians with its beautiful mosaic benches, a 25-foot painted steel and wood sculpture by artist James Surls, historic photographs and elements from Market Square's early days, an attractive dog park, as well as Lauren's Garden, dedicated to the memory of Houstonian Lauren Catuzzi Grandcolas, who died aboard Flight 93 on September 11, 2011. One of the biggest draws is the kiosk for Niko Nikos (page 81), where you can buy delicious baklava, wine, falafel, and other Greek treats to eat in the park. Special events, including movie screenings hosted by the Alamo Drafthouse, are held here throughout the year; visit the website to learn about upcoming events.

Parking is usually available on the streets around the park. There's additional parking in Market Square Garage at 300 Milam.

✳MEMORIAL PARK
6501 Memorial Dr., at the southeastern intersection of I-10 and Loop 610
(713) 863-8403
memorialparkconservancy.org
Located on what was once Camp Logan, Memorial Park is dedicated to the memory

of US soldiers who died in World War I. Wooded trails and a central location just east of Memorial and west of downtown make this 1,500-acre park one of the most popular places to run in Houston. In total, there are more than 20 miles of trails here, the most popular of which is the 2.9-mile Seymour Lieberman Exercise Trail made of crushed granite and packed earth. The lighted trail includes several exercise stations, restrooms, and water fountains—including some for the many dogs who visit with their humans. Runners can also practice their speed on a 0.25-mile asphalt-timing track. The rest of the trails are largely used for hiking, in-line and roller-skating, biking, and even horseback riding. Some trails are more challenging than others, making the park an attractive place for everyone from mountain bikers and others trying to build leg muscles to more leisurely riders and hikers. Some of the most scenic trails can be found along the Buffalo Bayou, which runs along the park's southern border.

The recreational possibilities here extend far beyond the trails. Located just off the Seymour Lieberman Exercise Trail at 1500 Memorial Loop is the Memorial Park Tennis Center, where you can practice your serve on 18 courts or a practice wall, take lessons, and participate in tournaments and tennis leagues. Golfer? You can play at the Memorial Park Golf Course (1001 Memorial Loop Dr. East), a 250-acre, 18-hole course that attracts more than 60,000 people each year. The park also has a sand volleyball court, baseball fields, a croquet field, picnic facilities, and a playground.

Prefer an indoor workout? Get a daily or monthly membership at Memorial Park Fitness Center, located in the park at 6402 Arnott. Next to the fitness center is a 33-meter outdoor pool, which is free and open to the public from Memorial Day to Labor Day. Additional information about the tennis center, golf course, and fitness center can be found in the "Recreation" chapter.

Memorial Park's nature and wildlife offerings are also a big draw. Lizards and raccoons abound, along with native plant and animal life. Unfortunately, the recent drought has killed many of Memorial Park's most beautiful natural assets—its trees—but the Memorial Park Conservancy has been raising money to plant new trees.

Among the areas of the park that has been hardest hit by the drought is the Houston Arboretum & Nature Center, a beautiful nature reserve whose 5 miles of nature trails are filled with forest, wetland, pond, and meadow habitats filled with native plants and animals. Learn more about the Arboretum, which is located on the park's western edge at 4501 Woodway Dr., on page 195.

Many events are held at Memorial Park throughout the year. The most notable of these is the Bayou City Art Festival in March.

Visit the Memorial Park website to download park maps. Free parking is available in several lots around the park.

> **i** Want to grab something to eat at Memorial Park? Visit Becks Prime (page 71) for a delicious burger—whether you prefer one of the beef, ahi tuna, or black bean variety. The casual restaurant is located in the golf course clubhouse at 1001 E. Memorial Loop Dr.

*SAM HOUSTON PARK
1000 Bagby, between McKinney St. and Allen Pkwy.
(713) 837-0311
houstontx.gov/parks/ourparks/
samhoustonpark.html

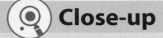 **Close-up**

Armand Bayou Nature Center

The country's largest urban wildlife refuge is located just southeast of Houston in Pasadena. Named after Gulf Coast wilderness conservationist Armand Yramategui, **Armand Bayou Nature Center** may not be a park in name, but it offers many of the attractions and activities that make other local parks popular, including canoeing, hiking, and even pontoon boat cruises. These are just some of the ways that you can learn about different wildlife and the ecosystems in which they live. Hike along the Martyn, Karankawa, Marsh, Prairie, or Lady Bird Trails, where you'll learn about the forest, prairie, marsh, and natural bayou habitats that were once abundant in the Houston area. Or walk along the center's boardwalk, where you can explore exquisite butterfly gardens and a farm site inhabited by about one dozen European families during the mid-1800s. Once a month near the full moon, the nature center offers Owl Prowls. These moonlit (and flashlight-lit) walks will take you through the woods in search of owls. Armand Bayou offers additional evening walks to look at nighttime creatures, such as raccoons and possums. One Friday a month, the center offers Prairie Night Rides—hayride tours that offer a glimpse at armadillos, rabbits, deer, and other nocturnal creatures. These special activities cost an additional $8 for visitors 6 and older. Guests under 18 must be accompanied by an adult. Reservations are required.

Throughout the year, the park offers educational programming for local students and scout groups and hosts birthday parties and guided hikes for kids. During the winter and summer, Armand Bayou also holds nature camps for kids.

Armand Bayou Nature Center is located at 8500 Bay Area Blvd., Pasadena (281-474-2551; abnc.org). General admission costs $4 for visitors 13 to 59 years old and $2 for kids ages 4 to 12 and seniors 60 and older. Kids 3 and under get in free. Free parking is available on-site. Closed Mon and Tues.

Sam Houston Park is the city's oldest park. Located on the northwest edge of downtown, the 20-acre park was established in 1899 at the request of Mayor Sam Brashier. The park lies on land where, in 1847, Nathaniel Kellum built what's now the oldest surviving house in Houston. Since 1954, the park has been largely known as the site of several Victorian homes and other historic buildings. Many Houstonians visit Sam Houston Park to learn about the city's early history at the Heritage Society (page 134). The park's close proximity to City Hall—along with its gardens, trails, and charming lily pond—also make it a popular spot for picnicking or throwing a Frisbee.

Many festivals and events are held in Sam Houston Park throughout the year. Among them: the Houston International Festival in April, Art Car Parade VIPit Party in May, the Bayou City Art Festival in October, and Via Colori Street Painting Festival in November. See the "Annual Events" chapter for more information on these events.

Free parking is available off Allen Parkway as you enter downtown. The parking lot is behind a big white brick building—the Kellum-Noble House.

SESQUICENTENNIAL PARK
400 Texas Ave.

sesquicentennialpark.org

As its name suggests, this downtown Theater District park was established to celebrate the 150th birthday of both Houston and Texas in 1986. Sesquicentennial Park runs along Buffalo Bayou, and though it's less of a recreation destination than most other local parks, it's worth a visit if you have extra time downtown. A peaceful sanctuary in the midst of the city, the 22.5-acre park is filled with grassy slopes for afternoon picnics and frolicking, as well as bridges, cascading waterfalls, meandering sidewalks, native plants, natural water pools, and spectacular views of downtown. Those in need of a quiet space to contemplate can gaze out on Buffalo Bayou and watch canoers and kayakers paddle by or stop at the park. Art lover? You'll appreciate Dean Ruck's photographic display on the railings overlooking Buffalo Bayou, as well as the "seven wonders." Each of the seven wonders is a 70-foot-tall pillar featuring 150 children's drawings that illustrate the city's history of agriculture, energy, medicine, transportation, manufacturing, philanthropy, and technology.

Sesquicentennial Park's beauty makes it a popular place for weddings, special events, and photo shoots. Many downtown events are also held here throughout the year. Parking is available in the Theater District parking garages; the most convenient is garage number 8. Parking costs up to $9 during the week and $7 for special events and on weekends. See the downtown parking map on page x.

i Take lots of water whenever you visit parks here. When the mercury starts to soar—especially in sparsely shaded parks—it's easy to get dehydrated quickly.

TERRY HERSHÉY PARK
15200 Memorial Dr., at Memorial Mews St.

(281) 496-2177

pct3.hctx.net/parks/terryhershey.aspx

Like George Bush Park and Cullen Park, Terry Hershey Park sits on flood control land in west Houston. The park, previously known as Buffalo Bayou Park, was renamed in 1991 to recognize conservationist Terry Hershey, who successfully fought to prevent the paving and channeling of Buffalo Bayou in the 1960s.

Today Terry Hershey Park is a popular place to bike and train for marathons. The park's trails, which stretch from TX 6 to the Sam Houston Tollway, now measure nearly 11 miles. Trees and breeze blowing off the bayou help cool a good chunk of these trails, but many sections aren't well shaded. There's also quite a bit of litter along the trails. Harris County continues to expand the park to make it easier for west Houston residents to bike to the Metro's Addicks Park and Ride Lot.

Terry Hershey Park also has a playground, picnic areas, and green space for throwing a Frisbee. Although the park runs along Buffalo Bayou, it's not safe to swim or drink the water here.

i Love to canoe or kayak? Buffalo Bayou Conservancy hosts several events revolving around boating on the bayou. Among them: a 15-mile canoe and kayak regatta in March, canoe and kayak trips, and a dragon boat competition. For details, visit buffalobayou.org or call (713) 752-0314.

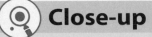

Close-up

Dog Parks

Maybe your dog is getting a little stir-crazy. Or maybe you just want your furry friend to socialize. Whatever the case, there's plenty of space for your dog to run free, sniff, and socialize at Houston's more than one dozen off-leash dog parks. One dog park—**Boneyard Dog Park & Drinkery** (page 101)—actually serves beer so humans can have fun and socialize while their pups play. Some local dog parks—like the Discovery Green Dog Park, the Market Square Dog Run, and Millie Bush Dog Park at George Bush Park—occupy a small, gated section of a larger made-for-humans park. Others are freestanding parks.

No matter which dog park you visit, be sure to take water and clean up after your dog. Poop bags and water are available for the taking at many parks, but that's not always the case. Some parks, such as Congressman Bill Archer Bark Park, prohibit owners from bringing in treats, so be sure to read the signs before entering the park.

Here are the names and addresses of several popular dog parks in the Houston area. Listed first are parks in Houston; parks in the major suburbs follow.

HOUSTON

Boneyard Dog Park & Drinkery
8150 Washington Ave.
(832) 494-1600
boneyardhouston.com

Buffalo Bayou Dog Park
2700 block of Allen Parkway at Studewood

Congressman Bill Archer Bark Park
3201 Hwy. 6, just north of Groeschke Rd.

Danny Jackson Family Dog Park
4828½ Loop Central Dr., inside Loop 610 just south of 59

Discovery Green Dog Runs
Downtown between McKinney and Lamar, 1 block east of Austin at La Branch Street
discoverygreen.com

Ervan Chew Dog Park
4502 Dunlavy, east of Shephard and south of Richmond

TRANQUILITY PARK
Downtown between Bagby and Smith Streets and Rusk and Walker Streets, across from City Hall and the Hobby Center

Named for the Sea of Tranquility, this small but lush green park pays homage to Houston's role in space history. Tranquility Park first opened in 1979 to commemorate the tenth anniversary of the first moon landing. Some three decades later, the park's entire

design subtly continues this celebration. Bronze plaques at the entrance include Neil Armstrong's first words from the moon—"Houston, Tranquility Base here. The Eagle has landed."—in 15 languages. There's also a replica of Armstrong's footprints on the moon. Even the park's grounds—green as they are—bear a slight resemblance to the moon: Mounds and craters dot the park and large stainless cylinders-turned-water-falls that resemble rocket boosters surround

Levy Park Dog Park
3801 Eastside, just south of Richmond

Maxey Bark and Run Dog Park
601 Maxey Rd., next to the Park and
Ride

Market Square Dog Runs
301 Milam
marketsquarepark.com

Millie Bush Dog Park
16756 Westheimer Pkwy.

Tanglewood Park
5801 Woodway between Augusta and
Bering

T.C. Jester Dog Park
4201 West T.C. Jester Blvd.

West Webster Dog Park
1502 West Webster

BELLAIRE
Officer Lucy Dog Park
4337 Lafayette, near Beechnut,
entrance off Edith St.

Deer Park
Ella and Friends Dog Park
500 W. 13th St. next to Jimmy Burke
Activity Center

KATY
Katy Dog Park
5414 Franz Rd.

KINGWOOD
AABY Bark Park
619 Lakeville Dr., off Russell Palmer Rd.
kingwoodkennels.com/dogpark.htm

PEARLAND
Independence Dog Park
3919 Liberty Dr.

Southdown Dog Park
2150 Country Place Pkwy.
pearlandparks.com/southdown.asp

THE WOODLANDS
Bear Branch Dog Park
5200 Research Forest Dr., west of I-45
thewoodlandsdogparkclub.org

Cattail Dog Park
9323 Cochrans Crossing Dr., across from
Palmer Golf Club House in Cattail Park
thewoodlandsdogparkclub.org

the giant Wortham Fountain. Towering trees line the park's perimeter and shade several wooden benches, where downtown office workers often eat lunch or decompress. Many special events and festivals, including the Houston Children's Festival (page 201) and the Houston International Festival (page 182), are held here throughout the year.

Parking is available in the nearby Theater District garages, including two located at Rusk near Bagby, one at the corner of Walker and Bagby Street, and one at Capitol Street and Smith. A map of these garages can be found on page x. Parking costs up to $9 during the week and $7 on weekends and holidays and during special events.

RECREATION

No matter how you prefer to get in shape and relax, you'll find plenty of recreational and fitness opportunities in Houston. Thanks to Houston's Buffalo Bayou location and its proximity to the Gulf of Mexico and area lakes, this is a great place to get your fill of water-based activities such as fishing, kayaking, canoeing, waterskiing, windsurfing, and boating. Prefer drier activities? Houston's got you covered there, too: Hunters can pursue deer, fowl, and other animals around these parts, and campers can pitch a tent or sleep in bunk beds at a few area parks. The miles of trails in the city's parks are great for runners, especially those training for races. Cyclist? You can use many of these same trails, as well as the local velodrome. Skaters can take advantage of several skate parks, join a roller or hockey league, or skate for fun at one of the local roller- or ice-skating rinks. And rock climbers can get their fix at two local rock-climbing gyms.

Is golf or tennis more your thing? With several public golf courses and tennis courts around the city, Houston offers plenty of opportunities to practice and play.

OVERVIEW

It would take several volumes to list and describe every possible recreational activity, league, and facility in town. But the activities and locales listed in this chapter are some of the most popular (in the case of facilities and activities) and best (in terms of facilities).

CAMPING

Savor the chance to sleep outdoors? **Lake Houston Wilderness Park, Brazos Bend State Park,** and **Lake Conroe** all boast campgrounds and cabins. Both Lake Houston Wilderness Park and Brazos Bend offer campsite facilities that sleep both small and large groups and include lantern lighting. You'll just need to bring your own camping equipment. Don't like roughing it? Lake Houston offers air-conditioned and heated

lodges. Learn more information about these parks in the "Parks" chapter.

The Lake Conroe KOA Campgrounds serve guests with their own RVs, as well as those who want to rent a cottage. Located just a few minutes from the lake, these camping accommodations include a health club, pool, and water slide. Learn more about the Lake Conroe KOA Campgrounds by calling (936) 582-1200 or visiting lakeconroekoa .com.

CYCLING

City ordinances prohibit biking on sidewalks where businesses are located, so biking here can be challenging. Luckily, recreational cyclists have plenty of other options. Not only is biking easy in more suburban residential areas; the majority of big parks here also include extensive trails for biking. Many of these trails are fairly flat, but mountain bikers and those looking to build some leg muscle can find more challenging trails on the southwest side of **Memorial Park,** which has a number of ravines. Color-coded maps at the park alert bikers to the difficulty of different trails. Memorial Park closes its Mountain Bike Trails when inclement weather makes them dangerous for riders. So, before visiting, call the park's Mountain Bike Trail Line (713-221-0499) to make sure the trails are open.

Training for a race? Head to **Cullen Park** (page 155) on the city's west side. This is the home of Alkek Velodrome, one of only about two dozen velodromes in the country. The banking of this 333-meter outdoor cement spans from 33 degrees around the turns to 9 degrees in the straights. Since opening in 1986, the Alkek Velodrome has been the site of a number of Olympic qualifiers; local races are also held here throughout the year. Learn more about these races on the Greater Houston Cycling Foundation's website (houstoncycling.org). See the "Parks" chapter for information about Memorial Park, Cullen Park, and trails at other Houston parks.

GOLF COURSES

Thanks in part to mild temperatures and a bustling business climate, golf courses abound in Houston. Although some are located in country clubs or areas that are off-limits to the general public, you've still got plenty of publicly accessible golf courses to choose from if you don't belong to a club. In total there are more than 50 public golf courses here. Seven of these—plus a junior training course—are operated by the Houston Parks and Recreation Department. Many of the nonmunicipal courses are located in the suburbs.

Generally local courses are open throughout the week and on weekends. Greens fees vary depending on the day of the week or time of the day you tee off. Some include golf cart rental; others don't. Most golf courses require advance reservations. And, since golfers tend to show up in droves when the weather is nice, it's best to reserve your time far in advance. Keep in mind that temperatures can be especially hot from noon to sunset during the summer.

Houston's got far too many public golf courses in Houston to discuss them all, so only a small sampling is included here. For a complete list of local golf courses, visit Golfersweb at golfersweb.com/golfhous.

HERMANN PARK GOLF COURSE
2155 N. MacGregor St., at Almeda Rd.
in Hermann Park
(713) 526-0077
hermannparkgc.com
One of the country's first desegregated courses, Hermann Park Golf Course is also one of the city's oldest and most popular courses. It was renovated in 1997 by golf architect Carlton Gipson, who designed several other attractive courses around Texas. Hermann Park Golf Course has a gold slope rating of 117 and a gold rating of 67.9. Like the rest of Hermann Park, the well-manicured course is filled with oak trees that offer small pockets of shade. The course's location makes it easily accessible from the Medical Center, the Museum District, and Rice University. Greens fees vary depending on the day and time, as well as the golfer's age. Generally, you'll pay somewhere between $8 (ages 17 and younger) and

$26.50 for adults Fri through Sun. Electric carts and range balls are available for rental.

MEADOWBROOK FARMS GOLF CLUB
23230 Meadowbrook Farms Club Dr., Katy
(281) 693-4653
meadowbrookfarmsgolfclub.com
Since opening in 1999, Meadowbrook Farms Golf Club has been widely regarded as one of Houston's best courses. That's partly because golf legend Greg Norman designed the par-72 course, which plays 7,100 yards. Expect your shot here to be challenged by trees, creeks, lakes, sod-wall bunkers, and white sands. The clubhouse offers a full-service grill. Lessons are available. Greens fees range from $49 to $89, depending on the day and time. Half cart rental is included. Make reservations online or by phone in advance.

MEMORIAL PARK GOLF COURSE
1001 E. Memorial Loop Dr., in Memorial Park
(713) 559-2000
memorialparkgolf.com
One of the best-rated municipal golf courses in Texas is located inside Memorial Park. Since opening in 1923, this 18-hole, 600-acre course has hosted the likes of Jack Nicklaus and Arnold Palmer. In 1995 the course was renovated to include a lighted driving course, putting and chipping greens, a golf museum, and a new clubhouse. A practice range and lessons are available for beginners and more experienced golfers looking to improve their game. The course is open in the evenings. Fees vary depending on the day, time, and the golfer's age, but they range anywhere from $10 for youth to $38 for adults on weekends and holidays. Balls

and carts can be rented for an additional fee. Call or visit the website to book your tee time.

WILDCAT GOLF CLUB
12000 Almeda Rd., off the South Sam Houston Tollway
(713) 413-3400
wildcatgolfclub.com
Located 10 minutes from downtown in southeast Houston, Wildcat Golf Club offers 36 holes of great golf. The club is home to two courses—the Highlands Course and the Lakes Course. Both offer picturesque views of the downtown skyline, big elevation changes, and fast greens, but the Lakes Course throws in some water to make things more challenging. Four putting greens give you a chance to practice before teeing off. Greens fees range from $39.90 to $63.75, depending on the time of day. Special rates are available for seniors and children. Call or visit the website to schedule your tee time.

WORLD HOUSTON GOLF COURSE
4000 Greens Rd.
(281) 449-8381
worldhoustongolf.com
This par-72, 6,700-yard course is one of the oldest courses in town. The 70.8-rated course offers challenges from 37 bunkers and water on 13 holes. It also has a 119-slope rating from the championship tees. On Wednesday through Saturday, the course's Ranch Grill serves burgers and sandwiches. Greens fees include golf cart rentals and range from $16 to $34. Special rates are offered for students, golfers under 18, and seniors 60 and older. Visit the website to book your tee time.

GYMS & WORKOUT FACILITIES

Houston's got dozens of gyms and fitness centers—some owned by the city, others private facilities that allow visitors to purchase a day- or sometimes even a week- or monthlong pass. Some even offer free day or week trial memberships.

Community Fitness Centers

The Houston Parks and Recreation Department runs four fitness centers and more than a dozen smaller community center weight rooms and gymnasiums around the city. Some are free; others charge a daily or monthly membership fee that's significantly lower than what private gyms charge. Hours vary, and most of the fitness centers have limited weekend hours. All four fitness centers, which require guests to be at least 18 years old, are listed here. Call to find out the schedule at your fitness center of choice.

A complete list of community center weight rooms and gymnasiums can be found on the Houston Parks and Recreation Department's website (houstontx.gov/parks/ourparks/fitnesscenters.html).

FONDE RECREATION CENTER
110 Sabine, just off Memorial Dr.
(713) 226-4466
Fonde Recreation Center is home to well-maintained basketball courts, where amateurs and pros alike team up for pickup games. Basketball isn't your sport of choice? The center also offers a weight room, aerobics and tai-chi classes, pickle games for seniors, volleyball and badminton games, and plenty of free activities. The downtown location makes this a convenient place to work out during lunch or before or after work. Fonde Recreation Center is free to the public.

JUDSON ROBINSON, JR., FITNESS CENTER AT HERMANN PARK
2020 Hermann Dr., off Main St.
(713) 284-1997
Work in the Medical Center or the Museum District? Or visiting someone at one of the Medical Center hospitals? Whatever the case, this Hermann Park-based fitness center is a great place to work out. There's a full gym and weight room, as well as a racquetball court. Monthly membership costs just $20; one-time and infrequent guests can pay $1.50 per half hour or $3 per hour to use the racquetball court. The center is closed evenings and on Sun; it's only open until 2 p.m. on Sat.

MACGREGOR FITNESS CENTER
5225 Calhoun, in MacGregor Park
(713) 747-8650
Located just south of the University of Houston's main campus in MacGregor Park, the MacGregor Fitness Center boasts a fully loaded weight room. A little cardio can be added to your workout with a pickup game in the covered, full-court basketball pavilion or a run on the 1.25-mile jogging trail located in the park. There are tennis courts available next door at the Homer Ford Tennis Center. Use of the fitness center is free; showers and lockers can be used at Homer Ford Tennis Center for 75 cents each. Closed on weekends.

MEMORIAL PARK FITNESS CENTER
6402 Arnot St., off Westcott St. on the eastern border of Memorial Park
(713) 802-1662
Memorial Park Fitness Center offers weights and aerobic machines, such as treadmills, stairmasters, and ellipticals, as well as opportunities to work with a personal trainer. You

can even swim laps at the swim center in the morning during the summer and at select times throughout the year. Call to find out when the pool is open for lap swim. Memorial Park Fitness Center is open daily, but it closes at noon on Sun. Monthly membership costs $20; daily memberships cost $1.75.

Private Gyms

Community centers are hardly the only gyms in town. Houston also boasts dozens of privately owned gym and personal fitness facilities. Chains such as Gold's Gym (goldsgym .com), Bally's (ballyfitness.com), and 24 Hour Fitness (24hourfitness.com) have several locations in and around the city. Houston also has several independent health clubs and gyms, many of which cost a little more than the larger chains. These gyms offer a broad range of workout equipment and classes and, for an additional cost, personal training. Here are a few of the most popular independent gyms in town.

THE DOWNTOWN CLUB
340 W. Dallas, at the Met
(713) 652-0700
1100 Caroline St., at Houston Center
(713) 654-0877
clubcorp.com/Clubs/The-Downtown-Club
The Downtown Club is the name for three different downtown facilities, two of which have extensive fitness facilities. The Downtown Club at the Met is home to a gym and weight room, group fitness classes, and courts for squash, basketball, tennis, and racquetball. The Downtown Club at the Houston Center offers a gym and weight room, basketball and racquetball courts, and group classes. Both also have a dining room

and snack bar. Visit the website for a free trial membership.

FIT ATHLETIC CLUB
1532 W. Gray St. at Waugh St.
(713) 782-9348
fithouston.com
Located between River Oaks and downtown, FIT Athletic Club is a popular place to socialize and work out. In addition to a state-of-the-art gym with great personal trainers, FIT offers yoga, Pilates, martial arts, cardio and conditioning, and cycling classes. Hungry after your workout? FIT's cafe serves healthy meals, snacks, coffee, comfortable couches, and Wi-Fi access. Visit the website for a free one-day pass.

MEMORIAL ATHLETIC CLUB AND
** AQUATIC CENTER**
14690 Memorial Dr.
(281) 497-7570
fitmac.com
Workout possibilities are endless at the Memorial Athletic Club, where you'll find racquetball and basketball courts, a weight room, and a cardiovascular center with treadmills, ellipticals, bicycles, and stairmasters galore. Yoga, Pilates, and spinning classes are offered in two aerobics studios; there's a jogging trail outside and two heated pools—one indoor and one out. Memorial Athletic Club also offers ballet, tumbling, jazz, and other fitness and conditioning classes for kids. Membership doesn't require a contract.

Memorial Athletic Club's sister club, MAC for Women, is just down the street at 14633 Memorial Dr. This location offers nursery care for babies so moms can work out and take Pilates classes. Call (281) 558-6691 for more information.

TIMBERLINE FITNESS
3939 Montrose Blvd.
(713) 523-7007
timberlinefitness.com

As one of Houston's pricier gyms, Timberline Fitness is a popular place to get in shape with the help of a personal trainer. This Montrose-area gym also offers machines for solo workouts, as well as Pilates, yoga, martial arts, and boot camp classes. Several membership options are available.

HUNTING

Hunting is a popular pastime in Texas, with thousands of people tracking deer, hogs, doves, turkeys, and other fowl each year. The Texas Parks and Wildlife Department requires all hunters to have a hunting license. Fees vary, depending on the license type, of which there are dozens. General hunting licenses for Texas residents cost $25, while general hunting licenses for nonresidents cost a hefty $315. Licenses can be purchased at sporting goods stores, bait and tackle stores, and many grocery stores and department stores. You can also buy a license on the Texas Parks and Wildlife Department website (tpwd.state.tx.us), where you'll also find a comprehensive list of different license fees and hunting regulations there. Beware: There's a $5 convenience charge for purchasing your license online.

There's very little government-owned land open for public hunting in Texas, so if you want to hunt, you'll most likely need to find some privately owned land. One option is to ask ranch- or land-owning friends or family to let you hunt on their property. Don't know anyone that fits the bill? You can buy what's known as a deer lease. That is, you can find a landowner in the area who will let

you hunt on their land for a certain period for a fee that they set. Area deer leases can be found by visiting local REI stores, which offer maps, ads, and other information about available deer leases. Houston has two REI locations—one in west Houston at 7538 Westheimer Rd. (713-353-2582) and the other in northwest Houston across from Willowbrook Mall at 17717 Tomball Pkwy. (832-237-8833).

i Check out the *Houston Chronicle*'s Outdoors page online (chron.com/sports/outdoors) to find the forecast for the upcoming hunting and fishing seasons, tips on good hunting and fishing spots, and what gear to use and where to buy or rent it.

ROCK CLIMBING

Houston's got two publicly accessible indoor rock-climbing gyms—Stone Moves Indoor Rock Climbing and Texas Rock Gym. The faux boulders at both of these first-class facilities will challenge you mentally as you maneuver your body and figure out where to put your hands and feet. Employees can spot you and hold the other end of your rope during your climb, but it's more fun to take along a buddy to help you out.

Each facility offers lessons to help you become a better climber. First-time climbers, rest assured: Both rock gyms will—literally—show you the ropes beforehand and help you out on the ground throughout the climb. In fact, Texas Rock Gym requires all first-time visitors to take a 20-minute ClimbSafe beginner's class for $7.50. Neither location has a minimum climbing age, but parents must sign a liability waiver for kids under 18.

Bring sturdy, tight-fitting tennis shoes or be prepared to pay a little extra to rent a pair at the gym. Also keep in mind that the required harness can't be worn with skirts or dresses. Rock climbing can be a little pricey, but a day pass is good for an entire day, even if you leave for lunch and come back.

A day pass at Texas Rock Gym is $15. That doesn't include the required harness, which you can rent for an additional $4. Climbing shoes can be rented for $6.

A day pass at Stone Moves costs $12. Harness rental costs $2, and shoe rental costs $3. Here are the addresses and contact details for Stone Moves and Texas Rock Gym.

STONE MOVES INDOOR ROCK CLIMBING
6970 FM 1960 Rd. West, in northwest Houston, east of Highway 249/Tomball Pkwy.
(281) 397-0830
stonemoves.com

TEXAS ROCK GYM
1526 Campbell Rd., off I-10 between Westview and Longpoint
(713) 973-7625
texasrockgym.com

RUNNING
Whether you're a noncompetitive jogger or training for a marathon, Houston is a great place to run. All of the city's parks include runner-friendly trails. Marathoners and distance runners tend to enjoy the long-running trails at Terry Hershey Park, and short-distance race runners will find the 0.25-mile concrete asphalt timing track at Memorial Park a good place to practice their speed. See the "Parks" chapter for additional information on these training sites and other running trails around Houston.

Throughout the year, several races, as well as one of the country's best marathons, are held in Houston. Learn about the Chevron Houston Marathon and other local races in the "Annual Events" chapter.

i Like to run races or need running buddies to help you maintain a running routine? Check out the Houston Area Road Runners Association's website (harra.org) for a list of upcoming races and more than two dozen local running clubs.

SKATING

Love to skate? You've come to the right place. Houston offers skating opportunities galore for skaters of all stripes—fast or slow, indoors or out, ice or concrete, flat surfaces or in skate parks.

Several skating rinks and ice-skating rinks are located around Houston. In addition to being fun places to take skating lessons or skate with friends, family, or a date, most ice-skating rinks also have ice-hockey teams that are open to the public. See the "Kidstuff" chapter for lists of local roller-skating and ice-skating rinks.

Women ages 21 and up who prefer to skate competitively off the ice can try out for one of four roller-derby teams—the Bayou City Bosse$, the Burlesque Brawlers, the Psych Ward Sirens, and the HaRD Knocks. Those who want a little more practice before trying out or who want something a little more laid-back can join the Houston Roller Derby Rec League. Learn more on the Houston Roller Derby website (houstonrollerderby.com).

Skating opportunities also abound on the trails of Houston's parks, which you can learn about in the "Parks" chapter. Up for a challenge or prefer to avoid the bikers and runners? Try one of Houston's six public skate parks. Each one caters to skateboarders, as well as in-line and old-school roller-skaters, with skate ramps and kicker benches, grind boxes, grindrails, and curbs. The names and addresses of Houston's skate parks are listed here. The Lee & Joe Jamail Skatepark is the city's first in-ground skate park; the other five are aboveground. Each of these is free to the public. Visit the City of Houston's Skate Parks page (houstontx.gov/parks/ourparks/skateparks.html) for additional information.

Central Houston

LEE & JOE JAMAIL SKATEPARK
103 Sabine St., in Buffalo Bayou Park/
Eleanor Tinsley Park (just east of downtown)
(713) 222-5500

East Houston

CLIFF TUTTLE PARK
6200 Lyons, just off I-10

CLINTON SKATE PARK
200 Mississippi St., in Clinton Park, just east of Loop 610

EASTWOOD SKATE PARK
5020 Harrisburg, in Eastwood Park

Northeast Houston

DYLAN DUNCAN SKATE PARK
3950 Rustic Woods

Northwest Houston

WATONGA SKATE PARK
4100 Watonga Blvd. off W. 43rd St.

TENNIS

Houston is home to dozens of tennis courts. Many are located inside member- or resident-only country clubs, schools, or neighborhood parks. But the Houston Parks and Recreation Department also owns three tennis centers—including one at Memorial Park. In total these three tennis centers offer 60 courts for the public, and they're all free to use. Each outdoor court is lighted, and shower and locker use is available for a small fee. The tennis centers have their own pro shops and offer tennis lessons, leagues, and tournaments for a relatively low fee. Call the appropriate center's pro shop to sign up for lessons or learn about upcoming events.

In addition to these three tennis centers, the Houston Parks and Recreation Department manages 205 publicly accessible tennis courts in dozens of neighborhood parks around the city. For a list of these courts, call the Houston Parks and Recreation Department's tennis office (713-803-1112) or visit houstontx.gov/parks/tennis.html.

Additional courts can be found in suburban neighborhood parks, such as Pasadena and more centrally located independent cities like Bellaire. If you live in one of these areas, contact your city to find the nearest neighborhood park with a tennis court. A list of the phone numbers and websites of other cities in the area can be found in the "Area Overview" chapter.

HOMER FORD TENNIS CENTER
(16 COURTS)
5225 Calhoun, in MacGregor Park in southeast Houston
(713) 842-3460

LEE LECLEAR (26 COURTS)
9506 S. Gessner Dr., inside Braeburn Glen Park in southwest Houston
(713) 272-3697

MEMORIAL PARK TENNIS CENTER (18 COURTS)
1500 Memorial Loop, in Memorial Park, just off the Seymour Lieberman Exercise Trail
(713) 867-0440

i Learn about tennis courts and clubs—private and public—and leagues around town by contacting the Houston Tennis Association (281-580-8313; houstontennis.org), an excellent resource for information and news about local amateur tennis activities.

WATER ACTIVITIES

Houston and the surrounding areas offer plenty of opportunities fishing, boating, waterskiing, surfing, Jet-Skiing, kayaking, and other water sports. While there aren't many places to boat or enjoy other activities that require waves within the city limits, there are miles of water within an hour's drive of Houston. Additional lakes and beach destinations are located within just a couple of hours of the city, though only the closest and most popular ones are listed here.

Fishing & Boating License Requirements

The Texas Parks and Wildlife Department regulates fishing and boating in the area. The department requires everyone 17 or older who wants to fish in public water to get a fishing license. A license is *not* required, however, if you're fishing at a Texas state park,

such as Brazos Bend State Park (page 163). The price of fishing licenses depends on whether you want to fish in freshwater or salt water. Residents pay $30 to fish in freshwater and $35 to fish in salt water, while nonresidents pay $58 to fish in freshwater and $63 to fish in salt water. Combination licenses that permit fishing in freshwater and salt water, as well as fishing and hunting license combo packages, are also available. Licenses can be purchased at dozens of locations around Houston, including sporting goods stores, gun shops, bait and tackle shops, and even grocery stores. They can also be purchased on Texas Parks and Wildlife Department website (tpwd.state.tx.us), although you'll be charged a $5 processing fee.

The department limits the number and size of fish you may take out of Texas waters; these numbers vary based on location and fish type. Visit the Texas Parks and Wildlife Department website to review these regulations before your trip.

Aspiring boaters under the age of 18 must take a boater education course before operating any kind of personal watercraft, any vessel over 10 horsepower, or a sailboat over 14 feet. Basic education courses start at $13. Additional information about boating education and requirements for buying and selling boats is available on the Texas Parks and Wildlife Department website (tpwd.state.tx.us) or by calling (800) 792-1112.

Safety Tips

Always wear a life vest and practice water safety when participating in water activities in and around Houston. Water can rise quickly, especially in lower-lying areas south of Houston and in Buffalo Bayou, so check the weather before you head out. It's not unusual for Houston weather to suddenly turn stormy. Also make sure someone on land knows you are on the water, just in case conditions get rough.

Where to Find Gear

Gear for water activities can be rented at vendors on the roads to the parks and bodies of water listed here, as well as at the sporting goods stores mentioned in the "Shopping" chapter. Additional shops can be found in the yellow pages or by contacting the appropriate visitor bureau (listed in the pages that follow). If you're in Houston in January, visit the Houston International Boat, Sport & Travel Show at Reliant Center. More details on this boating extravaganza are included in the "Annual Events" chapter.

Where to Go

Here are some of the most popular spots for water activities in and around Houston. Most don't charge for entry, but you must bring your own gear and, in some cases, pay for parking.

BRAZOS BEND STATE PARK
21901 FM 762, Needville
(979) 553-5102
tpwd.state.tx.us
Located about 30 miles southwest of Houston in Needville, Brazos Bend State Park offers plenty of fishing opportunities, though boats are prohibited. This 5,000-acre park runs along the Brazos River and has three lakes for fishing—Hale, New Horseshoe, and Forty Acre. There's also a fishing pier at Hale Lake, and New Horseshoe offers shoreline fishing. Among the fish you'll find: largemouth bass, catfish, crappie, sunfish, and carp. You don't need a license to fish here, but you will be charged general admission, which costs $7

for visitors 13 and older. Kids 12 and under get in free. Learn about additional activities at the park on page 143.

BUFFALO BAYOU
Various locations around Houston
(713) 752-0314
buffalobayou.org
Buffalo Bayou runs through Houston from Katy to the Houston Ship Channel. It's is a fun place to kayak, canoe, or fish without leaving the city. Popular fishing spots along the bayou include Buffalo Bayou Park and George Bush Park. In addition to plenty of mosquito fish, you'll find catfish and the occasional eel and bass in Buffalo Bayou.

Two of the easiest spots to launch a canoe or kayak are located in Buffalo Bayou Park, near downtown. See the Buffalo Bayou Park write-up in the "Parks" chapter for more information on kayaking and canoeing here. Haven't gone canoeing or kayaking in the Bayou before? You might find it helpful to take a guided morning kayak tour through the Buffalo Bayou Partnership. Call (713) 752-0314 or visit buffalobayou.org to learn more or sign up.

CLEAR LAKE/BAY AREA
South of Houston off I-45
Nicknamed the "Boating Capital of Texas," Clear Lake is the shining star of the Bay Area, which sits just south of Houston along Galveston Bay. This breezy inlet spans 2,000 acres and includes more than 9,000 marina slips, making it the country's third-largest basin for recreational boating. The Bay Area is also a popular spot for rowing, Jet-Skiing, waterskiing, and fishing. Among the most popular fish here are fingerling channel catfish and largemouth bass.

Want to rent a boat or take a fishing tour? Visit the Bay Area Houston Visitors Bureau online (visitbayarea houston.com) or call (866) 611-4688 for a list of companies that provide these services.

GALVESTON ISLAND
South of Houston off I-45

Galveston Island, located about an hour south of downtown, sits right on the Gulf of Mexico, making it a popular destination for lying on the beach, frolicking in the water, and enjoying water activities like boating, fishing, and surfing. Most of the beach here is open to the public, though some sections are closed off for guests at private resorts and residents of beachfront neighborhoods. Several beachfront parks charge a modest admission fee in exchange for use of the shower and bathroom facilities, as well as picnic areas just off the beach. The city permits surfing at several beaches, including those west of 91st Street, between the 17th Street and 21st Street rock groins, between the west edge of the Flagship Pier (25th Street) and 29th Street rock groins, and between the 29th Street and 53rd Street rock groins. Surfboards are available for rental at many shops on Seawall Boulevard, the main street running along the beach. Want to go fishing? Head out to any of the jetties along the beachfront or visit one of the city's commercial fishing piers—Seawolf Park Fishing Pier, the Galveston Fishing Pier, or the 61st Street Fishing Pier. Parking is available on Seawall Boulevard and other streets in Galveston. Watch the weather before visiting Galveston; tides can rise quickly here, making the rock groins and jetties dangerous places to be. For information on gear rental and the best spot for your favorite water activities, contact the Galveston Island Convention & Visitors Bureau at (409) 797-5145 or visit galveston.com.

LAKE CONROE
North of Houston off I-45

This human-made reservoir was completed in 1973. Today, thanks to its 157 miles of shoreline, Lake Conroe is one of Texas's most popular boating destinations—and a great place to go Jet-Skiing, waterskiing, sailing, and windsurfing. The best spots for sailing and windsurfing tend to be near the southern portion of Lake Conroe—the side closest to Houston—since winds are usually heavier here. Lake Conroe is also a popular place to go fishing. Channel catfish and bluegill are particularly abundant.

Visit lakeconroe.com for the low-down on recreation at Lake Conroe. You'll find information about upcoming events, as well as the best places to sail, fish, water-ski, kayak, and buy or rent gear.

LAKE HOUSTON
25 miles northeast of downtown, east of US 59

Lake Houston sits on the San Jacinto River, about 25 miles northeast of downtown. Impounded in 1954, this human-made lake spans nearly 12,000 acres. Many people come here to go boating and fishing. The lake is stocked with fish common to the area—mainly largemouth bass, white bass, white crappie, blue catfish, and bluegill. You can also kayak, canoe, camp, and hike on the north side of the lake in Lake Houston Wilderness Park, a city-owned and operated park that's discussed in more detail in the "Parks" chapter. Boaters, take note:

Unfortunately, it's not currently possible to enter the lake with your boat from the park.

YOGA & PILATES STUDIOS

Yogis, you can breathe easily: Opportunities to practice yoga and Pilates abound in Houston. In addition to classes offered at local gyms, there are many yoga studios around the city. Most studios offer classes early in the morning and in the evening on weekdays, as well as at various times on weekends. Usually, you can pay for individual classes or buy week-, month-, or yearlong passes. Here are some of Houston's best yoga and Pilates studios.

BIKRAM YOGA COLLEGE OF INDIA—HOUSTON
1854 Fountainview (Galleria area)
(713) 781-5333
2438 South Blvd. (Rice Village/West University)
(713) 664-5333
bikramyogahouston.com
Texas' first Bikram-certified studio offers hot yoga classes at two central locations.

DEFINE BODY & MIND
5781 San Felipe (Memorial)
(713) 780-7799
1945 W. Gray (River Oaks)
(713) 523-5800
1560 Eldridge Pkwy. (West Houston/ Energy Corridor)
(281) 496-4404
definebody.com
This popular studio combines Pilates, yoga, core strengthening, and ballet exercises. DEFINEbody classes focus on improving strength and flexibility by targeting all of the major muscle groups. DEFINEmind classes

focus on refreshing the body and calming the mind by helping students relieve tightness and reduce stress.

JENNYOGA
3641 Westheimer (River Oaks)
(713) 839-9642
jennyoga.com
JennYoga offers an array of vinyasa classes, ranging from power vinyasa flow to a vinyasa class devoted to strengthening students' hips and backs. A few Zumba and Forrest yoga classes are also available. The studio offers donation-based classes several times a week.

JOY YOGA CENTER
4500 Washington Ave. (Washington Corridor)
(713) 868-9642
joyyogacenter.com
Joy Yoga Center primarily offers Vinyasa classes, but you can also take Pilates, yoga for runners, Zumba, and yoga sculpt with weight classes here.

TEJAS YOGA
3930 Kirby Dr. (Upper Kirby)
(713) 807-7018
houstonyoga.com
Tejas Yoga teaches ashtanga classes primarily in the Mysore tradition. Beginners can also take basic ashtanga classes in the Led Primary Series.

YOGA ANANDA
1822 W. Alabama, Montrose
(713) 527-8280
yogaananda.com
Busy? Maximize the benefits of yoga at Yoga Ananda, where you can choose from Power Hour classes and Power Vinyasa Flow classes taught in the Baptiste Power Flow style.

i In February, renowned yogis and local yoga studios team up to host the Texas Yoga Conference. The three-day event features workshops, clinics, and talks on everything from teaching yoga to using backbends to open your heart to finding and embodying your purpose. Learn more at texasyogaconference.com.

✳YOGA ONE STUDIOS
3030 Travis St. (Midtown)
5750 Woodway (Galleria/Uptown)
(713) 522-0876 (Midtown)
(713) 239-2493 (Galleria/Uptown)
yogaonehouston.com
Yoga One Studios offers daily hot, Forrest, and vinyasa flow classes. You can also sign up for special clinics and workshops including a hot yoga posture clinic, partner yoga, and immersion courses. Babysitting is available for certain classes.

YOUR BODY CENTER
3605 Katy Fwy. (Heights)
(713) 874-0800
yourbodycenter.com
Your Body Center offers classes in Pilates, beginner and intermediate yoga, pre- and postnatal yoga, hatha, hot yoga, and even hot belly dancing. Massages are also available.

SPECTATOR SPORTS

S ports are a serious business in Houston—so serious, in fact, that the city opened three sports stadiums between 2000 and 2003 and a fourth in 2012. These state-of-the-art facilities immediately won national recognition, with the NFL choosing Houston's Reliant Stadium as the site of the 2004 Super Bowl, the MLB choosing Minute Maid Park as the site of its 2004 All-Star Game, the NBA tapping the Toyota Center to host its 2006 and 2013 All-Star Games, and the NCAA tapping Reliant Stadium to host the 2011 and 2016 Final Four tournament.

Of course, these big events aren't all Houstonians have to cheer about. In addition to professional football, baseball, basketball, soccer, and hockey teams, Houston is home to horse, greyhound, and drag racing tracks and countless NCAA Division I events at Rice University and the University of Houston. The city also hosts annual sporting events, such as the Meineke Car Care Bowl of Texas, Shell Houston Open golf tournament, and the US Men's Clay Court Championships. Like sports fans just about anywhere, Houstonians have had their share of heartache, but an exciting first trip to the playoffs by the Texans, a World Series appearance by the Astros, and championships won by the Rockets, Dynamo, Aeros, and Rice Owls (baseball) have given fans a few tastes of glory in recent years.

BUYING TICKETS

Tickets for most local sports events are sold through Ticketmaster (ticketmaster.com or 800-745-3000) and on-site; exceptions are noted accordingly. The ticket prices listed here don't include convenience charges, which can add an extra $7 or $8 to ticket prices. Keep in mind that prices included here are based on 2011–2012 rates; ticket prices often increase marginally every year or two. Almost all of the stadiums and other venues listed in this section are located within Houston city limits; exceptions are noted in the addresses where applicable.

Price Code

Price code is based on admission for one adult.

$................. Less than $15
$$ .... $15 to $35
$$$ .... More than $35

BASEBALL

HOUSTON ASTROS BASEBALL $–$$$
Minute Maid Park
501 Crawford, between Texas Ave. and Congress St.
(877) 927-8767
astros.com

After playing on AstroTurf under the Astrodome's closed domed roof for nearly 35 years, the Houston Astros now make their home at Minute Maid Park. In the early years, the move seemed to serve the team and its fans fairly well, though it's hard to say whether credit is due to Minute Maid Park's real grass and retractable roof, the stadium's downtown location, or big-name players like Roger Clemens, Andy Pettitte, Lance Berkman, Roy Oswalt, and Jeff Bagwell. More than three million fans came out to cheer on the 'Stros during the 2000 season—their first at Minute Maid Park—and the team made their first trip to the World Series in 2005, before being swept by the Chicago White Sox. Since then, the Astros have changed owners and lost some of their biggest-name—and controversial—players, and their record can leave something to be desired. But Houston's still full of die-hard fans, including former President George H. W. Bush.

The ballpark, which was named Enron Field before the Houston-based energy company filed for bankruptcy in 2001, is almost as much of an attraction as the Astros themselves. Nicknamed the Juice Box, Minute Maid Park was once the site of Houston's Union Station, which comprises the stadium's main entrance. Every time the Astros score a run or win a game, a full-size vintage train runs across 800 feet of track atop a wall on the stadium's left-field side. One of Minute Maid's most modern features is the World's Largest Sliding Glass Door. This 50,000-square-foot wall of hurricane-resistant glass spans across left field to make Minute Maid feel like an outdoor stadium even when the door is closed.

Hourlong tours of Minute Maid Park offer a close-up look at the press boxes, luxury suites, Union Station, the Astros' dugout, and other spots around the stadium. Tours cost $9 for adults, $7 for seniors 65 and up, and $5 for children 3 to 14. Visit the Astros' website for tour dates and times.

Located 1 block west of US 59, Minute Maid Park sits on the east side of downtown, just a few blocks northeast of the George R. Brown Convention Center and the Toyota Center. The stadium doesn't have its own parking garage, but paid parking lots and garages—not to mention the occasional open spot on the street—line the area. You can also take the METRORail, which stops on Main Street, 6 blocks from the ballpark.

The Astros play 81 home games from April through September. If the team makes the playoffs, their season extends into October. Tickets range from about $7 to $52.

Note: Texas Avenue near Crawford is closed to traffic for 20 minutes after every game, so plan to get picked up a few blocks away or along Jackson Street on the south side of Minute Maid Park.

> **i** Big appetite? Buy an All You Can Eat ticket to the Astros game. For $30, you'll get a mezzanine ticket and all the hot dogs, nachos, popcorn, peanuts, water, and soda you can pack in your belly.

BASKETBALL

✳HOUSTON ROCKETS
BASKETBALL $–$$$
Toyota Center
1510 Polk St. at LaBranch
(877) 622-7625
rockets.com
The Houston Rockets don't have quite the following that the Texans and Astros do,

but that seems to have more to do with Houstonians' affinity for football and baseball than anything else. The Rockets were the city's first major sports franchise to win a national championship—two, in fact—and one of the few to go to the playoffs nearly every year. In 1994 and 1995, Hall of Famer Hakeem Olajuwon led the Rockets to win back-to-back national titles. The road to both championships was bumpy and involved rallying back from deep holes in multiple playoff series, so when the Rockets finally won, Houston—known for its sports teams' tendency to choke under pressure—earned the nickname "Clutch City." The Rockets have experienced growing pains since then. But Rockets owner Les Alexander has continued to try to stock the team with some of the best (and biggest) players around. This high caliber of players makes for thrilling—if at times frustrating—visits to the Toyota Center and has helped secure several trips to the playoffs.

With all of the food at the Toyota Center provided by Levy Restaurants, dining options beat those at Houston's other stadiums. Food options range from Chinese to Mexican to salad to smoked meats to burgers and then some. The Toyota Center is located downtown, just a couple blocks east of US 59. It holds 18,300 fans during basketball games. Tickets range from $10 to $750. When games sell out, you can usually get in on the action by purchasing tickets through Flash Seats (rockets.flashseats.com).

Parking is available for $15 in the Toyota Tundra Garage next door to the Toyota Center. You can certainly find cheaper parking, though: Several garages within a few blocks of the stadium offer parking for $5 for many games. You can sometimes even find parking on the street within just 5 or 6 blocks of the Toyota Center.

The Rockets' season lasts from October through April, although it can extend into May or June if the team makes it deep into the playoffs.

i Arrive at the Toyota Center at least 30 minutes before tip-off to score giveaways at designated Rockets games. The free loot is often given to only the first 3,000 to 5,000 fans, so you've got to beat the crowd.

COLLEGE SPORTS

RICE UNIVERSITY $-$$
(713) 522-6957
riceowls.com

Rice University has 13 NCAA Division I teams, but the baseball team is by far the most successful of these. When the Rice Owls won the College World Series in 2003, they became the smallest school in 51 years to win a national championship at baseball's highest collegiate level. Since then, the team has continued to make appearances in the tournament, where the Owls finished third in 2006 and 2007.

The school's women's teams also fare pretty well, with the volleyball, soccer, tennis, and basketball teams advancing to their respective NCAA tournaments in the recent years. After a 45-year dry spell, Rice's football team played in bowl games in 2006 and 2008.

The Owls compete in Conference USA's Western Division.

Games and meets against the University of Houston, Texas A&M, and the University of Texas at Austin always draw large crowds.

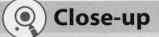 **Close-up**

Red Rowdies

After the Rockets ended the 2005-2006 season with a 15-26 home record, the team's coach at the time, Jeff Van Gundy, decided something had to be done to energize the crowd and help restore the home-court advantage. Borrowing a page from the San Antonio Spurs' "Baseline Bums," Van Gundy decided to round up the loudest, most rowdy Rockets fans. The team held auditions to find fans who fit the bill. Van Gundy bought season tickets for the 30 most impressive—that is, loud and colorful to the point of annoying—fans to sit behind the basket closest to the Rockets bench. The Red Rowdies were so loud during the preseason that player Tracy McGrady bought tickets for 20 more Red Rowdies. The move paid off: The Rockets went 28-13 at home during the 2006-2007 season.

Neither Van Gundy nor McGrady is with the Rockets anymore, but the Red Rowdies live on, with auditions for new Rowdies held each fall. Thirty minutes before each home game, the Rowdies gather at the Toyota Center's LaBranch entrance for their noisy ROMP. The Rowdies attend games clad in Rockets red and rarely sit down, which can be annoying for other fans in their section hoping to see and/or sit. But if you want to be in the heart of the action, section 114 is the place to be.

Tickets for these events cost $1 to $3 more than tickets to other games.

Rice's teams play at various facilities around campus, including Reckling Park (baseball), Rice Stadium (football), Tudor Fieldhouse (basketball), Jake Hess Tennis Stadium, and Rice Track/Soccer Stadium.

Baseball tickets range from $10 to $18 for adults ($5 for children). Tickets for men's basketball range from $15 to $30; tickets are $5 cheaper if you buy them before game day. Tickets for other events are also pretty cheap. Purchase tickets to all Rice sporting events on the school's website, by phone, or at the ticket office in Tudor Fieldhouse at 6100 Main St.

The campus is located across the street from Hermann Park and just a few blocks north of the Texas Medical Center. It's bounded by Main Street, Sunset Boulevard, Rice Boulevard, Greenbriar Street, and University Boulevard. Free public parking for

Rice athletic events is available in West Lot 4, which is accessible from University Boulevard and located between Greenbriar and Main Streets. Adjacent lots are also opened for football games.

UNIVERSITY OF HOUSTON $-$$$
(713) 462-6647 (box office)
uhcougars.com
With 16 intercollegiate teams, the University of Houston (UH) is almost always hosting some sporting event. Although the school's football and basketball teams have the largest following, events in nearly every sport see big turnouts, thanks to a large alumni base and the school's winning tradition. The University of Houston Cougars—aka the Cougs—currently play in the NCAA Division I's Conference USA; in 2013, they'll join the Big East Conference. UH's teams have won nearly three dozen conference titles since Conference USA formed in 1995.

The Cougars have also won 17 NCAA team titles—16 in golf—and 55 NCAA individual championships and played in 21 bowl games and 5 men's Final Four games. This success can be attributed at least partly to the caliber of athletes the school recruits and produces. The list of UH alumni includes NBA Hall of Famers (and former Houston Rockets) Hakeem Olajuwon and Clyde Drexler, track and field star Carl Lewis, former Dallas Cowboys coach Tom Landry, golfer Fred Couples, and Heisman Trophy–winner Andre Ware.

The football team plays at Robertson Stadium. The men's and women's basketball teams play at Hofheinz Pavilion and the baseball team plays at Cougar Field. All of these facilities are located on the UH campus, about 3 miles southeast of downtown at the intersection of I-45 and Texas Spur 5.

Ticket prices vary by sport. Football tickets range from $20 to $80. Men's basketball and baseball tickets range from $8 to $15; women's basketball tickets range from $8 to $20. Discounted tickets are available for kids. UH students get in to all regular season sporting events for free. Purchase tickets on the university's website, by phone, or at the ticket office on the first floor of the Athletics/ Alumni Center, next door to Hofheinz Pavilion. Parking is available in $5 and $10 lots around campus.

FOOTBALL

✳HOUSTON TEXANS
   FOOTBALL   **$$–$$$**
Reliant Stadium
1 Reliant Park, inner loop of the
southern portion of Loop 610 between
Kirby Street and Fannin Street
(866) 468-3926
houstontexans.com

When owner Bud Adams moved the Houston Oilers—the city's first NFL franchise—to Tennessee in 1997, Houston football fans were deprived of a team of their own for five long, agonizing seasons. In 2002 the city finally got a new team and a new stadium, complete with a retractable roof that's open on sunny days when the temperature is between 50 and 80 degrees Fahrenheit. Located just north of the South Loop near the intersection of Kirby Street and McNee, Reliant Stadium sits in Reliant Park, right next door to the Astrodome, the closed-domed stadium that the Oilers called home.

Since the Texans' arrival, Houston football fans have been making up for lost time and then some. The Texans consistently sell out games, and just about everyone comes to Reliant Stadium clad in red or navy (the team's colors) and ready to cheer. Many of the 71,500 fans tailgate outside the stadium starting as many as 4 hours before kickoff. Not surprisingly Reliant Stadium can be a tough place for the Texans' opponents to play; in recent years the Texans have won the vast majority of their home games. In fact, when the Texans played the franchise's first playoff game in January 2012, they won in decisive fashion, thanks in large part to an incredibly loud home crowd.

Tickets range from about $38 to $125. Since games sell out quickly, it's best to buy yours early.

Ticket holders with prepaid parking passes can park in the Miller Lite Parking Lots. There's no cash parking on-site, so be sure to purchase a parking pass when buying your tickets. No parking pass? You'll have to take a cab, bus, or the METRORail to the game. The METRORail stops at Reliant Park every 12 minutes on game day. Train tickets cost just $1.25 each way.

ℹ️ Visit the Texans' website or watch the sports segment of the local news before the game to find out if the roof will be open. If it will, take sunglasses and a sweatshirt or sweater. The stadium can get chilly if you're sitting in shaded areas and sunny if you're sitting in more open areas.

MEINEKE CAR CARE BOWL OF TEXAS $$-$$$
Reliant Stadium
1 Reliant Park, inner loop of the southern portion of Loop 610 between Kirby Street and Fannin Street
meinekecarcarebowloftexas.com
At the end of December, college football fans head to Reliant Stadium for the Meineke Car Care Bowl (formerly known as the Texas Bowl). This NCAA Division I bowl game features teams from the Big 12 and Big Ten.

Although the Meineke Car Care Bowl of Texas lacks the pomp and prestige of, say, the Rose Bowl, it's quickly becoming a Houston tradition. The 2011 bowl game pitted the Texas A&M Aggies against the Northwestern Wildcats and drew some 68,395 fans—the second-highest attendance in the bowl's history. The bowl kicks off with TexFest, a pregame carnival featuring horseshoes, tailgate competitions, washers, and food in the Reliant Stadium parking lot. Tickets start just under $20. Cash parking is available at the stadium for $20 to $30. See the Houston Texans listing on page 171 for directions and METRORail information.

GOLF

SHELL HOUSTON OPEN $$-$$$
Redstone Golf Club
5860 Wilson Rd., Humble
(281) 454-7000
shellhoustonopen.com
Since 1946, Houston has hosted the Shell Houston Open, a tournament on the PGA Tour. The event has moved around town over the years, and today it's played at Redstone Golf Club, located just outside of Houston in Humble. The tournament always draws some of the biggest names in golf, with recent winners including Phil Mickelson, Fred Couples, Stuart Appleby, and Vijay Singh.

The 6-day tournament is held in April. Tickets can be purchased (or, if necessary, reissued or transferred) and printed through the Shell Houston Open website. General admission is $20 for early rounds and increases to $25 for the final rounds.

Redstone Golf Club is located south of North Beltway 8 East, which intersects with US 59, just north of the city. Free parking is available on-site on Monday, Tuesday, and Wednesday. On Thursday and Friday, park in the ecopark lot at George Bush Intercontinental Airport for $5 and take a free shuttle to and from the tournament. The ecopark lot is located just off JFK Boulevard (the main road to the airport) at Greens Road.

GREYHOUND RACING

GULF GREYHOUND PARK $
1000 FM 2004, La Marque
(409) 986-9500
gulfgreyhound.com
The world's largest greyhound racing park is just 30 miles south of Houston at Gulf Greyhound Park. More than 10

million people have visited this four-level, air-conditioned park to cheer (and bet) on the dogs since Gulf Greyhound opened in 1992. In addition to the traditional win, place, and show wagers, the track offers daily double, pick three, trifecta, exacta, $1 superfecta, and a slew of other wager options. The park features both live racing events and simulcasts of races elsewhere in the world.

Many people enjoy the food here almost as much as the gambling. The Terrace Clubhouse on the park's second level serves fried Gulf shrimp, steak, salads, and desserts that can be eaten while watching the greyhounds race around the quarter-mile sand composition track below. Prefer something more akin to fast food? Take advantage of the concession stands on the park's first and second floors.

The park seats 6,600 but standing-room-only admission is available, enabling the park to hold up to 14,000 people. Races held Thurs through Sat evenings start at 7 p.m. On Wed, Sat, and Sun, the park holds matinee races. Wednesday matinees begin at noon; weekend matinees start at 1:30 p.m. The doors open 1 hour before all races.

Tickets are only sold on-site. General admission is $2; clubhouse admission is $3. Parking is free. To get to Gulf Greyhound Park from Houston, take I-45 South, then take exit 15. The park is 1 block west of the highway.

i Call in advance to reserve your table at the Terrace Clubhouse at Gulf Greyhound Park. Otherwise, your best dining option at the park may be a concession-stand hot dog.

HOCKEY

HOUSTON AEROS HOCKEY $-$$$
Toyota Center
1510 Polk St.
(713) 974-7825
aeros.com

Named after the city's successful 1970s World Hockey Association franchise, the Aeros debuted In 1994 as an International Hockey League (IHL) franchise. Today the IHL—at least the rendition that brought the Aeros to town—is no longer around, so the Aeros play in the American Hockey League as the primary developmental affiliate for the National Hockey League's Minnesota Wild. Despite the league change, the Aeros have maintained a winning tradition that began during the IHL days. In 1999 the team won the IHL Turner Cup and the Aeros continue to make the playoffs just about every year.

The team plays at the Toyota Center, having followed the Rockets there from the Compaq Center in 2003. From Chinese food to pizza to roast beef sandwiches and salad, the team's new home is full of food options that make Aeros games a popular destination for a night out, with or without the kids. The stadium can hold about 17,000 hockey fans, but games don't usually sell out. Tickets range from $13 to $79 if you purchase them in advance; prices increase on game day. The Aeros' season runs from October to April. Check out the Rockets listing in this chapter for information on parking around the Toyota Center.

HORSE RACING

SAM HOUSTON RACE PARK $-$$
7575 N. Sam Houston Pkwy. West
(281) 807-8760
shrp.com

Sam Houston Race Park hosts live thorough-bred races, as well as simulcasts of races held around the world. Each thoroughbred event features 10 races a night. This, combined with the park's alluring dinner options, makes the park a popular evening destination. Dinner options include a Texas-size buffet filled with carving stations, pasta and vegetable dishes, and a chocolate-fountain dessert bar. When there's not a race, the park often holds outdoor concerts featuring country, rock, and classic-rock musicians.

General admission starts at $6; kids 12 and under getting in for free. Special packages that include food start at $25 per person. Purchase tickets online, by phone, or at the ticket window. Parking ranges from $5 to $10.

The park is located in northwest Houston, just off the North Sam Houston Tollway at Fairbanks North Houston Road.. Live thoroughbred races take place from Nov through Apr on Thurs, Fri, Sat, and Sun nights. Races start at 7 p.m. on Thurs, Fri, and Sat and at 5 p.m. on Sun. The gates open at 10:30 a.m. on days when there are simulcasts.

MOTORSPORTS

ROYAL PURPLE RACEWAY $-$$$
2525 FM 565, Baytown
(281) 383-7223
royalpurpleraceway.com

Home to a 0.25-mile drag strip and a new 0.37-mile dirt oval track, Royal Purple Raceway (formerly Houston Raceway Park) hosts drag racing events. This Baytown area park holds 30,000 spectators. Some of the biggest crowds flock here for the National Hot Rod Association's prestigious O'Reilly Spring Nationals in late April or early May. Between the hot rods and the thousands of fans who show up to cheer and jeer, the park can get pretty noisy. But for those who love drag racing, the park—whose paved pit area holds about 400 pacing rigs—is a great place to get in on the action.

The park is located about 30 miles east of downtown Houston in Baytown. To get there, take I-10 East and exit at FM 565, going north.

Events are held year-round. Prices vary depending on the event, but tickets start at about $10 for most events. The exception is the O'Reilly Spring Nationals; tickets for this big-seller start at $30 for adults and $5 for kids. Parking prices also vary depending on the event, with rates ranging from $5 for smaller events to closer to $20 for O'Reilly Spring Nationals.

i In January, join nearly 200,000 Houstonians on the sidelines to cheer on 24,000 runners in the prestigious Chevron Houston Marathon and two others. Learn more on page 176.

SOCCER

HOUSTON DYNAMO SOCCER $$-$$$
BBVA Compass Stadium
1001 Avenida de las Americas
(713) 276-7500
houstondynamo.com

The Houston Dynamo are the newest team in town, and they're already one of the most successful. In their first two seasons—2006 and 2007—the Dynamo won the Major League Soccer Cup Championship. Of course, it didn't hurt that the team—previously known as the San Jose Earthquakes—had won two championships in their old hometown. When it moved to Texas, the Dynamo was originally going to be renamed Houston 1836—a tribute to the city's founding year. But the local Mexican community took issue with the name since 1836 is also the year that Texas separated from Mexico. So the franchise settled on Dynamo, a name that pays homage to Houston's energy sector and two previous Houston soccer teams, both named the Dynamos.

In any given season, the biggest draws are games against the other Major League Soccer (MLS) team from Texas—FC Dallas. The series of games the two play each season have been nicknamed the Texas Derby, or El Capitán Clasico. The team that wins the most games in the series is awarded a Civil War–era cannon called El Capitán. Unfortunately city regulations prohibit the Dynamo from firing the cannon in Houston.

After playing its first six seasons on the University of Houston campus, the Dynamo got its own downtown stadium to kick off the 2012 season. Dubbed the BBVA Compass Stadium, the new home of the Dyanmo seats 22,000. Ticket prices start at $24.

TENNIS

US MEN'S CLAY COURT
CHAMPIONSHIPS $$-$$$
River Oaks Country Club
1600 River Oaks Blvd.
(713) 874-6294
mensclaycourt.com

In early April the River Oaks Country Club hosts the US Men's Clay Court Championships, the last remaining Association of Tennis Professionals (ATP) tournament to be played on a clay court. The highly competitive championships have featured big names like Andy Roddick and Andre Agassi, as well as up-and-coming players. The tournament lasts a week, with matches held twice a day.

Tickets are sold on the tournament website. Prices increase as the tournament progresses; tickets to the earliest matches start at $20, and prices for the Finals start at $50.

Parking can usually be found on the side streets off River Oaks Boulevard. At night and on weekends, parking is available at Lamar High School (3325 Westheimer Rd., between Buffalo Speedway and Kirby). There's a free shuttle from the school to and from River Oaks Country Club.

ANNUAL EVENTS

Thanks to the hundreds of events held in Houston each year, you can always find something to do here. These events—many of them held year after year—are as diverse as the people of Houston themselves: There are car and boat shows, air shows, a marathon and other races, art events, cultural heritage celebrations, holiday events, food festivals, music festivals, shopping extravaganzas, the world's largest livestock show and rodeo, and even an art car parade.

OVERVIEW

Unfortunately, it would take several volumes to list all of the events that take place in and around Houston each year. So this chapter offers a sampling of some of the city's largest and quirkiest annual happenings. With a few exceptions, the events listed here are held in Houston. Many take place at downtown venues such as Discovery Green, the George R. Brown Convention Center, and Sam Houston Park; others are held in Hermann Park or Reliant Park. Some require venturing outside the city limits, though. These have been included because they draw so many people from Houston and the surrounding areas.

Almost all the events listed here are family friendly, and many offer special activities for kids. You can find a list of events for kids in the "Kidstuff" chapter.

Some events, such as the Ice at Discovery Green, begin in one month and end in another. These have been listed under the month in which they begin. Likewise, a Hanukkah event is listed in December, even though the holiday—and the corresponding event—occasionally falls at the end of November.

Events listed here are wheelchair accessible unless indicated otherwise. Call ahead and double-check, though, since some events change venues or accessibility offerings. The contact information provided here is for the event organizers. With a couple of noted exceptions, I've included the event location's street address.

JANUARY

CHEVRON HOUSTON MARATHON
George R. Brown Convention Center
1001 Avenida de las Americas, just off US 59 betwéen Polk Ave. and Texas St.
(713) 957-3453
houstonmarathon.com
Each January, Houston hosts its largest single-day sporting event: the prestigious Houston Marathon. Although the 26.2-mile marathon is the day's biggest draw, the Chevron-sponsored marathon is just one of three races held that day. There's also a half marathon sponsored by the petroleum company Aramco and a 5K run sponsored by El Paso Corporation. Participants are

encouraged to help raise money for more than 50 charities through the Run for a Reason program. In the program's first 17 years, runners and donors have raised more than $14 million.

The marathon begins downtown near Minute Maid Park and weaves through the Heights before heading down to Rice Village, west to the Galleria and Memorial area, and swinging back downtown by way of Memorial Park and Buffalo Bayou Park. All three races end downtown with festivities at the George R. Brown Convention Center.

During the races, masses of spectators cheer on the runners along White Oak Drive in the Heights, University Boulevard in West University, Post Oak and San Felipe, and Memorial Park. Visit the marathon website to find out approximately when the marathoners will be heading through your neighborhood.

Although the marathon is best known for its Sunday races, marathon weekend actually kicks off on Saturday with a kids' fun run sponsored by Texas Children's Hospital. About 5,000 youth ages 5 to 15 participate in the race, which also features a 1K adaptive run and walk for children with special needs.

Registration for the marathon and half marathon is capped at a combined total of 24,000 runners—13,000 for the marathon and 11,000 for the half marathon. Marathon and half-marathon registration opens in July and is determined by lottery. The 5K is capped at 4,500 participants. Registration prices change annually and by event.

HOUSTON INTERNATIONAL BOAT, SPORT & TRAVEL SHOW
Reliant Center
1 Reliant Park
(713) 526-6361
houstonboatshows.com

Serious boaters and campers flock to the Reliant Center each January and June for the Houston International Boat, Sport & Travel Show, better known as the Boat Show. With just shy of 500 exhibits and more than 150,000 attendees each year, this 10-day event is among the country's largest boat shows. Visitors get a sneak peek at more than 1,000 of the latest and greatest yachts, sailboats, and powerboats, as well as RVs and camping gear. Even better: attendees get special discounts. Industry leaders offer seminars on a variety of topics, and special presentations teach boating novices about boating safety and how to buy a boat. Taking the kids? When they get tired of looking at boats, let them help build a boat or go fishing in the Fish-O-Rama competition.

Admission is $10 for adults and $4 for kids under 12. Tickets can be purchased through Ticketmaster, or at the ticket window beginning 30 minutes before the show opens. Take note, though: only cash is accepted at the ticket windows. Cash parking is available at Reliant Park for $10. Want to save money and avoid the crowded parking lot? Take the METRORail. For directions see the Houston Texans write-up on page 171.

i Visit the Boat Show on Wednesday or Friday, and pay just $5 for adult admission and $5 for parking.

HOUSTON AUTO SHOW
Reliant Center
1 Reliant Park
(832) 667-1400
houstonautoshow.com
In the market for a new car, or just like to gaze at sleek new vehicles? Get your fix at the Houston Auto Show, where you'll find more than 500 of the hottest new domestic

and foreign cars and get sneak peaks at cars and trucks of the very near future. You can even test-drive some of the newest models. Children's entertainment is available at the Kids Fun Zone, a supervised play area with arts and crafts, a giant obstacle course, a Monster Truck Jump, and a 30-foot slide. The Auto Show is held at Reliant Center at the end of January or the beginning of February. Admission is $10 for adults; kids 12 and under get in free. Tickets can be purchased at the box office (cash only) starting 15 minutes before the show opens, or through Ticketmaster. Park at Reliant Park for $8, or take the METRORail to Reliant Park.

i Planning to attend the Auto Shop on a weekday? Get a coupon for $2 off the price of admission on the Auto Show website or at local care dealerships.

FEBRUARY

✳HOUSTON LIVESTOCK SHOW AND RODEO

Reliant Park
1 Reliant Park
(832) 667-1000
rodeohouston.com

You haven't really experienced Houston until you've been to the Livestock Show and Rodeo. This 3-week event starts in late February and runs through early to mid-March. Kicking off the world's biggest rodeo is the World Championship Bar-B-Que Contest. For 3 days, hundreds of teams compete to see who can make the best barbecue ribs, brisket, and chicken. More than 200,000 Houstonians turn out to get a whiff of the barbecue and enjoy free barbecue plates in the Chuck Wagon. There's live music each evening.

After the cook-off, the main event begins. Each night, a different big-name musician plays a concert at Reliant Stadium. Recent acts have included Beyonce, Kid Rock, and Blake Shelton. Every concert kicks off with real rodeo action—roping, riding, and yee-haws included. Some concerts sell out, so purchase tickets in advance if there's someone you want to see.

Many concertgoers head to Reliant Park early to check out the rest of the Livestock Show and Rodeo. At Reliant Center, you'll find milking, spinning and weaving, and cotton gin demonstrations and get an up-close look at the dairy goats, Brahmousin cattle, and Simbrah cattle in between checking out different livestock shows. Other highlights include a daily beef trivia contest, a burger toss, beef samples, and educational expos for ranchers. There's also plenty of rodeo getup and souvenirs to be purchased and food to be eaten at Reliant Center and Reliant Arena.

Outside, you'll find a Texas-size carnival, complete with roller coasters, Ferris wheels, cotton candy, and funnel cake galore. And kids can get a taste of life on the farm at the Kids Country Carnival, where you'll find pig races, a petting zoo, pony rides, live music, and a mechanical bull.

Tickets to the carnival, livestock and horse shows, shopping, and food areas cost $7 for guests 13 and up and $4 for kids ages 3 to 12. Tickets to the barbecue cook-off cost the same. Planning to attend the cook-off and other attractions (concerts excluded) multiple times? Consider buying a Houston Livestock Show Season Pass, which costs $25 per person. It gets you into the cook-off, carnival, and livestock and horse shows as many times as you want. Tickets to the rodeo concerts are sold through Ticketmaster and can be purchased on the rodeo website or

Close-up

Go Texan Day

Here in Houston, the Friday before the **Houston Livestock Show and Rodeo** kicks off—that is, the Friday of the cook-off—is **Go Texan Day**. That's when Houstonians don their best (and sometimes, kitschiest) Western getup—requisite denim, vest, bolo, cowboy boots and hat, and even spurs included. Schools around the city encourage their students and teachers to dress up and show up ready for rodeo-themed lessons and activities like square dancing. Those attending school or working along the city's major arteries, including Memorial Drive, get an added taste of the Wild West when they look out their windows and see more than 4,000 trail riders in 13 different trail rides coming into town from across Texas, Louisiana, and even Mexico. The trail riders make their way into town along various routes, but they all end up on Memorial Drive and head into Memorial Park. The trail riders begin entering the park between 10 a.m. and 5 p.m., when the Trail Ride Awards Ceremony is held. The trail riders' arrival makes for some serious traffic throughout much of the day, but against the backdrop of Houston's skyscrapers and freeway system, it's a sight that shouldn't be missed.

After camping out at Memorial Park for the night, the trail riders rise early Saturday morning and ride the last 5 miles down Memorial Drive to downtown. There, dozens of trail riders, stagecoaches, area marching bands, and local dignitaries march the streets of downtown for the Rodeo Parade before the trail riders head to Reliant Park for the main event.

by phone. They'll cost you anywhere from $18 to $300. All rodeo concert tickets include admission to Reliant Stadium, Reliant Arena, Reliant Center, and the carnival. Cash parking is available at Reliant Park for $7 during the day on weekdays and for $12 on weekday evenings and weekends.

MARCH

RIVER OAKS GARDEN CLUB AZALEA TRAIL

River Oaks Garden Club Forum of Civics and other locations in the River Oaks area
2503 Westheimer Rd.
(713) 523-2483
riveroaksgardenclub.org/AzaleaTrail.cfm

Each spring Houston neighborhoods brighten up with pink, white, purple, red, and yellow azalea blooms. For 3 days in early March, the River Oaks Garden Club celebrates these flowers by offering tours of seven of the city's most beautiful mansions and azalea-filled gardens. Most of these sites are relatively close, but few are actually within walking distance of one another. Only two sites—the River Oaks Garden Club Forum of Civics Building & Gardens and the Bayou Bend Gardens—are wheelchair accessible. Tickets to a single site can be purchased for $5; a ticket for all seven sites can be purchased for $20 during the event or for $15 in advance. Proceeds benefit conservation, horticulture, and beautification efforts around the city. Tickets can be purchased at the River Oaks Garden Club, Randall's, Rice Epicurean grocery stores, the Museum of Fine Arts, Houston, and several nurseries around the city. You can find a full list of ticket outlets, as well as the addresses of the seven sites, on the event website.

FOTOFEST BIENNIAL
1113 Vine St., Ste. 101 (headquarters)
(713) 223-5522
fotofest.org
Held in even-numbered years, this internationally acclaimed festival and conference celebrates photography and other image-heavy art. Each FotoFest has a different social or aesthetic theme of global relevance. The biennial, which was attended by some 265,000 people from 32 countries in 2010, runs for several weeks from mid-March to late April. Highlights include exhibits, a film and video series, a fine print auction, educational workshops, and reviews of participating photographers' and artists' portfolios by curators and critics. The events are held at more than 100 different venues, including museums, galleries, and even retail establishments. Event prices vary. Visit the website or call FotoFest headquarters for schedule and event pricing information.

✳BAYOU CITY ART FESTIVAL
March: Memorial Park
October: Downtown around City Hall
bayoucityartfestival.com
Whether you like good art or just want something fun to do here in March or October, put the Bayou City Art Festival on your must-do list. The semiannual event is regarded as one of the country's best art festivals—and for good reason. More than 300 artists and crafters from around the country participate, and all of them must

apply and win the approval of the festival jury. The semiannual festival is held along a 1.1-mile loop in Memorial Park for 3 days during late March; in mid-October a 2-day show is held downtown in front of City Hall around Hermann Square and at Sam Houston Park. In addition to gallery-quality art of all media, both shows feature cooking demonstrations from some of the city's top chefs, food and wine samplings, artist demonstrations, live musical and dance performances, and the Creative Zone, where kids make crafts such as mini art cars and wax hand sculptures. Admission is $12 for guests 12 and up; kids under 12 get in free. All festival profits benefit local charities. Although both festivals are held outdoors, pets aren't allowed.

Unfortunately, there's no public parking in Memorial Park for the Bayou City Art Festival. But you can take a free shuttle to and from Northwest Mall (located on Loop 610 North at 18th Street). On Saturday and Sunday, there's also free shuttle service between the park and three locations downtown—Memorial Drive at Rusk Street, Smith Street at Capitol Street, and Rusk Street at Smith Street. Parking information for the October festival can be found in the "October" section of this chapter on page 188.

APRIL

JAPAN FESTIVAL
Japanese Garden at Hermann Park, just west of the Jesse H. Jones Reflection Pool
(713) 963-0121
japan-fest.com
Each April nearly 20,000 people head to Hermann Park's serene Japanese Garden for the Japan Festival. This 2-day event celebrates

Japanese culture with traditional Japanese dance performances, food from local Japanese restaurants, martial arts demonstrations, and opportunities to learn about ikebana, origami, calligraphy, and anime. Admission is free, as is parking, which is available in several lots around Hermann Park. Or take the METRORail to the Rice U/Hermann Park stop. For more information on parking in or visiting Hermann Park, see the Hermann Park write-up on page 146.

US MEN'S CLAY COURT
CHAMPIONSHIPS
River Oaks Country Club
1600 River Oaks Blvd.
(713) 874-6294
mensclaycourt.com
In early April, the River Oaks Country Club hosts the US Men's Clay Court Championships, the last remaining Association of Tennis Professionals (ATP) tournament to be played on a clay court. The highly competitive championships have featured established tennis pros like Andy Roddick and Andre Agassi, as well as up-and-coming players. The tournament lasts a week, with matches held twice a day.

Tickets are sold on the tournament website. Prices increase as the tournament progresses; tickets to the earliest matches start at $20, and tickets for the Finals start at $50.

Parking can usually be found on the side streets off River Oaks Boulevard. At night and on weekends, tournament parking is available at Lamar High School, located at 3325 Westheimer Rd., between Westheimer and West Alabama and between Buffalo Speedway and Kirby. There's a free shuttle from the school to and from River Oaks Country Club.

BAYOU CITY CAJUN FESTIVAL
7979 North Eldridge Rd., accessible from I-10 or 290
(281) 890-5500
tradersvillage.com/en/houston
Red beans and rice. Gumbo. Boiled crawfish and fried alligator. Cajun sausage. Boudin. This is the stuff of the Bayou City Cajun Fest, hosted by Traders Village for one weekend each April. If the spicy food doesn't give the event a down-home feeling, the live music—fiddles included—and dancing in the rustic Traders Village establishment are sure to do the trick. Admission is free. Parking costs $3.

MENU OF MENUS EXTRAVAGANZA
Various locations
(713) 280-2896
menuofmenus.com
Each April winos, foodies, and beer lovers flock to the Houston Press's Menu of Menus Extravaganza. This popular 1-night event celebrates Houston's vibrant restaurant industry with samples from dozens of the city's best restaurants, as well as wine, beer, and spirits tastings. There's also live entertainment, a cash bar, and the opportunity to meet some of the city's most esteemed chefs. Participating restaurants and bars vary from year to year; each year's participants are featured in the *Houston Press*'s free Menu of Menus supplement, which hits newsstands a few days after the event. Menu of Menus has been held at several different venues over the past few years, so call or check the website to find out where it's being held.

General admission costs $40 if you purchase tickets in advance; admission costs $50 at the door. For $80 you can get in an hour early to sample signature dishes and gain access to the VIP room, which offers top-shelf liquor and pricey bottles of wine. Menu of Menus tends to sell out, so purchase tickets online in advance. All proceeds benefit local charities. Liquor flows freely here, so you must be 21 or older—and have a valid ID to prove it.

SHELL HOUSTON OPEN
Redstone Golf Club
5860 Wilson Rd., Humble
(281) 454-7000
shellhoustonopen.com

Since 1946, Houston has hosted the Shell Houston Open, a tournament on the PGA Tour. After moving around town over the years, the tournament is now played just outside of Houston in Humble at Redstone Golf Club. Shell Houston Open draws some of the biggest names in golf, with recent winners including Phil Mickelson, Fred Couples, and Vijay Singh.

The 6-day tournament is held in April. Tickets can be purchased through the Shell Houston Open website. General admission costs $20 early in the tournament and increases to $25 for the final rounds. Free parking is available on-site on Monday, Tuesday, and Wednesday. On Thursday and Friday, park in the ecopark lot at George Bush Intercontinental Airport for $5 and take a free shuttle to and from the tournament. The ecopark lot is located just off JFK Boulevard (the main road to the airport) at Greens Road.

✳HOUSTON INTERNATIONAL FESTIVAL
Downtown in City Hall, Tranquility Park, and Sam Houston Park
(713) 654-8808
ifest.org

The Houston International Festival—aka iFest—celebrates the city's diversity and encourages goodwill with the US' international trade partners. Each year's festival pays tribute to a different country with interactive exhibits, music, dance performances, fashion shows, cooking demonstrations, and food.

iFest is broken into six entertainment zones, each featuring music, art, and food from a different region. One zone is always reserved for the honored country. Other zones include Africa and the Caribbean, Texas/Latin America, International, Louisiana, and Jamaica. There's also a Kids Zone with a petting zoo, pony rides, inflatable games, a NASA exhibit, and festival treats like funnel cakes and candied apples.

More than 500 jewelry designers, photographers, painters, ceramicists, and other artisans sell their work throughout the iFest area. Some of the best art can be found along Fine Arts Avenue, a juried show featuring some of the country's most talented artists.

iFest is usually held for 2 consecutive weekends in late April; the Friday before the festival is iFest Preview Day. This free event takes place at City Hall during lunchtime and features an opening ceremony, concerts, and a chance to sample some of the international fare that will be served at the main event.

Admission costs $18 for ages 13 and up, and $3 for kids ages 3 to 12. Kids younger than 3 get in free. Tickets can be purchased on the festival website and at local H-E-B grocery stores. Food and drinks require iFest coupons, which can be purchased on-site for $1.50 each and $10 for sheets of nine.

Parking is available for $7 in the Theater District Parking Garages. The most convenient parking is available in Garage 2 at Rusk Street between Bagby Street and Smith Street and in Garage 3, located behind the

(Q) Close-up

Cinco de Mayo

Houston's large Hispanic population makes for lots of **Cinco de Mayo** celebrations on and around May 5. On that day in 1852, the Mexican army overcame steep odds to defeat the French at the Battle of Puebla. Today that victory is celebrated in different ways at venues and events around the city. At just about every Tex-Mex restaurant in town, for instance, Houstonians—many not quite sure what they're celebrating—show up for margarita specials and Mexican food galore.

Elsewhere around Houston, several family-friendly events celebrate Latino and Hispanic culture. Exact dates vary, as many venues celebrate Cinco de Mayo on the weekend closest to May 5. **Miller Outdoor Theatre** in Hermann Park celebrates with an afternoon full of mariachis and musical and dance performances. The event is always free. Visit the Miller Outdoor Theatre website (milleroutdoortheatre.com) for details.

Traders Village serves fresh fajitas, margaritas, live music, games, and community service exhibits for adults, and tasty treats and games for little ones. The event is free; on-site parking costs $3. Learn more on the Traders Village website (tradersvillage.com/en/houston).

Univision, the Spanish radio broadcasting network, sponsors one of the state's largest Cinco de Mayo celebrations downtown at the **George R. Brown Convention Center** (1001 Avenue of the Americas). The festive event features arts and crafts, tons of Mexican food, live Latino music, and games for the kids. Call (713) 407-1455 for details.

City Hall Annex at Bagby Street and Walker Street. Use the Downtown map on page x to navigate your way to these garages.

i Visit the iFest website a few weeks before the festival to get discounted admission tickets, which are good for any single day of the event.

MAY

✴ART CAR PARADE
Allen Parkway from Waugh to Bagby Street
(713) 926-6368
orangeshow.org/artcar.html
On the second Saturday of May, some 250 souped-up cars—airbrushed and decorated

in the loudest, most unexpected ways—make Houstonians *ooh, ah,* and laugh hysterically. A Toyota Rav4 turned into a hippopotamus? Check. A car transformed into a loader? Ditto. The parade runs along Allen Parkway from Waugh to Bagby Street, and it's free to watch. Even better views are available at the VIPit Party, held at the Heritage Society at 1100 Bagby St. The party starts a couple of hours before the parade and runs until the parade is over. Tickets cost $125 in exchange for one of the city's best views of the parade, drinks, food from some of Houston's best restaurants, and family-friendly activities. VIPit Party tickets help offset the costs of the parade and are available on the website.

Want a sneak peek of the art cars—and a look at some old favorites? Head downtown to Discovery Green (page 145) the evening before the parade for the Houston Art Car Parade Sneak Peek. This free event also features live music and other entertainment.

> **i** Check out art cars year-round at the ArtCar Museum (artcar museum.com), which features some of its own art cars, as well as other unusual contemporary art. The museum is located in the Heights at 140 Heights Blvd. Admission is free.

JUNE

HOUSTON PRIDE FESTIVAL AND PARADE
Montrose neighborhood along Commonwealh and Yoakum (festival)
Westheimer between Dunlavy and Crocker (parade)
(713) 529-6979
pridehouston.org
On the fourth Saturday in June, more than 50,000 of the city's gay, lesbian, bisexual, and transgender communities and supporters come out for the Houston Pride Festival and Parade. The colorful festivities—which wrap up the 7-day Pride Week—are held in Montrose, a neighborhood with a strong gay and lesbian community. The day begins with the festival, which is broken down into several sections: The Festival Latino section features traditional Latin cuisine and music from Houston's southern neighbors. The Gender Block shares information and exhibits geared toward transgender individuals, while Community Street offers lots of food options, crafts, and the main stage. Art exhibits—including crafts, sculptures, and other work available for sale—fill the artSpace section. There are also two kid-friendly areas: Kids

Zone is home to inflatable bouncers, face painting, balloons, and snacks, and the Family Retreat is an alcohol-free section featuring live, family-friendly music.

In the evening the festival ends and the Southwest's biggest pride parade begins. Each year's parade has a different theme, and participants vie for awards in categories such as Ruby Slipper (best walking), Stonewall (best social commentary), and Pink Diamond (best float for a for-profit). The community selects the parade's grand marshal through online voting. The parade, which draws more than 300,000 people each year, runs through Montrose on Westheimer Road between Dunlavy and Crocker Streets. Limited parking is available on side streets near the parade route.

Admission to the parade and festival is free, but donations are encouraged. Most exhibitors and food vendors only accept cash; there's an ATM on-site.

> **i** In the weeks and months leading up to the festival and parade, Pride Houston hosts several events, including a masquerade, Pride Superstar Finale, and a fashion show. Learn about these events at pridehouston.org.

JULY

✳FREEDOM OVER TEXAS
Eleanor Tinsley Park at Buffalo Bayou on Allen Parkway, just west of downtown
freedomovertexas.org
There are plenty of ways to celebrate the Fourth of July in Houston but Freedom Over Texas is the official celebration—that is, the one sponsored by the mayor's office. On Fourth of July afternoon, thousands of Houstonians begin staking out their spots

Close-up

Juneteenth

President Abraham Lincoln issued the Emancipation Proclamation in September 1862, but it wasn't until June 19, 1865, that Texans first learned that the slaves were free. Since 1980, **Juneteenth,** as that historic day is now called, has been an official state holiday in Texas. Offices don't actually close, but some employees use a floating holiday to take the day off. Twenty-eight other states have also made June 19 a holiday, but no state celebrates Juneteenth quite like Texas.

Celebrations of black culture and freedom take place throughout the Houston area and Galveston—the first Texas city to learn of the Emancipation Proclamation. Many churches hold special events, as do civic centers in some of the outlying areas. Some events are held on June 19; others take place on the days before or after.

One of the best celebrations in town is Houston's **Juneteenth Celebration,** sponsored by the Houston Institute for Culture. Held at Hermann Park's Miller Outdoor Theatre, this free event showcases blues, jazz, zydeco, brass band, funk, and gospel music by some of today's most talented black musicians. More than 8,000 turn out each year. Parking is available around Hermann Park, although you may have to drive around to find a space. Learn more at houstonculture.org/juneteenth or miller outdoortheatre.com, or by calling (713) 521-3686.

Another popular Juneteenth celebration is the **Freedom Parade,** which takes place downtown. The colorful parade is accented by boisterous music. Some parade participants also pass out flyers and carry banners about the impact of war and the death penalty on the African-American community today. The parade begins at Texas and Hamilton Streets. Learn more at neausa.org or by calling National Emancipation Association, Inc., at (832) 892-8780.

in Eleanor Tinsley Park at Buffalo Bayou and laying out their blankets and lawn chairs to watch patriotic and current musical performances by pop, Latin, country, oldies, and classic-rock artists. The festival also includes rides, games, and food booths. Around 9:30 p.m., the sky lights up with a magnificent 20-minute fireworks show that can be seen around much of the city.

Admission costs $8 per person; kids 2 and younger get in free. Adults can also get in free by donating one canned good per person at the gate; donations benefit the Houston Food Bank. Food, drink, and game vendors only accept special event coupons as payment. Packs of nine coupons can be purchased for $10. The city closes off many streets around the park on the day of Freedom Over Texas, so close parking can be tough to come by. Your best bet? Park in one of the Theater District parking garages downtown. The most convenient one is Garage 2, located along Rusk Street between Bagby and Smith Streets. See the Downtown map on page x. To avoid significant congestion on your drive to Freedom Over Texas, visit the event website or watch the local news to find out which streets have been closed off.

i Crowds don't usually show up for Freedom Over Texas until about 5:30 p.m. Find a better parking spot—and seating—by lathering on some sunscreen, bringing a bottle of water (or three) and a deck of cards, and showing up around 4 or 4:30.

✳FOURTH OF JULY AT MILLER OUTDOOR THEATRE
Miller Outdoor Theatre in Hermann Park
(713) 284-8350
milleroutdoortheatre.com
If you like a great symphony, fireworks, and money in your wallet, Miller Outdoor Theatre might be more your Fourth of July scene than Eleanor Tinsley Park. Each year thousands of Houstonians sit outside on blankets and lawn chairs and celebrate Independence Day with a night of all-American tunes performed by the Houston Symphony. Among the highlights: a rousing performance of Tchaikovsky's *1812 Overture* and a 16-cannon salute. The patriotic evening wraps up with a vibrant fireworks display. Admission is free. Refreshments and drinks are available for purchase, but it's even more fun to pack a picnic. Sit near the top of the hill and you might even steal a glimpse of the Freedom Over Texas fireworks display. See the Hermann Park write-up on page 146 of the "Parks" chapter for parking information.

ARTHOUSTON
Various locations
(713) 522-9116
arthouston.com
Each July more than 30 galleries participate in ArtHouston by launching new exhibits and hosting receptions toasting the work of up-and-coming regional artists and established artists from around the world. The works featured at these galleries span a variety of media, including painting, sculpture, drawing, photography, and mixed media. Not all of the participating galleries are within walking distance of one another, but many are clustered in the Museum District, the Heights, or along Gallery Row in Upper Kirby. All exhibits are free to the public. Visit the ArtHouston website for a map of participating galleries.

QFEST
Various locations
qfest.org
One of Houston's hottest gay, lesbian, bisexual, and transgendered cultural events takes place in late September. Originally, the event was known as the Houston Gay and Lesbian International Film Festival. But the name was changed to QFest in 2007 to reflect the festival's commitment not just to film but also to art and music. Despite the name change, the festival remains best known for showcasing full-length movies and shorts promoting sexual diversity and the work of LGBT and female filmmakers. Most films are screened at the Museum of Fine Arts Houston, Rice Media Center, or Discovery Green. Tickets cost $10 per movie for adults. Museum members and guests 65 and older get in for $8. Tickets are available through the QFest website or at the museum. For parking information, see the Museum of Fine Arts Houston write-up on page 123.

AUGUST

HOUSTON INTERNATIONAL JAZZ FESTIVAL
Discovery Green
1500 McKinney St.
(713) 839-7000
jazzeducation.org

Love some good jazz? You won't want to miss this darling of the Houston summer festival scene. Each August, Discovery Green hosts the Houston International Jazz Festival. And, as the festival demonstrates, jazz here really is an international form of music. This 3-day event showcases jazz musicians hailing from several continents. Be sure to bring a blanket to sit on, sunscreen, and sunglasses.

Tickets can be purchased in advance for $20 through Ticketmaster or at the gate for $25. Proceeds benefit Jazz Education, a local organization that promotes music education in schools.

*HOUSTON SHAKESPEARE FESTIVAL
**Miller Outdoor Theatre at Hermann Park
100 Concert Dr., just south of the
Houston Museum of Natural Science
(281) 373-3386
houstonfestivalscompany.com**
A perennial summer favorite, the Houston Shakespeare Festival takes place at Miller Outdoor Theatre in Hermann Park during the first part of August. Two different Shakespeare plays are performed every summer. Each play is performed multiple nights to accommodate the thousands of Houstonians who flock here. Many of them get their first exposure to Shakespeare through the festival, and many are repeat guests, some bringing along a picnic to eat before or during the performance. Whether you choose to bring a picnic, buy food on-site, or eat beforehand, be sure to bring blankets to sit on since the grass can be moist. The festival is free. See page 147 for information about parking around Hermann Park.

*THEATER DISTRICT OPEN HOUSE
**Various downtown theater locations
(713) 658-8938
houstontheaterdistrict.org**
Just before theater season kicks off, the Alley Theatre (615 Texas Ave.), Hobby Center for the Performing Arts (800 Bagby), Wortham Theater Center (501 Texas Ave.), and Jones Hall (615 Louisiana Ave.) all open their doors and raise their curtains to host a free open house. This free family event takes place on a Sunday afternoon in August and offers an opportunity to learn more about several of Houston's biggest performing arts organizations. Among the highlights: backstage tours, Q&As, special performances, an instrument petting zoo, and a scavenger hunt complete with prizes. Parking is available in the Theater District Parking Garage; see the map on page x.

i Want the full rundown of Houston happenings during your visit or permanent stay here? Go online to CultureMap (houston.culturemap.com) or 29/95 (29-95.com).

SEPTEMBER

*MUSEUM DISTRICT DAY
**Various locations in the Museum District
(713) 715-1939
houstonmuseumdistrict.org**
For one Saturday in September, thousands of Houstonians descend upon the Museum District to go museum hopping. That's because most of the museums in the Museum District offer free admission that day, enabling Houstonians of all ages to visit their favorite museums and discover new ones. Highlights include special docent-led tours, hands-on activities, demonstrations, and other special

events. Free shuttles provide transportation to any of the participating museums. Visit museumdistrict.org to download a schedule and find out about parking options.

OCTOBER

BAYOU CITY ART FESTIVAL
March: Memorial Park
October: Downtown in front of City Hall and along Walker, Bagby, and McKinney Streets
bayoucityartfestival.com
The Bayou City Art Festival is held downtown in front of City Hall around Hermann Square and at Sam Houston Park. See the listing on page 180 for details.

Parking for the Bayou City Art Festival downtown in October is available in the Theater District Parking Garages 2 (Rusk Street at Bagby Street), 3 (Walker Street at Bagby Street), and 5 (Capitol Street at Smith Street). Look at the Downtown map on page x to see exactly where these garages are located. All-day parking costs $7.

✳THE ORIGINAL GREEK FESTIVAL
Annunciation Greek Orthodox Cathedral
3511 Yoakum Blvd., 1 block east of Montrose between Harold and Kipling Streets
(713) 526-5377
greekfestival.org
It's all Greek to Houston for 4 days at the beginning of October. That's when the Annunciation Greek Orthodox Cathedral complex hosts The Original Greek Festival—not to be confused with the smaller Greek festival held in Clear Lake in May. Highlights include cathedral tours, Greek folk dancing, and the Athenian Playground, where kids play and enjoy crafts and other activities.

But the biggest draw is the food, including souvlaki, Greek salad, gyros, and other Greek food and pastries made by the cathedral's parishioners using generations-old recipes.

Admission costs $5; kids 12 and under get in free. Food isn't included in the price of admission. But some advance planning and $20 will get you a presale ticket, which includes admission and a dinner plate. Visit the cathedral in advance or call to order presale tickets.

There's no parking at the complex, but limited parking is available on the street. Just watch for the No Parking signs around the area. Your safest bet is to park at Lamar High School (3325 Westheimer, between Westheimer and West Alabama and between Buffalo Speedway and Kirby), and take the free shuttle.

HOUSTON WOMEN'S MUSIC FESTIVAL
Jones Plaza
601 Louisiana St., at Texas Ave.
hwfestival.org
Since 1995, the Houston Women's Music Festival has celebrated the artistic contributions of independent female musicians from the Gulf Coast region. Hosted by the Athena Art Project, this daylong event features performances by about 10 solo artists and groups, as well as wine tastings and food. Many artists also sell their work here. The festival is usually held in October, but it sometimes takes place in September. About 1,000 people—mostly women—attend each year. The event is held outside at Jones Plaza, so it tends to be hot and humid. Tickets cost $15 in advance and $22 at the gate. Parking is available for $7 in the Theater District Parking Garage in front of Jones Hall. Use entrance 4 on Texas Avenue or entrance 7 on Capitol Street.

*TEXAS RENAISSANCE FESTIVAL

21778 FM 1774, Plantersville
(800) 458-3435
texrenfest.com

Take a trip back to 16th-century England with a visit to the Texas Renaissance Festival. Held for 8 weekends in October and November, the festival features all things Renaissance: music, cuisine, games, rides, and dancing. There are even gardens designed to look like those of King Henry VIII and the English queen of fairies. The entire festival staff dresses in their best 1500s attire, making the glassblowing, blacksmithing, and metal forging demonstrations seem all the more authentic.

The festival is held in Plantersville, about 55 miles northwest of downtown. Sure, that's a bit of a drive, but it's worth every mile if you've got kids. Visit the website for directions from numerous points in the Houston area.

Tickets cost $25 for adults and $12 for kids 5 to 12. Children 4 and younger get in free. Weekend passes cost $35 for guests of all ages; family packages are also available. You can save several dollars by purchasing tickets in advance by phone, on the festival website, or at local H-E-B and Randall's stores.

i Extend the fun at the Texas Renaissance Festival by camping on-site beneath the trees. There's no air-conditioning, water, or restrooms, but the nearby Quickie Mart should satisfy most of your 21st-century snack food needs. Camping on-site costs $20 per vehicle with the purchase of a festival ticket.

WINGS OVER HOUSTON AIR SHOW

Ellington Airport, located just southeast of the Sam Houston Tollway/Beltway 8 at FM 1959 and TX 3/Old Galveston Road
(713) 266-4492
wingsoverhouston.com

At the end of October, the US Air Force Thunderbirds and Blue Angels put on a one-of-a-kind show. Planes swoop up and down like acrobats, fly in formations, and pull off some cheer-worthy landings. The 2-day show is held at Ellington Airport, an air base used primarily by the military and NASA. It's located about 15 miles south of downtown, near Pasadena and toward Clear Lake and Galveston Island. General admission costs $25 for adults and $5 for children ages 5 to 11. Discounts are available if you buy tickets in advance; the earlier you buy tickets, the cheaper they are. Kids under 5 get in free. Be sure to bring your own lawn chairs; the show is standing room only, unless you shell out $45 for an assigned seat at the so-called 50-yard line. For $125 you can get a seat in a covered area, reserved parking, and free food and drinks. Purchase and print tickets online or order them over the phone or at the gate; a convenience charge will be added to the price.

INTERNATIONAL QUILT FESTIVAL

George R. Brown Convention Center
1001 Avenida de las Americas, just off US 59 between Polk Ave. and Texas St.
(713) 781-6864
quilts.com

Quilters and quilt collectors, rejoice. Your little piece of heaven can be found downtown at the George R. Brown Convention Center in late October or early November. That's when the International Quilt Festival showcases thousands of beautiful quilts, cloth dolls, and other art made from fabric. Most are available for purchase. And, whether you quilt or just collect quilts, you'll find something that suits you in the catalogue of more than 400 demonstrations and classes. General admission costs $10 for adults and $8 for students and seniors 65 and over. Kids 10 and under get in free. For $35, you can get a full show pass, which gets you admission for all 4 days of the show, plus the preview night the evening before the main event.

i Ready to get into the Halloween spirit? Take Discover Houston Tours' Ghost Walk in late October. You'll learn about local urban legends, unsolved mysteries, and spooky stories about dead Houstonians. Call (713) 222-9255 or visit discoverhoustontours.com for details.

RE/MAX BALLUNAR LIFTOFF
Johnson Space Center
1601 NASA Pkwy.
(281) 488-7676 (Clear Lake Chamber of Commerce)
ballunarfestival.com
Houston, we have liftoff—of the hot air balloon variety, that is. In October, dozens of hot air balloons lift off at NASA's Johnson Space Center to celebrate our fascination with flight. The balloons participate in several competitions in hopes of being named Event Champion of the RE/MAX Ballunar Festival. This family-friendly event has a carnival aura, complete with concession stands, arts and crafts exhibits, live entertainment, skydiving exhibits, and the enchanting evening balloon glows, which light up the sky. Admission is $10 per vehicle, which includes admission to a NASA open house as well

as parking at the Lyndon B. Johnson Space Center. To reach the festival, take I-45 South and exit at NASA Parkway (formerly NASA Road 1). Take NASA Parkway east and follow the signs to the Johnson Space Center.

NOVEMBER

RUN IN THE PARK
Hermann Park
Fannin Street between North McGregor and Hermann Drive
(713) 524-5876
hermannpark.org
The Run in the Park is one of the ways that the Hermann Park Conservancy does its part to encourage Houstonians to get fit. Held in Hermann Park—the crown jewel of local parks—the event includes three races: a 5-mile run, a 2-mile walk for families, and a 1K kids' fun run. After the race, participants celebrate by enjoing live music and an array of healthy food options. Participants are encouraged, but not required, to raise money for the Hermann Park Conservancy. Registration is $25 if you register 3 weeks in advance or earlier and $30 if you register closer to race day. Visit the website to register. Parking is available in all lots inside Hermann Park as well as curbside around the park.

✳NUTCRACKER MARKET
Reliant Center
1 Reliant Park
(713) 535-3231
houstonballet.org/nutcracker_market
Whether you're serious about holiday shopping or just want to sample your way through dozens of food vendors, head to the Nutcracker Market. For 4 days in early November, more than 300 artists and

merchants from across the country—and a few from around the globe—kick off the holiday shopping season by peddling everything from Christmas ornaments to jewelry to knickknacks and food. With products ranging from kitschy to artsy to luxurious, the Nutcracker Market offers something for just about everyone on your gift list. Proceeds benefit the Houston Ballet Foundation. There are loads of food and alcohol vendors, as well as fashion shows and special events, which cost anywhere from $40 to $175 per person. Beware, though: With more than 65,000 shoppers attending each year, the crowds can be intimidating. General admission tickets cost $12 at the door and $11 if purchased in advance at any local Randall's store. Serious shoppers can get a 4-day pass for $40. Kids under 6 get in free, but strollers aren't allowed. Cash parking at Reliant Park will cost you another $10, but you can save money and avoid the crowded parking lot by taking the METRORail. For directions, see the Houston Texans write-up in the "Spectator Sports" chapter.

i Visit the Nutcracker Market for half-price by showing up 3 hours before closing. Just beware: there's a lot of ground to cover here, so 3 hours may not be enough if you're a serious shopper.

VIA COLORI STREET PAINTING FESTIVAL
Sam Houston Park at Bagby Street and Allen Parkway (downtown)
(713) 523-3633
houstonviacolori.com
The streets around Sam Houston Park look like they belong in an art museum the weekend before Thanksgiving. That's when more than 175 artists—hobbyists and professionals alike—"paint" the streets around Sam Houston Park as part of the Via Colori Street Painting Festival. The festival provides them with pastels, and they create elaborate illustrations and designs on the concrete. Each "square" the artists color corresponds to a donation made to the Center for Hearing and Speech, which teaches children with hearing issues to speak and listen without using sign language. Houstonians show up in droves to watch the artists work their magic during this free event. Although the art is the main draw, there's also live entertainment, kids' activities, and food and drinks. Want to color the streets of downtown Houston in the festival? If you're college-age or older, you can sign up on the Via Colori website beginning in May. Participation is free.

H-E-B HOLIDAY PARADE
Downtown
(713) 654-8808
hebparade.com
Start your Thanksgiving morning with a trip downtown for the H-E-B Holiday Parade. Each year nearly 400,000 Houstonians rise early to cheer on colorful floats and high flying balloons, marching bands, and the Houston Texans Cheerleaders and the Rockets Power Dancers as the parade travels some 20 blocks through downtown. Little ones also get a thrill from seeing the hottest cartoon characters of the moment and Santa, as well as local celebrities and athletes. The parade begins at Minute Maid Park at Hamilton and Texas and ends up at Rusk and Crawford Streets, a block north of Discovery Green. See the parade website for a route map. The parade is free to the public, but reserved seats are available through the

website for $14. Parking is available on the street and in many garages and paid lots throughout downtown.

UPTOWN HOLIDAY LIGHTING
Uptown District/Galleria
Post Oak Boulevard between San Felipe Street and Westheimer Road
(713) 621-2504
uptown-houston.com
After filling up on their favorite Thanksgiving foods, thousands Houstonians and their out-of-town visitors head to Uptown to watch the lighting of the 80 trees along Post Oak Boulevard. The festive evening also includes a fireworks display, Christmas music, and visits by reindeer, elves, 12-foot-tall snowmen, and even Santa. Concession stands also sell carnival foods like kettle corn, cotton candy, and funnel cakes for those who still have some room in their stomachs. The free festivities kick off at 4 p.m. on Thanksgiving afternoon, and the trees remain lit throughout the holiday season, making Post Oak Boulevard a lovely—if sometimes congested—route to and from the Galleria for holiday shopping. Free parking is available at the Galleria mall, Williams Tower, and several adjacent buildings and shopping centers.

ICE AT DISCOVERY GREEN
Discovery Green
1500 McKinney St., between La Branch St. and Avenida de Las Americas
theiceatdiscoverygreen.com
Snow is rare in Houston, but the Ice at Discovery Green might almost make you forget that. From Thanksgiving to Martin Luther King Jr. Day, a 7,200-square-foot ice-skating rink is set up at Discovery Green, with a smaller area for younger children to play in the snow. The festive rink features art glass railings and mural kiosks, and is powered entirely by renewable energy. Other highlights include live music, open-air movies, a gift shop, and seasonal treats, like hot cocoa. Admission is $10 plus tax, which includes skate rental. Beginners can take 20-minute skating lessons for $25. Ten-visit passes are available for $84, or you can by a season pass for $124 per person. Parking is available at meters near Discovery Green and in paid lots and parking garages.

i Have an IKEA FAMILY card? Take it to the Ice at Discovery Green on Thursday and get $2 off admission.

MAYOR'S HOLIDAY CELEBRATION AND TREE LIGHTING
City Hall
901 Bagby St., between Walker and McKinney Streets
(832) 393-0868
houstontx.gov/mayorsholiday/index .html
In late November or early December, Houston's mayor kicks off the holiday season outside City Hall. Held around the reflection pool, the celebration includes musical, theatrical, and dance performances before the lighting of the City Hall Christmas tree. The evening wraps up with a fireworks display, creating a spectacular backdrop for the newly lit tree. The event is free and open to the public. See the City Hall write-up on page 135 for parking information.

DECEMBER

CITY HALL MENORAH LIGHTING
City Hall
901 Bagby St., between Walker and
McKinney Streets
(713) 777-2000
chabadhouston.org

During the 8 nights of Hanukkah, the Chabad-Lubavitch Outreach Center of Houston sponsors menorah lightings around the city. The biggest of these takes place outside City Hall, where a giant menorah stands to commemorate the Jewish festival of lights. In addition to a symbolic lighting, the evening boasts Hanukkah treats like jelly rolls and latkes, craft demonstrations, and live entertainment. The lighting may be held anywhere from late November to the end of December, depending on when Hanukkah falls. The event is free and open to the public. See the City Hall write-up on page 135 for parking information.

i City ordinances don't allow dogs in city parks and plazas. So, leave Fido at home for events held downtown or at city parks.

MEINEKE CAR CARE BOWL OF TEXAS
Reliant Stadium
1 Reliant Park, inner loop of the
southern portion of Loop 610 between
Kirby Drive and Fannin Street
meinekecarcarebowloftexas.com

Held at the end of December in Reliant Stadium, this event, a Houston favorite, features teams from the Big 12 and Big Ten

Conferences. Pre-game festivities include a carnival with plenty of games, and tailgating competitions, plus the consumption of plenty of stadium food favorites and libations, all of which happen right in the parking lot. There is a fee for parking and tickets start at just under $20. See the full listing on page 172 for additional details, as well as an alternative way to get to the stadium.

i Want a really great view of the illuminated Art Car parade, minus the crowds? Reserve a room at the Hilton Americas (1600 Lamar) and watch from above.

*GLOWARAMA
Discovery Green
1500 McKinney St.
discoverygreen.com

Downtown Houston lights up in more ways than one on New Year's Eve, thanks to Discovery Green. When the sun goes down, the park begins ringing in the New Year with a variety of family-friendly activities. The main event, though, is the illuminated art car parade. Houstonians young and old line the streets around Discovery Green to cheer as cars decorated like everything from peacocks to boats drive down the street, honking and—in some cases—tossing beads to bystanders. Throughout the evening, several musicians perform at Discovery Green. Glowarama is free. Prefer to stay in for New Year's Eve? The entire event airs on local television stations, so you can enjoy the highlights without leaving the couch.

KIDSTUFF

Houston is a great place to be a kid. The mild weather deserves some of the credit since it makes for endless opportunities to run around outside and play in the water. Credit also goes to Houston's loads of parks and playgrounds, festivals and carnivals, water parks, skating rinks and bowling alleys, and spots to see unusual animals. Houston even has theaters especially for kids.

In this chapter, you'll find some of the most fun ways for your kids to blow off some steam here. With categories highlighting carnivals and festivals, parks and playgrounds, mental stimulation, physical activities, circuses and other shows, and animal hot spots, you're sure to find something that satisfies even the pickiest child.

OVERVIEW

The activities listed here are by no means all-inclusive. There are plenty of other neighborhood destinations and spots in the exurbs where kids can have fun. The ones listed here draw some of the biggest crowds and tend to put big smiles on little faces. You might notice some overlap between this chapter and the "Annual Events" and "Attractions" chapters. That's because many attractions and events are perfect for kids but are also worthy of a visit even if you don't have children in tow. Likewise, be sure to give the "Annual Events" and "Attractions" chapters a second look even if your kids are tagging along. Many activities in those chapters—especially the San Jacinto Battleground State Historic Site (page 138), the Houston International Festival, the Art Car Parade, the Wings Over Houston Air Show, the RE/MAX Ballunar Liftoff Festival, the H-E-B Holiday Parade, the Uptown Holiday Lighting, and Glowarama (all listed in the "Annual Events" chapter)—also make for great family outings. Be sure

to find out about options for family fun at Hermann Park and Discovery Green, too. Both are listed in the "Parks" chapter.

If a visit to the toy store is your child's idea of fun, you're in luck: Houston has plenty of great ones. You can find a good list in the "Shopping" chapter, which also includes a section on children's clothing stores.

Price Code

Entertaining your kids can be pricey if you go to a carnival or a family fun center where you have to pay for each game and activity, not to mention food. But you can easily entertain kids here for less than $15. This chapter includes activities for every budget—even if that budget is $0. Free parking is available on-site unless noted otherwise.

$....................Less than $8
$$ ....$9 to $12
$$$ .... More than $12

WHERE THE WILD THINGS ARE

Horses. Butterflies. Sharks. Pigs. Panda bears. Name your child's favorite animal and there's almost certainly at least one opportunity to see it in action here. Houston, after all, is home to a world-class aquarium and zoo, as well as a fantastic nature center. And in late February and March, the Houston Livestock Show & Rodeo comes to town, with plenty of cattle, bulls, horses, and other livestock ready to be watched and petted. These aren't the only places to see exotic creatures, though. You can also watch butterflies flutter by and insects creep around at the Houston Museum of Natural Science, which is described in the "Mental Buzz" section of this chapter. Here are some of the best places to take your kids to see their favorite creatures in Houston.

DOWNTOWN AQUARIUM $–$$$
410 Bagby St., at Memorial Dr. (Downtown)
(713) 223-3474
aquariumrestaurants.com/downtown aquariumhouston
Houston's Downtown Aquarium is a popular spot for school field trips, birthday parties, and family fun. Here you'll find eight one-of-a-kind "adventure exhibits," including The Gulf of Mexico exhibit, which offers a look at the nurse sharks, snapper, and other aquatic creatures that live around the gulf's offshore rigs. Also available for viewing are international exhibits, which include a sunken temple that showcases everything from pythons to tigers. To feed your hungry little marine biologists, visit the on-site Aquarium restaurant, where you'll dine surrounded by a 150,000-gallon aquarium. The Aquarium is also included on the Houston CityPass

(page 121). See the full listing on page 132 for additional information about exhibits, pricing and parking.

> **i** Take the kids to the free Art Car Trophy Workshop in mid-March or early April. They'll get to make their own wacky art—er, trophies—for winners of the Art Car Parade (held in May, see the "Annual Events" chapter). Find out the date and sign up on the parade website (orangeshow.org/artcar .html).

✳HOUSTON ARBORETUM & NATURE CENTER
4501 Woodway Dr., on the western edge of Memorial Park
(713) 681-8433
houstonarboretum.org
If your kids love to catch bugs, watch birds, and discover new things, be sure to take them to the Houston Arboretum & Nature Center. Located on the western edge of Memorial Park, this 155-acre nature preserve is a fun place to explore the creatures living in forest, pond, wetland, and meadow habitats as you walk along the shady trails. Guided tours and hands-on activities here are also a great opportunity for you and the kids to learn about nature and conservation. During spring break and in the summer, the arboretum offers camps where kids as young as 3 years old can learn about everything from tadpoles to ecology. The arboretum, which also hosts scout troops and school groups, is a fun place to have an amphibian, bird, or snake-themed birthday party. Admission is free, but donations are encouraged. Free on-site parking is available.

*HOUSTON LIVESTOCK SHOW AND RODEO (FEB–MAR)

Reliant Park, on the north side of the South Loop between Kirby Drive and Fannin Street
rodeohouston.com

When it comes to the Houston Livestock Show and Rodeo, the chili cook-off and concerts are the biggest draws for many adults. Not so for kids and teens, who tend to prefer the animals, rides, and cotton candy. At Reliant Center the kids can watch milking, spinning and weaving, and cotton gin demonstrations and get an up-close look at the dairy goats, Brahmousin cattle, and Simbrah cattle. And yes, your kids can pet them. Don't worry if your little ones show up looking like city slickers: They'll leave looking like they belong—that is, if they can talk you into buying some of the rodeo gear and souvenirs for sale at the livestock show.

When the kids get tired of the livestock show, head to the rodeo carnival, which is filled with roller coasters, Ferris wheels, merry-go-rounds, cotton candy, and funnel cake galore. Also be sure to stop by the Kids Country Carnival so your kids can get a taste of life on a farm. They'll have the chance to ride a mechanical bull, cheer on some cute oinkers in the pig races, visit the petting zoo, and ride ponies.

Tickets are $7 for guests 13 and up and $4 for kids ages 3 to 12. Kids under 3 get in free. Planning to attend the livestock show and carnival multiple times? Consider getting a Houston Livestock Show Season Pass, which costs $25 per person and gets you into the cook-off, carnival, and livestock and horse shows as many times as you want. Cash parking is available at Reliant Park for $7 during the day on weekdays and for $12 on weekday evenings and weekends.

*HOUSTON ZOO

6200 Golf Course Dr., at North MacGregor Dr. in Hermann Park
(713) 533-6500
houstonzoo.org

Family fun starts at the Houston Zoo, home to more than 4,500 animals. Here you can introduce your little ones to all the usual suspects, as well as rare breeds like greater kudu, sifaka, and giant eland.

One of the hottest exhibits here is the African Forest, where ostriches, rhinos, chimps, giraffes, and other creatures roam. Get a close-up look at the 6.5-acre exhibit by taking a 1-hour guided safari tour. Tours must be scheduled 3 weeks in advance and cost $35 for nonmembers and $15 for members.

Another big hit is the John P. McGovern Children's Zoo, where your kids can pet sheep and goats, play on the playground, ride a wildlife carousel, and explore different habitats. Also popular is the new 4-D Experience—short 3-D family-friendly films that include effects such as mists, bubbles, scents, and lights.

Each day, the zoo also hosts more than two dozen kid-friendly "Meet the Keeper" talks. Zookeepers from different sections of the zoo tell the kids about the animals they work with and, in some cases, offer hands-on demonstrations.

On Thursday mornings at 9:15, you can get some exercise and learn about the animals as you push your newborn- to 3-year-old children through a section of the zoo. Dubbed Wild Wheels, the hour-long stroll concludes in the Children's Zoo, where the kids can pet and play with the animals. Wild Wheels costs $8 per child; parents get in for $12.

On Wednesday and Saturday mornings, little ones can participate in the Natural Beginnings programs. During these hour-long sessions, kids learn about animals through songs, games, stories, and the occasional hands-on demonstration. Classes cost $25 per child and require advance online registration.

Whenever you visit the zoo, save time to feed the ducks at the duck pond, rent a pedal boat and ride around the duck pond, and take the kids for a ride (or three) on the Hermann Park Railroad—an open-air, kid-size train that travels around Hermann Park, just outside the zoo. The sleek red train runs from 10 a.m. to 6:30 p.m. every day and costs $2.50 per ride.

General admission is free for infants, $9 for kids ages 2 to 11, $13 for ages 12 to 64, and $7 for seniors 65 and up. The zoo stops admitting visitors 1 hour before closing each evening. During daylight saving time (from Mar to Nov), the zoo is open from 9 a.m. to 7 p.m., and during Central Standard Time (from Nov to Mar), it is open from 9 a.m. to 6 p.m.

Free parking is available in a lot on Golf Course Drive; paid parking can be found near the Houston Museum of Natural Science or at Memorial Hermann Medical Plaza at 6400 Fannin St. You can also take the METRORail to the Memorial Hermann Hospital/Houston Zoo stop.

i Avoid the zoo on Martin Luther King Jr. Day, Presidents' Day, Columbus Day, the day after Thanksgiving, and New Year's Day. The zoo is a mob on these days because just about every kid in town is out of school.

MENTAL BUZZ

Houston's got plenty of brain food for little Einsteins, aspiring meteorologists, mad scientists, future astronauts, and dinosaur lovers. Several of the city's museums, as well as Space Center Houston, offer exhibits and hands-on activities that are sure to keep inquisitive little minds asking questions. There's even a museum just for kids. Here are some of the best spots to take your little ones to learn while having tons of fun.

＊CHILDREN'S MUSEUM OF HOUSTON $
1500 Binz St., at La Branch St. (Museum District)
(713) 522-1138
cmhouston.org

Got young kids? If you only take them to one place in Houston, make sure it's the Children's Museum of Houston. Every moment here is a learning experience—and a fun one, at that. Kids are encouraged to use their imaginations and touch the 14 exhibits, which engage all five senses to teach them about everything from math to the environment.

In the Kidtropolis, USA exhibit, kids learn about money management and personal responsibility by running a city for kids by kids. Aspiring architects enjoy visiting the Invention Convention exhibit, where they can invent and build contraptions ranging from Styrofoam cups and water bottles to colored gels and gears. Got kids with lots of energy? Send them straight to the Power Play exhibit, a 3-story installation that teaches kids about their bodies and the importance of physical fitness. Here kids can climb the 40-foot Power Tower, or find out how strong they really are at the Grip It station.

The Children's Museum also hosts special events and workshops throughout the year. Among them: story time, face painting, puppet shows, and special holiday celebrations like the Halloween Monster Mash Bash. Not only do kids get to make scary 3-D monster sculptures, spider hats, ghost bubbles, and slime; there's also the *Ronald McDonald Magic Show* and a chance to dance as DJ Beetlejuice plays his favorite Halloween tunes, "Monster Mash" included. Kids can even trick-or-treat—in or out of costume—right inside the museum, where they can collect treats and toys from each exhibit.

Usually, special events like Monster Mash Bash are included in the price of admission, which costs $8 for everyone age 1 or older. Kids under 1 and museum members get in free. Seniors ages 65 and up pay $7. On Thursday evenings from 5 to 8 p.m., everyone gets in free. The Children's Museum of Houston is also included on the Houston CityPass (page 121).

Parking is available in the museum garage, which charges $6 for 1 hour of parking, $7 for 2 hours, and $7 for 3 hours or more. Closed Mon.

i **Think your child is too young to enjoy the Children's Museum? You might be wrong. The second floor of the museum has space and activities for children who have just begun crawling.**

✳THE HEALTH MUSEUM $
1515 Hermann Dr., between LaBranch and Crawford Streets, just east of the Hermann Park Golf Course (Museum District)
(713) 521-1515
thehealthmuseum.org
Are your kids fascinated by their bodies? With a variety of interactive exhibits and activities

designed to help visitors better understand their bodies, The Health Museum is one of the city's can't-miss spots—and a place sure to entertain even the littlest guests.

"You: The Exhibit" offers a one-of-a-kind chance to see one's own internal organs in real time using a body scanner. Elsewhere in the exhibit, kids can learn how living in Houston affects their bodies. The Amazing Body Pavilion gives curious little visitors the chance to walk through an enormous human body and discover the importance of keeping arteries unclogged, the brain challenged, and bones exercised. Inside the McGovern 4-D Theater, you and the kids can watch films about the body—and don't worry, these are nothing like those old movies you watched in biology class. These movies come complete with real scents, rain, lightning, and, of course, surround sound. Little brainiacs love the Challenge Gallery, where they can test their reflexes, play some Dance Dance Revolution, and work some puzzles. The museum hosts additional fun exhibits and events throughout the year.

Admission costs $8 for adults and $6 for kids ages 3 to 12 and seniors 65 and up. Kids 2 and younger get in free. The museum is also included on the Houston CityPass (page 121). Parking is available in the museum parking lot for $3 with the purchase of admission. Metered parking is also available along the streets surrounding the museum. Closed Mon, except from June through Aug.

i **Find out about upcoming kids' events in the Houston area online at Kid's Directory (kids-houston.com) and GoCityKids (gocitykids.parents connect.com).**

✳HOUSTON MUSEUM OF
NATURAL SCIENCE $$–$$$
1 Hermann Circle Dr., between Caroline
and San Jacinto Streets in Hermann Park,
just east of Main and Fannin Streets
(713) 639-4629
hmns.org

From dinosaurs to insects to butterflies, the Houston Museum of Natural Science is a big hit with kids. One of the museum's biggest draws is the Cockrell Butterfly Center and Brown Hall of Entomology, where kids become mesmerized as the butterflies flutter around, sip nectar, and rest inside a simulated tropical rain forest, complete with a 50-foot waterfall and exotic plants. If your kids are true insect lovers, don't miss the Brown Hall of Entomology, which is filled with live insects and spiders of all varieties, including walking sticks, cockroaches, and tarantulas. Kids can also play with insect-themed toys and read insect-themed books.

Little adventurers might also like watching a fast-moving, adventure-filled IMAX film about nature in the Wortham Theater. Most IMAX films are screened just once or twice a day, so check the schedule online or call (713) 639-IMAX before your visit. IMAX movies do sell out, so purchase tickets in advance and line up early for good seats.

Inquisitive kids with some patience may also enjoy some of the museum's permanent exhibits, which cover astronomy and space, oil and energy, chemistry, paleontology, shells, Texas wildlife, rare gems and minerals, and the requisite dinosaurs. The museum hosts two or three special exhibits at any given time, though these are usually geared more toward adults and older kids. Recent special exhibits have featured the famous Lucy fossil and given visitors the chance to try their hand at forensic science.

A McDonald's is located inside the museum, just in case you need to refuel.

General admission is $15 for adults and $10 for college students, seniors 62 and up, and kids ages 3 to 11. The museum is also included on the Houston CityPass (page 121). Admission to the Cockrell Butterfly Center and Wortham Theater IMAX movies requires the purchase of additional tickets, which cost $8 for the butterfly center for adults and $11 for an IMAX movie for adults. Seniors, students, and children under 11 pay $7 to see the butterflies and $9 to see an IMAX movie.

Paid parking is available in the museum garage on Caroline Street; museum members pay $5 and nonmembers who show their museum ticket stub pay $10. Limited parking is available on the streets around the museum. The METRORail stops 3 blocks from the museum at the "Museum District" stop.

JOHN C. FREEMAN WEATHER
MUSEUM $
5104 Caroline St., between Southmore
Blvd. and Palm St., 3 blocks east of Main
St. in the Museum District
(713) 529-3076
weathermuseum.org

Have an aspiring meteorologist in your brood? Be sure to visit the John C. Freeman Weather Museum, the country's only museum dedicated to weather. It's run by meteorologists from the Weather Research Center, a Houston-based nonprofit organization devoted to educating the public about weather and weather safety. The hands-on activities make this museum particularly popular with kids. Among the highlights: opportunities to record a weather broadcast in a simulated studio, touch a simulated tornado vortex in the Tornado Chamber, and watch meteorologists perform experiments in the Weather Wizard Corner. You and the kids can even learn how tornadoes form and track hurricanes using satellite images of Hurricanes Katrina and Rita.

Self-guided tours are $5 for adults, $3 for students and seniors, and free for kids 3 and younger. Admission is free on Thurs from noon to 4 p.m. Parking is available on the streets around the museum. Closed Sun.

SPACE CENTER HOUSTON $$$
1601 NASA Pkwy.
(281) 244-2100
spacecenter.org

For an adventure that's out of this world, take the kids to Space Center Houston, the visitor center of NASA's Lyndon B. Johnson Space Center. This 100-building complex is where all US astronauts train. It's also the home of NASA's Mission Control, which directs all space shuttle missions and International Space Station activities.

Space Center Houston offers dozens of hands-on and informational exhibits and activities tracing the history of spaceflight. In the Blast Off Theater, kids will feel like they're traveling in space as simulated shuttle exhaust blows into the room while large monitors air live updates about and the exploration of Mars and astronauts' training activities. Visit the Feel of Space exhibit to see how astronauts shower, eat, and live on the space station. Then, head to Kids Space Place to let the kids practice flying a space shuttle. Other can't-miss exhibits feature old spacesuits, artifacts, and space shuttle hardware.

Get the scoop on what you're looking at in each exhibit by taking an Astronaut Audio Tour. These digital tours are narrated by astronaut greats like John Glenn, Gene Cernan, Shannon Lucid, and Eileen Collins. Special versions are available for kids.

General admission to Space Center Houston is $22.95 for adults, $21.95 for seniors 65 and older, and $18.95 for kids 4 to 11. Save $5 by purchasing and printing your tickets online before your visit. Space Center Houston is also included on the Houston CityPass (page 121).

For a little extra money, you can give the kids one of these unique experiences at Space Center Houston:

During **Lunch with an Astronaut,** your family can eat lunch with an astronaut, hear first-hand war stories, and get a personalized lithograph. Tickets cost $49.95 per adult and $29.95 per child; each ticket includes general admission. Tickets must be purchased online in advance. Spaces are limited.

For a closer look at the Johnson Space Center's day-to-day operations, take the **Level Nine Tour.** This 4- to 5-hour tour will take your family inside Mission Control and give you a close-up look at the space vehicle mock-up area, as well as the Space Environment Simulation Lab and the Neutral Buoyancy Lab where the astronauts train. You'll even get to eat lunch in the cafeteria where astronauts and NASA employees eat. Purchase tickets in advance online. Tours are offered Mon through Fri, but only 12 people are allowed on each one. Tickets cost a hefty $89.95 per person, and kids under 14 aren't allowed on the tour.

During the summer, spring break, and other school holidays, the center hosts day-long, half-day, and weeklong day camps and scout camps where kids can participate in hands-on activities and check out special space exhibits. Prices vary.

Space Center Houston is located about 25 miles south of downtown near Clear Lake. To get there, take I-45 South toward Galveston, then take exit 25 for NASA Parkway/TX 1. Drive east and follow the signs for the Johnson Space Center.

CELEBRATION BUZZ

What kid doesn't like a good festival, carnival, or other celebration? Just about every festival listed in the "Annual Events" chapter of this book includes activities geared toward kids, but a few events are especially popular among—or in some cases designed just for—kids. Among them: the Easter Orange Hunt, two outdoor kids' festivals, and the Renaissance Festival. Also fun is the Houston Livestock Show and Rodeo, listed in the "Where the Wild Things Are" section of this chapter. The excitement doesn't have to stop when these seasonal events wrap up, though. The Kemah Boardwalk in the Houston Bay Area is home to a huge amusement park and, of course, cotton candy. Here are some of Houston's best festivals, carnivals, and special events for kids.

EASTER ORANGE HUNT AT THE
ORANGE SHOW (MAR/APR)   FREE
The Orange Show Monument
2402 Munger St.
(713) 926-6368
orangeshow.org/events.html
Want your kids to go easy on the Easter candy? Skip the traditional Easter egg hunt and opt for the Orange Show Center for Visionary Art's Easter Orange Hunt. Held on the Saturday afternoon before Easter, the zany event features a maze of hidden oranges and the occasional piece of candy. There's also an Art Car Trophy Workshop,

where kids can make trophies for the winners of the Art Car Parade in May (page 183). The Orange Show's Easter Orange Hunt is free; there's also free on-site parking. To get there, take I-45 south toward Galveston, then take exit 43A toward Telephone Road. Merge onto the Gulf Freeway and take a right at Munger Street.

HOUSTON CHILDREN'S FESTIVAL
(APR) $
Downtown Houston
houstonchildrensfestival.com
Imagine a weekend packed with games, rides, kiddie karaoke, live music, arts and crafts, science experiments, a petting zoo, and autographs and hugs from the likes of Dora the Explorer and Mickey Mouse. That's the Houston Children's Festival, a weekend-long extravaganza that overtakes the streets and sidewalks of downtown Houston in early April. With more than 300 activities and thousands of Houston kiddos and their families, it's the largest outdoor children's festival in the country.

Admission is $10 at the gate; kids three and younger get in free. There are plenty of free activities, but the cost of the festival can add up quickly. Food, drinks, and many games and rides cost between $1 and $5 each. To pay for these, buy a pack (or several) of nine food, drink, and ride coupons for $10. All event proceeds go to Child Advocates, an organization that supports abused children.

The most convenient place to park is Theater District Parking Garage 2 at Rusk Street between Bagby Street and Smith Street and Theater District Parking Garage 3 behind the City Hall Annex at Bagby Street and Walker Street. Parking in these, or any of the other Theater District parking garages, is $7 during the festival. See the Downtown map on page x.

ℹ️ Get $2 off admission to the Houston Children's Festival by purchasing your tickets in advance online or showing a McDonald's receipt when you purchase your tickets.

KEMAH BOARDWALK $$–$$$
215 Kipp Ave., Kemah
(877) 285-3624
kemahboardwalk.com
About 30 miles south of downtown, follow the crowds of Houston families and young couples to the Kemah Boardwalk. There are dining options for families (and options for an adults-only evening out), live music, games and rides, shops, and tranquil views of Galveston Bay. There's something for everyone in the family to enjoy. See the full listing on page 137 for additional attractions and details.

KIDS DAY ON BUFFALO BAYOU
(OCT) FREE
Sabine-to-Bagby Promenade downtown
(713) 752-0314
buffalobayou.org/kidsday.html
Help your kids discover a new outdoor hobby—or enjoy an already existing one—at Kids Day on Buffalo Bayou. Held downtown in October, it's a fun way to celebrate the outdoors and the many recreational possibilities Houston offers. Sure, you'll find the requisite face painting, jugglers, and arts and crafts activities. But you and the kids will also have your pick of boat rides and scavenger hunts along Buffalo Bayou, kayaking demonstrations, fishing lessons, skateboarding and hiking opportunities, and the chance to meet local professional athletes. Plus,

you and your little gardeners can help plant wildflowers to make the bayou even prettier.

Admission is free. The festival usually runs from 10 a.m. to 2 p.m. The Sabine-to-Bagby Promenade is downtown along Buffalo Bayou between Sabine Street and Bagby Street just south of I-45 and north of Tranquility Park. Parking is available in City Lots H and C, both of which are located off Memorial Drive at Houston Avenue as you enter downtown.

TEXAS RENAISSANCE FESTIVAL
(OCT/NOV) $$–$$$
21778 FM 1774, Plantersville
(800) 458-3435
texrenfest.com
Want to show the kids what 16th-century England was like? For 8 weekends in October the Texas Renaissance Festival brings that long-ago era to you through staff dressed in period costumes, music, cuisine, games, rides, and dancing, as well as glassblowing, blacksmithing, and metal forging demonstrations. The festival is held in Plantersville, about 55 miles northwest of downtown. See the full listing on page 189 for additional details.

CURTAIN CALLS

Whether your kids love clowns, ice skaters, ballerinas, and stage actors, they're sure to get their fix here. In Houston, there's almost always some sort of kids production going on. Some are put on by big tours; others are the work of small local theaters that stage productions especially for kids.

For those who love clowns and animals, **Ringling Bros. and Barnum & Bailey Circus** comes to Houston's Reliant Stadium about once a year. The circus typically stays in town for about 10 days. Tickets are often hard to come by, so keep the kids smiling by buying yours early. Tickets are sold through Ticketmaster (ticketmaster.com). Find out about the circus's next stop in Houston on the Ringling Bros. website at ringling.com.

Got aspiring figure skaters? Or do your kids just love all things Disney? Either way, you'll want to get tickets for **Disney on Ice,** which comes to town once or twice a year. Each tour has a different theme, like princesses, *High School Musical,* or *Finding Nemo.* Shows are held at Reliant Stadium. There are usually 8 or 9 performances over about 5 days, but it's a good idea to get tickets early so you can see the performance you want in the seats you want. Tickets are sold through Ticketmaster.com. Find out about the next Disney on Ice show at disney.go .com/disneyonice.

Another big-ticket show is the Houston Ballet's annual performance of *The Nut-cracker.* Even if your kids aren't wowed by the ballerinas' leaps and twirls, they're likely to get a little starry-eyed as Clara, Franz, and the Sugar Plum Fairy impart this classic story of holiday cheer. Visit the Houston Ballet website (houstonballet.org) and see the Houston Ballet description on page 110 of the "Performing Arts" chapter for more information.

i **Think your kid has a future in Hollywood—or on Broadway? Sign him or her up for acting classes at Theater Under the Stars (page 118) or HITS Theatre in the Heights (713-861-7408; hitstheatre.org).**

Some of the best children's performances in town are put on by smaller local theaters. On Saturday, for instance,

Company OnStage's Children's Theater holds professional-caliber performances of classics like *The Princess and the Pea* as well as contemporary scripts like *The Little Mermaid.* Company OnStage hosts two Children's Theater performances each Saturday—one at 11 a.m., the other at 1:30 p.m. Each show runs for about 5 weeks. Tickets cost $8 and can be reserved at companyonstage.org or by calling (713) 726-1219. The theater is located in southwest Houston at 536 Westbury Sq. near the corner of West Bellfort and Burdine.

Also popular is **InterActive Theater Company,** which brings kids from the audience into every performance. Shows here range from classics like *A Christmas Carol* to historical tales like *Harriet Tubman's Freedom Train* and *The Story of the Lone Star State* to contemporary scripts like *The Little Mermaid.* The theater is located in the Heights at 1548 Heights Blvd. Tickets cost $8; parking is free. Visit the website (interactivetheater.org) or call (713) 862-7112 to find out about upcoming performances and times. Advance reservations are required.

If your kids love books, such as *If You Give a Pig a Party* and *Sideways Stories from Wayside School,* take them to **Main Street Theater.** The Theater for Youth here puts on adaptations of popular children's books that are guaranteed to make you and the kids laugh. Recent shows have included *Superfudge, How I Became a Pirate,* and *Pinkalicious.* Tickets to Theater for Youth shows cost $5. Unfortunately the theater doesn't admit guests under 3. Tickets can be purchased by phone (713-524-6706) or online (mainstreettheater.com). The theater has two locations—one in Montrose, the other in Rice Village—but Youth Theater performances are held at the Montrose location at 4617

Montrose Blvd. in the Chelsea Market complex behind Danton's Gulf Coast Seafood Kitchen. However, the theater is planning to move into a single location at 2540 Times Blvd., so call before you visit to see if they've moved.

BOWLING

With Houston having its share of rainy Saturdays (and Tuesdays and Sundays . . .), local bowling alleys can be a good place to take the kids—or host a rainproof birthday party. Most local bowling alleys here are pretty typical, with bumpers and ramps to help the kids bowl. There's also added fun to be had bowling in Conroe at America's Incredible Pizza Company and in southwest Houston at Houston Fun Plex. Both offer activities in addition to bowling; see the "Family Fun Centers" section in this chapter for details.

Since the Houston area has so many bowling alleys, there's not room to discuss each one. Here you'll find the locations, phone numbers, and websites of several local bowling alleys inside the city limits. The bowling alleys listed under broad ordinal categories are located pretty far from downtown. Call ahead for pricing and hours. Go online or consult the yellow pages to find a bowling alley if you live or are staying in the outlying suburbs.

Bellaire

PALACE BOWLING LANES
4191 Bellaire Blvd.
(713) 667-6554
palacebowlinglanes.com

Downtown

LUCKY STRIKE
1201 San Jacinto St.
(713) 343-3300
bowlluckystrike.com

> **i** Avoid 300 Houston and Lucky Strike in the evening if you've got little ones in tow. The waits here can be long since young adults flock to both of these bowling alleys after work and on weekend nights for the loud music and mixed drinks.

Memorial

300 HOUSTON
925 Bunker Hill Rd., just off I-10
(713) 461-1207
3hundred.com

North Houston

DIAMOND LANES
267 N. Forest Blvd., off I-45
(281) 440-9166
amf.com/diamondlanes

Northwest Houston

DEL MAR LANES
3020 Mangum Rd.
(713) 682-2506
delmarbowlinglanes.com

WILLOW LANES
19102 Hwy. 249
(281) 955-5900
amf.com/willowlanes

WINDFERN LANES
14441 Northwest Fwy.
(713) 466-8012
amf.com/windfernlanes

CLEAR LAKE LANES
16743 Diana Ln.
(281) 488-1331
amf.com/clearlakelanes

FAMILY FUN CENTERS

Sometimes the easiest way to keep kids entertained is to take them somewhere that offers a variety of games and activities, such as go-karts, minigolf, and bounce houses. That way, if they get bored with one activity, there are four more they can try. Here are a few popular fun plexes in the Houston area. All four are geared toward younger kids and/ or kids in early elementary school.

CHUCK E. CHEESE'S $$–$$$
5535 Weslayan
(713) 666-9802
chuckecheese.com

From Skeeball to balls to jump in to, to skill games to arcade games to rides for tots to prizes, Chuck E. Cheese's knows the way to every kid's heart. And it doesn't just stop with the entertainment. There's plenty of pizza to go around. Chuck E. Cheese's has several locations in Houston, and the attractions and prices vary by location. One thing's for sure, though: The cost can add up quickly, so bring extra cash.

HOUSTON FUN PLEX $$–$$$
13700 Beechnut St.
(281) 530-7777
houstonfunplex.com

This newly renovated fun complex is Texas's biggest indoor family fun center. In addition to the usual rides, go-karts, arcade, and concession food, Houston Fun Plex offers a skating rink and a bowling alley. The price you pay depends largely on which activities you

do—and the number of times you do them. The best deal is the $11.99 all-day fun package, which gets your kids 10 ride admissions, as well as either skating or playport (a soft play center where they can run and play).

INCREDIBLE PIZZA COMPANY $$–$$$
230 S. Loop 336 West, Conroe
(936) 441-2222
ipcconroe.com

Imagine a place where your kids can go bowling, play minigolf, ride bumper cars and go-karts, play air hockey and Skee-Ball, win big stuffed animals, jump around in the gym, and ride a little train. Then throw in a huge buffet with more than 30 kinds of pizza. That little slice of kid heaven is Incredible Pizza Company. Not surprisingly this is a very popular place for birthday parties. A buffet purchase is required for admission. The buffet costs $7.99 for ages 13 to 54, $5.99 for kids 12 and under, and $4.99 for adults 55 and up. Bring extra money. The activities here require a constant cash flow.

MONKEY BIZNESS $
9750 W. Sam Houston Pkwy. North (next door to Coldwell Banker)
(832) 237-0100
monkeybizness.com

With 15,000 square feet, Monkey Bizness lives up to its name, giving younger kids plenty of room to do what they do best—run, jump around, play, and have fun. For little ones, the biggest draws here are custom-made inflatable play zones, including a huge obstacle course and a 24-foot slide. There's also an air hockey table and rock climbing, although the latter is usually only open during birthday parties and on special holidays. Speaking of birthday parties, this is a great place to have one: You just bring the cake. Admission for open play is $7.50 for kids ages 1 to 18; parents get in free. Kids under 1, as well as kids under 2 with a paying sibling, get in free. Show up before 11 a.m. on Monday, Thursday, or Friday, and you'll pay just $5 per child.

FUN RUNS

TEXAS CHILDREN'S HOSPITAL KIDS' FUN RUN (JAN)
Pre- and postrace festivities held at George R. Brown Convention Center 1001 Avenida de las Americas, just off US 59 between Polk Ave. and Texas St. (713) 957-3453
chevronhoustonmarathon.com/kidsRun
Each January more than 200,000 people—both runners and spectators—come out for Houston's largest single-day sporting event: the prestigious Houston Marathon, which is always held on a Sunday mid-month. But marathon weekend actually kicks off the day before. That's when Texas Children's Hospital sponsors the 3K Kids' Fun Run (and walk), which covers part of the marathon course and wraps up at the official Chevron Houston Marathon finish line. About 5,000 local youth ranging from 5 to 15 participate in the event, which also features a 1K adaptive run and walk for children with special needs. Parents can register their children for the Kids' Fun Run 1K and 3K races online for $10 per child or at the George R. Brown Convention Center on race day for $15 per child. There's no fee for accompanying your child in the race.

RUN IN THE PARK (NOV)
Hermann Park
Fannin Street between North McGregor and Hermann Drive
(713) 524-5876
hermannpark.org

The Run in the Park is one of the ways that the Hermann Park Conservancy does its part to encourage Houstonians to get fit. Held in Hermann Park, the event includes three races: a 5-mile run, a 2-mile walk for families, and a 1K kids' fun run. After the race, participants celebrate with live music and healthy snacks. Registration is $25 if you register 3 weeks in advance or earlier and $30 if you register closer to race day. Visit the website to register. Parking is available in all lots inside Hermann Park as well as curbside around the park. For parking information, see the Hermann Park write-up on page 146.

PARKS & PLAYGROUNDS

Kids got jungle gym fever? You've got options. Many Houston neighborhoods have smaller parks with the requisite monkey bars, swings, and slides. Some even have pools, tennis courts, and basketball courts, though these are often only available to members of the neighborhood association.

The most noteworthy neighborhood park is **Firetruck Park at Southside Place** (3743 Garnet St. between Edloe and Auden Streets). In addition to the usual playground equipment, it's home to a 1935 fire truck. This isn't the kind of antique you should discourage your kids from touching, though. This fire truck is meant for climbing, sliding, and letting little imaginations run wild. The park also has a pool and tennis courts, but access is limited to neighborhood residents who belong to the Southside Park Association.

Of course, you don't have to scope out neighborhood parks to find a good jungle gym or slide here. Most of the city's parks also have a good playground or two. Check out the "Parks" chapter to learn about some

⊕ Close-up

Rock Climbing

If your kids are always showing you how strong they are or are climbing around like monkeys, Houston may have just the challenge for them. The city is home to two publicly accessible indoor rock-climbing gyms—**Stone Moves Indoor Rock Climbing** and **Texas Rock Gym.** Both cater to kids (and parents) with walls and classes geared toward beginners. **Monkey Bizness,** a 15,000-square-foot family fun center just for kids, also has a 24-foot rock climbing wall, although it's open to the public for climbing only sporadically, typically during spring break and other holidays. See the Monkey Bizness write-up on page 205 and call ahead (832-237-0100) to find out when rock climbing will be available next.

Visit any of these rock-climbing walls and odds are your child will beg for a sequel. He or she might even demand a trip to rock-climbing camp or a rock-climbing birthday party. Not only is rock-climbing fun but it also challenges kids mentally as they plot their next move. Unfortunately, rock climbing isn't one of those activities where you can kick back and watch while your kids burn off steam. As your child uses a rope, a belt, and his or her arms and legs to climb up and down a faux rock wall, you'll hold the other end of the rope to keep your child from falling onto one of the cushion-like mats. Don't worry, though. Our rock gyms emphasize safety and will—literally—show you and your child the ropes beforehand and help you out on the ground throughout the climb. In fact, Texas Rock Gym requires all first-time visitors to take a 15- to 20-minute ClimbSafe beginner's class for $7.50.

There's no minimum age to climb at either location, but Texas Rock Gym requires kids to be at least 10 years old to attend one of its rock-climbing day camps. And anytime your child visits either rock gym, you'll have to sign a liability waiver.

Comfortable shoes are a must, whether you're climbing or just holding the rope. Climbers are required to bring a pair of sturdy, tight-fitting tennis shoes—or rent a pair at the gym for $6. Keep in mind that the harness that climbers must wear can't be worn with skirts or dresses.

Rock climbing can be a little pricey, but a day pass is good for an entire day, even if you leave for lunch and come back. A day pass at Texas Rock Gym is $15. That doesn't include the required harness, which can be rented for $4. A day pass at Stone Moves costs $12. Harness rental costs $2, and shoe rental costs $3.

Here is the contact information for Stone Moves and Texas Rock Gym:

Stone Moves Indoor Rock Climbing
6970 FM 1960 Rd. West, in northwest Houston, east of TX 249/Tomball Parkway
(281) 397-0830
stonemoves.com

Texas Rock Gym
1526 Campbell Rd., off I-10 between Westview and Longpoint
(713) 973-7625
texasrockgym.com

of Houston's great parks, many of which have playgrounds designed to accommodate kids of all physical abilities, including those in wheelchairs.

No matter which parks you visit, be sure to pack extra juice boxes and water during the summer. Temperatures can get very hot, and running around outside may make your kids overheat faster than you'd expect.

SKATING

Ice-Skating

It may be hot and humid here most of the year, but Houston's still a great place to take the kids ice-skating. The city is home to several ice-skating rinks. Some of the local rinks, like the Aerodome Ice Skating Complex, are destinations themselves. Others, like the rinks at the Galleria and Memorial City malls, can be a fun treat when the kids are tired of shopping and running errands. And the Ice at Discovery Green and the Ice Rink at The Woodland Town Center are set up outside during the winter holidays, adding to the season's festive spirit.

Houston's ice-skating rinks cater to families with kids of all ages and skill levels. Beginner ice-skating lessons are available at every rink, but you usually have to call ahead to sign up for classes or private lessons. Most rinks here offer figure-skating and ice-hockey classes; a couple also offer hockey leagues. And most are happy to host your child's next birthday party—assuming you fit the bill, of course.

Even if your kids aren't taking classes, ice-skating requires some advanced planning. That's because most rinks here have very limited hours for public skating. Call ahead or go online to find out about the latest hours, since these can change monthly

and seasonally. Free parking is available at all of the rinks listed here, although you may need to park on the street or in a paid garage when visiting the Ice at Discovery Green. See the "Parks" chapter to learn more about parking around Discovery Green.

The rinks listed here aren't the only ones in town, but they're some of the best and, for the most part, centrally located.

AERODROME ICE SKATING COMPLEX
8220 Willow Place Dr. North, at
Willowchase (northwest Houston, off TX
249, just northeast of FM 1960)
(281) 847-5283
aerodromes.com
Take even the littlest hockey and figure skater wannabes to the Aerodrome's rink, and they just might get a head start on their skating careers. That's because the Aerodrome features open skating hours, beginner figure-skating and ice-skating lessons, and ice-hockey classes that teach kids basic ice-skating skills and body control.

Throughout the year the Aerodrome hosts themed evenings and special events. On Friday evenings, take the whole family for Friday Night Live. That's when the Aerodrome dims the lights, plays lively music, and breaks up the ice-skating with games and dancing on the ice. No matter when you visit, admission is $7 and skate rental is $3.

✳ICE AT DISCOVERY GREEN
(NOV–JAN)
Discovery Green
1500 McKinney St., between La Branch
St. and Avenida de Las Americas
theiceatdiscoverygreen.com
Spread holiday cheer by taking your kids to Discovery Green between Thanksgiving and Martin Luther King Jr. Day. That's when a

7,200-square-foot ice-skating rink known as The Ice at Discovery Green is set up in Houston's beloved downtown park. Little ones who prefer to play in the snow can do just that in a special snow play area set up just for them.

Admission is $10 plus tax, which includes skate rental. Take extra cash for seasonal treats like hot cocoa and apple caramel cider. Beginners young and old can take 20-minute skating lessons for $25. Ten-visit passes are available for $84, or you can by a season pass for $124 per person. Parking is available around Discovery Green at meters and in paid lots and parking garages.

THE ICE RINK AT THE WOODLANDS TOWN CENTER (NOV–JAN)
Northeast corner of Lake Robbins Drive and Six Pines Drive in The Woodlands Town Center, The Woodlands
(281) 419-5630
thewoodlandsicerink.com
Living or staying near The Woodlands? There's no need to drive all the way into town to visit The Ice at Discovery Green. You can have just as much fun at the Ice Rink at The Woodlands Town Center, which is open from mid-November to mid-January. Much like the Ice at Discovery Green, the Ice Rink has a separate rink for kids 5 and younger. Admission is $9.50 on weekdays and $10.50 on weekends. Admission is $5 on weekdays and $6 on weekends for kids 5 and younger. Skate rental is included.

ICE SKATE USA
Memorial City Mall
902 Memorial City Way
(713) 463-9296
iceskatememorialcity.com
Ice Skate USA joined Houston's ice skating scene in 2003 when it was added as part of Memorial City Mall's remodeling. To ensure your kids actually get to skate here, though, you have to plan your trip just right. The public skating schedule varies by month and season; during the year, the rink doesn't stay open for public skating past 4 or 5 p.m., except on Friday evenings. When the rink isn't open for public skating, it's typically used for classes for beginners, aspiring figure skaters, and ice-hockey players. Visit the website for class schedules, as well as the current month's open skating schedule. Admission is $7; skate rental costs $3. Free parking is available at the mall.

✳ICE AT THE GALLERIA
The Galleria—Level 1
5015 Westheimer Rd.
(713) 621-1500
iceatthegalleria.com
Olympic skater Evan Lysacek named this one of the country's 10 best places to skate. But that's not the only reason this rink is tops. Ice at the Galleria also gets kids: This rink, located on the first floor of the Galleria mall, doesn't make kids wait to go ice-skating. In fact, it's the only rink in town that's open to the public 7 days a week, offering opportunities to skate every morning, afternoon, and evening. Public skating is a no-go for 2 or 3 hours each day, though, so check the website or call ahead to make sure the rink will be open during your visit.

Ice at the Galleria offers beginner ice-skating classes for kids as young as 3, as well as summer camp and ice-hockey and figure-skating classes. Ice at the Galleria also offers private lessons.

Admission is $14, which includes skates. Socks are required if you're wearing the rental skates. So, if your kids show up sockless, you'll need to purchase socks for $3.

Free parking is available in the Galleria parking garages.

SUGAR LAND ICE & SPORTS CENTER
16225 Lexington Blvd., Sugar Land,
about 25 miles from downtown off US 59
(281) 265-7465
sugarlandice.com

This isn't the most conveniently located ice-skating rink in town, but it's considered one of the best, especially for kids who love hockey or figure skating. In addition to in-house hockey developmental leagues for kids ages 7 to 12 and an all-girls hockey club for girls 8 to 18, Sugar Land Ice & Sports Center offers drop-in sessions, where young hockey players of all levels can come play with their equipment and work on their skills. The center also offers classes for kids ages 4 and older.

One rink here is open for public skating about 4 hours each day. With all of the classes and other activities going on, the center's schedule is pretty packed and constantly changing. So, call for current public skating times. It costs $10 to skate here on weekdays and Friday afternoons, and $12 to skate on Friday nights, weekends, and holidays. Skate rental is included.

Roller-Skating

Houston is home to several roller-skating rinks, some which host Mommy and Me or family skating times. The rinks often change their hours—and even the days they're open—depending on the month or season. Most are open primarily on the weekends and a couple of weekdays during the school year. And just about all of them are open throughout the summer, spring break, winter break, and other school holidays.

Occasionally the rinks host themed events, such as retro music nights or dress-up days. Call ahead or go online, where applicable, to find the schedule for the rink you want to visit.

Admission prices

The price of admission varies from one skating rink to the next. But you'll usually pay somewhere between $3 and $7 per person, depending on the day and time. Admission is usually priciest on Friday and Saturday evenings; weekday mornings and afternoons tend to be the least expensive. You can rent skates—both in-line and old-school roller skates—for $2 or $3 at most rinks. Many rinks offer group and private skating lessons; most also host birthday parties and other special events.

There are close to two dozen roller-skating rinks in the greater Houston area. But in the interest of space, the list here only includes those inside the city limits, though most of these are located in more suburban areas. For additional rinks, look in the yellow pages. With the exception of Houston Fun Plex, which features a variety of activities for children, all locations listed here are stand-alone skating rinks.

North Houston
AIRLINE SKATE CENTER
10715 Airline Dr., just southwest of
George Bush Intercontinental Airport
(281) 448-7845
airlineskatecenter.com

Northeast Houston
LOCKWOOD SKATING PALACE
3323 E. Lockwood Dr.
(713) 673-2232

Southeast Houston
ALMEDA SUPER RINK
10750 Almeda Genoa Rd., off I-45, just
southeast of William P. Hobby Airport
(713) 941-7000

West Houston
BEAR CREEK ROLLER RINK
5210 TX 6 North
(281) 463-6020
bearcreekskate.com

DAIRY ASHFORD ROLLER RINK
1820 S. Dairy Ashford, between
Westheimer and Briar Forest
(281) 493-5651
skatedarr.com

HOUSTON FUN PLEX
13700 Beechnut St., just west of Eldridge
Pkwy.
(281) 530-7777
houstonfunplex.com

> **i** Have a child who likes to glam it up? Consider having a birthday party at Olive Anne & the Pink Pokka Dot. This Heights shop throws unique parties that can revolve around pedicures and facials (seriously), karaoke, disco, tea parties, and more. Call (713) 802-2021 or visit pinkpokkadot.com for details.

WATER PARKS

When the mercury starts to rise, spending the day at a water park is a fun way to cool down. Houstonians used to have a few water parks to choose from, but some have closed in recent years. If you're willing to make a little bit of a drive, though, you can give your family a memorable day of sliding, floating, tubing, and swimming at one of two nearby water parks. Both are open primarily in the summer, but they're usually also open on certain holidays and weekends in the spring and early fall. Visit the websites or call for schedules.

SCHLITTERBAHN GALVESTON WATER PARK
2026 Lockheed St., Galveston
(409) 770-9283
schlitterbahn.com/gal

Got a day to spare and want to escape the city? Consider heading to Galveston (about a 45-minute to 1-hour drive) and visiting Schlitterbahn. This popular water park is divided into three zones with German-sounding names: Blastenhoff and Surfenburg are the outdoor areas, and Wasserfest is a heated indoor area. Each zone is filled with a range of slides and activities that are sure to please everyone from the biggest adventurers to the littlest tykes to those craving a lazy day. Toddlers love to slide down the short Beached Boat Slide, splash around in the shallow activity pool in the Wasserfest Kids' Area, and get sprayed with water as they slide down some more tot size slides in Tiki Tikes. Got older kids? They'll love Schlitterbahn's huge slides, whitewater adventure, and even bodysurfing in the Boogie Bahn. When you need a break from the water, head over to Kristal Beach and sit in a lounge chair on the sand beside Kristal River. Or pay a visit to Arcadia, where video games, Dance Dance Revolution, and air-conditioning await kids (and parents) who need to escape the sun but still have energy to burn. Schlitterbahn sells food and drinks, but you can save money by bringing your own cooler with food and drinks.

The entire park is open from late April to late September. From March to April and late September to December, only the indoor section of the park is open. Ticket prices vary. During the indoor season, day passes for adults and kids 12 and up cost $25.99, and passes for kids 3 to 11 and seniors 55 and over cost $20.99. Summer day passes are $37.99 for kids and adults ages 12 and up and $29.99 for kids ages 3 to 11. Tickets can be purchased on-site, but you can avoid the lines by ordering them online.

i Schlitterbahn tends to get pretty crowded, especially in the summer and on weekends. So, arrive early and, if at all possible, visit on a weekday to avoid long waits.

SPLASHTOWN HOUSTON
21300 I-45, Spring
(281) 355-3300
splashtownpark.com
SplashTown doesn't have quite as many rides, slides, and activities as Schlitterbahn, but it's still a popular choice among water park fans young and old. Little ones can climb net ladders on Treehouse Island, swing and play in the Blue Lagoon Activity Pool, and swim past the relatively authentic-looking crocs at Crocodile Island. Bigger kids—that is, anyone 48 inches or taller—can float on a raft along the river, ride in the eye of a tornado while traveling down a 132-foot tunnel, or go for a wild ride on the Ripqurl tube slide. The park is about 30 minutes north of downtown on I-45 North. Admission at the gate is $34.99 for adults and $26.99 for guests 62 and older as well as guests 48 inches and under. Kids 2 and younger get in free. You can save $5 off adult tickets by purchasing them online, though you'll incur a $5 processing fee for each ticket order. Parking is $10 per car.

SHOPPING

Whether you're a serial shopper, need some retail therapy, or just shopping out of necessity, you're sure to find whatever you want or need in Houston. In fact, many people travel here from other parts of Texas and even from other countries just to restock their closets.

OVERVIEW

This chapter highlights stores you might not discover without this book. These are primarily independent stores and smaller local and regional chains that give the city its unique flavor. Many are places where you can find special, one-of-a-kind items.

In the pages that follow, you'll find just about every kind of store you could need or want. That includes antiques stores and commercial art galleries, thrift and resale shops, comic book shops, flea markets, toy stores, baby gear stores, jewelry stores, shoe stores, gift shops and garden shops, sporting goods stores, music shops, bookstores, and clothing stores for men, women, and children. You'll also find a rundown of farmers' markets and specialty food stores around the city. And since no trip to Texas would be complete without a pair of boots, I've also included a list of shops that sell cowboy boots and hats—used, new, and custom-made.

The stores listed here are hardly the only ones in town, but they are some of the best. They span from inexpensive to luxurious, giving you options no matter what your budget is.

The stores are organized by type and then by neighborhood, or, in the case of less-central locales, the general geographic direction. Many stores included here are located in the Heights, Rice Village/West University, Memorial, Upper Kirby, Montrose, or around the Galleria area. All of these areas are discussed in the "Area Overview" chapter and can be found using the maps in this book.

Some stores have multiple locations. For these stores, only one location—usually the most central one—is listed, though additional locations are mentioned in the write-up.

MALLS & SHOPPING CENTERS

As you make your way around Houston, you're likely to notice many familiar stores, ranging from inexpensive retailers like Payless and Target to higher-end shops like Tiffany and Neiman Marcus. Most of these are located in strip malls, shopping centers, and malls. The best and most prestigious mall in the city is the **Houston Galleria** (713-966-3500; simon.com), located at 5085 Westheimer Rd., just off West Loop 610

South. Among the tenants: David Yurman, Prada, Neiman Marcus, Nordstrom, Apple, and less-expensive shops, such as Ann Taylor, Gap, Banana Republic, Urban Outfitters, J. Crew, Macy's, Dillard's, and Gymboree. Many other stores—most chains, some not—are located on streets around the mall. Smaller, more specialized chain stores like Williams-Sonoma, Anthropologie, Lucy, Restoration Hardware, Pottery Barn, and James Avery, can be found about a mile east in the **Highland Village** shopping center (Westheimer Road between Mid Lane and Weslayan Street; shophighlandvillage.com).

Another popular shopping area in the area is the high-end **River Oaks Shopping Center** (West Gray and South Shephard; riveroaksshoppingcenter.com), which boasts a mix of local stores and chains like Barnes & Noble, Ann Taylor, Gap, and Sur La Table. Just a couple of miles south is **Rice Village** (ricevillageonline.com), just across from Rice University. The area is home to nearly 300 shops, ranging from local gift shops and baby stores to chains like La Creuset to Urban Outfitters to Banana Republic and Victoria's Secret.

Other popular malls in the area include **Memorial City Mall** in Memorial (303 Memorial City; 713-464-8640; memorial citymall.com), which is anchored by Target, Macy's, and Dillard's. It has the usual mall chain stores, such as Abercrombie & Fitch and American Eagle, as well as an Apple store. Drive a couple miles west along Memorial Drive, and you'll end up in **Town & Country Village** (12850 Memorial Dr.; town andcountryvillage.com), an outdoor shopping area that includes big chains like Barnes & Noble, Restoration Hardware, Gap, and Chico's. Between Town & Country Village

and I-10—just a few hundred yards, really—is **CityCentre** (800 Town & Country Blvd.; citycentrehouston.com). This new mixed-use development is home to restaurants, condos, and shops such as Sur La Table, Anthropologie, Paper Source, Free People, and Urban Outfitters.

This is hardly a complete list of the malls and shopping centers in Houston. But they are some of the most popular and central ones. And since most stores in these malls aren't unique to Houston and can easily be found by going online or calling, they're not the focus here.

ANTIQUES

Galleria

MORTON KUEHNERT AUCTIONEERS & APPRAISERS
4901 Richmond Ave. (near the southeast intersection of Loop 610 and Richmond Ave.)
(713) 827-7835
mortonkuehnert.com

If you're looking for one-of-a-kind antique furnishings, art, fine jewelry, silver, porcelain, or architectural finds from around the world, pay a visit to Morton Kuehnert Auctioneers & Appraisers. The company holds estate auctions every Thursday at 7 p.m., and each one features antique, estate, contemporary, and/or traditional pieces. Attendance and bidding are free, and there's no minimum bid. The company's staff is happy to help first-time bidders. Visit Morton Kuehnert's public gallery on Wednesday or Thursday to check out the items up for auction that week. Closed Sun.

i Check out antiques from more than 150 dealers at the Houston Antiques Dealers Association's shows, held each spring and fall at the George R. Brown Convention Center. Learn about upcoming shows by visiting the association's website (hadaantiques.com) or calling (713) 764-4232.

Heights

CAROLINE THOMPSON'S ANTIQUE CENTER OF HOUSTON
9950 Hempstead Road
(713) 688-4211
antiquecenteroftexas.tripod.com
See thousands of antiques under one roof at Caroline Thompson's Antique Center of Houston. This 120,000-square-foot warehouse space features more than 200 dealers offering a diverse selection of antiques, including furniture, decor, china, silver, jewelry, and old toys. Take a break by getting a sandwich or a drink at the center's full-service restaurant, the Radio City Cafe.

Midtown

*ADKINS ARCHITECTURAL ANTIQUES & TREASURES
3515 Fannin St. at Berry St.
(713) 522-6547
adkinsantiques.com
Located in a 3-story house dating back to 1912, Adkins Architectural Antiques & Treasures has been helping Houstonians, movie studios, restaurant owners, and photographers find period design pieces and architectural treasures since 1972. Among the embellishments offered here: old street lamps, patio furniture, doors, Anduze French pottery, and ornamental fixtures—many of

which come from notable homes and buildings that have been renovated. You can also find some unique garden decor here. Adkins has a full wood shop that restores customers' architectural antiques.

Montrose

TEXAS JUNK COMPANY
215 Welch St.
(713) 524-6257
For more than 2 decades, Houstonians have gone to Texas Junk Company to find everything from yard art, old picture frames, and telephones to cowboy boots, animal hides, and reptile skin. Browse this well-organized warehouse's ever-changing selection to find unique gifts—and things you never knew you needed. The store can get hot in the summer so visit earlier in the day if possible. Texas Junk Company is only open on Fri and Sat, though this changes seasonally.

i The best way to go antiquing in Montrose is to walk along Westheimer between Woodhead and Dunlavy Streets, where small antiques stores abound.

Upper Kirby

MADE IN FRANCE
2912 Ferndale St., at W. Alabama St.
(713) 529-7949
madeinfranceantiques.com
If you want to give your home a French country feel, visit Made in France. This shop's yellow walls and checkered floors are lined with fine French antiques, including furniture, paintings, and tapestries. Made in France doesn't change its inventory much; new shipments arrive from France each April and November. Closed Sun and Mon.

ART GALLERIES

Montrose

BARBARA DAVIS GALLERY
4411 Montrose Blvd.
(713) 520-9200
barbaradavisgallery.com
For 30 years, Barbara Davis Gallery has been the place to go for groundbreaking contemporary art. The gallery boasts an extensive lineup of emerging artists, as well as established artists doing bold new things. Among the artists represented by the gallery are Andrea Bianconi, Paul Fleming, Julie Soefer, and Joe Mancuso. Closed Sun and Mon.

DE SANTOS GALLERY
1724 Richmond Ave.
(713) 520-1200
desantosgallery.com
Fine art photography is De Santos Gallery's *raison d'être*. Located inside a contemporary stucco building, the gallery touts work from the United States and abroad, but it shows a particular affinity for Spanish photographers. The gallery is particularly interested in helping new photography aficionados build their collections. Closed Sun and Mon.

Rice Village & West University

GREMILLION & CO. FINE ART
2501 Sunset Blvd.
(713) 522-2701
gremillion.com
For more than 30 years, Gremillion & Co. has brought Houstonians an extensive selection of sophisticated sculpture, art furniture, paintings, and printmaking. And the gallery is doing something right because its contemporary American art is considered some of the country's best. Art here is displayed in two galleries—the main gallery and the annex. Both are available for rental for special events. Closed Sun and Mon.

River Oaks

TEXAS GALLERY
2012 Peden St.
(713) 524-1593
texgal.com
Texas Gallery is considered one of the city's best galleries. Here you'll find avant-garde and more contemporary works by artists from around the country. The gallery has featured notable New York artists, such as abstract painter Elizabeth Murray, contemporary painter Jeff Elrod, and contemporary landscapist Ellen Phelan. But the gallery is true to its name and strives to feature work by Texas artists, too.

Upper Kirby

GOLDESBERRY GALLERY
2625 Colquitt St., at Lake St.
(713) 528-0405
goldesberrygallery.com
Goldesberry Gallery is the city's premiere source for craft-based fine art. The gallery represents local, regional, and national artists who create three-dimensional pieces in ceramics, glass, fiber, wood, metal, painting, mixed media, and collage. Goldesberry also showcases handcrafted jewelry. Closed Sun and Mon.

HOOKS-EPSTEIN GALLERIES
2631 Colquitt, at Lake St.
(713) 522-0718
hooksepsteingalleries.com
Hooks-Epstein Galleries has been around since 1969, making it one of the city's

longest-operating galleries. Many of the best art collections in the city include pieces acquired here. Hooks-Epstein specializes in representational American, European, and Latin works from the 19th and 20th centuries. Closed Sun and Mon, except by appointment.

JOHN CLEARY GALLERY
2635 Colquitt, at Lake St.
(713) 524-5070
johnclearygallery.com
If you love photography, a visit to John Cleary Gallery is a must. The gallery is committed to showcasing and selling top-notch photography above all else, which makes for a diverse collection. You'll find everything from vintage prints by famed photographers, like Henri Cartier-Bresson, Elliott Erwitt, and Dorothea Lange, to new work by contemporary photographers, like Brent Phelps and David Fokos. Closed Sun and Mon, except by appointment.

MEREDITH LONG & COMPANY
2323 San Felipe
(713) 523-6671
meredithlonggallery.com
Described by the *Houston Chronicle* as "a pillar in the landscape of Houston art," Meredith Long & Company is the gallery that many significant private art collectors turn to when they want to add to their collections. Meredith Long & Company specializes in 19th- and 20th-century American art. That includes modern, contemporary, and sporting pieces. Among the many artists whose work Meredith Long & Company has exhibited and sold: Thomas Cole, Georgia O'Keeffe, Alexander Pope, and Mark Rothko. Closed Sun and Mon.

MOODY GALLERY
2815 Colquitt, at Lake St.
(713) 526-9911
moodygallery.com
Since Betty Moody opened this gallery in 1975, it has showcased work by contemporary American artists working in a variety of media. The emphasis here, though, has always been on work produced by artists working in Texas and artists with some sort of connection to Texas. As a result, Moody Gallery is considered one of the best places in Houston to find work by Texas artists. Many artists represented by Moody Gallery are recognized nationally or even internationally, but the gallery also represents emerging and mid-career artists. Closed Sun and Mon.

BABY GEAR & GIFTS

Galleria

*BABY'S & KID'S 1ST FURNITURE
5575 Richmond Ave.
(713) 785-8511
babys1st.com
Looking for nice nursery furniture? Baby's & Kid's 1st Furniture should definitely be on your list of stores to visit. Higher-end brands like Young America and Munire are this store's bread and butter. Whether you're buying furniture, a car seat or stroller, bedding, or baby gifts here, you'll probably end up paying a little more than you might otherwise. But you can save money by shopping during the store's big post-Thanksgiving sale, or by signing up for Baby's 1st's e-newsletter, which will keep you in the loop about deals and sales. Baby's 1st also offers infant CPR classes and will check your car seat to make sure it's installed correctly. That's true even if you don't buy from them. There are four

locations in the Houston area, including one in Sugar Land and one in Rice Village.

Rice Village

NEST & COT
2401-B Rice Blvd.
(713) 429-5246
nestandcot.com
If you love unique home decor, you won't want to miss Nest & Cot. This high-end shop features inspired baby and children's furniture, as well as a custom line of linens, lighting, and window treatments that instantly upgrade the look and feel of any nursery or child's room. Nest & Cot also boasts beautiful baby gifts that are sure to impress. Closed Sun.

*RIGHT START
2438 Rice Blvd.
(713) 807-7300
rightstart.com
Need a stroller or car seat? Right Start's knowledgable staff will help you find the perfect one for your car and lifestyle. This bright store also sells some of the best brands when it comes to high chairs, activity sets, educational toys, blankets, diaper bags, and just about everything else you could need for a baby or toddler. This is a great place to register for an upcoming birth or to select a baby gift. They'll even gift wrap your finds for you.

BOOKSTORES

Downtown

BROWN BOOKSHOP
1517 San Jacinto St.
(713) 652-3937
brownbookshop.com
Brown Bookshop has been around since 1946, making it one of Houston's oldest bookstores. This bookshop doesn't cater to the general interest, though. Books here are geared toward engineers, electricians, construction workers, computer scientists, and other technical professionals. If you can't find the technical publication, codes, or standards that you need, just ask. Brown Bookshop might be able to order it for you. Closed Sun.

The Heights

KABOOM BOOKS
3116 Houston Ave., at Bayland
(713) 869-7600
kaboombooks.com
Until Hurricane Katrina came and the owner fled west, Kaboom Books was a New Orleans establishment. Now Houstonians are reaping the benefits of this bookstore's well-organized collection of hard-to-find, scholarly, children's, and used books by authors ranging from Danielle Steele to Henry Miller. The prices are reasonable. Have books to sell? Bring them here: Kaboom will usually give you more for your books than competitors like Half Price Books.

Montrose

DOMY BOOKS
1709 Westheimer Rd.
(713) 523-3669
domystore.com
Don't go to Domy Books looking for the latest bestseller. This popular hipster hangout primarily sells off-the-beaten-path art and comics from around the world. Domy also has a good selection of first-edition books, zines and hard-to-find periodicals,

and other media. During your visit, check out the quirky art on display in the gallery.

✴HALF PRICE BOOKS
1011 Westheimer Rd. (Montrose)
(713) 520-1084
halfpricebooks.com

If you've ever visited a Half Price Books, you probably know that these stores are great places to find both rare and popular books at steep discounts. The family-owned chain has nine stores in and around Houston and two in particular are worthy of a visit: the Montrose location and the store in Rice Village (2537 University Blvd.; 713-524-6635). Both have especially good selections ranging from cookbooks to novels to literary theory and everything in between, thanks in part to the large number of students and bookish types living nearby. The Montrose store can also be a fun place to people watch, though seating is limited.

ISSUES MAGAZINE STORE
3425 S. Shepherd
(713) 521-9900

It's not exactly a bookstore, but Issues caters to Houston's reading population. Here you'll find mainstream magazines like *Vogue, GQ,* and *Martha Stewart Weddings* sandwiched between indie and obscure magazines, scholarly journals, and literary journals, like *Bitch, Farm Ranch Living,* and *JPG.* Issues also offers a selection of gay and straight pornography. Beware, though: There's not really room to sit and read here, and there's no coffee shop to speak of, so plan to stand or buy and take your finds home.

Rice Village & West University

✴BRAZOS BOOKSTORE
2421 Bissonnet
(713) 523-0701
brazosbookstore.com

Brazos Bookstore is dedicated to maintaining what it calls a "careful, intelligent book selection." This includes a unique collection of literary fiction and nonfiction, biographies, poetry, history, literary criticism, philosophy, travel, art, and architecture books. The knowledgeable staff is happy to make suggestions or help you find exactly what you're looking for. The small store also holds a number of author events and has a monthly book club. Recent authors showcased here include Siddhartha Mukherjee *(The Emperor of All Maladies: A Biography of Cancer),* Andre Dubus III *(House of Sand and Fog),* and Emily Fox Gordon *(Are You Happy? A Childhood Remembered).* On the first Wednesday of each month, Brazos hosts free book club meetings that are open to the public.

MURDER BY THE BOOK
2342 Bissonnet St.
(713) 524-8597
murderbooks.com

Since 1980, Murder by the Book has offered one of the largest collections of mystery books around, including many signed first editions. Titles here include everything from Agatha Christie classics to Patricia Cornwell and Michael Connelly to graphic thrillers. A three-time nominee for *Publishers Weekly's* Bookseller of the Year honor, Murder by the Book hosted more than 200 author signings in 2011. Murder by the Book also hosts a free book club once a month; visit the website for details.

BOOTS & WESTERN WEAR

Galleria

THE HAT STORE
5587 Richmond, at Chimney Rock
(713) 780-2480
thehatstore.com
Looking for the perfect cowboy hat? Visit the Hat Store, where you can order custom-made, hand-shaped hats in more than 25 colors. Although cowboy hats are the shop's specialty, the Hat Store also offers hats in a variety of shapes and styles, including felt hats, fedoras, and dress hats. Among this family-run business's happy clients: former president George H. W. Bush and former NBA basketball star Shaquille O'Neill. Closed Sun.

PINTO RANCH
1717 Post Oak Blvd.
(713) 333-7900
pintoranch.com
This spacious Western wear store sells what it bills as "Fine Western Wear." That includes Stetsons, boots, jewelry, buckles, jeans, Western shirts, and rhinestone- and turquoise-covered dresses and blouses—everything you might ever need to look Western chic for a hoedown or rodeo. Decorative logs inside and out give the store a rustic, ranchlike feel, so you'll get in the mood to buy.

Montrose

TEJAS CUSTOM BOOTS
208 Westheimer Rd.
(713) 524-9860
tejascustomboots.com
When celebrities want a one-of-a-kind pair of cowboy boots, Tejas Custom Boots is the place they call. In fact, former Houston Rockets basketball star Hakeem Olajuwon purchased more than 30 pairs made to fit his size 22 feet. Boots here can be made from ostrich, alligator, or other exotic leather. Tejas also makes leather belts and buckles. Although the boots here are some of the finest around, they're definitely not cheap. Prices start at $750 per pair.

Southwest Houston

WHEELER BOOT COMPANY
4115 Willowbend
(713) 665-0224
wheelerboots.com
Since opening in 1960, this family-run custom-boot business has created one-of-a-kind boots for everyone from celebrities to ranchers and Texans with a strong sense of personal style. Master boot maker Dave Wheeler sees each boot as a piece of art and makes them according to customers' specifications. The world-renowned company has been written up in magazines ranging from *Playboy* to *Forbes*. Closed Sun and Mon, expect by appointment.

West Houston

CAVENDER'S BOOT CITY
12141 Katy Fwy. (between Memorial and Katy)
(281) 597-1110
cavenders.com
This Texas chain is owned and run by a family of ranchers who dress in Western wear themselves, and make sure the clothes sold at Cavender's stores are authentic and durable. With a large selection of boots, blouses, shirts, and denim, Cavender's caters to everyone from farmhands to those looking to dress up for a Western-themed gala. There are eight locations in the greater Houston area; see the website to find the location nearest you.

ℹ️ Find a pair of unique cowboy boots at a steep discount at Texas Junk Company, listed in the "Antiques" section of this chapter.

COMICS & COLLECTIBLES

Upper Kirby & Greenway

NAN'S GAMES & COMICS TOO
2011 Southwest Fwy. at Greenbriar
(713) 520-8700
Get in touch with your inner geek at Nan's Games & Comics Too. In addition to comic books and figures aplenty, you'll find a huge collection of board games, many of which you've probably never heard of. Nan's also have a great selection of novelty toys. The shop's shelves can be tough to navigate at times, but the staff is happy to help. Beware, though: Nan's can be pricey.

THIRD PLANET
2718 Southwest Fwy., near Lakewood Church
(713) 528-1067
third-planet.com
From *Star Wars* to *Superman* to everything obscure and in between, Third Planet is the best place in town to find out-of-print comic books. You can also find rare comic figurines and novelty toys here—that is, if you're willing to spend some time browsing. Third Planet has so much merchandise that toys here are stacked from floor to ceiling. Luckily, the staff is very helpful. Third Planet occasionally hosts author events. Call ahead or visit the website for details.

Washington Corridor

BEDROCK CITY COMIC COMPANY
4602 Washington
(713) 862-0100
bedrockcity.com
Three of Bedrock City's four Houston stores aren't in the most convenient locations, but they're well worth the trip if you're a true comic fan. Here you'll find an extensive collection of comic books, old and new, as well as a great selection of figures and collectibles from your favorite series. The friendly staff here knows their comics. See the website for details on the other three locations.

FARMERS' MARKETS

Downtown

CITY HALL FARMERS MARKET (WED)
901 Bagby
(713) 880-5540
urbanharvest.org
Perhaps Houston's most urban farmers' market is the one outside City Hall on Wed from 11 a.m. to 1:30 p.m. The market, which is open from late Feb until early summer, offers businesspeople a chance to mingle and get some fresh air while stocking up on local fruits, vegetables, flowers, and tasty sandwiches and other lunch items.

The Heights

✳CANINO PRODUCE CO. (DAILY)
2520 Airline Dr.
(713) 862-4027
caninoproduce.com
Canino Produce is a bit like a farmers' market on steroids: Everything about this place is bigger and better. At the front of the complex is a grocery store that stocks a variety of beans, oils, rice, spices, herbs, eggs, and

more. Once you've finished there, you could easily spend an hour or two checking out the local fruits and veggies sold by dozens of farmers who set up shop out back. Produce varies depending on the season and what's fresh, but you're likely to find everything from kale to pecans to jicama to juicy mangos to melons and pomegranates—many from Texas, but some shipped from other parts of the country.

Highland Village

HIGHLAND VILLAGE FARMERS MARKET (SUN)
2720 Suffolk Dr.
urbanharvest.org
On Sun from 10 a.m. to 1 p.m., crowds flock to Highland Village for one of the city's newest farmers' markets. Many of the vendors who sell at the Eastside, Rice, and City Hall farmers' markets also set up shop here. That means you can expect great produce, as well as fresh flowers, seafood, soaps, breads, and cheeses.

Upper Kirby

⁂EASTSIDE FARMERS MARKET (SAT)
Behind the office building at 3000 Richmond, between Kirby and Buffalo Speedway
(713) 880-5540
urbanharvest.org
Eastside Farmers Market is open every Sat from 8 a.m. to noon, rain or shine, and it's widely considered the best farmers' market in town. In addition to mouthwatering seasonal produce from local farms, Bayou City sells grass-fed meats, honey, coffee, orchids, baked goods, Gulf seafood, organic eggs and turkeys, handmade soaps, and more. The market is constantly adding new vendors,

especially ones who practice organic and sustainable growing. There's usually live music and plenty of free samples, making this a festive place to visit on a Saturday morning.

Rice Village & West University

⁂RICE UNIVERSITY FARMERS MARKET (TUES)
2100 University Blvd.
farmersmarket.rice.edu
On Tues afternoons from 3:30 to 7 p.m., Rice University hosts its farmers' market. But this is no ordinary college farmers' market. This one boasts everything from fresh-caught Gulf seafood, handmade cheeses and breads, French macarons, gourmet infused oils and vinegars, and fresh seasonal fruits and veggies. Many of the vendors here are also at Eastside Farmers Market on Saturday.

Sugar Land

SUGAR LAND TOWN SQUARE (THURS)
2711 Town Centre Blvd.
urbanharvest.org
On Thursday from 4 to 7 p.m., Sugar Land residents stock up at their new farmers' market. Many of the same farmers who sell at Eastside, City Hall, and Highland Village are here, so you can expect a good selection of homegrown produce and flowers, as well as homemade baked goods, seafood, and more.

> **i** Want to grow your own garden? Urban Harvest—the organization behind the Eastside, City Hall, Sugar Land, and Highland Village farmers' markets—offers gardening education classes for adults and youth. Visit urbanharvest.org or call (713) 880-5540 for details.

FLEA MARKETS

North Houston

SUNNY FLEA MARKET
8705 Airline Rd.
(281) 447-8729
sunnyfleamarket.com
More than 50,000 people visit the Sunny Flea Market each weekend, making it one of the country's largest open-air markets. If you're willing to spend time sifting through the goods here, you can find rare vinyl records, old Nintendo sets, and garage sale–type goods to cowboy hats and beauty supplies. Most vendors will gladly bargain with you. There are also produce stands, tax prep services, pony rides, and an old-fashioned carousel. You can also find plenty to eat here, including fresh cooked churros, fajitas, Chinese food, and chicken on a stick. The market is open every Sat and Sun from 8 a.m. to 6 p.m.

Northwest Houston

TRADERS VILLAGE
7979 N. Eldridge Rd.
(281) 890-5500
tradersvillage.com/en/houston/
fleamarket
Traders Village isn't just one of the oldest flea markets in town; it's one of the most popular. Each weekend more than 2,500 dealers show up to sell everything from old tires, silk plants, and collectibles to army surplus items, crafts, and comic books. There are also more than 15 food stands that sell spicy fajitas, huge turkey legs, homemade corn dogs, cake, ice cream, beer, and more. Traders Village is open every Sat and Sun from 7 a.m. to dusk.

GARDEN SHOPS

The Heights

✳ANOTHER PLACE IN TIME
1102 Tulane at W. 11th
(713) 864-9717
anotherplaceintime.com
Named the best small nursery in town by the Houston Chronicle, Another Place in Time sells beautiful orchids, tropical plants, herbs, annuals, and perennials. The knowledgeable staff can help you find plants for your garden's unique growing conditions. Stop in the gift shop for Texas-made candles in all shapes and scents, vintage and decorative pottery, garden decor and seasonal decorations.

✳BUCHANAN'S NATIVE PLANTS
611 E. 11th
(713) 861-5702
buchanansplants.com
Buchanan's Native Plants specializes in organic gardens and, as the business's name suggests, native trees, shrubs, and plants—that is, those that can survive serious heat and humidity. Buchanan's also sells lovely wildflowers, antique roses, and heirloom vegetables. Visit the garden shop for unique garden art, bird feeders, wind chimes, candles, jewelry, scents, and crafts.

**JOSHUA'S NATIVE PLANTS AND
 GARDEN ANTIQUES**
502 W. 18th St. at Nicholson
(713) 862-7444
joshuasnativeplants.com
Looking for plants that can survive Houston's heat and humidity? This is the place to go. Joshua, the nursery's owner, visits local farms each week to scope out and purchase new plants, which he then sells

to customers. Joshua's Native Plants is also home to an 8,500-square-foot warehouse filled with antiques, American and European pottery, handblown glass, unique gifts, concrete landscape pieces, recycled tumbled glass, and fountains. Closed Mon.

River Oaks

✳THOMPSON & HANSON
3600 W. Alabama
(713) 622-6973
thompsonhanson.com
This upscale nursery sells both native and unusual annuals and perennials, as well as attractive—if pricey—pots. Thompson & Hanson also offers landscape design services that can give your garden a whole new look. Visit the garden shop for jewelry, French-inspired gifts and home decor, antiques, and other odds and ends. And, if you have time, grab a bite at Tiny Boxwood's—the nursery's outstanding cafe. You'll find a delicious range of sandwiches, salads, pizzas, and pastries. Get details on Tiny Boxwood's on page 62.

GIFT SHOPS

Galleria & Uptown Park

BERING'S
6102 Westheimer Rd.
(800) 237-4647
berings.com
Walking into Bering's, you might mistake this for just another hardware store. But that's hardly the case. In addition to pet supplies and outdoor, patio, and hardware products, Bering's sells beautiful china, crystal, and silver. Other highlights include a good selection of kitchenware, coffee, unusual candy, gifts and toys for babies and children, and a large selection of Jon Hart luggage and accessories. Bering's also offers an extensive selection of stationery and invitations for special events. Despite the high-end items for sale, though, the customer service here can be lacking, especially when it comes to wedding registries and stationery. Bering's has a second location in West University.

✳HANSON GALLERIES
5000 Westheimer Rd., #106
(713) 552-1242
hansongalleries.com
Handblown perfume bottles. Meticulously crafted earrings and necklaces. Glass cheeseboards. Wooden kaleidoscopes and hand-carved boxes. These are just a few of the artisan gifts you'll find at Hanson Galleries. You'll also find one-of-a-kind wall art, dazzling glass vases and bowls, and unusual scarves and ties. Since everything here is handcrafted, it can be tough—but not impossible—to find anything under $50. Free gift wrap is available. Hanson Galleries has a second location in Memorial City Mall (746 Memorial City Mall; 713-984-1242). Both locations are closed Sun.

LÉRÁNT
5000 Westheimer Rd.
(713) 626-1377
shoplerant.com
Silver, china, picture frames, and other high-end home gifts can be found at this shop across from the Galleria. Léránt also offers a good selection of Judaica, including handcrafted menorahs and mezuzahs. Watch your step and leave strollers at home: The narrow store is lined with breakables. Closed Sun.

*THE MONOGRAM SHOP OF HOUSTON
5860 San Felipe St.
(832) 251-8771
monogramshophouston.com

Houston has many monogram stores, but this is one of the very best. From towel wraps to duffle bags to coolers, the Monogram Shop of Houston sells plenty of gifts ready to be monogrammed. The store also sells a wide selection of personalized sorority and college gear, as well as seasonal gifts, baby and children's gifts, jewelry, hand lotions, and Vera Bradley bags. Added bonus: the saleswomen will gift wrap your purchases for free. Closed Sun.

OUT OF THE BOX
5709 Woodway Dr.
(832) 252-6222

Out of the Box isn't a big store, but it makes up for its size with an enormous array of gifts. The selection here includes bath and body products, stationery, flip-flops, kitchen decor, decorated aprons, jewelry, toys, home gifts, and baby blankets. Many of these gifts can be monogrammed. Closed Sun.

Memorial

HEART'S DELIGHT GIFTS
8 Woodlake Sq.
(713) 974-0591
heartsdelightgifts.com

Shopping for someone who likes hearts? Or love them yourself? Either way, this is the place to go. Heart's Delight sells jewelry, vases, frames, and other gifts for the home, and most—though not all—of them involve hearts. The store also carries quite a bit of merchandise by Brighton, Jeep Collins, and Jon Hart, as well as a sizeable selection of Christian gifts. Closed Sun.

i In late October and early November, dozens of stores around the city offer the Houston Holiday Shopping Card. In exchange for a donation of $70 or more to the American Cancer Society, you'll get a card that gives you a 20 percent discount on all of your purchases at participating stores during a predetermined 11-day period.

*INITIALS GIFTS AND MONOGRAMMING
12454 Memorial Dr.
(713) 465-3700
initialsgifts.com

Whether you're looking for a special baby gift or a graduation present, you'll find lots of options here—most available with a monogram. That includes everything from Gund lovies to blankets to robes to luggage tags. The prices may seem a little high, but that's because the price of the monogram is included.

THE VILLAGER
9311 Katy Fwy.
(713) 461-2022

Looking for a gift? If you're not sure exactly what you want, The Villager just might have the answer. The selection here includes a little of everything—stationery, jewelry, bath scents, serving dishes, mosaic picture frames, and Christian-inspired gifts. This popular Memorial gift shop also sells cards, women's clothing, Vera Bradley bags, unique seasonal decor and gifts, children's toys, and baby gifts. The saleswomen will wrap your gifts for free. Closed Sun.

Montrose

✳CANDYLICIOUS
1837 W. Alabama St.
(713) 529-6500
Need to feed a sugar addiction? Head directly to Candylicious. Here you'll find M&Ms, jelly bellies, rock candy—both on the stick and off—in a variety of colors, novelty toys, retro candy, and some unusual types of candy you've probably never tried. Candylicious also sells carefully crafted baskets and gift packages combining different candies for every kind (and age) of sweet tooth. Candylicious has a second, much smaller shop inside The Chocolate Bar in Rice Village (2521 University Blvd.; 713-874-1988).

Rice Village & West University

✳IMPROMPTU
2358 Bissonnet at Morningside
(713) 807-9696
impromptuhouston.com
Impromptu isn't a big store, but you could spend an hour in here and still miss something. That's not to say the store is cluttered; it just has a big array of unique merchandise, ranging from candles that look like wine corks to soap on a rope scented with coriander to jewelry, baby gifts, and sun hats. Gifts here are very reasonably priced and can be wrapped at no extra charge.

✳LA TASTE
2417 Rice Blvd.
(713) 520-0027
Prepare to be soothed by lavender and other scents inside La Taste, where you'll find bath soaps, gels, lotions, and even bath confetti. The French-inspired shop sells well-known brands like L'Occitane, as well as scents from less familiar brands. La Taste also sells

colorful—if pricey—French pottery for the kitchen and bathroom, unique candies, and dried flowers and potpourri. Free gift wrap is available.

✳OLIVINE
2405 Rice Blvd.
(713) 622-7776
olivineliving.com
This French-inspired store offers a variety of beautiful lifestyle items—beaded jewelry, bedding, furniture, glasses for the bathroom or bedside, candles and body scents, baby clothes, and even unique dog leashes. You may have to sift through the linens in this cozy store to find exactly what you want, but the salespeople are very helpful.

✳PH DESIGN SHOP
2414 Rice Blvd.
(713) 522-8861
phdesignshop.com
Got a stationery, greeting card, or journal addiction? Get giddy at the sight of all things letterpress? Head directly to PH Design Shop. This small shop sells letterpress cards and stationery, notebooks, desk products, gifts, and other paper products with funky designs. The shop also has a full-service graphic-design studio that will custom design invitations and announcements for weddings, bar and bat mitzvahs, holidays, births, and other special events.

✳SURROUNDINGS
1710 Sunset Blvd.
(713) 527-9838
surroundingshouston.com
Looking for eclectic contemporary and ethnic gifts that are reasonably priced? Surroundings has got you covered. Wooden tables, painted and designed by artist David

Marsh, are scattered throughout the spacious shop. These are often used to showcase some of the store's other goods: one-of-a-kind painted lamps and mirrors, Talavera pottery, painted crosses, salt and pepper shaker sets in the form of animals, textiles, handpainted mugs, and bowls made from tree stumps. Surroundings also offers a great selection of inexpensive earrings, including some from Latin and South America. The owners are frequently at the store and, like the rest of their staff, are knowledgeable and great at dishing out gift suggestions. They'll even gift wrap your purchases for free. Closed Sun except during the winter holiday season.

*THE VILLAGE FIREFLY
2422 Rice Blvd.
(713) 522-2808
villagefirefly.com
Artsy and unique gifts abound at The Village Firefly, where you'll find an affordable and frequently changing selection of wall art, jewelry, Texana, seasonal decor, and home gifts ranging from glass cutting boards to painted gourds to papier-mâché dogs. Everything sold here is made by artists from the US, many hailing from the Gulf Coast region. The shop owner knows about each piece and artist, and she'll gladly tell you all about them.

River Oaks

EVENTS
1966 W. Gray
(713) 520-5700
eventsgifts.com
This large River Oaks shop is considered one of the premier places in Houston to register for and buy elegant gifts, including china, silver, crystal, linens, and handblown glass and

pottery. Events also sells unique handmade jewelry, specialty photo albums, and ornamental gifts for men and women. Nothing here is cheap, but you can find some fairly inexpensive tchotchkes. Closed Sun except during the winter holiday season.

*INDULGE
2903 Saint St.
(713) 888-0181
indulgedecor.com
Pamper someone special with a gift from Indulge. This shop, which makes its home in a French garden, sells unique jewelry, linens, soaps and scents, baby gifts, children's toys, furniture, glassware, home decor, and garden gifts that owner Cynthia Davis carefully selects during her trips to New York and France. Even if you don't buy anything, the beautifully decorated shop is worthy of a look. Just watch where you step; the owner's dogs often roam around or nap on the floor. Closed Sun.

PAULA FRIDKIN DESIGNS
2022 W. Gray
(713) 490-1070
paulafridkindesigns.com
Costume jewelry and relatively inexpensive yet chic handbags are among the biggest sellers at Paula Fridkin Designs. The shop also sells a hodgepodge of gifts, ranging from candles and notepads to the latest in flip-flop fashion. New products arrive every day.

Upper Kirby

KUHL-LINSCOMB
2424 W. Alabama
(713) 526-6000
kuhl-linscomb.com
This unusual shop spans some 70,000 square feet and occupies five different buildings,

three of them old houses. Each building showcases a different type of product. The best of these is the main showroom, which houses unique gifts, beautiful—if pricey—handmade jewelry, quirky books, and delicious-smelling lotions and bath products. The other showrooms feature unusual contemporary furniture, linens, and other home decor.

GROCERY & SPECIALTY FOOD STORES

Downtown

PHOENICIA SPECIALTY MARKET
1001 Austin St.
(832) 360-2222
phoeniciafoods.com
Downtown residents were thrilled when Phoenicia opened in 2011, and understandably so. This pristine grocery is a foodie paradise, thanks to its meats and seafood, delicious cheeses and coffee, freshly made pita bread, cooking demonstrations, rustic pizzas and other gourmet foods to go. The market even has its own beer and wine bar, where you can sip your favorite drink and nibble on appetizers. There's a second location in West Houston (12141 Westheimer Rd.; 281-558-8225).

i You can't purchase beer or wine before noon on Sunday in Texas so plan ahead if you need to pick up a bottle or a six-pack for a Sunday gathering.

The Heights

ASIAN MARKET
1010 W. Cavalcade St.
(713) 863-7074
asiamarket-hou.com

Cheese, Please

Can't resist great artisanal cheese? Visit the **Houston Dairymaids** warehouse to sample and buy handmade mozzarellas, goat cheese, feta, and other varieties made from unpasteurized milk whenever possible. The warehouse is open on Fri and Sat. For details, call (713) 880-4800 or visit houstondairymaids.com.

Hard-to-find Asian spices are easy to find at Asian Market, which supplies groceries to local Thai, Laos, and Cambodian communities. It's not the best-looking store in town, but you can find plenty of fresh galangal, chilis, Kaffir lime leaves, and Thai basil for reasonable prices. The market also sells some of the best-prepared (and most-authentic) Thai food in Houston.

✳REVIVAL MARKET
550 Heights Blvd. at White Oak
(713) 880-8463
revivalmarket.com
Talk to meat-a-tarians, and they'll probably tell you they love Revival for its incredible meats—all-natural, locally sourced ones at that. But you don't have to be a carnivore to love this little specialty food store. That's because Revival sells all sorts of irresistible produce and homemade cheeses, pickles, and jams from local farmers and food artisans. You can also grab a good cup of coffee—or a delicious sandwich made with locally sourced products. No matter what you buy, Revival hopes you'll leave with a better understanding of where your food came from and why local is best.

Highland Village

✳CENTRAL MARKET
3815 Westheimer Rd.
(713) 386-1700
centralmarket.com

Central Market is a big slice of foodie heaven. Here you'll find some of the best fresh-baked breads and tortillas in town, an overwhelming array of tasty prepared foods and sandwiches, hard-to-find spices and gourmet foods, an extensive beer and wine selection, and staff who can help you find the perfect bottle for your meal. Central Market also sells gift baskets and flower arrangements with some of Houston's prettiest blooms. You can even take cooking classes from some of the region's best chefs. This may not be the best place to do your regular grocery shopping, though. Central Market can be a little pricey though, and it doesn't carry most of the standard name brands or household items that you find at other grocery stores.

Central Market's parent store, H-E-B, recently opened locations in Memorial (9710 Katy Fwy.; 713-647-5900), West University (5225 Buffalo Speedway; 713-218-1800), and Montrose (1701 W. Alabama; 713-529-2475) that offer many of the same specialty foods, spices, and vast beer, wine, and cheese selections as Central Market. They also sell the standard name brands.

i Additional Asian groceries and shops can be found in West Houston along Bellaire Boulevard between Boone and Fondren.

Memorial

✳99 RANCH MARKET
1005 Blalock Rd.
(713) 832-8899

"Incredible" just begins to describe this Asian market. You'll find everything from sushi to unusual fruits and vegetables to knickknacks and Japanese candies to all of your favorite Asian foods, species, and ingredients here. Added bonus: 99 Ranch Market is inexpensive.

i Need a nice bottle of wine? Stop into one of the dozens of Spec's Liquors locations around Houston. You'll find wines from around the globe, as well as knowledgeable staff who can help you find the perfect wine for your meal. Visit the website (specsonline .com) to find the nearest location.

SUPER H-MART
1302 Blalock Rd.
(713) 468-0606
hmart.com

One of the best Pan-Asian groceries in town, Super H-Mart has a huge selection of Asian foods and spices. The large assortment of Korean, Chinese, and Japanese food products include everything from Korean pickles to garlic-infused Chinese cabbage to sushi-grade fish, as well as deliciously prepared Asian dishes. Super H-Mart is very clean and well arranged and the prices are very reasonable.

West Houston

✳LEIBMAN'S WINE & FINE FOODS
14529 Memorial Dr.
(281) 493-3663
leibmans.com

Leibman's offers some of the best in gourmet food and wine. At this West Houston store, you can order a delicious sandwich or soup for lunch, pick up a nice bottle of wine and some gourmet cheese, or order

🔍 Close-up

Love Etsy? Try this local equivalent: Roundtable Goods

Etsy addict? Head directly to Roundtable Goods. This newcomer on the Houston shopping scene brings together the works of more than a dozen artisans and bakers under one roof.

Among the goodies you'll find at this Heights shop: digital art prints, jewelry, quilts, handmade clothes, gluten-free cupcakes, skin care products, and even cat accessories. Many products can be custom ordered.

The best part? You can actually find a good gift for $20 here. That's because Roundtable Goods' mastermind, Juanita Baker, wants to make it affordable to choose local art over items sold at big retail stores.

Baker, a clothing designer who sells her hand-sewn fashions under the Festive Nest Designs label, hand-selected the artists whose work is available at Roundtable Goods. Each artisan helps run the store and designs his or her own display.

Capitalizing on its vendors' many talents, Roundtable Good plans to offer a variety of services, including sewing classes, event planning, and even a handcrafted gifts and floral delivery service.

Roundtable Goods is currently open only on weekends from 10 a.m.–6 p.m. on Saturday and 1–5 p.m. on Sunday. The shop may eventually offer weekday hours, though, so call for the latest schedule.

Roundtable Goods
238 W. 19th Street, Suite A-2 (inside the Corridor Shops)
roundtablegoods.blogspot.com

gourmet gift baskets and party platters. Leibman's also caters and offers special menus and foods for major holidays.

JEWELRY STORES

Bellaire

I W MARKS
3841 Bellaire
(713) 668-5000
iwmarks.com
I W Marks bills itself as Houston's "Hometown Jeweler," and rightfully so. For more than 30 years, this family-owned business has been South Texas's largest independent jeweler—and a popular place to buy wedding

and engagement rings. The more than 100 showcases here house diamonds, platinum, semiprecious stones, gold, and watches manufactured by the likes of Tag Heuer, Bertolucci, Omega, and Raymond Weil. Closed Sun.

Galleria

✴A.A. BENJAMIN
1775 St. James Place, Ste. 105
(713) 965-0555
aabenjaminjewelry.com
Looking for a one-of-a-kind engagement ring or another special piece of jewelry? Schedule a visit to visit A.A. Benjamin. Twice named the "Best Place to Buy an Engagement

Ring" by the *Houston Press* and the "Best Place to Buy Estate Jewelry in Houston" by *HTexas* magazine, this small Galleria-area shop sells exquisite estate, period, and antique jewelry, much of it designed in the art-deco, Georgian, and Edwardian styles. If you can't find exactly what you want, owner Amy Lawch will work with you to design exactly the piece you want. A A Benjamin also does jewelry appraisals. Open by appointment only.

✳ZADOK JEWELERS
1749 Post Oak Blvd., at San Felipe
(713) 960-8950
zadokjewelers.com
For seven generations, the Zadok family has been in the fine jewelery business, which means you get some serious expertise—not to mention great service—at this family-owned jewelry shop. Zadok's has an extensive collection of everything from platinum and gold wedding and engagement rings to Swiss watches by more obscure and creative designers like Gregg Ruth, Roberto Coin, and Yvel, as well as familiar names like Bulgari, Ebel, Montblanc, Baccarat, and Lalique. Closed Sun.

Upper Kirby

PAST ERA FINE ANTIQUE JEWELRY
3433 W. Alabama
(713) 641-3433
pastera.com
The daughter of London jewelers, Past Era owner Marion Glober handpicks each piece she sells and goes as far as Europe to find many of her collection's exquisite pieces. The items she chooses are a big part of the reason so many brides-to-be, antiques collectors, and those looking for a special piece of jewelry head here for one-of-a-kind rings, earrings, necklaces, brooches, bracelets, and

objects dating as far back as the 17th century. The store's extensive offerings include many pieces designed in the Georgian, Victorian, arts-and-crafts, art-deco, Edwardian, and belle-epoque styles. Closed Sun and Mon.

KIDS' CLOTHING

Galleria & Uptown Park

LITTLE LORDS N' LADIES
6100 Westheimer
(713) 782-6554
littlelordsladies.com
Want your child to look runway-worthy? Little Lords N' Ladies sells clothes that fit the bill for boys ages 0 to 7 and girls 0 to 14. You'll also find the perfect jewelry and other accessories here. You can even get your child's hair cut here. Just beware: you will pay more than you would at other kids' chains. Closed Sun.

MINT BABY
1121–09 Uptown Park Blvd.
(713) 622-3580
From taffeta dresses to tutu skirts and cute shorts and shirts, Mint Baby sells children's couture fit for a portrait session or special event. And new parents—as well as gift givers—can find everything they need for their little ones, from hip diaper bags to beautiful bedding. Service here is great, but that's to be expected, given how pricey most of the merchandise is. After shopping for baby, head next door to Mint (listed in the "Women's Clothing" section) to find clothes for Mom. Closed Sun.

SECOND CHILDHOOD
1922 Fountainview
(713) 789-6456
secondchildhoodtexas.com

This aptly named children's store sells new and used clothes and shoes for young kids—and buys your kids' old clothes on consignment. Most clothes here have been gently worn, but they're good quality and tend to run anywhere from about $4 to $20. A big play area in the middle of this small store is filled with toys that will occupy the kids while you look through the racks. Pregnant? You can also find a limited selection of maternity clothes here. Closed Sun.

The Heights

TULIPS AND TUTUS
833 Studewood
(713) 861-0301
tulipsandtutus.com

Forget trends and labels. This ecofriendly shop encourages kids (and their parents) to embrace their individuality by giving them loads of options. Style and fun are never sacrificed, though: The clothes, tutus, and toys sold here are among the cutest in town and the service and prices here are terrific. Free gift wrapping is available.

Montrose

LITTLE PATOOTIES
2608 Westheimer, near Kirby
(713) 520-8686
littlepatooties.com

Like children's outfits that look like they're meant for adults? Little Patooties is the store for you. Here you'll find boys' and girls' couture ranging from formal evening wear to casual styles. Sizes are available for infants through preteens. Closed Sun.

Rice Village & West University

✳HIP HOP LOLLIPOP
6207 Edloe
(713) 218-7800
thehiphoplollipop.com

Hip Hop Lollipop sells some of the most hip, casual clothes in town for young girls, tweens, and women. And the store is constantly increasing its cute quotient with new merchandise. At the back of the store, Hip Hop Lollipop hosts birthday parties that make little girls go gaga. Among the themes: Groovy Girl Rock Star, Hannah Montana, Glamour Girl, PJs and Pancakes, and Spa Party. Closed Sun.

✳PURPLE MANGO
2410 Rice Blvd.
(713) 529-9188

Cute, brightly colored clothes rule at this well-organized Rice Village shop. In addition to an array of clothes for toddlers and young kids, Purple Mango sells backpacks, bags, bows, tutus, and kids' shoes. Be sure to check out the dressing rooms, which resemble a fairy tale castle. Closed Sun.

MEN'S CLOTHING

Galleria & Uptown Park

A. TAGHI
5116 Westheimer
(713) 963-0884
ataghi.com

Need slacks, suits, sport coats, shirts, or shoes—or better yet, all of these? A. Taghi offers plenty of options from brands such as Zanella, Mobro, Santoni, and Bruno Magli. If you don't want to look through the neatly manicured racks to find exactly what you need, the salespeople will do it for you.

They'll also make sure that the clothes you select fit perfectly.

M PENNER
1180-06 Uptown Park Blvd.
(713) 527-8200
mpenner.com

Recognized by *Esquire* magazine as one of the best stores in its class, M Penner sells men's suits, slacks, sport coats, and sportswear by designers such as John Varvatos, Luigi Borrelli, Tailorbyrd, and Versace. Can't find exactly what you're looking for? You're in luck: M Penner custom designs clothing. You can also find shoes by Alden, Michael Toschi, and Romano Martegani here. Closed Sun.

Upper Kirby & Greenway

NORTON DITTO
2425 W. Alabama, at Kirby
(713) 688-9800
nortonditto.com

Since 1908, Houston men have looked to Norton Ditto for fine clothing, including shoes, dress shirts, coats, pajamas, suits, sport coats, slacks, and casual wear. Among the brands you'll find here: Trussini of Italy, Orvis, Tommy Bahama, Cole Haan, and Kenneth Gordon. If none of the brands available suit your needs, Norton Ditto's Custom Shop can design clothes especially for you. Don't have time to stop by to get fitted for your custom clothing? Someone from Norton Ditto will gladly come to you. Closed Sun.

MUSIC SHOPS

Midtown

SIG'S LAGOON
3622-E Main St.
(713) 533-9525
sigslagoon.com

Named after the late *Houston Press* and *Houston Chronicle* columnist Sig Byrd, this campy Midtown music shop boasts a large collection of local and more obscure music on CD and vinyl. They even host in-store performances by many touring and local musicians. You can also find novelty toys here.

Montrose

SOUND EXCHANGE
1846 Richmond, at Hazard St.
(713) 666-5555
soundexchangehouston.com

You won't find the latest top-40 tunes at Sound Exchange, but you will find an enormous selection of hard-to-find blues, punk rock, jazz, obscure folk, psychedelic and rock, experimental, and local music. Some of this comes in CD format, but a sizeable chunk of the store's inventory is vinyl. Ask the staff for recommendations; they're likely to introduce you to some great new tunes. Sound Exchange also repairs turntables and appraises CD and record collections. The store will even buy your old CDs and records—if the staff thinks your music is hip enough.

SOUNDWAVES
3509 Montrose Blvd.
(713) 520-9283
soundwaves.com

Part surf shop, part music shop, Soundwaves sells a large selection of rock, country, classical, and jazz tunes, just about all on CD. The store has a very small selection of records and a selection of used CDs that's nearly as tiny. Soundwaves also has a decent DVD selection, including a shelf of used DVDs. There's a small coffee stand inside the store, but there's nowhere to sit while you sip. Soundwaves has two additional locations—one in the Clear Lake (1331 Bay Area Blvd., Webster; 281-332-4200) and another near the Heights (20 E. Crosstimbers; 713-694-6800).

Northwest Houston

VINAL EDGE RECORDS
13171 Veterans Memorial Dr., near FM 1960
(281) 537-2575
vinaledge.com
Located in far northwest Houston, Vinal Edge Records isn't particularly convenient for most people, but it's worth the drive if you collect vinyl records. It doesn't even matter what kinds of music you like—the collection here is so expansive that you're sure to find something. Beware, though: Finding your treasure may require thumbing through the countless cardboard boxes lining the floor. Vinal Edge is constantly getting in new records, so the collection here is constantly growing and changing.

River Oaks

ALL RECORDS
3211 Edloe St.
(713) 524-4900
For more than 20 years, All Records has been one of Houston's leading independent music stores. It sells everything from classical and international music to big band, rock, pop, and folk. And the shop sells plenty of retro media—cassettes, CDs, and an expanding vinyl collection. Owner Fred Allred is always happy to talk music and will order anything you can't find. Closed Sun.

Upper Kirby & Greenway

✳CACTUS MUSIC
2110 Portsmouth St., at Richmond
(713) 526-9272
cactusmusictx.com
For many years, Cactus Records stood next door to the now-defunct Bookstop at Alabama Theatre as a staple of the Houston music scene. That record shop closed in 2006, but a few former Cactus staffers later reincarnated the store, naming it Cactus Music and setting up shop near the old location. The new Cactus is every bit as good as the old one. You can find tons of independent and obscure music here, along with an extensive collection of Texas and Houston music. A lot of this music is available on CD, but Cactus also has an entire room of vinyl. Cactus frequently hosts in-store performances by local musicians and bigger acts peddling their latest album.

SHOE STORES

Galleria

BRUCETTES SHOES
4920 San Felipe
(800) 229-0022
brucettes.com
Have narrow or wide feet? Brucettes has got you covered. This small Galleria-area shop has a big selection of dress, casual, and even tennis shoes in sizes 2 to 15 in widths ranging from AAAAA to WW. Many are made by well-known brands such as Stuart Weitzman, Nina, and Keds. The store also has a decent selection of dyeable and bridal shoes, as well as handbags. Brucettes has a second location in Friendswood. Call (713) 941-1170 for more information on that location.

Rice Village

ARIEL'S VILLAGE SHOE SHOP
2507 Rice Blvd.
(866) 528-8424
arielsvillageshoeshop.com

Ariel's Village Shoe Shop specializes in comfortable shoes, especially those designed for people with diabetes or orthopedic problems. Among the brands sold here are Rockport and Birkenstock. The store's resident pedorthist can also design custom orthotics. Ariel's Village Shoe Shop does shoe and luggage repairs, as well as fabric dyeing. Closed Sun.

PREMIUM GOODS
2416 Times Blvd.
(713) 523-8825
premiumgoods.net

Looking for a pair of Nikes, Adidas, or Pumas in all the latest colors? Premium Goods is the place to go. Just don't expect to find your next pair of running shoes. Aside from a few pairs of Air Jordans, most shoes sold here are meant purely to make a fashion statement. The store sells a limited selection of men's and women's clothing. Closed Sun.

SPORTING GEAR

Bay Area

SOUNDWAVES
1331 Bay Area Blvd., Webster
(281) 332-4200
soundwaves.com

Soundwaves doubles as a music store and Texas's largest surf and skate shop. Here you'll find more than 600 surfboards, some used. You'll also find Reef sandals and board shorts, women's clothes by Quicksilver, and all the latest skaters' shoes. Soundwaves has additional locations in Montrose and Northwest Houston.

Bellaire

AUSTIN CANOE & KAYAK
5822 Bissonnet
(713) 660-7000
austinkayak.com

Whether you're looking for a whitewater kayak, a fishing kayak, a sit-on-top kayak, or a canoe, you'll find it at Austin Canoe & Kayak, better known as ACK. This small Texas chain rents and sells just about every kind of kayak and canoe imaginable, plus all of the accessories you need, whether you're taking a ride down the Buffalo Bayou or heading to Clear Lake. Rentals range from $30 and $55 a day for 1 to 2 days and $25 to $50 a day for 3 or more days. You can also rent paddles, cell phone cases, and dry bags.

Galleria

IFLY, THE ANGLER'S EDGE
5000 Westheimer Rd.
(713) 993-9981
ifly.org

This small store is packed with everything you could need for fly fishing. Here you'll find a large selection of poles, fishing line, and men and women's clothing by brands such as Patagonia, as well as a few unique gift items such as carved wooden boxes. The store's travel services team can also help plan your next fly-fishing trip. There's a second location downtown (728 Travis St.; 713-224-4359).

✳WHOLE EARTH PROVISION CO.
2501 Post Oak Blvd.
(713) 526-5440
wholeearthprovision.com

Whole Earth Provision Co. sells a hodge-podge of products—travel and spirituality books, wind chimes, sunglasses, children's puppets and toys, hammocks, and camping gear, like stoves, cook sets, and luggage. That includes many products by TOMS, Birkenstock, and North Face, as well as some more obscure lines. Not only are the durable and functional items here useful for an active lifestyle; many of them also make great gifts. There's a second location in the Upper Kirby/Montrose area (2934 S. Shepherd Dr.; 713-526-5226).

Memorial

FISHING TACKLE UNLIMITED
8933 Katy Fwy.
(713) 827-7762
fishingtackleunlimited.com
Whatever kind of fishing you prefer, you'll find tons of gear at Fishing Tackle Unlimited. The store has aisles and aisles of gear for fly, in-shore, freshwater, and offshore fishing, including tough-to-find tackle and accessories. You can also buy kayaking gear and rent kayaks for $50 a day. Need clothes for your next fishing expedition? Head into Fishing Tackle Unlimited's Flywater Outfitters shop for brands like G. Loomis and Abel. The store has a second location in southeast Houston near the Bay Area (12800 Gulf Fwy.; 281-481-6838; fishingtackleunlimited.com). Closed Sun.

i Can't find what you need at any of the sporting gear stores listed here? Several major sporting goods chains are also located in Houston, including Sports Authority, Academy, Bass Pro Shop, REI, and Gander Mountain. Go online or consult the yellow pages to find a location near you.

TOY STORES

Galleria

TOYS TO LOVE
1715 Post Oak Blvd.
(713) 599-0099
toystolove.net
With everything from remote-control dinosaurs to art project kits to toy cars to cute T-shirts to PJs to stuffed animals, Toys to Love lives up to its name. You could spend hours here and not see everything. The store also helps put together special gifts, including Easter baskets. Free gift wrap is available.

Memorial

IMAGINATION TOYS AND SHOES
6531 Woodway
(713) 932-8000
imaginationtoysandshoesonline.com
Imagination Toys and Shoes sells toys and cute shoes for everyone from infants to preadolescents. While you shop, the kids can run loose and let their imaginations run wild at the Thomas the Train table or in the kids' play kitchen. Some of the toys and shoes here can be a little pricey. If you're looking for something in a particular price range, just tell the salespeople, who will gladly help you find something. Free gift wrap is available. There's a second location in the Bellaire/West University area (3849 Bellaire Blvd.; 713-662-9898).

✳LEARNING EXPRESS
12850 Memorial Dr.
(713) 465-8697
learningexpress.com
No matter your price range, you can do all of your gift shopping for kids at Learning Express Toys. This popular store sells stationery, toys and games, stickers, and

personalized gifts galore. The salespeople are happy to help you find the perfect toy or gift—and wrap it for free. You can even register for gifts for an upcoming baby shower or birthday party. This Texas franchise has four stores in the Houston area, including locations in Pearland, The Woodlands, and Katy.

Rice Village

FUNDAMENTALLY TOYS
2401 Rice Blvd.
(713) 524-4400
fundamentallytoys.com
Since opening in 1995, Fundamentally Toys has specialized in toys and games that help little ones develop their minds and bodies. This well-organized store sells books, as well as a range of children's gifts. Fundamentally Toys will even host a themed birthday party for your child. The staff takes care of the registry, decorations, cupcakes, and fun; you just show up. Free gift wrapping is available.

VINTAGE, THRIFT & RESALE SHOPS

Galleria

ENCORE
1852 Fountain View Dr. at Winrock
(713) 334-9327
encorehouston.com
Want high-end clothing at reasonable prices? Visit Encore. You'll find well-maintained clothing and accessories by Prada, Louis Vuitton, Gucci, David Yurman, Manolo Blahnik, and Tracy Reese—all secondhand. Owner Terry Rambin, a former Tootsies employee, will help you put together the perfect outfit. Closed Sun and Mon.

The Heights

RETROPOLIS
321 W. 19th St.
(713) 861-1950
If you live and breathe vintage, Retropolis is the place for you. Frequently named Houston's best vintage shop, this 2-story Heights store sells a hodgepodge of retro clothes, accessories, records, and novelty items. Just beware: the clothes are thrown together, so you'll have to hunt to find something special. But if you're willing to look, you're likely to find a few keepers. Prices aren't the lowest in town, but they're fairly reasonable considering the quality and uniqueness of the clothes.

Montrose

BLUE BIRD CIRCLE
615 W. Alabama
(713) 528-0470
thebluebirdcircle.com/ResaleShop.aspx
It's not uncommon to find brands like Banana Republic and Talbots on the racks at Blue Bird Circle. Clothes here are clean and well organized. Although the prices aren't the best in town, Blue Bird Circle does mark down clothes the longer they're on the floor. The store also offers some nice used furniture, wall art, and other home items. Closed Sun.

CHARITY GUILD RESALE SHOP
1203 Lovett Blvd.
(713) 529-0995
charityguildshop.org
Need to put together a memorable costume? The Charity Guild Resale Shop—not to be confused with the nearby Guild Shop—is a good place to do just that. In addition to great accessories, Charity Guild

offers a solid selection of vintage and newer clothes, including wedding dresses. Prices are marked down regularly, but the best items tend to get snapped up before they're marked down. Closed Sun.

THE GUILD SHOP OF ST. JOHN THE DIVINE
2009 Dunlavy St.
(713) 528-5095
theguildshop.org
Whether you're looking for a good deal or an unusual piece of decor, you'll find good options at this Montrose shop. The Guild Shop has a sizeable selection of previously owned clothes, rugs, jewelry, dishes, lamps, and even lithographs and original art. You can also find nice furniture here, some of which is antique. Prices are cheap, but if you wait a week or two, you can probably get what you want for even less—that is, if someone else doesn't beat you to it. Want to sell some of your old stuff on consignment? Be sure to call ahead. Closed Sun.

i There are tons of thrift shops in Montrose, including several on Westheimer between Woodhead and Mandell. Park your car and walk around the area to find the treasure you've been looking for, as well as things you didn't know you needed.

Rice Village & West University

MEN'S RESALE BY THE VILLAGE
2437 Bissonnet St.
(713) 522-5645
Want to look like a million dollars without shelling out more than $20 or $30? For men, Men's Resale by the Village is the place to

go. This well-organized shop sells previously worn men's clothing, especially suits, slacks, dress shirts, and sport coats. Much of the merchandise here is by designers such as Zanella and Zegna, so you'll usually pay a little more than the $2 to $3 you might spend at other thrift shops. Closed Sun.

i Looking for unique, globally inspired furniture that won't break the bank? Head to Rice Village and check out Nadeau (2414 University Blvd.; 713-942-9310; furniturewithasoul.com) and El Paso Import Co. (6121 Kirby; 713-807-9559; elpasoimportco.com).

Upper Kirby

MORE THAN YOU CAN IMAGINE
2817 Westheimer Rd.
(713) 668-8811
mtyci.com
Want to dress like Carrie Bradshaw without breaking the bank? Shop at this aptly named consignment shop. More Than You Can Imagine sells secondhand clothes, shoes, accessories, and even home decor by designers such as Louboutin, Prada, Juicy Couture, and Louis Vuitton. Sizes range from 0 to 20. Although everything here was previously owned, many items have never been worn. Yet, even for these items, the price is just a small fraction of what you'd pay retail. Closed Sun.

WOMEN'S CLOTHING

Galleria

A. TAGHI
5116 Westheimer Rd.
(713) 963-0884
ataghi.com

A. Taghi, as its tagline suggests, sells "fine clothing for men and ladies." Here you'll find shoes and casual and formal wear by designers such as Zanella, Brioni, Belvest, and even some clothes designed by A. Taghi. The salespeople are great about finding your size and pairing separates. They'll also make sure that the clothes you choose fit just right.

MINT
1121-7 Uptown Park Blvd.
(713) 977-4460
minthouston.com
From the moment you ring the bell to enter Mint, you'll see just how exclusive—and serious about fashion—this women's boutique is. The clothes here range from casual slacks and blouses to colorful suits and sundresses by designers like Hugo Boss, Moschino Jeans, and Cynthia Rose. Just about everything is pricey. Mint also has a small selection of jewelry and accessories. Mint Baby is located next door. Closed Sun.

M PENNER
1180-06 Uptown Park Blvd.
(713) 527-8200
mpenner.com
Whether you're looking for a fine dress, suit, or casualwear, you'll find lots of options at M Penner. Among the designers sold here are Badgley Mischka, Hugo Boss, and Paul Smith. Closed Sun.

✳LANGFORD MARKET
2715 University Blvd.
(713) 520-5575
langfordmarket.com
Cotton and silk dresses, jeans, and trendy blouses are just some of the fashionista-worthy items you'll find at this spacious Rice Village boutique. Much of the casual clothing here is vintage inspired, and most of it is reasonably priced. Langford Market also sells panties, swimsuits, jewelry, and other accessories. The store is decorated with comfortable chairs and contemporary paintings, and all of them are for sale. The hip salespeople wear outfits worthy of emulation, and they'll gladly help you put together one of your own. Langford Market has additional locations in Memorial City Mall (303 Memorial City; 713-461-8503) and The Heights (249 W. 19th St.; 713-880-1515).

VILLAGE GIRLS BOUTIQUE
2509 Rice Blvd.
(832) 368-0240
villagegirlsboutique.com
Looking for something fun to wear to a dressy casual party or for a night on the town? You'll find chic options at Village Girls Boutique. The dresses, blouses, sweaters, skirts, and jewelry here are every bit as bright and fun as the fuchsia-hued walls. You won't find much by familiar designers, but everything is reasonably priced and stylish. Closed Sun.

River Oaks

ALEXANDRA KNIGHT
3622 Locke Ln.
(713) 527-8848
alexandraknightonline.com
Actresses like Hilary Swank and Michelle Williams have purchased modish leather handbags from former *Vogue* and *Vanity Fair* stylist Alexandra Knight, who designs her unique handbags right here in Houston. If you call ahead, you can visit her West University studio to purchase a handbag or talk to her about custom designing one just for you.

i Love a good knockoff handbag and costume jewelry that won't cost you more than a few dollars? Visit Harwin Drive from Hillcroft to Gessner Road, where cheap perfume, knockoffs, and other quirky fashion finds abound.

MUSE
2411 W. Alabama St.
(713) 520-6873
musehouston.com

Muse is a fun place to shop for funky clothes and accessories you won't find anywhere else in Houston. In addition to brands such as YA-YA, Nanette Lepore, and Tracy Reese, Muse sells dresses, tops, skirts, and pants by New York– and Los Angeles–based designers like B with G, Calypso, Christopher Fischer, and Swati Argade. You can easily complete your look here—or give one outfit multiple looks—with Muse's voguish jewelry, handbags, and accessories. Added bonus: You'll get lots of personal attention, both on the sales floor and while you're trying on your finds in the boudoir-inspired dressing rooms. Closed Sun.

Upper Kirby & Greenway

NORTON DITTO
2425 W. Alabama, at Kirby
(713) 688-9800
nortonditto.com

Norton Ditto has long been known for its men's clothing, but now it's added a women's department to boot. And, much like the men's department, the women's department offers high-end business and casual clothes by brands such as Audrey Talbott. Closed Sun.

✳TOOTSIES
2601 Westheimer Rd. at Kirby
(713) 629-9990
tootsies.com

Tootsies is Houston's premier women's boutique. While some women come here for casual wear and jeans, others look to Tootsies for fine suits and ball gowns. No matter what you're looking for, you'll have your pick of esteemed American and European designers and styles ranging from classic to contemporary. The sales staff can help you complete the look with some of Tootsies beautiful jewelry, accessories, and shoes. Tootsies also has an excellent alterations department.

LIVING HERE

In this section we feature specific information for residents or those planning to relocate here. Topics include real estate, education, health care, and much more.

RELOCATION

People move to Houston for many different reasons: Some, like my stepfather, come for the promise of warm weather year-round. Others come for job opportunities in aerospace, architecture, medicine, law, business, education, or the arts. Many choose Houston for the low cost of living, the good quality of life, and the countless cultural, social, and culinary offerings. Others come because they already have family here, or because they've heard this is a good place to raise a family. And more than a few come here to get an education and never leave.

No matter why you've decided to move—or are thinking about moving—to Houston, chances are you'll find your niche in this city of millions of opportunities and people.

You're also likely to see why Houston topped *Kiplinger*'s 2008 list of the "Best Cities to Live, Work and Play."

OVERVIEW

From an economic standpoint, Houston is about as good as it gets. The city's cost of living index is 89.4—well below the national average of 100 and the lowest of 27 metropolitan areas with more than 2 million residents. Between April 2010 and April 2011, the city's energy, health-care, and technology sectors helped create 51,000 new jobs—more than any other city in the country except Dallas. Those new hires had their choice of affordable housing—some new, some old, almost all significantly less expensive than comparable homes in other cities of Houston's size.

While Houston hasn't entirely escaped the economic struggles of recent years, it has weathered the storm far better than most of the country. And recession or not, there's no state income tax here in Texas.

Houston is also committed to providing residents a great quality of life. In the last decade, the city has given downtown the most magnificent of makeovers, building a serene urban park, new sports stadiums, and a light-rail system. New restaurants, clubs, hotels, and residential developments have been quick to move in and make downtown a place where Houstonians want to spend their time.

The city isn't stopping here, though: In the next few years, Houston will be adding more light-rail lines, making it even easier to get around downtown. Elsewhere in the city, you'll find all of those other things that make for a good life: quality primary and secondary schools, world-class colleges and universities, some of the best health-care facilities in the world, great grocery stores and farmers' markets, festivals, shops, live music, restaurants, parks, and playgrounds.

Your quality of life depends on more than just finding the right city. You also have to live in the right place in that city—a place that caters to your needs, wants, and pocketbook. So where should you live in Houston? The metropolitan area is filled with dozens of neighborhoods, subdivisions, and suburbs that continue to expand along with Greater Houston's population, which has grown nearly 26 percent since 2000.

Navigating This Chapter

In the pages that follow, you'll learn about some of the most desirable neighborhoods in the Houston area. You'll also learn about real estate agencies and other resources that can help you find your new home, whether you are renting or looking to buy. Keep in mind that most neighborhoods aren't for everyone. If you're young or you and your family like to be in the middle of the action, you may be happier in a central, happening area like Midtown, the Heights, or downtown. Likewise, if space, swimming pools, and a lower mortgage are important to you, Pearland, Katy, Sugar Land, or The Woodlands may be the best neighborhood for you.

This chapter also covers some of the things you'll need to do once you move to Houston—things like registering your car, registering to vote, licensing your pet, getting a driver's license, and finding a place of worship. In subsequent chapters you'll learn about education, child care, higher education, and health care—all factors that could affect your decision about where to live.

NEIGHBORHOODS

Houston and the surrounding areas are filled with dozens of neighborhoods, ranging from eclectic urban communities with lofts and luxury hotels to distant suburbs with houses with swimming pools. To help you start making decisions about where to live—or at least where to start looking—I've included a few of the most desirable and popular residential neighborhoods in this section. Most housing in these neighborhoods is single-family homes.

However, most neighborhoods also have some apartments and condos. Apartments here tend to be located in large complexes with on-site management. Many have gyms, laundry rooms, and pools, and most include parking—often gated.

With so many neighborhoods and rapidly growing suburbs, it's impossible to list every desirable neighborhood here. So as you read the following pages and begin to search for a place to live, keep in mind that this is just a starting point. Houston is full of neighborhoods and suburbs that would be great places to call home.

For additional insight on these neighborhoods, be sure to study the "Area Overview" chapter. And if you have school-age children, check out the "Education and Child Care" chapter, too.

Bellaire

Located just off the Loop, Bellaire is an independently run city. While there's a strong sense of community here, Bellaire is hardly disconnected from the rest of Houston. Residents enjoy easy access to the Medical Center, downtown, and the Galleria, as well as other inner-Loop neighborhoods. This makes Bellaire an attractive option for many doctors, as well as professionals who work downtown or in the Medical Center. The area, which is home to a couple of synagogues and the Jewish Community

Center, is also home to a sizeable Jewish community.

The City of Bellaire is primarily residential, although many retail businesses and restaurants can be found here, too. Single-family homes comprise more than 94 percent of the housing in Bellaire, but there are some apartments in the area. While Bellaire has a number of 1950s and 1960s ranch homes, there has been a trend toward tearing these down and building bigger houses in recent years. The median home value here in 2009 was $506,397.

Bellaire is served by the Houston Independent School District, and most students are zoned to attend Bellaire High School. Learn more about Bellaire at ci.bellaire.tx.us.

Clear Lake

The crown jewel of Houston's Bay Area is Clear Lake, about 20 miles southeast of Houston on I-45. Many residents work at nearby NASA, and a good number enjoy sailing, waterskiing, and other water-based recreational activities on Clear Lake and Galveston Bay. Housing in this family-oriented area ranges from smaller, older homes to large new homes in planned communities. There are even some houses right on the water, although you'll usually pay a premium for that kind of location.

The broad array of single-family homes in Clear Lake makes for quite a variation in pricing: You can find homes here for anywhere from $150,000 on up to $3.5 million for newer mansions. Most homes, though, fall well below the $1 million mark, with the average price of Clear Lake houses at $269,794 in 2009.

The area is served by Clear Creek Independent School District and Dickinson Independent School District. Learn more about Clear Lake at clearlakearea.com.

Cypress

Located about 20 miles northwest of downtown off US 290, Cypress is an unincorporated area of Harris County. Extraterritorial jurisdiction gives the City of Houston control over this major suburban area. Cypress is divided into many neighborhoods and subdivisions, such as Jersey Village, Klein, and Copperfield.

Up until the 1950s, Cypress was farmland. As a result, most houses here are pretty new; they range from smaller two- and three-bedroom homes to larger brick houses. Many Cypress neighborhoods are master-planned communities with their own recreational facilities and offerings, such as parks and neighborhood swimming pools. There's quite a bit of commercial development in the area, including an outlet mall with 145 stores.

The median single-home value here is more than $200,000; the median condo value is just under $200,000. Two school districts serve the area—Cypress Independent School District and Klein Independent School District.

Downtown

Downtown's revitalization in the early 2000s resulted in many new lofts and luxury condos. Many Houstonians are now opting to move downtown because it means easy access to the office. Residents also enjoy light-rail, sidewalk, and underground tunnel access to some of the city's best offerings, including the Theater District, the Houston Rockets and Astros, great restaurants and clubs, and parks like Discovery Green.

The overwhelming majority of downtown housing is condos; the median downtown condo value is $258,000. Rent downtown ranges from roughly $1,000 per month for a studio on up to more than $11,000 per month for luxury penthouses. More than two-thirds of downtown residents are married, although there's also a sizeable population of young single professionals.

Children living downtown are zoned to attend school in the Houston Independent School District. For a list of downtown lofts and condos, visit downtownhouston.org.

Galleria & Uptown

The Galleria area is anchored by the Houston Galleria mall and the many restaurants, shops, hotels, and other businesses that surround this prestigious shopping district. Since the 1990s, many new residential developments have cropped up in the Galleria/Uptown area, and most are luxury high-rise condos, condos, apartments, lofts, and town houses. In fact, nearly half of the residences here are condos; just over one-third are single-family homes. More than a third of the neighborhood's residents are single, and many are young professionals.

The median condo value in the Galleria area is just under $200,000, while the median value for single-family homes is more than $500,000. Rent for the area's apartments ranges from about $800 per month for small, just-the-basics apartments farther away from the Galleria to as much as $5,000 a month for luxury rentals with a doorman and other amenities.

While close proximity to great shopping and dining is part of the neighborhood's allure, many people move here for easy access to other parts of the city. Located just off the West Loop, the Galleria area is just minutes from downtown, the Medical Center, Memorial, River Oaks, and many other central locations around the city. Children in the area are zoned to attend school in the Houston Independent School District.

i Houston floods often, so make sure you buy flood insurance if you rent or buy a home here. Not all insurance companies provide this, so you may have to shop around. It will only take one storm for you to realize that your effort was worth every hour and penny.

The Heights

The Heights is one of the city's most unique and historic neighborhoods, making it an attractive option for many people in search of a fairly central location with an eclectic vibe. While many older homes around the city have been bulldozed and replaced with cookie-cutter homes, that hasn't been the case with the Heights. In the 1970s Heights residents began a campaign to restore the beautiful Victorian homes—some mansions—in their neighborhood. Residents here tend to be very community minded and know one another's faces, if not names. The neighborhood even has its own civic association and opera, as well as a neighborhood fun run and arts events throughout the year.

Single-family houses comprise more than 90 percent of the housing in the Heights, where the median home value is just under $300,000. These homes include a mix of old bungalows, Victorian homes, and enchanting cottages.

The Houston Independent School District serves the Heights. Learn more about the neighborhood at houstonheights.org.

Katy

Over the last two decades, Katy has attracted large numbers of families with master-planned communities, such as Cinco Ranch, Memorial Parkway, and Grand Lakes. Located about 25 miles west of downtown off I-10, these affluent communities boast amenities such as swimming pools, golf courses, parks, rec centers, and playgrounds.

More than 90 percent of housing in Katy is single-family homes, which are fairly large in many of the developments. Condos make up less than 1 percent of housing here; apartments make up the rest. A median home price of $162,107 makes Katy an affordable option for many people who want relatively easy access to downtown.

In the last few years, there's been tremendous commercial development, with a number of retail vendors and restaurants setting up shop in Katy. Part of what's now considered the Katy area is located in the City of Katy, which is an independent municipality; the rest is an unincorporated area controlled by the City of Houston. Children in the area are zoned to attend school in the Katy Independent School District.

Kingwood

Located in northeast Houston about 23 miles from downtown, Kingwood is home to several master-planned communities. The neighborhood—which was annexed by the City of Houston in 1996—is divided into several heavily wooded villages.

Housing is comprised largely of single-family homes, but nearly a quarter of residents here rent apartments, condos, or houses. The median home value is close to $150,000.

Each year, the community holds several events in Town Center Park. Among them are Mardi Gras, Fourth of July, and picnics. Most of Kingwood is located in Harris County, but a small part is in Montgomery County. Students are zoned to attend school in the Humble Independent School District. Learn more at kingwood.com.

Medical Center & South Loop

Some of the most affordable, centrally located apartments in Houston can be found near the Texas Medical Center. Many Medical Center staff and students live in new developments along Hermann Park or in the nearby South Loop area, which runs along South Main and Fannin Streets near the Reliant Center. Developers have moved in and begun renovating older apartments and building new, yet affordable ones. Apartments and condos can be rented in the area run from anywhere from $800 to $4,200 per month, although you'll also find some rentals outside this range.

The neighborhood is easily accessible on the METRORail and has a number of METRO bus stops. There are many retail businesses and restaurants here, too. Children in the South Loop are zoned for the Houston Independent School District.

Memorial

This wealthy neighborhood on Houston's west side is dotted with large houses, beautiful landscaping, and old trees. Many of the houses in Memorial were built 50 years ago, but contractors have begun to tear down some of the original houses and replace them with enormous homes. Single-family homes in Memorial are among the most expensive in Houston, with many homes selling for $1 million or more. The median condo value here is more than $200,000. While housing here consists largely of single-family homes, a number of upscale apartment complexes have cropped up recently, with rents ranging from $1,000 to upwards of $2,500.

Memorial is divided into many smaller neighborhoods, and in a few cases, independently run villages with their own municipal governments. In 2008 Forbes.com named two of these villages—Bunker Hill and Hunters Creek—"Top Suburbs to Live Well." Memorial has several prominent residents, including former baseball All-Star Roger Clemens.

Most of Memorial is zoned for the Spring Branch Independent School District, although some parts of the area are zoned for the Houston Independent School District. Many Memorial parents send their children to private schools, such as The Kinkaid School and Second Baptist Church. People who can't quite afford a Memorial mortgage or rent often live on the north side of I-10 in Spring Valley. This enables families to send their children to Spring Branch schools and pay less for housing. The median home value in Spring Valley is close to $500,000, but you can find less expensive homes in the area.

Midtown

This mixed-use area is considered one of Houston's most hip neighborhoods, with popular bars and restaurants lining the area. That wasn't always the case for Midtown, though. Until the 1990s, Victorian-style homes dating back to the early 20th century lined the streets of this urban neighborhood. Today upscale apartments, town houses, and lofts have replaced them.

Midtown residents are largely 20- and 30-somethings who work downtown or in the nearby Medical Center, but you'll find families here, as well as a large Vietnamese population. Close to half of Midtown's residents are single, and about 60 percent of residents live in single-family homes. Another 30 percent live in condos. The median home value is close to $230,000; the median condo value is more than $125,000. Apartments in Midtown range from about $1,100 per month to more than $3,000 per month. Midtown youth attend school in the Houston Independent School District. Learn more at houstonmidtown.com.

Montrose

If you want to be close to downtown, Rice University, Midtown, River Oaks, the Medical Center, or the Museum District, Montrose is an attractive option. The neighborhood, which has a large gay and lesbian population, is one of the city's most diverse. However, many new apartments and condos have recently been built in the eastern part of Montrose near Midtown, pricing out many of the artsy types and students who have historically called this eclectic neighborhood home.

In their stead are a growing number of young professionals. About half of Montrose's residents are single and about two-thirds live in single-family homes, which range from restored mansions dating back to the early 1900s to cute cottages. Even as Montrose has become a pricier place to live, it has remained eclectic and community oriented. Many families now live in the area, particularly in Neartown, a neighborhood with tree-lined streets and homes that range from mansions to cottages. Among Montrose's former residents are reclusive aviator

Howard Hughes and US President Lyndon B. Johnson.

The median Montrose home value is close to $400,000. Apartments here range from about $800 per month to $2,500 per month. The neighborhood is served by the Houston Independent School District.

i Visit swamplot.com for the latest news on Houston real estate, architecture, home design, and renovation.

Pearland

One of the fastest growing cities in the country, Pearland is located about 20 miles south of downtown. The independent city is filled with master-planned communities with parks and recreational facilities, as well as retail locations. Residents also enjoy relative quietude, a family-friendly community, and easy access to jobs in the Medical Center and downtown via TX 288. Plus, with a median home value of just under $200,000, larger homes here tend to be more affordable than those in more central locations. Pearland is served primarily by the Pearland Independent School District, but parts of the area are served by the Alvin Independent School District. Learn more at cityofpearland.com.

River Oaks

Located inside the Loop, River Oaks is in one of the country's wealthiest zip codes, and it's got huge houses and incomes to show for it. The median home here is more than 3,600 square feet, and close to a quarter of River Oaks residents make $800,000 a year or more. Many belong to the exclusive River Oaks Country Club.

Most River Oaks houses are older stately mansions embellished with lavish landscaping. The median single-family home is appraised at more than $1 million. Although single-family homes make up the majority of River Oaks housing, there are some condos and apartments in the area.

The Houston Independent School District serves River Oaks. Many children in the neighborhood attend Mirabeau B. Lamar High School, considered one of the area's best public high schools. A number of other youth here attend St. John's School, the city's most elite private school, also located in River Oaks.

Sugar Land

Situated about 20 miles southwest of downtown, Sugar Land is an independent municipality in Fort Bend County. The city is home to master-planned communities with houses built within the last 20 years. Each community has retail and recreation facilities, such as tennis courses, golf courses, pools, and clubhouses. Many people move here because they can get a bigger home for less than they might pay in Houston.

The median home value here is close to $200,000. But there are plenty of homes in Sugar Land that cost in the millions, making this a popular place for professional athletes to live. In 2008 Forbes.com named Sugar Land one of the "Top Suburbs to Live Well" (along with two Memorial neighborhoods) and in 2006 *Money* magazine ranked Sugar Land third on its list of "100 Best Cities to Live in the United States."

Sugar Land is served by the Fort Bend Independent School District. Learn more on the city's website at sugarlandtx.gov.

i Want to compare rates on utilities as well as home phone, cable TV, satellite TV, and high-speed Internet providers? Visit movehouston.com.

West University Place

This area just west of Rice University is one of Houston's wealthiest neighborhoods. Technically, West University Place—aka West U—isn't even part of Houston since it has its own local government and has never been consolidated into the City of Houston.

Many streets here are lined with large oak trees, and homes here are eclectic in design and steep in price. Houses vary in size, but many have small yards. More than 85 percent of the housing here is single-family homes; another 9 percent is condos. The median home value in West U is close to $800,000.

Most West U residents are professionals (and in some cases, Rice professors) with families who appreciate the neighborhood's proximity to the Medical Center, Museum District, Hermann Park, and downtown. In 2009, the median household income was more than $180,000. Children in West U are zoned to attend school in the Houston Independent School District and its well-regarded Mirabeau B. Lamar High School. Learn more about West U at westu.org.

The Woodlands

Located nearly an hour northeast of downtown off I-45, this master-planned community offers a serene retreat from the city. The Houston exurb, as its name suggests, is highly wooded and beautiful, with plenty of community-oriented offerings and amenities. The vast majority of Woodlands residents are families living in single-family homes, although there are some condos and apartments in the area. The median home value is close to $280,000.

Residents often choose The Woodlands, in part, because it's less expensive than living in the city. The area has its own mall, several golf courses, a country club, and plenty of other recreational facilities. The Woodlands is served by three school districts: Tomball, Conroe, and Magnolia. Learn more at thewoodlands.com.

REAL ESTATE AGENCIES & RESOURCES

Finding a new home can be a big endeavor, especially in a city the size of Houston. Luckily, Houston's got thousands of knowledgeable Realtors who can help you buy or sell a home or rent an apartment or loft. In this section, you'll find a list of a few of the biggest and best-known real estate brokerage firms in the area. At these firms and many others, you'll find Realtors who speak many languages, so if you need someone who speaks a language other than English, just ask. Keep in mind that this list is by no means all-inclusive. Dozens of other reputable companies and agents can also help you find a new home.

For additional agents and agencies, contact the **Houston Association of Realtors (HAR).** This free service can help you find real estate agents and a new home, whether you're looking to buy or rent a house, condo, loft, or apartment. Visit har.com to search for houses, apartments, real estate companies, or agents or call (713) 629-1900 for free assistance.

Many Realtors distribute publications from a series called *Houston Newcomer Guides,* which highlight everything you need to know about moving to areas such as Clear Lake, Fort Bend County (where Sugar Land is located), Northeast Houston, Northwest Houston, West Houston, and the area along TX 288 South, which includes the Texas Medical Center and Pearland. You can also request a free paper copy or view the electronic version online at houstonnewcomerguides.com.

Also be sure to check out the real estate ads in Sunday's *Houston Chronicle* (chron .com/realestate).

Looking for an apartment? Check out **Apartment Whiz,** which offers free apartment locating services. Call (713) 688-5585 or visit apartmentwiz.com to get started.

You can also grab a free copy of ***Apartment Guide*** magazine at most grocery stores. While you're at it, you may also want to grab a copy of the Houston Press (houston press.com) and the Greensheet (thegreen sheet.com) and look for apartments in their respective classified sections.

CENTURY 21 BALLARD & ASSOCIATES
5930 Hwy. 6 North, Ste. A-1
(281) 855-6100
century21ballard.com
Veteran property manager and licensed Realtor Darrell Ballard opened Century 21 Ballard & Associates in 1991. Today the firm has more than 30 agents who speak many different languages, including Arabic, French, Spanish, German, and Italian. Located on the west side of town, Century 21 Ballard & Associates sells homes and helps buyers find homes in Cypress, Houston, and Katy.

CENTURY 21 PREMIER GOLD PROPERTIES
8118 Park Place, Ste. 300, Houston
(713) 644-0084 (Houston office)
century21premiergold.com

With almost 100 agents who speak more than two dozen languages, Century 21 Premier Gold Properties is Houston's largest Century 21 firm. Agents here specialize in relocation, construction, resales, vacant land, and rentals. The firm serves the Greater Houston area, including Sugar Land and Spring. Visit the website for additional locations.

CENTURY 21 ROSS GROUP
12623 Jones Rd.
(281) 469-7677
century21ross.com
The Century 21 Ross Group has been recognized for its sales volume and excellent service. It serves the Clear Lake, Cypress, Houston, Kemah, Klein, Nassau Bay, River Oaks, Spring, Tomball, and Seabrook areas.

COLDWELL BANKER UNITED
houston.cbunited.com
Coldwell Banker United has nearly 20 offices in the Houston area. Each office serves a different area of Houston or one of the suburbs. Among the neighborhoods covered by these offices are Kingwood, Greenway Plaza, the Heights, Clear Lake, Bellaire, Pearland, Katy, The Woodlands, and Memorial. Visit the website or consult the phone book to find the office for the neighborhood you're interested in.

GREENWOOD KING PROPERTIES
3201 Kirby Dr. (Upper Kirby)
(713) 524-0888
greenwoodking.com
Greenwood King is one of the foremost names in Houston's high-end real estate market. The private firm, which was founded in 1984, has three offices and nearly 200 agents. Greenwood King provides financial support for a number of community

organizations and schools and founded the Lobby, the city's only full-service real estate resource center for homeowners. Although Greenwood King specializes in expensive homes, these properties aren't limited to just a few neighborhoods. Agents here help clients buy and sell houses and condos all over the Greater Houston area and surrounding counties. Visit the website for additional locations.

JOHN DAUGHERTY REALTORS
520 Post Oak Blvd., 6th Floor
(713) 626-3930
johndaugherty.com

Since its founding in 1967, John Daugherty Realtors has led the way in home sales in neighborhoods such as Bellaire, West University, Memorial, and River Oaks. More than 150 agents currently work for the firm, whose office is in Uptown. While John Daugherty Realtors specializes in high-end real estate, the firm has been branching out to serve emerging neighborhoods and cater to clients with a broad range of budgets and lifestyles.

KELLER WILLIAMS METROPOLITAN
550 Post Oak Blvd., Ste. 350
(713) 621-8001
kwmet.com

Keller Williams Metropolitan has more than 300 agents, many of whom are multilingual. They sell and help clients buy homes all over the Greater Houston area.

MARTHA TURNER PROPERTIES
12506 Memorial Dr. (Memorial)
(713) 520-1981
marthaturner.com

This privately owned real estate company is a big player in Houston's high-end market. In 2010 Martha Turner Properties booked more than $1.2 billion in closed sales transactions. Although Martha Turner Properties is known for its success in the high-end market, the company helps clients in all price ranges buy and sell homes. The company has several offices around the Greater Houston area and works with home buyers, sellers, developers, and builders. Martha Turner publishes *PROPERTIES*, a full-color magazine featuring articles and listings of interest to local home buyers and sellers. Copies can be picked up at the Martha Turner offices. Visit the website for locations.

INFORMATION FOR NEWCOMERS

New to the Houston area? Here are a few things you need to know:

Pet Licenses

The City of Houston requires that all dogs and cats have and wear a license. You can purchase your pet's license by filling out an application online at petdata.com/cs/hst and submitting it by mail. Or you can get a license in person at the animal shelter at 3200 Carr St., located north of downtown, just off US 59 North; call (713) 229-7300 for hours.

i Dog lovers, beware: Houston doesn't permit households to have more than 3 dogs older than 6 months.

Whether you acquire a license in person or by mail, you'll need to provide your pet's rabies vaccination certificate, as well as your spay/neuter certificate, if you have one. Licenses cost $60 a year for pets that have not been spayed or neutered and $20 a year for pets that have been. With a valid ID, seniors ages 60 and up can license their pet for $5 the first year and $2 every year after that. There's no fee for the first year license for seeing/hearing assistance pets; subsequent years cost $2. You must purchase your license within 30 days of moving to the city and renew your license within 30 days of your previous license's expiration or your pet's most recent rabies vaccination.

Houston also requires all pets to be on a leash or in a fenced yard. If your pet is found roaming the streets—or hanging out in an angry neighbor's yard—he or she may be impounded, and you may be fined up to $100.

Auto Insurance

The State of Texas requires liability insurance coverage for all vehicles. The minimum requirement is $30,000 for bodily injury for each injured person, $60,000 per accident, and $25,000 for property damage. You'll need proof of liability coverage to obtain or renew your Texas driver's license, register your car, and get your vehicle inspected.

A new database called SafeTexas (texassure.com) makes it easier for police to verify insurance coverage. So, if you're driving without valid insurance, you'll probably get a ticket when you get pulled over.

i You must have liability insurance before you can register your vehicle or get your driver's license.

Vehicle Registration

The State of Texas requires new residents to register their vehicles and get Texas license plates within 30 days of moving to the

state. Before registering, you'll need to visit a state-approved Safety Inspection Station for a vehicle safety inspection and a visual verification of the vehicle identification number. To find the Safety Inspection Station nearest you, visit txdps.state.tx.us/vi/inspection/new_locator.asp or look in the yellow pages under "Automobile Inspection Stations."

i Have a good driving record? You may be able to renew your driver's license online. If you're eligible to do so, you'll receive a notice in the mail when it's almost time to renew your license.

At the inspection station, you'll receive a Vehicle Identification Certificate, which you must then submit to the Harris County Tax Office along with an Application for Texas Certificate of Title and your out-of-state title or registration. You can get your Texas vehicle registration in person at any Harris County Tax Office or by mail; you'll also need to supply proof of liability insurance. Registering your vehicle will require paying a new resident fee of $90, or a sales tax fee of 6.25 percent of the price you paid for the vehicle. The Harris County Tax Office is downtown at 1001 Preston. Call (713) 368-2000 or visit the website (hctax.net) for more information.

Once you've registered your vehicle, you'll have to renew your registration each year and keep a registration sticker on your vehicle window. You can renew your registration at the tax office or online at txdmv.gov.

Vehicle Inspection

Texas requires all vehicles to be inspected each year. Your first inspection will occur during the vehicle registration process. After that, you can get your car inspected at the same Safety Inspection Station you visited initially, or at one of many gas stations and oil change businesses around the area.

Inspections include both safety and emissions testing. Safety testing costs $14.50; emissions testing costs up to $39.75. You'll need to provide proof of insurance to get an inspection.

Driver's Licenses

The State of Texas requires all permanent residents to get a Texas driver's license within 90 days of moving to the state.

Eighteen or older and already have a driver's license? You'll need to take proof of identity and social security number, proof of Texas vehicle registration, and proof of liability insurance. You can find a complete list of acceptable forms of ID on the Texas Department of Public Safety's website (txdps.state .tx.us). To get your Texas license, you'll also have to pass a vision exam, hand over your out-of-state license, and be thumbprinted. Applicants under 18 with a valid license from another state must also supply proof that they've completed a driver's education course and verification of current enrollment and attendance in school.

The fee for a driver's license is $25 for adults 18 and older. Licenses must be renewed every 6 years. New Texans under 18 pay just $16 for a license but must pay $6 to renew their license each year until they turn 18.

i Avoid a hassle and an even longer wait by taking cash when you visit the Department of Public Safety to get your license.

The Texas Department of Public Safety has several locations at which you can obtain or renew a driver's license; the're listed here. Take note: None of these locations are open on the weekend, though most are open until 7 p.m. at least one day a week. Hours vary by day and by location, so visit txdps.state.tx.us or call for the hours of your preferred location.

12220 S. Gessner (Southwest)
(713) 219-4100

4545 Dacoma (Northwest)
(713) 683-0541

10503 Grant Rd. (Northwest)
(281) 890-5440

1601 Townhurst (West)
(713) 465-8462

9206 Winkler (Southeast)
(713) 943-0631

8825 Tidwell (Northeast)
(713) 633-9872

15403 Vantage Pkwy. East, Ste. 300
(North)
(281) 449-2685

i Got questions about licensing your dog or voting, or need to report a minor water line break? For these and other non-emergency needs, call 311. You'll quickly be connected with the appropriate city service that can solve your problems.

Registering to Vote

You may register to vote in Texas by calling (713) 368-8683 and requesting an application or by downloading an application from tax.co.harris.tx.us and mailing it to the Tax Assessor-Collector and Voter Registrar. You can also register to vote in person at 15 Tax Office branch locations around the city. Call (713) 368-2000 to find the office closest to you. If you live outside of Harris County, you can download an application from the Texas secretary of state's website (sos.state.tx .us) and mail it to the address listed on the application.

Religious Institutions

With thousands of places of worship and religious organizations, the Greater Houston area serves just about every religion and denomination. The city's churches, synagogues, temples, and mosques have congregations ranging from the low hundreds to several thousand, so you can find a place to worship that suits your preferences.

You can find a complete list of Houston's many houses of worship and religious organizations at houston.com/religion/business-directory or by consulting the yellow pages.

Jewish? You may also find the **Jewish Federation of Greater Houston** (houston-jewish.org; 713-729-7000) and the **Jewish Community Center** (jcchouston.org; 713-729-3200) to be useful resources for getting involved in the community.

Muslim? You may find the **Islamic Society of Greater Houston** (isgh.org; 713-524-6615) helpful as well.

EDUCATION & CHILD CARE

Whether you're moving to Houston with children or just planning to raise a family here in the future, you may be concerned about the city's education and child-care offerings. Rest assured: Houstonians place a high value on education and child care. No matter how unique your child's learning needs are, you'll almost certainly find an appropriate school or child-care facility here. Between the more than two dozen school districts, 300 private schools, and 1,500 licensed day-care facilities that serve the area, Houston is home to many excellent learning environments. Here you'll find schools that cater to just about every demographic and neighborhood. Read on to learn about the city's public-school, private-school, preschool, and day-care offerings.

PUBLIC SCHOOLS

If you haven't quite grasped how big Houston is yet, the public education system should give you some idea: Some 26 school districts serve Harris County. (Six of these districts lie only partly in the county.) By far the biggest district is the Houston Independent School District, which also happens to be the largest district in Texas and the seventh largest in the country.

Many Houston suburbs, such as Katy, have their own school districts. These districts vary in size and the number of schools within them. Some include charter schools and magnet schools. Students are typically required to attend school in the district in which they live, although some magnet schools and charter schools make exceptions to this rule.

i Before deciding where to live, check out the ratings of local school districts on the Texas Education Agency's website: tea.state.tx.us.

Public schools here are typically organized in three levels: pre-K through 5th grade (elementary school), 6th through 8th grade (middle school), and 9th through 12th grade (high school). Texas children aren't required to attend kindergarten, unless they're at least 6 years old on September 1.

The curriculum and activities for all grade levels are regulated by the State Board of Education and Texas Education Agency. Among these regulations: Classes for kindergarten through 4th grade never have more than 22 students per teacher. While wealthier districts try to maintain comparable class sizes for the older-grade levels, some poorer districts may have closer to 30 students in a classroom.

Curriculum Requirements

Just like their counterparts elsewhere in the state and country, public school students here are required to take many aptitude and achievement tests throughout the course of their K-12 education. Beginning in the spring 2012, Texas started moving to a new standardized test, the State of Texas Assessment of Academic Readiness (STAAR). The new testing regimen will assess students in grades 3-8 in math and reading each year and in writing, social studies, and science once each in elementary and middle school. STAAR will require high school students to take end-of-course assessment tests in all of their math, science, English, geography and history classes. You can learn more about the STAAR requirements at tea.state.tx.us/student.assessment/staar.

To graduate, Texas high school students must earn at least 26 course credits and pass the STAAR tests and all of their classes. However, students with special challenges or who attend lower-performing schools may only be required to complete 22 credits. The requisite 26 credits include 4 years of English, math, and science; 3.5 years of social studies, including three history classes and a US government course; economics; at least 2 years of a foreign language; a year and a half of physical education; a semester of speech or another communications course; a technology course; a fine arts class; and several electives.

Because there are so many school districts in the Houston area, it's impossible to discuss them all in the space of a chapter. A few notable districts are listed here to give you a flavor for the educational terrain here.

Enrollment

Contact your local school district to enroll your child in a public school in Houston. You'll need a copy of your child's birth certificate, immunization records, social security number, and proof of residence to enroll him or her in school.

Not sure what district you're zoned in? Find out by contacting the Harris County Department of Education (713-694-6300; hcde-texas.org).

School Districts

HOUSTON INDEPENDENT SCHOOL DISTRICT
4400 W. 18th St.
(713) 556-6005
houstonisd.org
Houston Independent School District—better known as H.I.S.D.—serves more than 300 square miles of the city and parts of the suburbs. So, if you live in Houston or Bellaire, odds are high that your child is zoned to attend an H.I.S.D. school. The district served more than 202,000 students in 2009–2010. About 62 percent of the district's students are Hispanic, 27 percent are black, 8 percent are Caucasian, and 3 percent are of Asian origin. The district has a strong bilingual education program.

Like other urban districts of its size, Houston Independent School District has its share of problems, ranging from underperforming schools to dropouts to schools in need of repair. The district's high dropout rate appeared to decline considerably in the late 1990s and early 2000s, but an audit of these numbers revealed that the district misreported and misrepresented their dropout rates. And a recent audit encouraged the closing of nearly half of the district's 100-plus magnet schools.

Some of the best schools in the district are magnet schools, such as the High School for Performing and Visual Arts, the Michael E. DeBakey High School for Health Professions, and Carnegie Vanguard, which serves gifted and talented students. To attend an H.I.S.D. magnet school, students must apply and be selected from a competitive applicant pool. These schools, which began as a way to encourage integration three decades ago, give otherwise indifferent or at-risk students the chance to attend a school that focuses on something they're passionate about. They also give talented students the chance to hone their gifts at a young age. (Just ask Beyoncé. She's a graduate of the High School for Performing and Visual Arts.) Budget concerns have forced the district to curtail bus transportation for magnet-school students living 2 miles or farther away from their school, causing some Houstonians to worry about additional cuts.

H.I.S.D. also operates more than 20 charter schools, which tend to have higher achievement standards than other schools. That's at least partly because H.I.S.D. charter schools are exempt from many of the regulations that other schools in the district are required to follow. Want to send your child to an H.I.S.D. charter school (which shouldn't be confused with the many independently run charter schools throughout Texas)? You'll have to apply. If there are more applicants than available spots, students are selected by lottery.

KATY INDEPENDENT SCHOOL DISTRICT
6301 S. Stadium Ln.
(281) 396-6000
katyisd.org
The Katy Independent School District serves a 181-square-mile area west of Houston's city limits, predominately in the city of Katy. This is one of the state's fastest-growing school districts. Currently the district's 53 schools enroll more than 60,000 students, about

43 percent of whom are Caucasian and 34 percent of whom are Hispanic.

Although close to 34 percent of Katy students are considered at-risk, students in the district—on the whole—perform consistently well on the statewide TAKS test. Many schools in the district receive "exemplary" or "recognized" ratings in the Texas accountability system each year. The suburban district is particularly known for drawing in volunteers from the community to mentor students and give them fresh perspectives and opportunities.

SPRING BRANCH INDEPENDENT SCHOOL DISTRICT
955 Campbell Rd.
(713) 464-1511
springbranchisd.com
The Spring Branch Independent School District—aka S.B.I.S.D.—enrolls more than 32,000 students on the city's west side. The district's 44-square-mile area covers the Memorial area, as well as an area north of the Katy Freeway and west of 290. S.B.I.S.D. serves everyone from wealthy students to poorer students living in apartments, though it's rare that both groups are represented in large numbers at the same school. More than half of Spring Branch students are Hispanic and close to a third are Caucasian.

Spring Branch's 45 campuses include four high schools, an alternative high school, a charter middle/high school, seven regular middle schools and a middle school–only charter, 26 elementary schools for grades K through five, and five schools for children in pre-K. While high schools like Northbrook and Spring Woods have historically had some problems with underperforming students, many of the district's schools are quite good. Memorial High School, for

LIVING HERE

instance, is consistently rated one of the best high schools in the country in national rankings. Nearly half of the district's schools have been named National Exemplary "Blue Ribbon" Schools by the Department of Education. And in 2009, S.B.I.S.D. produced 16 National Merit Scholarship Finalists and 18 Semifinalists.

PRIVATE SCHOOLS

The Houston area is home to more than 300 private schools, giving you options galore for educating your child outside the public school system. Some independent schools serve students from preschool through high school; others offer only high school classes. Many schools are affiliated with a particular religion or religious organization; others are secular. The city is home to several schools for students with learning and physical challenges, as well as schools that serve gifted types. The price tags at these schools vary almost as much as their focuses and their student bodies. Many private schools require students to wear uniforms.

It's impossible to list all 300-plus private schools here, but the top-notch schools listed here should give you a flavor for the types of learning environments available in Houston. Use this list as a starting point, then find additional suggestions by consulting the yellow pages, friendly neighbors and colleagues, and houstonprivateschools.org, the website of Houston Area Independent Schools (HAIS). The HAIS is made up of 79 private schools in the area; its website includes information about each member school. Every fall the HAIS hosts a "preview" day, where parents and students can meet representatives from local private schools and boarding schools.

THE BRIARWOOD SCHOOL
12207 Whittington Dr.
(281) 493-1070
briarwoodschool.org
The Briarwood School serves students with learning and developmental disabilities through three different schools: The Lower School educates kindergarteners through sixth graders. Students in grades 7 through 12 attend the Middle/Upper School, while students ages 5 to 12 who have developmental delays attend the Tuttle School. Each school offers small classes, typically composed of fewer than 10 students. Teaching approaches are adapted to meet each child's individual needs. In addition to standard curriculum requirements in reading, math, science, and social studies, students take electives and participate in extracurricular activities. Briarwood also focuses on helping students build social and motor skills. The Briarwood School is located in west Houston.

THE EMERY/WEINER SCHOOL
9825 Stella Link
(832) 204-5900
emeryweiner.org
The Emery/Weiner School is a Jewish community school for middle- and high-school age students. The curriculum focuses on both general and Jewish studies. The school also emphasizes *Tikkun Olam*—the Jewish value of repairing the world—through community service requirements and opportunities. Students often participate in experiential learning opportunities, including trips to Poland, Israel, and elsewhere. Classes are small, which makes for a close-knit community. This southwest Houston school recently built a new $14 million campus, featuring art and music studios, a

high-tech audio/video room, and top-notch computer and science labs.

EPISCOPAL HIGH SCHOOL
4650 Bissonnet
(713) 512-3400
ehshouston.org

Episcopal High School enrolls approximately 640 students and offers a 7-to-1 student-to-faculty ratio. The school, which is affiliated with the Episcopal Diocese of Texas, requires students to participate in daily chapel and sacred studies. While religion is a big part of the curriculum, the school also emphasizes academics, the arts, and athletics. The 35-acre campus is located in Bellaire.

THE FAY SCHOOL
105 N. Post Oak Ln.
(713) 681-8300
thefayschool.org

This challenging preparatory school serves students from age 3 to fifth grade. Small nurturing classes and individualized attention help students discover and hone their intellectual, physical, social, ethical, and artistic abilities. Students study math, social studies, Spanish, music, language arts, library, multimedia, and art. The Fay School's first-class facilities include an outdoor classroom—a screened-in area where students learn while interacting with the environment.

THE KINKAID SCHOOL
201 Kinkaid School Dr.
(713) 782-1640
kinkaid.org

The Kinkaid School educates bright—and typically wealthy—students from preschool through high school before sending many of them off to the Ivy League. About 1,280 students are enrolled here each year, and admission is highly competitive. In addition to fulfilling standard curriculum requirements, students can take classes in subjects such as Chinese, philosophy and ethics, art history and philosophy, astronomy, JAVA and robotics, and filmmaking. The school also offers top-notch extracurriculars and competitive teams in everything from debate to lacrosse to football. The campus is located in Memorial and is divided into three separate schools—Lower School, Middle School, and Upper School. Each school has its own classrooms, faculty, and close-knit community.

> **i** Thinking about sending your child to a charter school? Check out the list of Houston charter schools—some public, some private—at charterstexas.org.

ST. JOHN'S SCHOOL
2401 Claremont Ln.
(713) 850-0222
sjs.org

Considered one of the best—if not the best—private school in Houston, St. John's School is a college preparatory school serving students from kindergarten through high school. Students here often end up going to some of the country's best universities. The admissions process at this River Oaks school is highly competitive and academics are rigorous. Regardless of what grade they're in, students take classes in math, science, language arts, social studies, and the arts. The school also has a number of athletic teams and extracurricular events. Particularly ambitious students in grades 10 through 12 can undertake an Independent Studies Project, where they spend a semester or year studying a subject of interest in-depth and at their own pace.

CHILD CARE & PRESCHOOLS

There are hundreds of licensed child-care centers in the Greater Houston area—1,500 in Harris County alone. Some are national chains such as Crème de la Crème, Kindercare Learning Center, and LaPetite Academy. Many community organizations such as the YMCA, churches, synagogues, and other religious institutions also offer excellent child-care and preschool programs. A small sampling of local child-care programs can be found in the next few pages.

Before enrolling your child in a child-care program or preschool, be sure to visit the school and do some research to make sure the school is licensed and hasn't had any health or safety violations. If you don't know any other local parents yet, contact the referral agency listed at the end of this section. A representative can help identify the best early childhood programs for your child.

i Not sure whether a child-care provider is licensed? Search the Texas Department of Family and Child Protective Services' database at dfps .state.tx.us/child_care, then look into licensing history and compliance with health and safety standards by calling (866) 892-4453.

Child-Care Providers

BECKER EARLY CHILDHOOD CENTER
1500 Sunset Blvd.
(713) 535-6400
beckerschool.org
The Becker Early Childhood Center is the preschool of Congregation Emanu El, a Reform synagogue across the street from Rice University. There's often a waiting list to attend the school, which serves more than 200 children ages 15 months to 5 years. While many of the children are Jewish and come partly for the Jewish education and programming, many non-Jewish families send their children here, too. Becker is accredited by the National Association for the Education of Young Children.

i Many public schools offer prekindergarten programs. Consult your school district to find out if your local elementary school offers this option.

ESPERANZA SCHOOL
1100 Roy St.
(713) 868-3276
esperanzaschool.com
This popular school in the Heights offers child care for kids ages 6 weeks through pre-K, as well as after-school and summer camp programs for children in elementary school. Esperanza also offers child care on Saturday evenings for kids ages 18 months to 10 years.

KIPLING STREET ACADEMY
1425 Kipling St.
(713) 529-4472
kiplingstreetacademy.com
This popular Montrose child care center and private preschool boasts beautiful, state-of-the-art facilities and web cams that parents can use to check up on their kids throughout the day. Kipling Street is dedicated to making its programming educational and begins teaching children sign language in the toddler class. Kipling Street is opening a second location at Memorial and Shepherd in the fall of 2012.

KOMPANY KIDS
2030 Post Oak Blvd.
(713) 621-4006
kompany-kids.com
Kompany Kids serves children ages 6 weeks to prekindergarten. The classes have low teacher-to-child ratios. Children eat hot, healthy meals that are prepared at the school. The center is located in the Galleria area.

i **Looking for a nanny or babysitting services? Contact the Motherhood Center (713-963-8880; motherhoodcenter.com). This local organization offers nanny and babysitter referrals for new parents.**

MONTESSORI SCHOOL OF
DOWNTOWN
Various locations
(713) 520-6801 (downtown/Medical
Center campuses)
montessoridowntown.com
Since opening its first campus downtown in 1984, the Montessori School of Downtown has opened a second downtown campus and additional campuses in Midtown and the Clear Lake and Pearland suburbs. The school ascribes to the Montessori philosophy. Programs are available for infants, toddlers, preschoolers, and elementary school students through the 5th grade. Summer programs are also available.

Referral Agencies

COLLABORATIVE FOR CHILDREN
3800 Buffalo Speedway, Ste. 300
(888) 833-6805
collabforchildren.org
As a member of the Texas Association of Child Care Resource and Referral Agencies, Collaborative for Children helps parents find quality child care and provides resources related to child development and learning. This nonprofit organization offers parenting classes and supports and trains early childhood teachers and care providers. The Collaborative for Children works to improve early childhood care and education through policy initiatives, too. Visit the website or call to speak with a consultant who can guide you in your search for a child-care program or other early childhood resources.

HIGHER EDUCATION

No matter what you want to study or where you are in your life, Houston is a great place to continue your education. Close to a dozen colleges and universities, three major community college systems, and several nationwide technical institutes and distance-learning universities have campuses here.

With some of the world's leading hospitals located in Houston's Texas Medical Center, many of these colleges and universities offer students an unrivaled opportunity to study medicine. Two medical schools—Baylor College of Medicine and the University of Texas Health Science Center at Houston—are located in the Texas Medical Center, as is Prairie View A&M College of Nursing. Plenty of other professional, graduate, and associate's degree programs in the health sciences are available through the University of Texas Health Science Center at Houston, the Texas A&M Institute of Biosciences and Technology, and local community colleges.

There are also plenty of opportunities to work on a law degree or an M.B.A. in Houston. In addition to the business programs at the large universities here, Houston is home to satellite M.B.A. programs affiliated with Tulane University, Texas A&M University, and the University of Texas at Austin. Two of the city's universities have their own law school, and a third university—South Texas College of Law—is a law school unto itself.

OVERVIEW

Houston educates far more than doctors, nurses, lawyers, pharmacy technicians, and physician's assistants. Here you'll find higher-education institutions that educate college students, older adults, and recent high school graduates or GED recipients pursuing associate's degrees and future doctors and medical practitioners, aspiring lawyers and M.B.A.s, established professionals seeking continuing education credits, as well as curious adults who just want to learn something new. Those seeking a Christian education also have two options in Houston.

Many institutions of higher education here offer night classes and special programs geared toward students who work full-time and have families. The city's colleges and universities also cater to students of all financial backgrounds and offer a good deal of financial aid. A few of the universities here are pricey private schools, but many are public schools, with low tuition rates for students from Texas and still-reasonable prices for those who come here from elsewhere in the country or the world. Unless indicated otherwise, tuition prices listed in this chapter are based on 2011–2012 rates.

Here you'll find a rundown of colleges and universities in Houston—including medical, law, and business schools—followed by community colleges. Several national technical colleges and distance-learning programs such as the University of Phoenix and ITT Technical Institute have campuses in Houston. These campuses can be found by doing a search online.

COLLEGES & UNIVERSITIES

BAYLOR COLLEGE OF MEDICINE
1 Baylor Plaza (Medical Center)
(713) 798-4951
bcm.edu
Baylor College of Medicine—also referred to as BCM or Baylor—consistently ranks among the top 25 medical schools in the country. This is due in part to the school's location in the heart of the internationally acclaimed Texas Medical Center, allowing for affiliations with several outstanding teaching hospitals. While groundbreaking research projects and teaching (and learning) opportunities are abundant at these affiliated hospitals, significant research is also undertaken at Baylor, which receives more than $400 million in research support. This funding helps support Baylor's more than 90 patient-care and research centers.

Several Texas colleges—including Baylor University in Waco and Rice University in Houston—offer joint bachelor's degree/ MD programs with the medical school. This enables high school seniors to be provisionally accepted to Baylor when they apply to college, allowing them to later avoid the stress of applying to medical school.

Baylor College of Medicine shouldn't be confused with Baylor University, a Baptist university located in Waco, about 90 minutes north of Austin in central Texas. Although the medical school became affiliated with Baylor University in 1903, it became an independent institution in 1969.

Baylor enrolls approximately 3,000 students, the majority of whom are medical students, postdoctoral fellows, and physicians completing their residency training. The school also trains about 600 students pursuing PhDs, as well as a smaller number of nurse anesthesia and physician assistant students. Students seeking an MD have the option of also pursuing a second degree—a PhD, a master of business administration, a master of public health, or a law degree. Tuition and other enrollment fees vary depending on the program, the student's year in the program, and, in some cases, whether the student is a Texas resident. Out-of-state medical school students pay between $22,500 and $33,000 a year, while Texas residents pay between about $16,000 and $20,000 a year. PhD students pay just over $27,000 per year, while physician assistant students pay $29,000 their first year, with tuition prices dropping in subsequent years. Nurse anesthetist students pay more than $16,500 during their first year.

HOUSTON BAPTIST UNIVERSITY
7502 Fondren Rd., just off US 59
(281) 649-3000
hbu.edu
Houston Baptist University—also known as Houston Baptist or HBU—prides itself on providing a solid liberal arts education infused with Christian ideals. The university isn't a liberal arts school in the true sense, though: Undergrads can choose from more than 40 majors in music, business administration, liberal arts, and the sciences. The university also offers both bachelor's and associate's degree programs for aspiring nurses, as well as teacher certification and

master's degree programs in Christian counseling, accountancy, psychology, theology, business and management, liberal arts, and education. With only 2,500 undergrads and graduate students, Houston Baptist offers small classes with lots of personal attention. Almost all HBU students are Christian, and most attend school full-time. Many undergrads live on campus during their first couple of years of college. Annual fees for tuition and room and board total about $33,000.

PRAIRIE VIEW A&M COLLEGE OF NURSING
6436 Fannin St. (Texas Medical Center)
(713) 797-7000
pvamu.edu/pages/290.asp
The main campus of Prairie View A&M—a member of the Texas A&M University system—is located in a small town northwest of Houston, but the College of Nursing makes its home in the Texas Medical Center. Currently, the College of Nursing is expanding its programs and facilities to give students and professors even better research and learning opportunities.

Undergrads must first complete their basic science/prenursing requirements on the main campus or another university, then transfer to the College of Nursing. Graduate students may pursue degrees that will allow them to work as family nurse practitioners, nursing administrators, or nursing educators.

An historically black university, Prairie View A&M was the first university west of the Mississippi River to admit black students to nursing school when the College of Nursing opened in 1918. Today the student body is still predominately black, but the College of Nursing's 8,000 students also represent a number of other racial and ethnic backgrounds.

College of Nursing students pay Prairie View A&M tuition rates, which are relatively low and are determined by the number of credit hours a student takes. Undergrads pay about $23,600 per year for tuition, room and board, and other fees; graduate students pay about $21,600 per year.

RICE UNIVERSITY
6100 Main St., at Sunset Blvd. (Museum District)
(713) 348-0000
rice.edu
Rice University is one of Houston's educational gems. Thanks to its large endowment, small classes, and top-notch professors, the university consistently ranks among the top 15 universities in the country. Rice enrolls just over 3,000 undergrads in six schools—architecture, engineering, humanities, music, natural sciences, and social sciences. About 2,300 graduate students enroll in research-centered PhD and master's degree programs, as well as in professional degrees in the sciences and business management. Undergraduate tuition was $34,900 per year in 2011–2012; this price doesn't include room and board or other fees. Tuition varies for the different graduate programs, but most graduate students receive some sort of fellowship or tuition waver.

The Susanne M. Glasscock School of Continuing Studies offers top-notch educational opportunities for older adults and professionals, who can take professional development courses, work toward certificates in a wide range of fields, and take enrichment courses on everything from wine to music to personal finance. The school also offers foreign language and English as a Second Language courses for businesspeople and non-businesspeople, as well as a limited number of classes for high school students. The Glasscock School also offers an evening master of liberal studies degree program, where adults study the humanities, sciences, and social sciences. Tuition and fees vary.

SOUTH TEXAS COLLEGE OF LAW
1303 San Jacinto St., at Clay St. (downtown)
(713) 659-8040
stcl.edu

When South Texas College of Law opened in 1923, it was Houston's first law school and Texas's third. The school was originally geared toward people who worked full-time and needed to be able to take classes in the evening. But today about two-thirds of South Texas students enroll full-time. A small number participate in the 3 + 3 program with Texas A&M University, which allows undergrads to receive both a bachelor's and a law degree in 6 years, with 3 years spent at each institution. One-third of South Texas students are enrolled part-time, most taking evening classes so they can work or care for their families. A small number of part-timers enroll in daytime classes, as space permits. South Texas admits new students in both the fall and the spring. Each year South Texas enrolls less than 400 new students, close to a quarter of which are minorities.

The school has a particularly strong trial law program. The Trial Advocacy Program frequently ranks in the *US News & World Report's* top 10, and the mock trial team has won the American Association for Justice's Student Trial Advocacy Competition and the National White Collar Crime Mock Trial Invitational in recent years.

Annual tuition was just over $26,000 for full-time students for the 2010–2011 academic year; part-time students paid $17,760 for tuition during the same period.

TEXAS A&M UNIVERSITY INSTITUTE OF BIOSCIENCES AND TECHNOLOGY
2121 W. Holcombe Blvd. (Texas Medical Center)
(713) 677-7700
ibt.tamhsc.edu

Texas A&M University's Institute of Biosciences and Technology gives aspiring biomedical science scholars the chance to work with leading scientists and other biomedicine and biotechnology practitioners. The institute offers a PhD program in biomedical sciences, which requires students to develop theoretical and practical research skills. Students specialize in one of four areas: cell and developmental biology, microbiology and immunology, environmental and molecular genetics, or biochemistry and molecular biology. Each senior faculty member has a relationship with at least one biotechnology company, giving students access to cutting-edge research and trailblazers in their field.

The institute's students are enrolled in the Texas A&M University System Health Science Center's Graduate School of Biomedical Sciences. Graduate education is supported by research grants and outside awards. All entering students receive 12-month stipends for up to 5 years.

TEXAS A&M UNIVERSITY MAYS BUSINESS SCHOOL EXECUTIVE MBA PROGRAM
CityCentre complex (Memorial)
(888) 551-9998
emba.tamu.edu

Texas A&M's Mays Business School now offers an executive MBA program in the City-Centre complex in Memorial. The program seeks to mold students into strong managers, helping them hone skills in communication, problem solving, self-management, financial acumen, and teamwork. Classes are held on Friday and Saturday of alternating weekends in the fall and spring. There are no summer classes. In addition to class time at CityCentre, students are required to spend a week at Texas A&M's College Station campus at the beginning of the program and another week in Washington, D.C., where they can see federal policies in action.

Students enrolling in August 2012 paid $74,500 for the 2-year program. This relatively low tuition gives the Mays MBA students one of the highest returns on investment, according to the *Wall Street Journal*. Applicants are required to have at least 10 years of professional work experience, with at least 7 of those involving increasing and significant managerial responsibilities.

TEXAS MBA AT HOUSTON
University of Texas Health Science Center
7000 Fannin St.
(512) 471-7698
mccombs.utexas.edu/mba/houston
Houston professionals can earn an MBA from the top-ranked University of Texas McCombs School of Business without moving to Austin. Students take team-based classes taught by McCombs faculty year-round on alternating weekends for 2 years. Students take 48 credit hours of business, management, and accounting coursework. Each academic year also includes a week at the University of Texas' Austin campus; the first year also includes a trip abroad.

Applicants must have at least 2 years of full-time, post-undergraduate work experience to be considered for the program. The total program cost for students entering in August 2011 was $86,000.

TEXAS SOUTHERN UNIVERSITY
3100 Cleburne St. (Third Ward)
(713) 313-7011
tsu.edu
With more than 9,500 students, Texas Southern University is one of the country's largest black colleges. Historically, the university has produced 27 percent of all black pharmacists in the country as well as the majority of Houston's black lawyers and teachers in the Houston Independent School District. Most Texas Southern students are native Texans, but a growing number of students hail from other states and abroad.

Texas Southern is home to nine schools and colleges, including programs in the liberal arts, education, and sciences, as well as the Barbara Jordan–Mickey Leland School of Public Affairs, the College of Pharmacy and Health Sciences, the Jesse H. Jones School of Business, the Tavis Smiley School of Communications, and the Thurgood Marshall School of Law, which *US News & World Report* recognized as the country's most diverse law school.

The 150-acre campus is situated in the Third Ward, an historically black neighborhood near downtown. Tuition is relatively low, but it varies, depending on the number of credit hours, field of study, whether the student is a graduate student or undergraduate, where the student lives, and whether the student is a Texas resident.

TULANE UNIVERSITY FREEMAN SCHOOL OF BUSINESS—HOUSTON
1700 W. Loop South at San Felipe St.
(Galleria)
(866) 885-2636
houston.tulane.edu

You can now earn a graduate degree in business from Tulane University's Freeman School of Business without spending more than a few weekends in Louisiana. The school offers three tracks—a 23-month professional MBA, an 18-month executive MBA for managers and executives, or a 14-month master of finance program. Classes meet on Friday and Saturday of alternating weekends. Students in the executive and professional MBA programs are also required to participate in international seminars; all students must participate in a couple of seminars at Tulane's New Orleans campus.

The programs are geared toward professionals with at least 2 years of full-time work experience. Tuition and fees vary depending on the program.

UNIVERSITY OF HOUSTON
4800 Calhoun Rd., (Southeast central Houston)
(713) 743-2255
uh.edu
With more than 39,800 students enrolled in more than 300 undergraduate and graduate programs, the University of Houston (U of H) is Houston's largest university. The campus is located in southeast central Houston; it's not affiliated with the University of Houston—Downtown, the University of Houston—Clear Lake, or the University of Houston—Victoria.

Undergrads can choose from 120 majors and minors, as well as pre-professional programs in law, medicine, and pharmacy. U of H also offers nearly 200 graduate programs, including especially strong programs in optometry, law, pharmacy, creative writing, clinical psychology, kinesiology, and business.

Thanks to a strong alumni base and a huge endowment, U of H students—aka Cougars—enjoy a wealth of resources, opportunities, and sports teams. The university is constantly undertaking renovations to ensure its students and faculty enjoy the most state-of-the-art facilities. Courses are offered both during the day and in the evening to serve U of H's many nontraditional students.

Tuition and room and board was a little over $19,000 a year for in-state students and just shy of $25,000 for out-of-state students for the 2010–2011 school year.

UNIVERSITY OF ST. THOMAS
3800 Montrose (Museum District)
(713) 522-7911
stthom.edu
This small Catholic school sits on the edge of Museum District, which makes for an attractive campus with easy access to the local arts and culture scene. The University of St. Thomas enrolls only about 3,750 students, about 1,600 of whom are undergraduates. St. Thomas's 32 undergraduate majors and minors include the standard fare, as well as more unusual offerings, such as environmental science and studies, pastoral studies, social justice, medieval studies, and Catholic studies. The university offers 10 graduate programs, including divinity, business, pastoral studies, and theological studies. With an 11-to-1 student-to-faculty ratio, St. Thomas offers small classes and a fairly close-knit campus. Although the university is a Catholic institution, only 60 percent of students are actually Catholic. Tuition is fairly reasonable for a private university. Undergrads pay $832 per credit hour—around $12,000 per semester—and graduate students pay $940 per credit hour,

which comes out to around $14,000 per semester. These costs don't include room and board or other fees.

UNIVERSITY OF TEXAS HEALTH SCIENCE CENTER AT HOUSTON
7000 Fannin St. (Texas Medical Center)
(713) 500-4472
uthouston.edu

The Health Science Center is the main health science arm of the University of Texas, one of the state's two largest university systems (the other being Texas A&M University). Thanks to its Texas Medical Center location, the Health Science Center offers unrivaled learning and research opportunities for students pursuing just about any career in the health sciences. In fact, no other university in Texas has as many health science schools on one campus. Students here can pursue a variety of degrees in the UT Dental Branch, the Graduate School of Biomedical Sciences, the School of Public Health, the School of Nursing, the School of Health Information Sciences, and the Medical School. With the exception of a few certificate programs, the Bachelor of Science in dental hygiene, and the Bachelor of Science in nursing, all of the Health Science Center's programs are geared toward graduate-level students.

The closely affiliated University of Texas MD Anderson School for Health Professions offers certificate and bachelor of science degrees in eight health professions. These include clinical laboratory science, cytogenic technology, cytotechnology, diagnostic imaging, histotechnology, medical dosimetry, molecular genetic technology, and radiation therapy.

The Health Science Center offers several joint degree programs, including a master of social work with a master of public health and a doctor of law with a master of public health in conjunction with the University of Houston. Health science professionals also have opportunities to earn continuing education credits and participate in educational community service opportunities.

Tuition varies by program and by the student's year in the program. Out-of-state students pay roughly 4 times as much as Texas residents, but their tuition is still relatively low. Visit the Health Science Center's website for a complete tuition breakdown.

COMMUNITY COLLEGES

HOUSTON COMMUNITY COLLEGE
Various locations
(713) 718-2000
hccs.edu

Houston Community College, also known as HCC, is the primary community college system serving the Houston area. HCC serves Houstonians living in seven area school districts—Houston Independent School District, Stafford Municipal School District, Spring Branch, Alief, North Forest Independent School Districts, Katy, and the part of Fort Bend Independent School District that covers Missouri City. The HCC system serves more than 70,000 students through six colleges: Central College, Coleman College for Health Sciences, Northeast College, Northwest College, Southeast College, and Southwest College. With the exception of Coleman, which is located in the Texas Medical Center, each college's name corresponds to the region of the Houston metropolitan area that it serves.

Each college, aside from Southeast, has at least two campuses. In total HCC offers courses in about 70 fields. All of the colleges in the Houston Community College system also offer distance-learning classes. Course offerings vary by campus to some extent, but about all of them offer liberal arts and science courses that fill basic requirements at most universities. The exception is Coleman, where classes prepare students to work in about 20 different health-science fields.

None of HCC's campuses offer housing, but students can participate in university-wide sporting events and attend film screenings, guest talks, and other special activities. Tuition varies depending on where the student makes his or her permanent residence and the number of credit hours. Students who live in one of the seven school districts served by HCC pay the lowest price. In the fall of 2011, the cost for 15 credit hours was $1,011 for in-district students, $2,016 for out-of-district students, and $2,263.50 for out-of-state students.

LONE STAR COLLEGE SYSTEM
Various locations
(832) 813-6500
lonestar.edu
With 90,000 students, the Lone Star College System is one of Texas' largest and fastest-growing community college systems. Lone Star's six campuses and six centers serve north Houston and areas just north of the city limits in Harris and Montgomery Counties. The six Lone Star colleges are in CyFair, Kingwood, Montgomery, North Harris County, Tomball, and University Park.

Through Lone Star College–University Center, students can complete their associate's degrees at one of Lone Star's campuses, then work toward their bachelor's and even master's degrees at one of six of the area's

biggest universities. Lone Star also offers GED prep classes, as well as dual-credit and tech-prep programs for high school students looking to earn some college credits.

Tuition varies depending on where the student makes his or her permanent residence and the number of credit hours taken. Students who live in one of the following school districts pay the lowest prices: Aldine, Conroe, Cypress-Fairbanks, Humble, Klein, Magnolia, New Caney, Splendora, Spring, Tomball, or Willis. Students who live in Texas but outside of these districts pay nearly twice as much. During the 2010–2011 academic year, the annual average cost of attendance was $10,092 for students living at home and $12,192 for out-of-district students living at home. Rates vary for students living on-campus or off-campus in an apartment.

SAN JACINTO COLLEGE
Various locations
(281) 998-6150
sjcd.edu
For 50 years, the San Jacinto College community college system has been serving East Harris County residents zoned for the Channelview, Deer Park, Galena Park, La Porte, Pasadena, Sheldon, and Clear Creek School Districts. The college has three campuses—one near NASA and the Texas Medical Center, one in north Harris County, and a third just southeast of Houston in Pasadena. There are also seven extension centers.

Each campus offers courses that can be transferred to four-year colleges, as well as continuing education courses and job-training programs that prepare students for careers in industries such as agriculture, food, natural resources, hospitality, and construction. SanJac, as the college is nicknamed, also offers dual-credit programs for high school students, as well as GED courses. For students who work full time or have family obligations that prevent them from attending classes on weekdays, all three colleges offer the Weekend College—that is, Friday, Saturday, and Sunday classes offered during the morning, afternoon, and evening. SanJac offers students more extracurricular activities and campus activities than other community colleges in the area.

Tuition varies depending on the students' permanent residence location and the number of credit hours. In the spring of 2012, 16 hours of course credits cost $743 for in-district students, $1,143 for out-of-district Texas residents, and $1,943 for out-of-state students. These prices don't include books, housing, or additional fees required for some courses.

HEALTH CARE

Need to see a doctor? You've come to the right place. Houston is home to dozens of hospitals and urgent-care facilities—many of which are so good that people travel from across the globe to receive treatment. Hospitals here conduct groundbreaking medical research and surgeries time and again, consistently earning them recognition as top hospitals in the country—and the world.

OVERVIEW

Most of Houston's best hospitals are located in the Texas Medical Center, the world's largest medical complex. Located inside the Loop near Hermann Park, this 1,000-acre medical complex is home to 14 renowned hospitals and two specialty institutions, three medical schools, six nursing schools, and schools of dentistry, public health, pharmacy, and most other health-related professions.

Together, hospitals in the Medical Center perform more heart surgeries than any other place in the world. The Texas Medical Center isn't just a leader in cardiology, though. Other top-ranked specialties here include cancer, pediatric care, woman's health, urology, gastroenterology, endocrinology, psychiatry, and neurology. The Medical Center is also home to two level-one trauma centers.

While the Medical Center is the center of Houston's medical universe, it's hardly the only place to receive great medical care in Houston. Many hospitals in the Texas Medical Center now have satellites in the suburbs and other parts of Houston. A sampling of some of the city's best hospitals can be found in this chapter.

Urgent Care & Walk-In Clinics

Fortunately not all symptoms and medical circumstances demand a trip to the hospital. Several urgent-care/walk-in clinics around the area serve patients with relatively minor medical problems like broken bones, the flu, and asthma attacks. You'll find a list of some of these clinics in this chapter.

The city and county health departments also operate several community health clinics that cater to lower-income Houstonians. Interested in visiting one of these facilities? Consult the "Health Departments" section in this chapter.

Physician Referral Services

Need help finding a doctor? Whether you need a general practitioner or specialist, physician referral services listed in this chapter can help. Keep in mind that Houston is home to thousands of doctors and dozens of hospitals, so this list—like the clinic list and hospital list—is hardly exhaustive. Use this chapter to start your search for a doctor or a medical facility, but don't discount the value of seeking doctor recommendations from friends and colleagues who have lived in Houston for many years.

At the end of this chapter is a list of important emergency numbers such as poison control, animal control, and the local rape crisis hotline.

HEALTH DEPARTMENTS

HARRIS COUNTY PUBLIC HEALTH AND ENVIRONMENTAL SERVICES
2223 W. Loop South
(713) 439-6000
hcphes.org
Harris County Public Health and Environmental Services promotes health and seeks to prevent injury and illness throughout Harris County. The department provides resources for the community to learn about communicable diseases, prenatal care, HIV screening, and immunizations, as well as how to avoid unhealthy conditions created by storms and other environmental conditions. Also handled by the department: the all-important mosquito control. Four health clinics run by the department provide preventative health-care services for low-income residents. Call the department or visit its website for a list of clinics.

HEALTH AND HUMAN SERVICES DEPARTMENT
8000 N. Stadium Dr.
(832) 393-5169
houstontx.gov/health
The Houston Department of Health and Human Services works with the community and health-care providers to promote good health and health services among Houstonians. In particular, the department's programs seek to help prevent communicable diseases like the flu, HIV, and H1N1

(swine flu). The department also leads public health programs; monitors environmental conditions, such as air quality and allergens; oversees animal control; and inspects local restaurants and food establishments. To help Houstonians access to quality health care, the Health and Human Services Department operates preventative-care clinics and primary-care clinics for low-income residents. For a list of clinics, call the department or visit houstontx.gov/health/HealthCenters.

HOSPITALS

BEN TAUB GENERAL HOSPITAL
1504 Taub Loop (Medical Center)
(713) 873-2000
hchdonline.com/en/services/locations/pages/ben-taub.aspx
Owned and operated by the Harris County Hospital District, Ben Taub General Hospital is one of the country's elite level-one trauma centers in the county and the only hospital in the Medical Center with a 24-hour psychiatric emergency room. With 586 beds, Ben Taub treats more than 100,000 emergency room patients each year, making it one of the country's busiest trauma centers. Ben Taub also provides outpatient care in numerous specialties, including endocrinology, neurosurgery, obstetrics and gynecology, diabetes, dermatology, cardiology, radiology, urology, and gastroenterology. The staff is made up of faculty and residents from Baylor College of Medicine.

CHILDREN'S MEMORIAL HERMANN HOSPITAL
6411 Fannin (Medical Center)
(713) 704-5437
childrens.memorialhermann.org

Children's Memorial Hermann Hospital recently expanded to include 240 beds, making it one of the largest pediatric hospitals in the United States. The hospital has an emergency room just for pediatric patients and Houston's largest level-one trauma center for treating pediatric patients. Though Children's Memorial Hermann Hospital is known for its work in trauma, transplants, cardiac care, and neuroscience, it handles everything from neonatal care to common childhood ailments and injuries to transplants and potentially fatal diseases and injuries. The hospital is home to the Children's Heart Institute and the Children's Neuroscience Center, as well as a woman's center, which provides prenatal and maternal care and ob/gyn and breast-health services. The hospital has additional campuses in Katy, Memorial City, Sugar Land, The Woodlands, and five other locations around Houston. Call or visit the website for details.

MEMORIAL HERMANN HOSPITAL
6411 Fannin (Medical Center)
(713) 704-4000
memorialhermann.org
With 11 hospitals around the Houston area, Memorial Hermann Hospital is Texas's largest hospital system. And in 2012, it was named one of the top 15 health systems in the country by Thompson Reuters. Anchored by its Texas Medical Center campus, the system operates the country's busiest level-one trauma center, 8 cancer centers, 3 heart institutes, 27 sports medicine and rehabilitation centers, a substance abuse treatment center, 21 patient imaging centers, 8 breast care centers, 25 sports medicine and rehabilitation centers, 10 surgery centers, a substance abuse treatment center, the Life Flight air ambulance program, Houston's only burn treatment center, a children's hospital, and a neuroscience institute. Visit the website to find additional hospitals and specialty facilities.

i Parking in the Texas Medical Center can be confusing, especially for first-time visitors. So, download a map at tmc.edu and figure out where to park before your visit.

METHODIST HOSPITAL
6565 Fannin St. (Medical Center)
(713) 790-3311
methodisthealth.com
Anchored by its Texas Medical Center campus, the renowned Methodist Hospital system is known for groundbreaking research in areas ranging from transplants to heart attack diagnosis time to cancer treatment to genetic therapy to brain aneurysm repair. Methodist is perhaps best known for its excellence in breast health, cardiology, neuroscience, orthopedics, and cancer treatment. The Medical Center location has 864 beds; the entire system has 1,561. Visit the website for locations.

ST. JOSEPH MEDICAL CENTER
1401 St. Joseph Pkwy. (Downtown)
(713) 757-1000
sjmctx.com
When it opened in 1887, St. Joseph Medical Center was Houston's first hospital. Today it provides comprehensive medical and surgical care, including neonatal and pediatric care, women's care and baby delivery, behavioral care, intensive care, neurosurgery, orthopedics, and diabetes management. St. Joseph also has a level III emergency department. This teaching hospital has 420 beds

and is staffed by more than 600 board-certified physicians.

ST. LUKE'S EPISCOPAL HOSPITAL
sleh.com
6720 Bertner Ave. (Medical Center)
(832) 355-1000
VisitStLukesHouston.com
17200 St. Luke's Way (The Woodlands)
(936) 266-2000
VisitStLukesWoodlands.com
1317 Lake Pointe Pkwy. (Sugar Land)
(281) 637-7000
VisitStLukesSugarLand.com

Since it was founded by the Episcopal Diocese of Texas in 1954, St. Luke's Episcopal Hospital has become one of the country's best hospitals and one of the world's leaders in heart surgery and the treatment of heart disease. The Texas Medical Center location has 640 beds, including 143 in the intensive care unit. In addition to providing outstanding cardiac care, St. Luke's is known for specialties such as neurology and neurosurgery, gastrointestinal disorders, geriatrics, endocrinology, respiratory disorders, urology, and kidney disease. The Medical Center campus, which is located in iconic O'Quinn Medical Tower, trains residents at Baylor Medical School. St. Luke's is the principal hospital in the St. Luke's Episcopal Health System, which includes the Texas Heart Institute, hospitals in the Woodlands and Sugar Land, St. Luke's Diagnostic & Treatment Center, several urgent-care clinics, and Kelsey-Seybold Clinic, which provides primary care and specialty care in an outpatient setting. The Medical Center, Woodlands, and Sugar Land locations are listed here; visit the website or call to find additional facilities.

TEXAS CHILDREN'S HOSPITAL
6621 Fannin St. (Medical Center)
(832) 824-1000
18200 Katy Fwy. at Barker Cypress (West Houston)
(832) 227-1000
texaschildrens.org

With 474 beds and more than 20,000 admissions a year, Texas Children's Hospital is the country's largest children's hospital and a global leader in pediatric care. The hospital's specialty care centers focus on cancer, fetal care, cardiology, maternity care, neurology, and newborns. *US News & World Report* has ranked Texas Children's Hospital in 10 pediatric specialties, including cardiology, diabetes and endocrinology, gastroenterology, neonatalogy, urology, neurosurgery, cancer, and orthopedics. Among Texas Children's trailblazing feats: inserting the world's smallest pacemaker in a child and operating on conjoined twins. Texas Children's is affiliated with Baylor College of Medicine. Texas Children's recently opened a satellite location in West Houston; find additional facilities on the website.

UNIVERSITY OF TEXAS MD ANDERSON CANCER CENTER
1515 Holcombe Blvd. (Medical Center)
(877) MDA-6789 (all locations)
mdanderson.org

People from around the world visit the University of Texas MD Anderson Cancer Center for cancer treatment. Ranked the number-one cancer care hospital in the country by *US News & World Report* for 9 of the last 11 years, MD Anderson is also nationally ranked for its treatment of cancer specialties, including ear, nose, and throat; gynecology; urology; gastroenterology; pediatrics; and

Emergency Phone Numbers at a Glance

Abuse and Neglect Hotline
(800) 252-5400

Adult Protective Services–Aged and Disabled
(713) 767-2700

Animal Control
(713) 229-7300

Children's Protective Services
(713) 664-5701

Domestic Violence Hotline
(713) 528-2121

Harris County Hospital District's 24-Hour Nurse Help Line
(713) 634-1110

Household Hazardous Waste Hotline
(713) 551-7355

Health and Human Services Department
(832) 393-5169

Houston Rape Crisis Hotline
(713) 528-7273

Mental Health/Mental Retardation Crisis Clinic
(713) 970-4600

Missing Persons Information
(713) 884-3131 (non-emergency)
911 (emergency)

Poison Control
(800) 222-1222

Police/Ambulance
(713) 461-9992 (nonemergency)
911 (emergency)

Sexual Assault Hotline
(713) 528-7273

Suicide Prevention Hotline
(713) 228-1505
(800) 784-2433

Teen Crisis Hotline
(713) 529-8336

Texas Runaway Hotline
(888) 580-4357

Youth Crisis Hotline
(800) 448-4663

---

endocrinology. A leader in cancer research, MD Anderson evaluates more cancer-fighting drugs than any other institution in the country, enabling patients to participate in clinical trials that often extend or save their lives. MD Anderson has nearly 600 beds at its Medical Center location; it served more than 108,000 patients from September 2010 through August 2011. MD Anderson has additional locations in Sugar Land, Katy, The Woodlands, and the Bay. Visit the website for additional locations.

THE WOMAN'S HOSPITAL OF TEXAS
7600 Fannin (Medical Center)
(713) 790-1234
womanshospital.com
Since opening in 1976, The Woman's Hospital has been the state's leading hospital dedicated solely to the care of women and newborn infants. The Woman's Hospital of Texas specializes in gynecology, regular obstetrical care, high-risk pregnancies, and minimally invasive surgery. The hospital, which delivers more babies than any other hospital in Harris County, is renowned for its Neonatal Intensive Care Unit and its exceptional success rate with babies weighing

1,500 grams or less at birth. Thanks to a recent 145,000-square-foot expansion, The Woman's Hospital now has 397 beds and 36 labor and delivery rooms. The Woman's Hospital has a network of six neighborhood physician satellite offices called The Woman's Place; call or visit the website to find the nearest location.

URGENT CARE & WALK-IN CLINICS

Whether you've cut your finger or broken a bone, you probably don't want to sit in the ER for hours. Luckily, dozens of urgent-care facilities here treat minor illnesses and injuries, saving you the time and hassle of waiting in a hospital emergency room. The clinics treat medical problems, such as burns, broken bones, migraines, swallowed objects, splinters, urinary tract infections, fever, and the flu. They also provide immunization and diagnostic services. Although it's a good idea to call ahead, you don't need an appointment to visit one of these clinics, where you'll be treated by board-certified physicians and licensed nurses. Most accept health insurance plans with major insurance companies, as well as Medicare and Medicaid.

Following are a handful of Houston's many urgent-care clinics. Most are open 7 days a week. 24 Hour Emergency Room and St. Luke's Community Emergency Center are open 24 hours. Houston Urgent Care, Texas Urgent Care, and Wells Walk-In Clinic close relatively early in the evening, so call ahead to make sure the clinic will be open when you visit.

HOUSTON URGENT CARE
1826 Wirt Rd. (West Houston)
16125 Cairnway, Ste. 100 (Northwest Houston)
(832) 428-4546 (both locations)
urgentcarehouston.com

ST. LUKE'S COMMUNITY EMERGENCY CENTER
6363 San Felipe St., at Winrock (Memorial)
(713) 972-8300
2727 W. Holcombe (West University)
(832) 355-7525
11713 Shadow Creek Pkwy. (Pearland)
(713) 793-4600
stlukesemergency.com

TEXAS URGENT CARE
10906 FM 1960 West, at Jones Rd. (Northwest Houston)
(281) 477-7490
texasurgentcare.com

EMERUS 24 HOUR EMERGENCY ROOM
1635 South Voss Rd., at San Felipe (Memorial)
(713) 972-0911
16000 Southwest Fwy., Ste. 100 (Sugar Land)
(281) 277-0911
24727 Tomball Pkwy., Ste. 120, Tomball (Northwest of Houston)
(281) 516-0911
24houremergencyroom.com

i Kelsey-Seybold Clinic and Baylor Clinic (Baylor College of Medicine's adult outpatient care facility) both offer excellent primary and specialty care. To find a doctor or schedule an appointment, contact Kelsey-Seybold (713-442-5440; kelsey-seybold.com) or Baylor Clinic (713-798-1000; baylorclinic.com).

WELLS WALK-IN CLINIC
10311 N. Eldridge Pkwy. (Northwest Houston)
(281) 890-3822
wellswalk-inclinic.com

> ℹ️ Military veteran? Get 24-hour telecare by calling the Michael E. DeBakey VA Medical Center at (713) 794-8985.

REFERRAL SERVICES

Whether you're new to town or a longtime Houstonian, finding a good doctor can be tough. Here is a list of hospitals and organizations that provide referral services those looking for local physicians and specialists. Most participating doctors are affiliated with specific hospitals and many teach at Baylor College of Medicine or the University of Texas Health Sciences Center.

BAYLOR CLINIC PHYSICIAN REFERRALS
(713) 798-1000
baylorclinic.com

HARRIS COUNTY MEDICAL SOCIETY REFERRAL SERVICE
(713) 524-4267
hcms.org

HCA HOUSTON NETWORK REFERRAL SERVICE
(888) 624-9456

MEMORIAL HERMANN HOSPITAL REFERRAL SERVICE
(713) 222-2273
memorialhermann.org

PLANNED PARENTHOOD
(713) 522-6363
plannedparenthood.org

TEXAS CHILDREN'S HOSPITAL REFERRAL SERVICE
(832) 824-7700 (primary care physicians)
(832) 824-1111 (pediatric specialists)
texaschildrens.org

ST. LUKE'S EPISCOPAL HOSPITAL PHYSICIAN REFERRAL SERVICE
(832) 355-3627
stlukes.com

THE WOMAN'S HOSPITAL OF TEXAS REFERRAL SERVICE
(281) 438-4357
womanshospital.com

INDEX

HELP US KEEP THIS GUIDE UP TO DATE

We would love to hear from you concerning your experiences with this guide and how you feel it could be improved and kept up to date. Please send your comments and suggestions to:

editorial@GlobePequot.com

Thanks for your input, and happy travels!

INSIDERS' GUIDE®

The acclaimed travel series that has sold more than 2 million copies!

Discover: Your Travel Destination.
Your Home. Your Home-to-Be.

Albuquerque

Anchorage &
 Southcentral
 Alaska

Atlanta

Austin

Baltimore

Baton Rouge

Boulder & Rocky Mountain
 National Park

Branson & the Ozark
 Mountains

California's Wine Country

Cape Cod & the Islands

Charleston

Charlotte

Chicago

Cincinnati

Civil War Sites in
 the Eastern Theater

Civil War Sites in the South

Colorado's Mountains

Dallas & Fort Worth

Denver

El Paso

Florida Keys & Key West

Gettysburg

Glacier National Park

Great Smoky Mountains

Greater Fort Lauderdale

Greater Tampa Bay Area

Hampton Roads

Houston

Hudson River Valley

Indianapolis

Jacksonville

Kansas City

Long Island

Louisville

Madison

Maine Coast

Memphis

Myrtle Beach &
 the Grand Strand

Nashville

New Orleans

New York City

North Carolina's
 Mountains

North Carolina's
 Outer Banks

North Carolina's
 Piedmont Triad

Oklahoma City

Orange County, CA

Oregon Coast

Palm Beach County

Palm Springs

Philadelphia &
 Pennsylvania Dutch
 Country

Phoenix

Portland, Maine

Portland, Oregon

Raleigh, Durham &
 Chapel Hill

Richmond, VA

Reno and Lake Tahoe

St. Louis

San Antonio

Santa Fe

Savannah & Hilton Head

Seattle

Shreveport

South Dakota's
 Black Hills Badlands

Southwest Florida

Tucson

Tulsa

Twin Cities

Washington, D.C.

Williamsburg & Virginia's
 Historic Triangle

Yellowstone
 & Grand Teton

Yosemite

**To order call 800-243-0495
or visit www.Insiders.com**